Eleanor of Provence

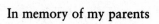
In memory of my parents

Eleanor of Provence
Queenship in Thirteenth-Century England

Margaret Howell

First published 1998

2 4 6 8 10 9 7 5 3 1

Blackwell Publishers Ltd
108 Cowley Road
Oxford OX4 1JF
UK

Blackwell Publishers Inc.
350 Main Street
Malden, Massachusetts 02148
USA

British Library Cataloguing in Publication Data

A CIP catalogue record for this book is available from the British Library.

Library of Congress Cataloging-in-Publication Data
Howell, Margaret.
  Eleanor of Provence: queenship in thirteenth-century England / Margaret Howell.
    p. cm.
  Includes bibliographical references and index.
  ISBN 0-631-17286-6
  1. Eleanor of Provence, Queen, consort of Henry III, King of England, *c.*1223-1291. 2. Great Britain–History–Henry III, 1216-1272. 3. Civilization, Medieval–13th century.
  4. Queens–Great Britain–Biography. I. Title.
DA228.E44H69   1997
941.03'4'092–dc21   97-6679
[b]

                                                                                                        CIP

Typeset in Sabon on 10/12pt
by Pure Tech India Ltd, Pondicherry
Printed and bound in Great Britain by MPG Books Ltd, Bodmin, Cornwall

This book is printed on acid-free paper

Contents

Plates

Figures

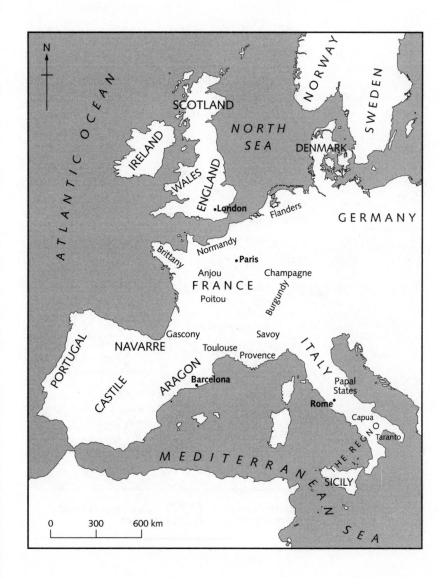

Western Europe in the thirteenth century

France and neighbouring regions in the thirteenth century

England and Wales in the reign of Henry III

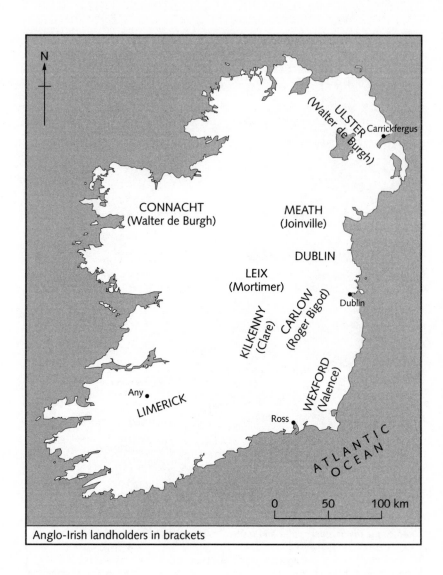

N

CONNACHT
(Walter de Burgh)

ULSTER
(Walter de Burgh)

Carrickfergus

MEATH
(Joinville)

DUBLIN

LEIX
(Mortimer)

KILKENNY
(Clare)

CARLOW
(Roger Bigod)

Dublin

Any

LIMERICK

WEXFORD
(Valence)

Ross

ATLANTIC
OCEAN

0   50   100 km

Anglo-Irish landholders in brackets

Ireland in 1265

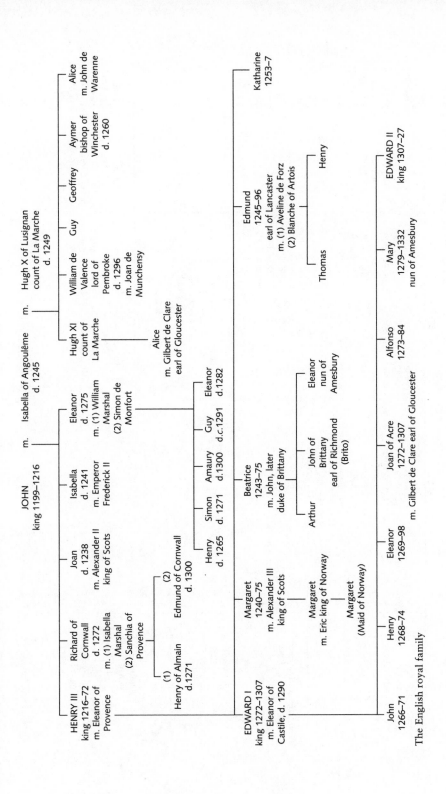

The English royal family

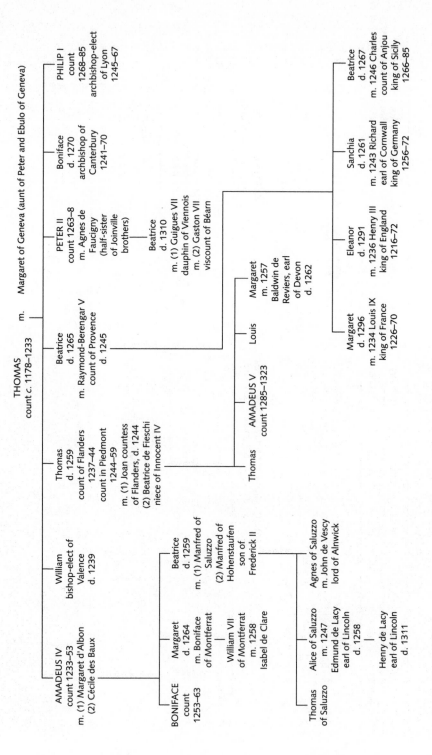

The house of Savoy

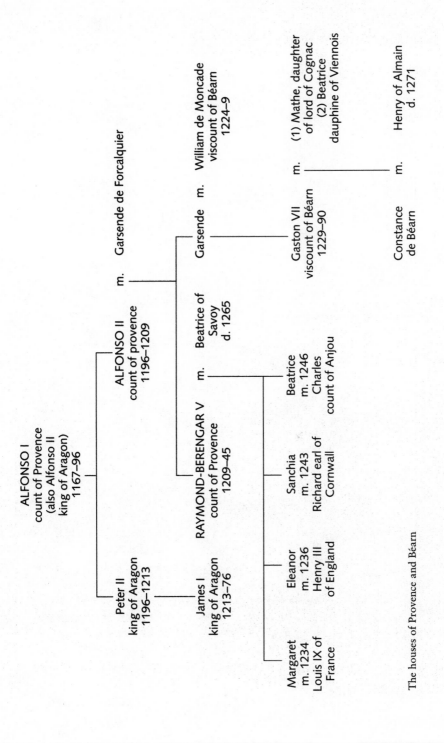

The houses of Provence and Béarn

Preface

Apart from professional historians, few people have heard of Eleanor of Provence. This book is an attempt to restore identity to a remarkable queen of England who, in her own day, was described by the word *virago*. Until recently, thirteenth-century specialists have tended to be slightly dismissive in their comments. Sir Maurice Powicke believed that Eleanor exercised influence over her husband but that she was not 'particularly ambitious or self-assertive' (1953);[1] in fact she was both, in high degree. Professor Tout sighed over the deficits in her household accounts and judged her 'an unthrifty housewife' (1920);[2] yet finance was one of her strong points. If one moves back to the nineteenth century one founders on two dated and very inaccurate chapters in Agnes Strickland's *Lives of the Queens of England* (1851). Here Eleanor of Provence is caricatured as a vain, extravagant and opinionated young woman who gained a hold over the will of her 'feeble-minded' husband, Henry III; although Strickland concedes that Eleanor's character improved 'as she advanced into the vale of years'.[3] This is the only substantial account of Queen Eleanor's life, although there have been other brief summaries, and a more sustained and well-informed essay by Martha Biles in the Festschrift to Harold Snellgrove (1983).[4] There has been no biography.

This lack of attention is strange, since Queen Eleanor was a woman of great vitality, with an unusually exciting life-story. Queen of England at the age of twelve, she was a loyal marriage partner for thirty-six years

[1] Powicke, *Thirteenth Century*, 73.
[2] Tout, *Chapters*, i. 255.
[3] Strickland, *Lives of the Queens of England*, i. 356, 407.
[4] Biles, 'The Indomitable Belle', 113–31.

and proved a deeply affectionate but dominating mother. Having promoted her Savoyard kinsfolk and their policies at the English court in the 1240s and 1250s, she became a highly significant political figure in the struggle between the king and the baronage; she encouraged the use of contingents of foreign knights to strengthen the royal power in England in moments of crisis; she gathered an army in the Low Countries, negotiated confidently with Louis IX of France and with the papacy, and by her energy and commitment helped to bring about the overthrow of Simon de Montfort and the rescue of her husband and eldest son from his control. She was widowed in 1272, showed herself vigilant over her rights as a dowager, and in 1286 entered the Wiltshire nunnery of Amesbury in a well-managed withdrawal from the world. There she died in 1291.

Eleanor of Provence was a European. Familiar with the county of Provence in her childhood, she also came to know Gascony well, especially the great port of Bordeaux, and she bore the title of duchess of Aquitaine as well as that of queen of England. She knew Paris, too, which she visited on two glittering state occasions, and for brief periods in 1264/5. Fontevrault, Pontigny, Chartres and the north-eastern towns of St Omer, Amiens and Boulogne were all part of her experience. The range of her social and diplomatic contacts stretched across the Continent; one of her uncles was count of Savoy, another count of Flanders, another archbishop-elect of Lyon; her eldest sister was queen of France and a younger sister was married to Henry III's brother and briefly became queen of Germany; her eldest daughter was queen of Scotland; she was in touch with them all, and her purpose was not simply to exchange courtesies but to move events. Politics and diplomacy were frequently intermingled with familial concerns. The court of Rome, of course, had its own matchless international network, and she knew her way about that too.

For Eleanor of Provence, personal relationships mattered more than abstract issues. She was normally on good terms with her husband, although there were occasional moments of sharp friction, and the tensions in her relations with her eldest son were at times politically damaging. Even so, a passionate loyalty to the well-being of her family was the strongest motive in her life. Her many friendships meant much to her. Some were close working relationships, as with her uncle Peter of Savoy, but her religious life was sustained by friendships too, notably that of the forthright Franciscan scholar Adam Marsh.

The sources for Eleanor's life range from the staple chronicles of English thirteenth-century history to a great mass of archive materials. From the records of the English chancery and exchequer comes remarkably detailed evidence for the setting of her daily life, the well-furnished apartments, the secluded gardens, the clothes, the jewels, the messengers who came and went so frequently. Her own letters, notably those to her eldest son, survive mainly from the period of her widowhood, but they reflect as nothing else can, the image of her personality, intelligent, decisive, courageous, and infused with a tremendous zest for life and interest in people. The chapter on Eleanor as queen mother gives only some indication of the extensive evidence relating to the period 1272–91, particularly in regard to her property. To have treated this fully would have required a longer book, which was not possible. The wealth of evidence in the English archives has been so great that, regrettably, I have done no more in continental archives than examine the main printed collections. There may therefore be much interesting material still to come to light.

It will be clear from my footnotes that this book could not have been written without the bedrock support of recent specialist work on English thirteenth-century history. The political developments of the 1250s and 1260s and the role of the Savoyards in that period have been greatly elucidated by the work of Huw Ridgeway, including his unpublished D.Phil. thesis, by two seminal articles by David Carpenter on the significance of the 1258 crisis and on the 'Statute' against aliens, and finally by John Maddicott's new interpretation of the personality and significance of Simon de Montfort. The work of Simon Lloyd and Clive Knowles has helped to clarify the post-Evesham period, and on the Lord Edward, I am indebted to Robin Studd's unpublished as well as his published work, to Hilary Wait's thesis on Edward's household and resources and to Michael Prestwich's biography of Edward I.

Personal academic debts are obviously many. Huw Ridgeway introduced me to the Thirteenth Century England conferences at Newcastle upon Tyne (now held at Durham) and I have profited greatly from both his insights and his extensive knowledge. John Parsons has given generous, detailed help in a steady flow of letters from Toronto to Oxford; Robin Studd, with great kindness, lent me his own copy of his Ph.D. thesis and helped with several Gascon references; John Maddicott was good enough to allow me to read his biography of Simon de Montfort, step by step, before it was published. To Michael Clanchy I owe my introduction to Blackwell Publishers and a very useful criticism of my first scheme for the book. Among those who have helped on specific topics, or have given long-term encouragement, I would mention particularly David d'Avray, Robert Stacey and Barbara Harvey. To all these I offer my warm thanks.

My greatest debt of all is to David Carpenter who first told me I ought to write a life of Eleanor of Provence, and has never relented. He has given unstinted critical help throughout, and finally he read a first draft of the whole book, making invaluable suggestions at that stage. His steady encouragement has seen me through.

For more general criticism, help and encouragement I owe much to Doris James and Elizabeth May, who both read the text in full. Elizabeth May has also given valuable help with the index. Finally I am indebted to Blackwell Publishers for inviting me to write this book and for their care in preparing it for publication. I have especially appreciated the perceptive editorial guidance of Tessa Harvey.

                                                                    M.H.

Abbreviations

AM	*Annales Monastici*
BIHR	*Bulletin of the Institute of Historical Research*
BL	British Library
CChR	*Calendar of Charter Rolls*
CCR	*Calendar of Close Rolls*
CIM	*Calendar of Inquisitions Miscellaneous*
CLR	*Calendar of Liberate Rolls*
CM	*Matthaei Parisiensis Chronica Majora*
CPL	*Calendar of Papal Letters*
CPR	*Calendar of Patent Rolls*
CR	*Close Rolls*
Cron. Maiorum	*De Antiquis Legibus Liber: Cronica Maiorum et Vicecomitum Londoniarum*
DBM	*Documents of the Baronial Movement of Reform and Rebellion*
DNB	*Dictionary of National Biography*
EHR	*English Historical Review*
Flores	*Flores Historiarum*
HMC	Historical Manuscripts Commission
JHSE	Jewish Historical Society of England
JMH	*Journal of Medieval History*
King's Works	R. A. Brown, H. M. Colvin, and A. J. Taylor, *The History of the King's Works: The Middle Ages*
Robert of Gloucester	*The Metrical Chronicle of Robert of Gloucester*
RS	Rolls Series
TCE	*Thirteenth Century England*

TRHS   *Transactions of the Royal Historical Society*
VCH   *Victoria County History*
WAM   Westminster Abbey Muniment

Note on Money

References to money are given in £ s d sterling, unless otherwise stated. The mark was worth 13s 4d (two-thirds of a pound). The exchange rates for foreign currencies have been calculated in line with the tables provided by Dr Peter Spufford in *Handbook of Medieval Exchange* (Royal Historical Society, London, 1986).

1

Childhood, Marriage and Coronation

On 14 January 1236 Eleanor of Provence was married to King Henry III by Archbishop Edmund Rich at Canterbury. It was the most significant single event in her life, dividing her childhood in her father's court in Provence from her adult life as queen of England. She had very recently disembarked at Dover, to marry a man she had not yet met and to become queen of a country she had never before seen. She was twelve years old.[1]

The medieval county of Provence, from which Eleanor had come, stretched along the Mediterranean seaboard from the fertile plains of the Rhône valley in the west to the foothills of the Alps in the east, with the River Durance forming the northern boundary. It was an area favoured with clear air and a beautiful and varied terrain. Eleanor's father, Raymond-Berengar V, assertive and capable, had ruled the county since 1219 and he also claimed suzerainty over the neighbouring county of Forcalquier to the north of the Durance.[2] He held these lordships as a vassal of the Emperor Frederick II. The count's capital was Aix-en-Provence but he also favoured Brignoles, nearer the coast, where he built a new palace in 1223, the probable year of Eleanor's birth. Unlike

---

[1] CM, iii. 335–6. Eleanor was probably born in 1223. Matthew Paris, writing under 1236, but referring to the negotiations of October 1235, describes her as 'jamque duodennem'; in his *Historia Anglorum*, ii. 386 he describes her as 'fere duodennem' when she comes to England. See Sivéry, *Marguerite de Provence*, 19, and Parsons, 'Mothers, Daughters, Marriage, Power', 67. Agnes Strickland is incorrect in suggesting that she was almost fourteen, *Lives of the Queens of England*, i. 356.

[2] For Provence under Raymond-Berengar V, see Baratier, *Histoire de la Provence*, 154–63, 178–9.

his predecessors he visited even the more remote parts of his territories, sometimes presumably accompanied by his family.[3] Raymond-Berengar V was the last of a line of counts, Catalan by birth, who had controlled Provence since 1112 when Raymond-Berengar III, count of Barcelona, married the Provençal heiress Douce. The various descendants of Douce came to rule not only in Provence and Barcelona but also, through a further advantageous marriage, in the kingdom of Aragon. Although ensuing divisions of power among siblings came near to depriving Eleanor's father of his legitimate inheritance, he survived a hazardous minority, which included captivity in an Aragonese castle and an exciting rescue operation, to become count of Provence in his own name in 1219.

It may have been in the same year that Raymond-Berengar V married Beatrice of Savoy.[4] This was a politically astute alliance with the county which bordered his own lands to the north and east, but beyond this the marriage had results of far-reaching importance in the history of western Europe in the next half century. Beatrice was a gifted woman, with marked diplomatic skills, but her prime importance lay in her six remarkable brothers. Their father, Count Thomas of Savoy, a man of strong will and political vision, had married the daughter of the count of Geneva, one of the many shrewd steps which he took towards extending his influence and consolidating his scattered lordships in the Helvetian Alps and the Lombard plain. Determined to secure the integrity of his patrimony, he obliged his five younger sons to take up careers in the Church. Amadeus, the eldest son, was to succeed his father as count of Savoy, but the others were installed in key benefices in churches within the Savoyard sphere of influence, at Valence, Vienne and Lyon in the Rhône valley, at Nantua and Belley further east, and at Geneva and Lausanne in the Pays de Vaux.[5] These Savoyard uncles of Eleanor of Provence were to play a crucial role in her career as queen of England.

The marriage of Raymond-Berengar and Beatrice was not an immediate success in terms of a family. First came two boys, probably twins, who were either stillborn or died very young.[6] After that there were no more sons, but four daughters, Margaret born in 1221, Eleanor in 1223, and then a younger pair, Sanchia and Beatrice, born about 1228 and 1231 respectively.[7] The absence of a son and heir focused attention on the four daughters. All four, like their mother Beatrice and their grandmother Margaret of Geneva, were renowned for their beauty, and all

[3] Sivéry, *Marguerite de Provence*, 12.
[4] Ibid., 11.
[5] Cox, *Eagles of Savoy*, 9–19.
[6] *Receuil des Actes des Comtes de Provence*, i, p. xxxvi.
[7] Sivéry, *Marguerite de Provence*, 11–12, 19.

four eventually became queens. Chroniclers and poets, including Dante himself, felt compelled to dwell on these dazzling facts which had so much the air of medieval romance. Even the English chronicler Matthew Paris, who could be sharp enough about these women individually, dwelt enthusiastically on the image of Beatrice of Savoy as a second Niobe.[8]

Eleanor of Provence owed much to her parents. Her energetic and forceful father, committed in his approach to the business of government, and her beautiful, intelligent and cultured mother helped to fashion her. Again she was probably much indebted to the companionship and affection of her eldest sister who left her father's household in 1234 to marry Louis IX of France. Eleanor and Margaret were on terms of close friendship throughout their lives, whether they were seeing each other much or little, and that friendship had far-reaching political significance.

The medieval concept of childhood, the treatment of children and their education are currently hotly debated. The conclusions of Philippe Ariès as to the lack of interest in the special features of childhood and the lack of parental affection for children in the cultural climate of medieval Europe have been strongly contested by several more recent writers. Notably, Shulamith Shahar has shown that childhood was conceived as a distinct stage in human development, with serious thought being given to child care and education.[9] Specifically in relation to Occitan culture, where we come close to the immediate environment of Eleanor of Provence, Linda Paterson has argued from the evidence of literature and chronicles that children were valued in their own right and often treated with affection and special care, although she points out that one hears far more of boys than of girls.[10] This, however, gives special interest to a text relating to paediatrics, the first to come from a source connected with the Occitan. It was written for Eleanor's mother, Beatrice of Savoy, as two chapters in the *Régime du corps*, which she commissioned from Aldebrandino of Siena in 1256. This date is much too late for Beatrice to have made use of this advice in rearing her own children, but she may well have had in mind the needs of her daughters, who were by this time mothers themselves. Evidently, in Beatrice's view, physical well-being, including the special needs of children, were matters appropriate for systematic exposition in a language (Old French) which made the subject accessible to women.[11] Aldebrandino's treatise, being closely based on

---

[8] *CM*, iii. 335; *CM*, v. 477, 654.

[9] Shulamith Shahar, in *Childhood in the Middle Ages*, 1–4, summarizes her criticism of P. Ariès, *L'Enfant et la vie familiale sous l'ancien régime* (Paris, 1960).

[10] Paterson, *The World of the Troubadours*, 280–6. For connotation of 'Occitan' see ibid., 1–9.

[11] Ibid., 295–6.

the work of the Arabic scholar Avicenna, has few surprises; the original-
ity lies in the attitude of Beatrice. Beatrice's interest in practical man-
uals finds an interesting parallel in her daughter Margaret's request to the
Dominican Vincent of Beauvais for a treatise on the education of children. This dates from the 1240s or 1250s and its approach is purely
conventional in clerical terms. It does give more attention than usual to
the education of girls, but claims that Vincent had advanced views on this
subject have rightly been dismissed; his work makes arid reading.[12] What
is significant is Margaret's desire for something more than haphazard
instruction. In this she was her mother's daughter. The close contacts
which Eleanor of Provence was later to establish with her own children
fit well into such a picture.

In bringing up her daughters in the 1220s, Beatrice of Savoy herself
would not have lacked traditional advice; but the traditions were conflicting. Vincent of Beauvais, mentioned above, and Giles of Rome,
another thirteenth-century Dominican, simply reflect a well-established
clerical tradition which stressed the careful seclusion of girls in order to
safeguard their chastity, and the prime importance of their moral education. The discipline of prayer and the study of Holy Scripture were to be
encouraged; reading and writing and the ability to speak adequately
should also be taught, along with textile skills and household management.[13] It remained a bleak programme, and it cannot have been the
whole picture. Between the ages of seven, when childhood ended, and
twelve, when a girl became marriageable, she, like her brothers, had to
be equipped for her future lifestyle. For this, prayer and chastity were not
enough. An aristocratic girl had to learn the basic social arts. She must be
able to choose clothes and jewels and learn how to wear them to good
effect; she must master horse-riding and the skills required in hawking, a
popular sport with women, and she must become practised in music and
dancing, in conversing with ease and in playing such socially popular
games as chess.[14] It is likely that she would become acquainted with
secular as well as religious literature. All of this required a subtle combination of formal instruction with some exposure to a social environment
in which these skills were practised and valued.

The young woman who emerged at the end of this exacting training
was popularly required to possess two special qualities, both of which

[12] Orme, *Childhood to Chivalry*, 106–9; Tobin, 'Vincent of Beauvais on the Education of
Women', 485–9.

[13] Orme, *Childhood to Chivalry*, 107; see also Duby, *The Knight, the Lady and the
Priest*, 259–61.

[14] Shahar, *Childhood in the Middle Ages*, 222; Paterson, *The World of the Troubadours*,
254–6.

call for further comment. The girl should be beautiful and she should be articulate. Eleanor of Provence, her mother, her sisters and her daughters were all described as beautiful. What did it mean? Superficially it seems that medieval chroniclers were entirely uncritical in attributing beauty to almost any young woman of high birth. Here one must avoid anachronisms. Thirteenth-century chroniclers frequently mention beauty and manner in close association, and the second might powerfully reinforce the first. Certainly, physical beauty in itself would be apparent and would be admired, and from Matthew Paris's superlatives it seems likely that Beatrice of Provence and her daughters had a generous measure of natural advantage.[15] He was prepared to descend to ribald comment on the appearance of Eleanor's aunt Garsende de Moncade, who had the misfortune of being extremely fat.[16] But in most cases manner counted for much. A French chronicler described Eleanor's sister Margaret on her arrival at Sens in 1234 as 'discreet and well taught from her earliest years'.[17] What he perceived was good breeding. In describing Eleanor, Matthew Paris uses the words *decor* and *venustissima*, which suggest a particular style of beauty.[18] We discern that Eleanor was graceful, charming and elegant. There seemed to be no danger that she would behave in an awkward or untoward way. Training of this kind did much to enhance whatever natural attractions a girl might possess. It was obviously highly valued.

So too was the power to communicate, not just adequately but with elegance and subtlety. Apart from the evidence in contemporary romances, the English chronicler Matthew Paris makes specific allusion to this accomplishment. Familiar with the values of aristocratic society, Paris noted the 'eloquence' of Cecilia de Sanford, the instructress of both Henry III's sister Eleanor Marshal and of his sister-in-law Joan de Valence.[19] The Emperor Frederick II, a man of sophisticated standards in cultural matters, had been delighted by the accomplished speaking of another of Henry III's sisters, Isabella, who became his empress.[20] The chronicler was indicating qualities of effortless style and confidence in expression, a skill which Eleanor of Provence and her sisters would have been expected to master.

That Eleanor was highly articulate is evident from the quality of her letter-writing at a later stage in her life, and since she shared this

[15] *CM*, iii. 335.
[16] *CM*, iv. 224, 293.
[17] *Les Grandes Chroniques de France*, 65.
[18] *CM*, iii. 335.
[19] *CM*, v. 235.
[20] *CM*, iii. 324.

facility with her sister Margaret, it presumably owed something to their early training. Eleanor's linguistic knowledge is a different matter. Culturally she belonged to Occitania, a region of many dialects, but where the language of the troubadours had been standardized, and the count's daughters would have been familiar with that.[21] Beyond this one must go cautiously. Both Eleanor and Margaret must have mastered quickly the French spoken at the courts of their husbands.[22] Later, in England, Eleanor would also have become familiar with yet another form of French, Anglo-Norman. Her knowledge of Latin is more difficult to assess. Since two religious works, originally composed in Latin, were recast for her in Anglo-Norman, it appears that she certainly did not have a full literary command of Latin.[23] Even so, it seems unlikely that an intelligent woman, apparently linguistically competent, receiving many letters written in Latin and deeply committed to an elaborate liturgical round, spoken and written in Latin, should not have acquired at least some working knowledge of the language.[24]

Ultimately the technical side of education mattered less than the systems of thought and belief in the light of which the education took place. Thirteenth-century Provence was heir to a distinctive culture. The greatest age of the troubadours had passed but the courts of the count and nobles were still steeped in its conventions. The count especially had to be seen to maintain this prestigious culture and new compositions were required and presented. Garsende de Forcalquier, Raymond-Berengar's mother, had been a notable patron of troubadours and so too were Beatrice of Savoy and the count's sister Garsende de Moncade, Eleanor's mother and aunt. Blacas, lord of Aups, and the young Italian troubadour Sordello were among those who wrote lyrics in honour of the Countess Beatrice, and Bertrand d'Alamanon lists some half-dozen aristocratic ladies in Beatrice's entourage who actively patronized troubadours.[25] The troubadour lyrics were marked by a strongly secular female image. The lady who could inspire *fin amors* could play on the feelings of others; she possessed nicety of judgement, a poised manner and marked *savoir-faire*. Not all troubadour compositions were love lyrics; some were debate poems and some satirical *sirventes*, which Raymond-Berengar found to his own taste. Each type demanded linguistic facility and

---

[21] Paterson, *The World of the Troubadours*, 2; Wolff, *Western Languages*, 147–51.

[22] Lodge, 'Language Attitudes and Linguistic Norms in France and England in the Thirteenth Century', 77–8, 80.

[23] See ch. 4, below.

[24] Clanchy, *From Memory to Written Record*, 188–90.

[25] Viard, *Béatrice de Savoye*, 32–5; Jeanroy, *La Poésie lyrique des Troubadours*, 174–6, 181–2.

presumed a social ambience in which witty comment and neat verbal interchange were appreciated.

The young Eleanor is also likely to have been acquainted with the Provençal epic and, beyond that, with the stories underlying Arthurian romance. Although Occitan literature was somewhat resistant to the full development of the chivalric ethic, with its distinctive linking of the virtues of knighthood and the erotic excitement of courtly love, the Arthurian legends themselves were very widely known and by the twelfth century were familiar in Catalonia, the country with which Eleanor's father and his entourage retained so many links.[26] We know that Eleanor later delighted in Arthurian and other romances. It is worth noting that in the summer of 1236, the year of her arrival in England, Henry III visited Glastonbury.[27] Since his visits there were rare, he may possibly have been taking Eleanor to see King Arthur's reputed burial place.[28] If this is speculation, it is reasonably sober speculation. What must be discounted in the light of modern scholarship is the frequently repeated assertion that Eleanor herself wrote a very indifferent romance poem called *Blandin de Cornouailles*, with the aim of catching the attention of Richard of Cornwall and Henry III. The association of the poem with Eleanor is in fact spurious.[29]

The culture of the troubadours and of the writers of romance was essentially secular. Quite distinct, but perhaps even more potent in shaping Eleanor's thought and feeling, was the religious tradition in which she was raised. In Provence the Church was the firm ally of the count. This bond reflected the count's political stance as well as his piety. In the sequel to the Albigensian crusade, the Church looked to Raymond-Berengar for support and viewed his neighbour, Raymond VII, count of Toulouse, with hostility. Raymond-Berengar's support for the authority of the bishops in Marseilles and Avignon and other cities of the lower Rhône made them his allies against popular disturbance and urban ambition.[30] These were facts which no doubt impinged on Eleanor's mind but they were not the influences which would have shaped her religious sensitivity. For this we must look to a distinctive feature of

---

[26] Keen, *Chivalry*, 40–1; Paterson, *The World of the Troubadours*, 71–3; Salter, *English and International*, 20.

[27] CPR 1232–47, 151.

[28] I owe this suggestion to the kindness of David Carpenter.

[29] For the view that Eleanor wrote the poem, see Fauriel, *Histoire de la Poésie Provençale*, iii. 92–4, cited by Orme, *Childhood to Chivalry*, 162, n. 103, and earlier followed by Strickland, *Lives of the Queens of England*, i. 357–8. For a more authoritative view, see J. Boffey, 'Women authors and women's literacy...', 176, n. 6 and the references cited.

[30] Baratier, *Histoire de la Provence*, 155–7, 178; Busquet, *Histoire de Provence*, 154.

Christian experience in Provence in the early thirteenth century. When Eleanor was born, St Francis of Assisi was still alive. The enthusiasm for the various orders of friars, particularly the Franciscans and the Dominicans, which was soon to sweep the royal courts and episcopal households of Europe, was only just beginning. Both orders were already welcomed at the court of Raymond-Berengar, and Eleanor, like her future husband, was to be an eager patron of both, but her devotion to the followers of Francis went deepest. Provence was much closer than England to the cultural environment of early Franciscan preaching and, when every reservation has been made, it is difficult not to believe that the personification of Lady Poverty touched the mainsprings of a society steeped in troubadour poetic traditions. It would hardly be surprising if Eleanor had a sense of affinity with the followers of Francis and a sensitivity to the emotional warmth of their preaching, which in each case drew its strength from her childhood in Provence.[31]

In addition to providing Eleanor with a rich cultural environment as she grew up, Raymond-Berengar may have contributed to the first awakening of her political sense. In bringing Provence under his control he had faced a formidable task with such energy and intelligence that he is said to have virtually transformed Provence into a modern state.[32] His assertion of his comital authority over both local lords and towns eager for self-government was unremitting. But his policies were not merely repressive. He provided Provence with a coherent administration and effective judicial machinery. His political vision was matched by close attention to business and a discriminating choice of agents. Edouard Baratier points out that whereas the court of Alfonso II, Raymond-Berengar's father, had been frequented by great lords, that of Raymond-Berengar himself was dominated by clerks and lawyers, drawn from social ranks below the nobility.[33] Eleanor, young though she was, may have been aware of the frequent threats to the count's authority, of his firm handling of opposition and of the type of men on whom he habitually relied in government.

In the spring of 1234 Raymond-Berengar, hard-pressed by his political rival Count Raymond of Toulouse, turned to the French Crown for support. His own feudal superior, the Emperor Frederick II, now at enmity with the papacy, was becoming more friendly with Raymond of Toulouse.[34] At the French court the young Louis IX was still guided in all

---

[31] Franciscan houses were established at Arles and Aix around 1200; Moorman, *A History of the Franciscan Order*, 65.

[32] Busquet, *Histoire de Provence*, 163.

[33] Baratier, *Histoire de la Provence*, 157.

[34] Fournier, *Le Royaume d'Arles et de Vienne*, 138–41.

things by his shrewd and politically assertive mother, Blanche of Castile, who had seen him through the dangers of his minority. Blanche recognized the political importance of Raymond-Berengar, with his impeccable orthodoxy, his courage and his efficiency as a ruler, as an element of stability in the Midi, where the French Crown had a foothold in the Languedoc, as an outcome of the Albigensian crusade. Blanche's ideas went further than this. Louis IX must marry and have heirs. A marriage with Raymond-Berengar's eldest daughter would bind the count himself firmly to French interests and possibly give Louis IX some claim on Provence if Raymond-Berengar had no male heirs. The outcome was an agreement of 13 February 1234 by which the count and countess of Provence submitted their differences with Raymond of Toulouse to the arbitration of Louis IX and his mother, on condition of the marriage of their eldest daughter to the French king.[35] The marriage took place at Sens on 27 May 1234 with great ritual splendour, feasting and chivalric displays, and Margaret was crowned queen of France on the following day. Significantly, she was given away, not by her father but by her uncle, William bishop-elect of Valence, one of the enterprising sons of Count Thomas of Savoy.[36] He was a man of daring political vision and he was no doubt mindful of the fact that in Raymond-Berengar's court there was another niece, Eleanor, equally pleasing, who was approaching marriageable age. The political considerations promoting the marriage of Margaret of Provence with the Capetian king, Louis IX, are obvious. Those which underlay the marriage of her sister Eleanor to Henry III of England are much less so. 'An odd choice' was Robert Stacey's brisk comment on Henry's decision to marry Eleanor.[37] It is time to unravel the story behind that choice.

When Henry III succeeded to the English throne in 1216 the greater part of the south-east of his kingdom, including London, was held by Prince Louis of France, the future Louis VIII, supported by English rebel barons. Louis was a serious contender for the English Crown. Although he quickly withdrew after the Treaty of Kingston in 1217, Henry could not readily forget the threat that had been posed by the Capetians. By the time Henry's minority ended in 1227 he was eager to recover the continental possessions which his father King John had lost and which had been judged legally forfeit in the French royal court in 1202. These were Normandy, Brittany, Maine, Anjou and Poitou. Henry's supreme wish

---

[35] *Receuil des Actes des Comtes de Provence*, ii, no. 200.

[36] Sivéry, *Marguerite de Provence*, 39–43.

[37] Stacey, *Politics, Policy, and Finance*, 180. In relation to what follows see ibid., 166–73 and Powicke, *Henry III*, 175–85; also Hajdu, 'Castles, Castellans and the Structure of Politics in Poitou, 1152–1271', 34–9.

was to recover effective control of Poitou. He was partially Poitevin himself, through his grandmother Eleanor of Aquitaine and his mother Isabella of Angoulême. After the death of Henry's father King John, Isabella made a second marriage, to Hugh de Lusignan, count of La Marche, the most powerful of the local lords of Poitou. This might have seemed promising for Henry's own prospects in Poitou, but the loyalty of Isabella's new husband vacillated between the kings of France and England according to his immediate self-interest. Henry III's ineffective and costly attempt to recover Poitou in 1230 had placed him no nearer to his personal goal and brought him discredit with his own subjects in England. However, at the time of his marriage, Henry still retained his control of the southernmost province of the former Angevin empire, Gascony, which together with Poitou had previously constituted the great duchy of Aquitaine. Gascony had a special prestige since it was held by Henry as an allod and had never been a fief of the French Crown.[38]

As in the reign of King John, the background to any military campaign for the recovery of the lost Angevin dominions was a network of continental alliances, and the most effective alliances were those reinforced by marriage. Accordingly, in 1235 Henry played his boldest stroke yet, with the marriage of his sister Isabella to the German Emperor Frederick II. This seemed an excellent move since Frederick was by far the most powerful ally that Henry could have, but it cost the king a very large dowry of £20,000.[39]

The king and his advisers naturally had his own marriage constantly in mind as the greatest asset of all; this was to be the trump-card in the diplomatic game and also the means of providing Henry and the kingdom with heirs. They were at it for ten years. Proposals for a marriage with a daughter of Leopold of Austria and later with a daughter of Peter of Dreux, count of Brittany, both failed, the latter being foiled by the vigorous intervention of Louis IX's mother, Blanche of Castile, who saw it as a clear threat to French interests.[40] The next plan got much further, so far in fact that thirteen years later Henry III was worried lest on this occasion he had come too close to a binding union with another woman for the legitimacy of his subsequent marriage with Eleanor of Provence to be absolutely beyond question.[41] In 1234–5 Henry was deeply and at first hopefully involved in negotiations for a marriage to Joan, heiress-apparent to the strategically important county of Ponthieu which lay

---

[38] Chaplais, 'Le Duché-Pairie de Guyenne', 5.
[39] *CPR 1232–47*, 188; *CM*, iii. 327.
[40] Powicke, *Henry III*, 178–9.
[41] See ch. 3, below.

between Normandy and Flanders. To acquire Ponthieu would have given the English king a very useful foothold to the north-east of France. Henry was determined that this time he should succeed; Blanche of Castile was determined that he should not.[42]

At some point before 8 April 1235 Henry III and Joan of Ponthieu had pledged themselves to each other by the *verba de presenti*.[43] When made before witnesses by two persons freely consenting and of canonical age, the *verba de presenti* constituted an absolutely binding commitment to marriage. According to canon law there was no going back on this, unless a just impediment to the union was discovered. The impediment envisaged was most often that of kinship within the prohibited degrees, as laid down by the Lateran Council of 1215.[44] Such an impediment did exist in the case of Henry's proposed marriage to Joan of Ponthieu, but Henry seemed reasonably confident that the pope would grant them the necessary dispensation, as was often done. On 8 April Henry was urging the count of Ponthieu to send his daughter to England for the marriage to be solemnized by the Church before Pentecost, 27 May, so that Joan might be crowned queen of England on that feast.[45] He wrote to Joan herself asking her to beg the pope to grant the necessary dispensation.[46] This proposal was soon overtaken by events.

Before the end of June Henry was playing a double game, which now involved the possibility of a marriage with Raymond-Berengar's second daughter, Eleanor. Eleanor's uncle William of Savoy evidently played a major role in the subsequent negotiations but we lack the evidence for the initial move. William held benefices in England and he had figured prominently, as we have seen, in the ceremonies of Margaret's marriage to Louis IX at Sens in the spring of 1234. In the following December we find him with Eleanor's parents in the Provençal city of Arles and, together with his brother Amadeus, now count of Savoy, he soon became closely involved in promoting an English royal marriage for Eleanor.[47] Only Henry's side of the correspondence remains extant but it seems that the Savoyard brothers had shrewdly made much of earlier links between England and Savoy in order to strengthen Henry's inclination to the match.[48]

The political benefits of a Provençal marriage to Henry are less obvious than those of a link with Brittany or Ponthieu. There were

---

[42] CM, iii. 327–8.
[43] *Foedera*, i. 216, 217 and 270 (letter of 27 October 1249).
[44] Brundage, *Law, Sex and Christian Society*, 331–41.
[45] *Foedera*, i. 216.
[46] Ibid.
[47] *Receuil des Actes des Comtes de Provence*, ii, no. 218; Cox, *Eagles of Savoy*, 46.
[48] *Foedera*, i. 217.

indeed drawbacks. Henry's main ally against the Capetians was the Emperor Frederick II, who was now on better terms with Raymond of Toulouse than with Raymond's chief adversary, Raymond-Berengar of Provence. Again, the marriage could do nothing for Henry's own relations with Raymond of Toulouse who so far had been the natural ally of Henry in the south of France. Financially the marriage was unpromising since Raymond-Berengar was not a rich man, and in territorial terms Henry could only look forward to a possible claim on a portion of Provence at best, and there was no certainty of that. Yet the prospect of a marriage alliance with Provence did have its attractions. Political allegiances in the Midi were fluid and Raymond of Toulouse was particularly unpredictable. It was above all the French Crown that Henry had to watch and he saw a marriage with Eleanor as countering the advantages which had accrued to the Capetians by Louis IX's marriage to Eleanor's sister Margaret. Again, through close contacts with Savoy and Provence, who together controlled most of the Alpine passes, Henry looked forward to establishing his influence to the south and east of France in an area which had great strategic importance in European politics, and Henry aimed to play a continental role.[49] By the early summer of 1235 Henry had developed a lively sense of the advantages of a marriage with Eleanor of Provence; but, whatever its attractions, he was in point of hard fact committed to marriage with Joan of Ponthieu, and that too had much to commend it. What he must not do was to lose both possible brides.

On 22 June 1235, therefore, Henry wrote to Amadeus count of Savoy and his brother William.[50] He assured them that he would dearly like to strengthen his friendship with them by a marriage with their niece. But there were problems, as they would be aware. He had pledged himself to marriage with the daughter of 'a certain nobleman' by the *verba de presenti*. This was surely a very big problem indeed, but Henry seemed reasonably sanguine. It now appeared, he said, that there was an impediment to that marriage. In fact Henry was aware that Louis IX and Blanche of Castile were ruining his prospects with Joan of Ponthieu by diplomacy in Rome and by threatening Joan herself.[51] He by now perceived that a swift change of tack was wholly desirable and on 16 July he urgently ordered his own envoys in Rome to cease their efforts to secure a dispensation for the Ponthieu match.[52]

---

[49] Stacey, *Politics, Policy, and Finance*, 180–1; Cox, *Eagles of Savoy*, 47.
[50] *Foedera*, i. 217.
[51] *CM*, iii. 328.
[52] *Foedera*, i. 218 (16 July).

Henry could now concentrate on Provence. Before 10 October 1235 the king had sent his envoys Richard le Gras and John of Gatesden to negotiate with Raymond-Berengar, and almost certainly to view the bride.[53] Fascinating details of this custom by which a prospective queen was vetted by the envoys of her future husband have been brought together by Dr Pierre Chaplais.[54] The practice seems a crude confirmation of Georges Duby's view that women in this period were treated as valuable objects, although we are assured by the English chronicler Matthew Paris that the viewing of Henry's own sister Isabella was done reverently, as it was no doubt in the case of Eleanor herself.[55] The likelihood that Gatesden had officially viewed the bride is strengthened by the detailed information that he was able to give Matthew Paris about Eleanor's parentage and about her person. On the basis of the envoys' favourable reports on their visit Henry quickly obtained assent to the marriage from a council of his lay and ecclesiastical magnates.[56]

A medieval aristocratic marriage always involved a property transaction. Henry III was required to make a settlement of dower on Eleanor of Provence at the moment when he took her as his wife 'at the church door'. Dower amounted notionally to a third part of the husband's property and if he died before her she would then enjoy this property for life, although she could not dispose of it. Dower might be 'nominated', that is, specified, or it might be unspecified, but in the case of a future queen a specified dower would be expected.[57] Henry now undertook that Eleanor should be dowered with 'the cities, lands and tenements' which had by custom been assigned to previous queens of England, but contingency provisions had to be made in case Henry predeceased not only his wife but his mother Isabella, the dowager of King John. In that case Eleanor would receive the following twelve towns and vills: Gloucester, Cambridge, Huntingdon, Droitwich, Basingstoke, Andover, Cheltenham, Godmanchester, King's Cliffe, Kingston, Ospringe and Lothingland.[58] In the grant which was finally entered on the charter rolls on 21 January 1236, Worcester and Bath had been added to that list.[59] Raymond-Berengar's own copy of the charter is still to be found in the archives of the *département* of the Bouches-du-Rhône.

---

[53] Ibid., i. 218 (10 October).

[54] Chaplais, *English Medieval Diplomatic Practice*, Part I, i. 89–93.

[55] Duby, *The Knight, the Lady and the Priest*, 134 and *passim*; CM, iii. 319.

[56] *Foedera*, i. 218 (10 October).

[57] Howell, 'The Resources of Eleanor of Provence', 380–2 and sources cited.

[58] *Treaty Rolls*, i, no. 23.

[59] CChR 1226–57, 218.

For his part, the father of the bride had to allot her a marriage portion, which would be made over to her husband for the benefit of the children of the marriage. As members of a full-scale diplomatic mission to Provence in October 1235, the king's proctors John fitz Philip and Robert de Mucegros were appointed to negotiate this sum. The king had given the matter anxious thought and he furnished his proctors with no fewer than six separate sets of letters, all dated 11 October 1235, each specifying a different sum, the amounts ranging from a hopeful 20,000 marks to a modest 3,000 marks.[60] When they had made the best bargain they could with Raymond-Berengar the proctors would then produce the appropriate set of letters. With matters thus prudently arranged, Henry suddenly decided that he could not tolerate a disappointment at this stage and wrote impulsively to his envoys on 19 October that even if they could extract no money at all from the count they must without fail bring his daughter Eleanor back to England to marry the king.[61] When Raymond-Berengar made his will in 1238, the amount designated as a marriage portion in the case of each of his two elder daughters was 10,000 marks.[62]

At the Provençal castle of Tarascon on 23 November 1235 Eleanor of Provence committed herself to Henry III by the exchange of the *verba de presenti*.[63] The promise was made on Henry's behalf by Robert de Mucegros, Eleanor's future steward, and Eleanor would presumably have made her own commitment in person, since she was present and she had reached the necessary age of twelve. All was now in readiness for her journey to England.

The first stage was accomplished when she reached the city of Vienne on the Rhône, where William of Savoy was dean of the cathedral, and here the marriage contract was apparently confirmed on 15 December.[64] William of Savoy then undertook the personal escort of his niece for the rest of her long journey and she was also accompanied by Henry's ambassadors and by her own large retinue, which according to Matthew Paris numbered 300 horsemen and would have included her ladies and personal attendants. Theobald of Champagne, that generous-hearted, imprudent troubadour, as a kinsman of Henry III, paid the expenses of the whole cavalcade for more than five days as they travelled north

---

[60] *Treaty Rolls*, i, nos 24, 25.

[61] Ibid., no. 26.

[62] *Receuil des Actes des Comtes de Provence*, ii, no. 292 A. See also *Ann. Dunstable*, 144.

[63] *Flores*, ii. 216.

[64] Ibid.

through his territories.[65] When Eleanor came to the borders of France itself, in the sense of the fiefs under the direct control of the French king, she is said to have received honourable protection from Louis IX, her sister Margaret and from the formidable queen mother, Blanche. Whether there was a personal meeting between Eleanor and members of the French royal family is not clear.[66] They may have sent individual envoys to greet her and escort her along her route. At last the Channel coast was reached, the winds were favourable and Eleanor and her retinue landed at Dover and arrived in Canterbury before they were expected. The king was already there to greet them, with an imposing following of magnates and prelates. Since the end of the Christmas festivities at Westminster he had been eagerly awaiting news of the return of his ambassadors and he now rushed to embrace them. Since Matthew Paris was keen to hurry on to his description of the coronation at Westminster he dealt briskly with the king's first meeting with Eleanor. 'Having seen the girl, he accepted her and married her at Canterbury.'[67]

For Eleanor herself Canterbury would have been more than a brief preliminary to Westminster. From what we know of Beatrice of Savoy one imagines that her daughter would have been prepared for her marriage realistically and would therefore have experienced no sense of shock that her future husband was a man of twenty-eight, her senior by sixteen years. Despite the slight defect of a drooping eyelid there is no reason to think that Henry was other than personable, but he had no chivalric reputation to stimulate the imagination of a young girl. To Eleanor he must surely have seemed old and she may have felt some envy for her sister Margaret, queen of France, whose husband was much nearer her own age. Yet Henry was king of England and he was a man with a fine sense of occasion. He would have taken trouble to see that his entourage was impressive and that the welcome to his future bride was performed with royal dignity. More than this, he was generous and warm-hearted and prepared to lavish care and affection on his wife. In any case, it was her business to please him. At Canterbury she bound herself to Henry III by the solemn sacrament of marriage, and almost certainly by the consummation of that marriage.[68] The betrothal at the church door and the nuptial mass in the cathedral would have been followed by the blessing of the marriage bed. Only six days separated the marriage at Canterbury from the coronation at Westminster, but their

---

[65] CM, iii. 335–6.

[66] Sivéry, *Marguerite de Provence*, 58.

[67] CM, iii. 336.

[68] This would have been important politically in establishing beyond doubt the validity of the marriage (see Brundage, *Law, Sex and Christian Society*, 235–6, 269).

personal relationship would have begun during that week. We are told by the confessor of Eleanor's sister, Queen Margaret of France, that Louis IX, following the prescription of canonists and theologians, had refrained from consummating his union with Margaret for the first three nights after the marriage had been celebrated.[69] If Matthew Paris is to be believed, the Emperor Frederick II, characteristically free of all such scruples, only waited for the hour when his astrologers informed him that the moment was absolutely right.[70] Neither confessor nor chronicler has left any record of the beginning of married life for Henry III and Eleanor of Provence.

On 20 January 1236 Eleanor was crowned and anointed as queen of England. The disjunction of the ceremonies of marriage and coronation, by this time common practice in the West, tended to a recognition of queenship as distinct from marriage, although wholly dependent upon it. In England, if the king had been crowned previously, the coronation of the queen was performed in the presence of the king in his full coronation regalia. This had been the case with the coronation of King John's second wife, Isabella of Angoulême, and it was current practice in France.[71] It had also been established that a queen of England, like the king himself, should be crowned at Westminster and by the archbishop of Canterbury, when this was practicable.[72] The coronation of a queen was a public act, affecting the whole community of the realm. In a dower instrument of 1204, King John had gone so far as to imply 'national' acceptance of his wife Isabella of Angoulême, 'queen by the grace of God, who was crowned in England by the common assent and will of the archbishops, bishops, earls, clergy and people of the whole kingdom as queen of England'.[73] The queen's coronation certainly needed to be witnessed by the great men of the kingdom and their presence may have been taken to signify assent as well.

The coronation of Henry III's queen was a magnificent state occasion and a brilliant spectacle, full of symbolic significance for the image of monarchy. It was the first occasion on which Henry III's undoubted flair for meticulously planned royal pageantry had full aesthetic scope. Matthew Paris relished the opportunity to describe it.[74] London was

---

[69] Guillaume de Saint-Pathus, *Vie de Saint Louis*, 129.

[70] *CM*, iii. 324.

[71] Richardson, 'The Marriage and Coronation of Isabella of Angoulême', 307; M. Facinger, 'Medieval Queenship: Capetian France', 18.

[72] Schramm, *A History of the English Coronation*, 39–40.

[73] *Rotuli Chartarum*, 128; for comment see Richardson, 'The Marriage and Coronation of Isabella of Angoulême', 307–11.

[74] *CM*, iii. 337–9; the details which follow are drawn from Paris's account and from an extract from the Red Book of the Exchequer, printed in *English Coronation Records*, 58–61.

crammed with people and decked out with silk hangings, flags and festive garlands, which heightened the mood of excitement and celebration. At certain points there seem to have been set pieces which delighted the chronicler by their ingenuity, but unfortunately failed to make him more explicit. The short daylight hours of an English January posed no problem for prolonged festivities since the city streets were ablaze with candles and lamps, but control of the crowds presented a security hazard. The constable of Chester kept eager bystanders in check with a virge 'when they pressed forward in a disorderly way', but the duties of William Beauchamp, the king's almoner, sound a harsher note; he had jurisdiction over the petty crimes of the poor and of lepers, with the power to sentence a leper to burning if one of them struck another man with his knife.

In sheer panache the cavalcade of the wealthy London citizens outdid everything. After trying out the speed of their horses in impromptu races they formed into disciplined troops and rode out to Westminster, splendidly attired in silk mantles worked with gold thread, the trappings of their horses burnished and shining. Ahead of them rode the king's trumpeters, their horns sounding, to the delight of the crowds. The mounted citizens carried with them 360 gold and silver cups to serve the king's guests at the coronation banquet, according to their established privilege.

At Westminster a more solemn note was struck, as the processions of the king and the queen walked from the royal palace to the abbey church over the special blue ray-cloth which was traditionally laid down for the occasion. The king was preceded by three earls bearing the swords of state, followed by the treasurer in a dalmatic, carrying the paten which was to be used at the coronation mass, and the chancellor in full pontificals carrying the special stone chalice of the king's regalia.[75] Two knights carried sceptres ahead of the king, but it is not entirely clear whether or not these were intended for presentation to the queen.[76] The king himself came last, in his full coronation regalia, and there was held above him a canopy of purple silk, secured at the corners on four silver lances, with a silver-gilt bell at each corner, the lances carried according to tradition by barons of the Cinque Ports.

Behind the king's procession came that of the queen, or more accurately of the young royal wife who was about to be crowned. Eleanor too walked beneath a silk canopy with silver lances and silver-gilt bells like

---

[75] *English Coronation Records*, 58; on the chalice see Carpenter, 'The Burial of King Henry III', 451, 455.

[76] Parsons, 'Ritual and Symbol', 63 and n. 13; and see n. 79, below.

that of the king, and hers too was borne by barons of the Cinque Ports. Almost certainly she would have worn her hair loose, falling upon her shoulders, and on her head a circlet of gold to keep her hair in order. Two bishops, chosen by the king, walked on each side of the queen to support her. It may be that her own regalia was carried in front of her, as was later the custom; we cannot be certain.[77] Inside the church the congregation of clergy, magnates and knights presented a colourful sight and no doubt expectancy and curiosity ran high. And since at the age of twelve perceptions have not yet been blunted by experience, it is likely that the ceremony of her coronation never entirely faded from Eleanor's memory.

At the church door the future queen paused while the archbishop recited the first prayer.[78] Its theme was significant in setting the tone for the whole service. After reciting the names of those biblical women who had been blessed in bearing sons of the line of King David, Sara, Rebecca and Rachel, the prayer culminated in celebration of the Virgin Mary who had been uniquely blessed in the fruit of her own womb. The emphasis on child-bearing within a royal descent was crucial to what was about to be enacted. Proceeding to the steps of the high altar, the future queen prostrated herself and the archbishop recited a further prayer. She then rose and knelt in preparation for the first and most potent ceremonial act, the anointing. The gold circlet was removed and the archbishop anointed her head with holy oil, an unction which exalted her to a new status and conferred spiritual gifts. Unction was followed by the blessing of the ring and by the placing of the ring on her finger and then by the blessing of the heavy gold crown of lilies. The raising of this crown and the placing of it on the queen's head was visually the high point of the ceremony. The new queen may also have been handed a sceptre and virge, the attributes of authority. The absence of any mention of this in the order of service which was probably followed for Eleanor's coronation does not mean that such a presentation did not take place.[79] On the great seal which Eleanor used until 1259 she is shown crowned and holding both virge and sceptre.[80]

---

[77] Some of these details are inferred from the fourteenth-century *Liber Regalis*; *English Coronation Records*, 100, 108.

[78] What follows is based on the second version of the third recension of the coronation order for a queen, Bruckmann, 'English Coronations, 1216–1308, 266–70. The order is printed in *English Coronation Records*, 37–9. I am indebted to John Parsons for invaluable help over the coronation orders for a queen.

[79] Parsons, 'Ritual and Symbol', 62–3. In a thirteenth-century manuscript, Edith, wife of Edward the Confessor, is shown receiving a sceptre from a layman at her coronation, *Estoire* (ed. James), 44, plate 18.

[80] Seal attached to BL Cotton Charter XVII. 6. For sceptres see Crouch, *The Image of Aristocracy in Britain*, 211–14.

A fuller consideration of queenship must be deferred until later in the book.[81] For the moment it is useful to consider what may have been immediately intelligible to Eleanor herself. The prayers related to hopes for her fertility in producing children for the English royal line; she was to be chaste within marriage and as a queen she was to be humble and compassionate and to imitate Queen Esther, who interceded with her husband for the welfare of her people. The visual imagery of the coronation service was as powerful as that of the marriage service; the ring of faith, the crown for glory, the unction for sanctification. By unction she was set apart for a special office and this could hardly have failed in its emotional impact. From this day onwards in letters and all other written instruments she would be addressed and would designate herself as *regina Dei gratia*, queen by the grace of God. Whatever efforts the Church may have made in the reform period of the eleventh and twelfth centuries to tone down the exaltation of royal state with which a coronation ceremony was inevitably imbued, they were surely effectively foiled by the Anglo-Norman tradition of the singing of the *Laudes Regiae* on these occasions. This was an invocation of Christ Triumphant. It began with the rousing affirmation 'Christus vincit, Christus regnat, Christus imperat' (Christ conquers, Christ reigns, Christ rules), followed by acclamations of the established powers ruling in this world as vicars of God. Henry III, with a keen sense of the majesty of his office, had the *Laudes* sung on all great royal occasions. At the coronation of his queen the chanting of the psalms and antiphons would have been performed by the monks of Westminster but it was a special group of the king's singers, led by one Walter de Lenche, who burst into this final triumphal paean of the *Laudes*.[82]

The day ended, as such days do, in a lavish feast, with unlimited quantities of venison, fish and many other delicacies. The wine was handed round freely by the Londoners, while the citizens of Winchester saw to the presentation of the food. Minstrels and entertainers gave first-rate performances.[83] But the queen herself is entirely lost to view; we do not even know whether she was present. Her part was over. There was some sharp watching over other men's privileges among the lay magnates, but the king prudently postponed the hearing of most of these conflicting claims to a later date. Conspicuous as one who did forcefully assert his ancestral right that day was Simon de Montfort, claimant to the earldom of Leicester, who acted as the king's steward 'although

---

[81] See ch. 11, below.
[82] Kantorowicz, *Laudes Regiae*, 173–5; Cowdrey, 'The Anglo-Norman *Laudes Regiae*', 43–4; *CLR 1226–40*, 255.
[83] *CM*, iii. 338–9.

Roger Bigod earl of Norfolk contested it'.[84] According to the same record the only right claimed in the queen's household was that of Gilbert de Sanford to act as her chamberlain. At the end of the day he was given 'the whole of the queen's bed, the basins and other things which the chamberlain has to deal with'.[85]

As Eleanor of Provence stood at the beginning of her career as queen of England, we may discern two ways in which she was pointed towards the future. The first was a petition which she made to the king on the day of her coronation that one William de Panchehall, who had been imprisoned for an offence against the forest law, should be pardoned.[86] This was clearly a set piece. Eleanor knew nothing of William de Panchehall and his troubles until she was directed to make this request to her husband. The custom of queenly intercession was widespread in western Europe and had its origins in the classical past, as Marjorie Chibnall has noted in recording an intercession made by the future Empress Matilda, daughter of the English King Henry I, shortly after her arrival at the imperial court.[87] At what point in the day Eleanor's request was made and how publicly is not known, but her role as an intercessor, already alluded to in the coronation service by the reference to Queen Esther, was reinforced.

The second pointer towards the future was a stained-glass window. In 1237 Henry III ordered a representation of the Tree of Jesse to be made for a window in the queen's bedchamber at Windsor.[88] The allusions in the coronation service to the fruitfulness of the eminent women of the line of David, culminating in the fruit of the Virgin's own womb, are here reflected in the royal genealogy of the Tree, with the Virgin and Child at its summit. In the queen's chamber this powerful image was placed permanently before the girl from whom royal sons were required. Here marriage and coronation seem to be fused into one overriding purpose. It has been claimed that queens were anointed not for their own sakes but simply towards the end of producing legitimate royal heirs for the kingdom, and Georges Duby has stressed that a woman's true throne was her marriage bed.[89] It may certainly be supposed that Henry III had placed

---

[84] Simon de Montfort held the honour of Leicester but did not receive the earldom until 1239, Maddicott, *Montfort*, 23.

[85] *English Coronation Records*, 58–61.

[86] *CR 1234–37*, 229.

[87] Chibnall, *The Empress Matilda*, 23–4. For further discussion of intercession see ch. 11, below.

[88] E 101/530/1, no. 23; Borenius, 'The Cycle of Images in the Palaces and Castles of Henry III', 42, 49; Parsons, 'Ritual and Symbol', 66–7.

[89] Stafford, *Queens, Concubines and Dowagers*, 134; Parsons, 'Ritual and Symbol', 61–2; Duby, *The Knight, the Lady and the Priest*, 234.

this image of royal genealogy deliberately and appropriately in the room in which he and his wife came together in the conjugal act.

2

The Young Queen

In the third year of his marriage Henry III was marked down as the victim of an assassination attempt. Henry believed the intention was to kill the queen too.[1] It happened at the royal palace at Woodstock in September 1238 and is vividly recounted by Matthew Paris, whose story, where it can be checked, is substantiated by other evidence.[2] A man pretending to be insane had thrust himself into the king's presence, calling upon Henry to resign to him his kingdom. The king restrained his servants from seizing the man and beating him, since he did indeed believe the intruder to be mad. In the middle of the night, however, the assassin climbed through a window into the king's bedchamber, armed with an unsheathed knife, and rushed at the royal bed. It was empty. By God's providence, as Paris says, the king was sleeping with the queen in her chamber. The man then began searching adjoining rooms, but his wild shouting had now disturbed one of the queen's damsels Margaret Biset, who was awake, reciting her psalter by candle-light. When she raised the alarm the king's attendants rushed to break down the door of the room where the assassin had barred himself in; he was overpowered and cast into chains. Under torture the man confessed that he had been sent by the outlawed William de Marisco to kill the king. This time there was no mercy; he was condemned to a brutal death.

The heroine of this incident was the queen's damsel Margaret Biset, who is described by Paris as very devout.[3] So she was, but not only

---

[1] CR 1237–42, 146.
[2] CM, iii. 497–8; Powicke, Henry III, 751–4.
[3] Flores, ii. 228.

because she read her psalter when others were asleep. Margaret came from a family distinguished by its loyal service to the Crown. Her personal kindness was remembered by Henry III's sister Isabella, and she gained permission to visit the unfortunate Eleanor of Brittany, daughter of King John's elder brother, Geoffrey, who was kept in close custody in Gloucester castle because of her possible entitlement to the throne.[4] Margaret was evidently compassionate as well as brave. The young queen's immediate gratitude to her for foiling the assassination attempt was natural, but Eleanor of Provence continued to remember. More than thirty years later it was at the queen's instance that Henry III confirmed a grant of property to the Biset leper foundation at Maiden Bradley, cherished by Margaret during her lifetime. When a royal escheator later questioned the grant the queen fended him off with the sharp warning that 'we regard the affairs of our religious house of Maiden Bradley as our own, because of our long-standing love for that house'.[5]

The presence of a woman such as Margaret Biset as an attendant on the queen indicates the tone at which the king aimed. Overall care of Eleanor's health and personal development was entrusted to an urbane and distinguished Englishman, Nicholas Farnham, qualified in medicine and theology and familiar with the schools of Oxford, Paris and Bologna. Until he left court to become bishop of Durham in 1241 he was the queen's moral guide, as well as her doctor.[6] As a support for her day-to-day living Eleanor was provided with a small household, topped by its own financial office, the queen's wardrobe.[7] Her first wardrobe-keeper was John of Gatesden, who had 'viewed' her in Provence, and her first household steward was Robert de Mucegros, who had spoken the *verba de presenti* on the king's behalf at Tarascon.[8] This continuity of contact reflects Henry's consideration in providing for his young wife.

The setting of Eleanor's daily life was equally the king's concern. He built or improved apartments for her in at least nine royal residences, and at the palace of Westminster he provided her with a finely appointed chamber and chapel.[9] The chamber walls were richly painted and on the mantel above the fire was an evocative figure of winter 'to be portrayed with such sad looks and miserable appearance that he may be truly likened to winter'.[10] Eleanor may well have hated English winters,

[4] *CPR 1232–47*, 103; *CR 1234–37*, 91, 224.
[5] BL Cotton MS Augustus II. 14; see also *CPR 1266–72*, 609.
[6] Talbot and Hammond, *Medical Practitioners*, 223–5; *CM*, iv. 158.
[7] Tout, *Chapters*, v. 232–6.
[8] *CLR 1226–40*, 366.
[9] *King's Works*, i. 125, 501–2, plates 28, 29.
[10] *CLR 1226–40*, 444.

having arrived in one of the wettest within living memory.[11] The spacious chapel, well-lit from eight lancet windows, was furnished with a Purbeck marble altar and font; on either side of the central lancet above the altar were the painted corbel heads of a young king and queen.[12] The Westminster suite was obviously regal and impressive, but Henry could command a range of styles and Eleanor's chamber in the Tower of London was painted over with roses on a white ground, perhaps the prettiest and most feminine of all her private rooms.[13]

Henry III's aesthetic sensibility was naturally stimulated by Eleanor's presence. He delighted in giving her presents; a silver platter with gold shields, emblazoned with the king's arms, a gold goblet enriched with enamel work, gold and jewelled rings, girdles and brooches.[14] But Henry's deepest satisfaction came when his aesthetic imagination was enhanced by his piety. He quickly drew Eleanor within the pattern of religious ritual by which he regulated his own life. In 1236, on the first feast of St Edward which they celebrated together, two rich brocades were offered on behalf of the king and the queen at the Confessor's shrine, and later Henry presented an image in gold of the queen herself.[15] In the next year, at the king's insistent petition, the name of Edward the Confessor, the last king of the Old English royal line, was added to the calendar of the universal Church. The cult of St Edward and the rebuilding of the abbey church at Westminster as a fitting setting for his shrine came to dominate Henry III's expression of his own piety and his distinctive style of kingship. He saw himself within a divinely ordained royal succession to which the saint/king gave incomparable lustre. Legends of the Confessor decorated many walls in the royal palaces. It was natural that the queen should be schooled in this devotion and her own intense personal hopes would have been focused on giving birth to another link in this line of kings.

The thoughtful attention of the king was of prime importance to Eleanor of Provence, but from the time of her arrival in England she derived additional support and consequence from the presence, at first intermittent but later virtually continuous, of one or other of her mother's able and politically-minded brothers. To class these men simply as royal favourites is an over-simplification. The very lack of subservience to Henry III on the part of the queen's Savoyard uncles is fundamental to an understanding of the developing relationship of Eleanor of

[11] *CM*, iii. 339–40.
[12] *King's Works*, i. 125.
[13] *CLR 1226–40*, 453.
[14] Ibid., 268, 276; *CR 1237–42*, 258; *CLR 1240–45*, 83, 120.
[15] *CR 1234–37*, 309; *CLR 1226–40*, 243.

Provence to her husband. They felt a strong obligation to the English king, but they all had interests elsewhere.[16] They could survive without Henry III, and when they wished they could take an independent stand. It was William of Savoy, as we have seen, the most senior of the clerical brothers, who helped to negotiate Eleanor's marriage and who accompanied her to England. According to the Dunstable annalist, he immediately became the king's chief counsellor.[17] His influence on the important financial and administrative measures taken by a newly-sworn royal council, established in April 1236, has been questioned, since the guiding intelligence here was almost certainly that of the king's chief justice, William Raleigh, an Englishman, but William of Savoy presumably secured the king's support for the new policies and undoubtedly understood and approved their thrust.[18] The reforms, although sound, roused opposition in the community and the blame may have come to rest with the king's counsellor from Savoy, who had already been loaded with privileges, including the custody of the earldom of Richmond.[19]

William left England in May 1238 to attend to his interests abroad and he did not return. The pope, eager to enlist his high abilities, promoted his election to the Flemish see of Liège in 1239, but William's career was cut short suddenly by his death at Viterbo in the same year.[20] While the appointment to Liège still hung in the balance, Henry III had been ruthlessly and clumsily active in trying to force the election of William to the wealthy English bishopric of Winchester. The king's bullying methods went contrary to the freedom of episcopal elections required by canon law; he alienated the reforming bishops in England and increased public suspicion and dislike of William of Savoy.[21]

Brief though it was, the career of William of Savoy in England affected the reputation of the queen. Matthew Paris entirely mis-states the case when he writes that the king, 'being under the influence of his wife', allowed this bishop to pull his kingdom to pieces and to eat up the produce of his own territories.[22] William of Savoy, in his own right and by virtue of his own ability and personal qualities, had secured Henry III's regard and favour. Yet the relationship between her husband and her uncle was profoundly important for Eleanor. It established her from the start under the protective influence of one of her mother's family; this

[16] Cox, *Eagles of Savoy*, 11–19; 95–107.
[17] *Ann. Dunstable*, 145–6.
[18] Stacey, *Politics, Policy, and Finance*, 96–100, 104–6.
[19] CR 1234–37, 310–11; CM, iii. 362–3.
[20] Cox, *Eagles of Savoy*, 69–70, 76–7.
[21] CM, iii. 493–5; Stacey, *Politics, Policy, and Finance*, 128–9; Powicke, *Henry III*, 270–1.
[22] CM, iii. 388.

was partially, but only partially, gain. She was the emblem of the Savoyard link, and William's unpopularity as an alien, favoured by the king to the detriment of Englishmen, redounded on her.

Meanwhile, Eleanor of Provence needed to note two other forceful personalities at her husband's court, the king's brother, Richard of Cornwall, and his brother-in-law, Simon de Montfort. The events surrounding Simon de Montfort's marriage in January 1238 show both men acting in character, and the queen had later to reckon with each of them. Simon was a highly accomplished and intelligent French nobleman, whose father and namesake had acquired notoriety for his cruelty and acquisitiveness in the suppression of the Albigensian heretics in the Languedoc. The younger Simon was imbued with something of his father's style of religious fervour but at this stage, as a younger son, he was motivated mainly by ambition. Although a Frenchman by birth and upbringing, he had secured Henry III's acceptance of a claim, derived from his grandmother, to a portion of the earldom of Leicester. He had risen high in royal favour and, after two unsuccessful attempts to make a prestigious marriage on the Continent, he focused on England and secured Henry's permission to marry the king's own sister Eleanor, widow of William Marshal earl of Pembroke.[23] Montfort was by now about thirty and Eleanor Marshal about twenty-three. The marriage was a splendid career step for Simon, but it was controversial. On the death of her first husband, Eleanor Marshal, influenced by her former instructress Cecilia de Sanford, had taken a vow of chastity in the presence of Archbishop Edmund. There could be no doubt that the archbishop would sternly resist Eleanor's re-marriage, which possibly explains why it was conducted secretly in the private chapel off the king's own chamber in the palace of Westminster. The English magnates were greatly angered by the secrecy, the absence of customary consultation and by the disparagement of the king's sister in marriage to a man of comparatively small fortune and modest position. Most angry of all was Richard of Cornwall, the king's brother, who had not been consulted on the marriage of his own sister. Allying with other disaffected magnates, Richard immediately raised a revolt against the Crown. The king was sufficiently alarmed to make one of his rare retreats to the Tower of London, but the revolt ended quickly when the king made it clear that he was prepared to buy his brother off. The king made an immediate payment of 6,000 marks towards the expenses of Richard's proposed crusading expedition, and this was only part of his fraternal generosity.[24]

[23] Maddicott, *Montfort*, 17–18; 21–9.
[24] *Ann. Tewkesbury*, 106; CM, iii. 475–9; Carpenter, 'Henry III and the Tower of London', 203; Stacey, *Politics, Policy, and Finance*, 123–6.

The queen may have made the useful discovery that Richard of Cornwall had his price.

Montfort's relations with the king were very soon to run into critical difficulties, which were to impinge on the queen, but in the course of 1238 Queen Eleanor was absorbed in a quite different matter. She had realized from the first that her husband depended on her to give him children, and above all to give him sons. In England no woman ruled in her own right as queen before the Tudor period and the history of the Empress Matilda had been a warning, not an encouragement. The deep anxiety which must have shadowed Eleanor's own mind in the first few years of her marriage is glimpsed in a casual remark of Matthew Paris under the year 1238 that 'it was feared that the queen was barren'.[25] In the autumn of that year the fear was removed; the queen was pregnant and the pregnancy was successful. On 17/18 June 1239, when she was still no more than sixteen years old, Queen Eleanor gave birth to a son, the future Edward I.[26] She had been remarkably fortunate. Her sister Margaret, queen of France, to her own great distress and her husband's disappointment, had to wait ten years after her marriage before she gave birth to an heir to the French throne. Eleanor of Provence had achieved the first step in what was required of her above all else, in the eyes of her husband and in the eyes of his subjects.

One accepts that Henry III was deeply gratified by the birth of his son, for personal and political reasons, but, more than that, he was overjoyed. He gave thanks to God, and the queen was at the centre of all his thanksgiving. His sensitivity to his wife's first experience of childbearing appears in his grant of an annual pension of £10 to Sybil Giffard, a woman experienced in court service, 'for her diligence exhibited towards the queen at the time of her confinement'.[27] The triumphal strains of 'Christus vincit, Christus regnat, Christus imperat' rang out from Walter de Lenche and his fellow clerks of the royal chapel to greet the day of Edward's birth, as they had greeted Eleanor's coronation.[28] The child, named after the Confessor himself, without regard to any Norman or Angevin forebears, was baptized by the papal legate Otto and confirmed by Archbishop Edmund in the presence of a group of bishops and earls, one of whom was Simon de Montfort. Simon was still high in the king's favour, having secured a papal dispensation for his marriage and having fathered a son who had been named after the king himself.[29] King Henry

25 *CM*, iii. 518.
26 Ibid., 539.
27 *CLR 1226–40*, 418.
28 Ibid., 406.
29 *CM*, iii. 539–40.

later gave 20*s* each to two boys who had been baptized on the same day as Edward and from the same font.[30] Yet there could be no certainty that the prince would thrive, and the king's anxiety is as apparent as his joy. A chaplain was appointed whose sole task was to celebrate the mass of the Virgin for the good estate and health of the king's son. To the same end, fifteen poor people were fed at Windsor on Christmas Eve, and a tunic of rich silk, made to fit Edward, was offered at St Mary's, Southwark.[31]

The celebrations surrounding Edward's birth reached their climax in the ceremony of the queen's purification on 9 August 1239. Five hundred tapers were lit before the shrine of St Edward and again the triumphal paean of the *Laudes* rang out.[32] A large gathering of noble ladies assembled in London to accompany the queen to her churching. The scene was set – but certainly not for the drama which was in fact to take place.[33] Henry's anger had suddenly been roused against Montfort and his wife. Perhaps Archbishop Edmund, who continued to deplore the marriage, had again appealed to the king's conscience; perhaps there had been too many malicious rumours that Montfort had forced the king's hand by seducing Eleanor Marshal. What is certain is that Montfort, with great imprudence, had become indebted for a sum of 2,000 marks to another of the queen's uncles, Thomas of Savoy. Thomas was not the initial creditor but the debt had been transferred to him. What rankled most deeply with the king was the fact that Montfort had apparently used the king's name as surety for this debt, without his permission.[34] Henry was furiously angry. When Montfort and his wife appeared in London for the queen's purification Henry rounded on them both with great violence, apparently in the archbishop's presence, accusing Simon of having seduced Eleanor before marriage, of using bribery at Rome to secure a dispensation for the marriage and of citing the king as surety for his debts.[35] In deep confusion and humiliation Simon and his wife fled the country. The queen could hardly have remained unmoved by the force of her husband's anger. On the occasion of a public ceremony of which she was the focus, the most splendid since her own coronation, she was witnessing court politics in the raw. But was she further involved? It is difficult to be sure. She would have a natural inclination to sympathize with her uncle Thomas of Savoy, even to speak for him, but there is no

[30] *CLR 1226–40*, 479.

[31] Ibid., 435, 442.

[32] Ibid., 404, 406.

[33] *CM*, iii. 566–7.

[34] *CR 1237–42*, 234–5; Maddicott, *Montfort*, 24–5; Cox, *Eagles of Savoy*, 99.

[35] *CM*, iii. 566–7. For Montfort's own account see Bémont, *Simon de Montfort* (1st edn), 333–4.

evidence for Powicke's surmise that 'probably the two Eleanors did not get on well together'.[36] They were later on terms of friendship.

Thomas of Savoy was the second of Eleanor's uncles to take advantage of her position as queen of England. Having abandoned his clerical career in February 1238 to marry Joan, countess of Flanders in her own right, he was now keen to maximize the traditional links between Flanders and England. He made a brief visit to England in August 1239, very close to the time of Montfort's sudden disgrace, in order to do homage to Henry III and then as his vassal to receive the money fief of 500 marks traditionally payable by the king of England to the count of Flanders.[37] The next year Count Thomas was back in England, in genuine need of money to pay the debts earlier incurred in supporting his brother William's candidature to the see of Liège. He pressed Henry for repayment of the debt owed him by Simon de Montfort, and the king, after paying 500 marks himself, made an immediate distraint for the remainder on Earl Simon's lands, an action which Simon was to resent bitterly.[38] Matthew Paris noted that on this 1240 visit Thomas went to Windsor to see the Lord Edward.[39] The queen would presumably have been at Windsor too, frequently staying there for long periods when the children were young. Thomas was reputed to be a genial man but one may doubt whether he went to Windsor simply to greet his niece and admire the baby. Eleanor of Provence was now a young woman of sixteen or seventeen, an age at which she was capable of some political understanding. She must already have known her husband well and she had experience of the internal politics of the court. Even more important, she now had a new personal motivation in watching over the future interests of that one-year-old baby who was heir to his father's throne. She was also, then as always, warmly disposed towards her mother's family. Thomas was a knowledgeable man. A vassal of the kings of England and France and of the emperor, he had learned to be supple in diplomacy. He had a good working knowledge of Flanders, a region highly distinctive in its economic, social and political complexion.[40] It was the area which was later to provide Eleanor of Provence herself with men who would fight and men who would lend money. Thomas would have been aware that the better informed his niece was, the more effectively she could work in the interests of those dear to her. Thomas may even have perceived in this young woman a marked interest in, and

---

[36] Powicke, *Henry III*, 204.
[37] *CM*, iii. 616–17.
[38] *CLR 1226–40*, 472; Bémont, *Simon de Montfort* (1st edn), 334.
[39] *CM*, iv. 20.
[40] Cox, *Eagles of Savoy*, 95–6.

potential aptitude for, the great art of politics. We can only speculate. What is certain in the light of later events is Eleanor's strong personal regard for Thomas, her apparent confidence in his judgement and her stalwart loyalty when he was imprisoned by his enemies.[41]

Soon after Count Thomas's visit to England, Eleanor of Provence gave birth to her second child, on 29 September 1240; the girl was named Margaret after the queen's sister. In the previous month the king had ordered the great hall at Westminster and a second smaller hall to be filled with poor people who were fed at the king's expense, 'for the queen who is near to her confinement'.[42] Again, the *Laudes* were sung to greet the birth, candles were lit and a specially fine candle worth five marks was provided for Eleanor herself to carry at her purification. In November the king gave presents of twelve ounces of gold both to his wife and to his daughter as a mark of his delight and his congratulations.[43]

Through her success as a mother Eleanor was now high in royal favour. The time was therefore propitious for the appearance of two more Savoyard uncles on the English scene. Peter arrived in England in December 1240 and Boniface was elected to the primatial see of Canterbury in February 1241, although he did not come to England for a further three years. What part the queen played in encouraging these new arrivals cannot be known with certainty. There may well have been Savoyard family scheming to which she contributed by judicious use of her influence with the king. Boniface's election to Canterbury was procured in response to pressure from Henry III, and Matthew Paris alleges that the king later wrote to the pope to seek confirmation for the appointment, 'urged by the queen'.[44]

Of all the uncles it was Peter of Savoy who proved to be the queen's outstanding mentor and collaborator in politics. He was fortunate to arrive at the English court at a moment when the two heavyweight personalities were absent. In December 1240 Richard of Cornwall and Simon de Montfort were both away on crusade. The king was free to open his unbounded liberality to the newcomer, without restraint. The result was a meteoric rise to influence and wealth, unmatched even by the example of William of Savoy. Peter's earlier career in the Pays de Vaux had given him experience of the kind typical in his family, some sharp fighting and a good deal of clever political manipulation, including his

[41] See ch. 6, below.

[42] *CR 1237–42*, 217.

[43] Howell, 'The Children of King Henry III and Eleanor of Provence', 62 and references cited.

[44] *CM*, iv. 103–5, 259.

own marriage to Agnes de Faucigny, which had enabled him to escape, like his brother Thomas, from a career in the Church.[45]

On his arrival in England Peter of Savoy was immediately received into the king's highest favour and most intimate counsels. On the January feast of St Edward he was knighted by the king together with fifteen other young noblemen, and in the next few months Peter was endowed with lands, honours and posts of influence which revealed the king's utterly untrammelled enthusiasm for this family of Alpine 'eagles'.[46] In May 1241 Peter received the honour of Richmond with the right to bequeath it to his heirs.[47] In September he was given the honour of Pevensey and custody of the lands of the late Earl Warenne in Surrey and Sussex.[48] In November he was placed in charge of Rochester castle and made warden of the Cinque Ports.[49] Peter himself had the wit to realize that there was danger in all this. Matthew Paris describes him as discreet and circumspect, qualities which his royal patron certainly lacked. Uneasy in his knowledge that the return of Richard of Cornwall was imminent, Peter decided to make at least a temporary withdrawal and to give back some of his castles to the king. What happened next is very odd indeed. The king recalled Peter from Dover and there was in fact no confrontation between Peter of Savoy and Richard of Cornwall.[50] According to Denholm-Young, Richard yielded, as Henry had done, to Peter's charm. That seems most unlikely as a total explanation. Richard of Cornwall, as we have seen, was a hard man, who yet had his price. It is certainly pertinent that he returned to England inclined to marriage with Peter's niece Sanchia of Provence, Raymond-Berengar's third daughter. The proposed marriage was clearly of great importance to the queen, and Peter of Savoy emerged before long as a prime facilitator.[51]

Before considering Sanchia's marriage, we must consider Peter's influence on the queen and the stimulus he gave to Eleanor's own political development. No doubt she had been making her own observations and learning all the time, but in Peter she had an ally with ideas, diplomatic skill, knowledge of the European as well as the domestic scene, and a large measure of political realism. Peter's later manipulation of Henry III's patronage to serve his own interests in Savoy had implications for

[45] Cox, *Eagles of Savoy*, 40–3, 82–6.
[46] *CM*, iv. 85–6; Cox, *Eagles of Savoy*, 108–9.
[47] Wurstemberger, *Peter der Zweite*, iv, no. 138.
[48] *Foedera*, i. 243.
[49] *CPR 1232–47*, 265–6.
[50] *CM*, iv. 177–8.
[51] Denholm-Young, *Richard of Cornwall*, 46, 50.

the queen, both good and bad, which need to be discussed in the next chapter, since Peter's activities gathered momentum after 1246. But even in this earlier period Peter had begun to introduce Savoyard protégés into England and to bring them within the queen's orbit.[52] Meanwhile there was another, even deeper issue than this. Peter realized from the first that the queen's position must be immovably grounded in her rights and influence as a mother. Control of, or participation in, all affairs relating to the heir to the throne should be Eleanor's aim, and both Peter and Eleanor knew that in this her arm could be considerably strengthened by Peter's own active participation in whatever concerned the Lord Edward. One facet of this policy was the establishment of Savoyards in posts of responsibility connected with Edward.[53] Already, before Peter's arrival in England, a Savoyard clerk from the household of William of Savoy, Walter de Dya, had been appointed as joint custodian of Edward, alongside the Englishman Hugh Giffard.[54] It was characteristic of Queen Eleanor that she was always on terms of warm accord with Hugh Giffard and his wife Sybil; English and Savoyards were readily integrated in the service of herself and her family. This was what Eleanor and Henry III himself wished and saw as appropriate. Even so, the Savoyard participation in Edward's affairs became more emphatic after Peter's arrival. In December 1241 Bernard of Savoy, possibly an illegitimate son of old Count Thomas of Savoy, had been appointed to the key position of keeper of Windsor castle where the royal children spent most of their time, and in 1244 lands set aside for the support of the Lord Edward were placed in Bernard's custody.[55] In both capacities Bernard was replaced in due course by Peter of Geneva, a Savoyard protégé of Peter of Savoy.[56] In 1249 Peter of Savoy himself became keeper of the lands allocated to Edward.[57]

The establishment of Queen Eleanor as the natural guardian of Edward's interests and the political implications of this, emerged strikingly in certain royal writs of 1241–2, relating to the control of royal castles in the event of Henry III's death. The king was planning an expedition to Poitou, which took place in the spring of 1242, in a further attempt to regain his continental possessions. The first writ, issued in February 1241, provided that if the king died, the present keeper of

---

[52] Ridgeway, 'Henry III and the "Aliens"', 81–6; 'Politics', ch. 1.

[53] This crucial feature of Savoyard policy was first pointed out by Huw Ridgeway, 'Politics', 63–5 and 'The Lord Edward', 90–3.

[54] *CR 1237–42*, 236.

[55] *CPR 1232–47*, 268, 418, 422; *CR 1242–47*, 178.

[56] *CLR 1245–51*, 155; Ridgeway, 'The Lord Edward', 91.

[57] *CPR 1247–58*, 52. See comments of Wait, 'Household and Resources', 8.

specified castles on the Welsh border was to deliver them to the queen for the use of Edward, the king's son and heir.[58] In April 1242 a series of similar writs, covering other key fortresses including the great stronghold of Dover itself, had the additional provision that if the queen was unable to come personally to receive any particular castle then it was to be surrendered to one of her uncles not in the fealty of the king of France.[59] This precluded Thomas of Savoy, but pointed pretty clearly to Peter. These remarkable provisions pointedly excluded Richard of Cornwall and any claims he might have been expected to make to the guardianship of Edward, should the king die. They placed Queen Eleanor, supported by her Savoyard uncles, centre-stage. She is now seen as something more than a successful wife and mother; she can be envisaged as a public figure, the guardian of her son's interests.

The persuasive influence of Peter of Savoy may possibly lurk behind another royal instrument of 1242. On 5 April the king granted his wife a charter promising that in the event of his own death she should have 'reasonable dower from all the king's lands, castles, rents and tenements acquired or hereafter to be acquired'.[60] Although the wording is imprecise, it opened the possibility of Eleanor's dower claims extending beyond the nominated dower of 21 January 1236. She was now a more considerable person than she had been hitherto.

In the early months of 1242 Eleanor was no doubt party to the plan for the second Anglo/Provençal marriage alliance, already mentioned.[61] Peter d'Aigueblanche, Savoyard bishop of Hereford, now one of the king's chief diplomats, was dispatched on a preliminary mission to Provence to explore the possibility of a marriage between Richard of Cornwall and Raymond-Berengar's third daughter, Sanchia. There is tantalizingly little evidence as to how and when this proposal originated. It is certain that Richard had met Raymond-Berengar on his way to embarkation for the Holy Land in 1240. He may have met Sanchia too on that occasion, but if so, he would have known that she had recently been betrothed to Guigues VII, dauphin of Viennois.[62] This came to nothing and in the following year Guigues was betrothed to a daughter of Peter of Savoy, an interesting point.[63] Scholars have suggested, partly on the grounds of Sanchia's reputed beauty, that Richard had quite simply fallen for her personal attractions and that there is no reason to

---

[58] *CPR 1232–47*, 244.
[59] Ibid., 280, 294.
[60] *CChR 1226–57*, 268.
[61] See n. 51, above.
[62] *CM*, iv. 46, 190; *Receuil des Actes des Comtes de Provence*, ii, no. 316.
[63] Cox, *Eagles of Savoy*, 123–4.

look for any political motive behind the alliance.[64] This seems a little wide of the mark. Richard of Cornwall was admittedly susceptible to female beauty, but he was too hard-headed and materialistic to have treated something as serious as marriage in a haphazard way. The political context of this marriage has been passed over far too casually. For the queen and her Savoyard relatives, Richard of Cornwall, unmarried and unsettled in respect of his territorial ambition, was an unstable element at court and a potential threat to their plans for the Lord Edward. He must be tamed. It seems certain that the king was persuaded of this too. Seen in this light, the second Anglo/Provençal marriage appears as a well-judged Savoyard coup. Shortly after 26 May 1242 Peter of Savoy left Henry III's war camp at Pons, empowered by Earl Richard to exchange the *verba de presenti* on his behalf with Sanchia at Tarascon.[65] Henry's readiness to release Peter at this moment reflects the king's view of the importance of the mission. On 17 July at Tarascon the marriage contract was concluded. The document bore five seals, those of the count and countess of Provence, Peter of Savoy, Philip of Savoy and Peter d'Aigueblanche.[66] It amounts to a pretty coherent pressure group. Sanchia was later escorted to Henry's temporary court at Bordeaux by her mother Beatrice and her uncle, Philip of Savoy.

The fact that Richard of Cornwall was a man who would drive a hard bargain indicates some frank discussion between himself and the king on the terms of this marriage before Richard would have been prepared to commit himself. He undoubtedly looked for an advantageous financial and territorial settlement from his brother and this he got, beginning with the promise of £3,000 as a marriage portion, but the details were not confirmed until after the end of the Poitou expedition.[67] Henry III looked to the marriage to strengthen even further his own bonds with the Provence/Savoy bloc, which was the pivot of his continental ambitions and it would identify Richard with the king's own diplomatic interests.[68] To Queen Eleanor the proposed marriage must have seemed particularly desirable. She would have been alive to all the diplomatic advantages and she must have hoped that the terms of a settlement for Richard of Cornwall would avert a clash between his territorial ambitions and the interests of her son Edward. On the personal side, she would have the

---

[64] Ibid., 114; Denholm-Young, *Richard of Cornwall*, 50. Raymond of Toulouse made a proposal of marriage with Sanchia in 1241, Fournier, *Le Royaume d'Arles et de Vienne*, 164–5.

[65] Wurstemberger, *Peter der Zweite*, iv, no. 154.

[66] *Receuil des Actes des Comtes de Provence*, ii, no. 356.

[67] CLR 1240–45, 198. See n. 84, below.

[68] Stacey, *Politics, Policy, and Finance*, 238; Clanchy, *England and its Rulers*, 232–5.

pleasure of having a sister in England, but not in a role that could possibly eclipse her own. The prospect was delightful.

However, in the early summer of 1242, on the eve of Henry III's expedition to Poitou, this marriage was still at the planning stage and Eleanor had many other things to occupy her. It had been decided that she was to accompany her husband on his Poitou expedition. She must have felt some misgivings, as she was nearing the end of her third pregnancy and she had the sad reflection that Henry's adversary was Louis IX, the husband of Eleanor's sister Margaret. The English force, together with the king and queen, embarked at Portsmouth on 9 May and they had a calm passage round the west coast of France. They disembarked on 13 May at Royan in Gascony, at the mouth of the Gironde. From there Eleanor withdrew to La Réole, some way up the Garonne, and later removed to Bordeaux, where she had the doubly anxious prospect of awaiting the birth of her third child and awaiting news of her husband. She evidently had a miserable time, which we glimpse from the comments of Simon de Montfort to the king some eight years later, recalling to Henry's mind the habitual faithlessness of some of his Gascon subjects. 'They did not have mercy on you when you were fleeing from the treachery and persecution of the French king, nor on the queen in her pregnancy, when she was lying ill at La Réole and when she was delivered at Bordeaux.' It came back all too vividly to the king. 'By God's head, you have told the truth, Earl.'[69] Despite all, Eleanor gave birth to a healthy daughter, Beatrice, named after Eleanor's mother, on 25 June, just before the main campaign began.[70]

This campaign was Henry III's response to Louis IX's investiture of his brother Alphonse as count of Poitou in June 1241. It was a disaster.[71] Henry was outnumbered and outmanoeuvred by the French on the southern borders of Poitou at Taillebourg, and might even have been captured but for his brother's presence of mind. Richard of Cornwall, seeing how things were, seized a pilgrim's staff and crossed the River Charente to make a personal appeal to King Louis for a short truce, which was granted. The English withdrew to Saintes further up the river and Henry, overwhelmed with gratitude to his brother, impulsively promised that Richard should have Gascony.[72] At Saintes Henry learned that he had been deserted by his main ally, his stepfather, Hugh X count

---

[69] CR 1237–42, 497–8; CM, v. 208–9.

[70] CM, iv. 224; Howell, 'The Children of King Henry III and Eleanor of Provence', 62.

[71] CM, iv. 209–13. For the best recent account see Stacey, *Politics, Policy, and Finance*, 182–200; see also Bémont, 'La Campagne de Poitou (1242–1243): Taillebourg et Saintes', 289–314.

[72] *Foedera*, i. 253; Denholm-Young, *Richard of Cornwall*, 47–8.

of La Marche. Hugh was by far the most powerful of the Poitevin lords and his desertion spelt the end of effective resistance to King Louis. Two of Count Hugh's sons sent messages to Henry to warn him of his imminent danger. The ensuing precipitate flight from Saintes to Bordeaux is vividly described by Matthew Paris. His description may well be unfair, but there was no denying that this campaign had been irretrievably damaging to the military reputation of the English king.

He was made to feel his failure, by the caustic remarks of Simon de Montfort and by the jibes of the troubadour *sirventes*.[73] The disaster and humiliation may have had their effect on the relationship of Eleanor of Provence and her husband. Eleanor was no fool, and her delight in chivalric ideals would have made her the more sensitive to her husband's damaged reputation, but there is no doubt that she stood by him. It is easy and obvious to point out that she had no alternative; of course not. But one can go a little further. The contemporary French chronicler Philippe Mousket comments that Henry returned to Bordeaux to his queen 'qui l'ounoura'.[74] This brief remark may well indicate what the support of his wife meant to Henry III at this point. Matthew Paris impatiently criticizes the king for lingering at Bordeaux in the company of his queen, who had given him a daughter.[75] It points in the same direction.

Henry III's promise at Saintes that he would give Gascony to Richard of Cornwall was a potentially devastating blow to the policies of the queen and Peter of Savoy in respect of their plans for a future appanage for Edward, plans which had presumably evolved in discussion with the king. Gascony would inevitably have been a key component in such planning. In short, the grant to Richard, impulsively made, must be revoked. And so it was. Matthew Paris reported the rumour that it was the queen who had secured that revocation.[76] This may have happened in the course of August 1242. The royal brothers certainly quarrelled sharply at this time, although not only over Gascony. At the end of September Richard left for home and one suspects that he was a bitterly disappointed man.[77] It may well have been the queen again who ensured in the following year that the county of Chester should not fall to Richard's grasp. Again there was a rumour to that effect and there is

[73] Bémont, *Simon de Montfort* (1st edn), 341; extracts from *sirventes* by Guilhem Montanhagol and Duran of Pernes, quoted by H.J. Chaytor, *The Troubadours and England*, 82–3.

[74] 'Fragment de la Chronique Rimée de Philippe Mousket' in *Receuil des Historiens des Gaules et de la France*, xxii. 77, line 30946.

[75] *CM*, iv. 229.

[76] *CM*, iv. 487.

[77] *CM*, v. 291–3; Denholm-Young, *Richard of Cornwall*, 48–9.

evidence which tends to support it.[78] On 17 August 1243, when Henry and Eleanor were still in Gascony, certain manors assigned to the queen in dower in 1236 were replaced by the county of Chester, together with Newcastle under Lyme and the advowson of Rocester Abbey.[79] This did not give the queen present control of Chester but it brought it within her orbit and excluded it from that of Richard of Cornwall. It was briefly granted to her second son Edmund in 1245 but was later to form an important part of Edward's appanage.[80] The first two witnesses to the new dower grant were Peter d'Aigueblanche and Philip of Savoy. The queen and her kinsmen were playing for high stakes in all this, for Richard of Cornwall could have become a dangerous enemy. Much would depend upon the king's generosity to his brother in the final marriage settlement for Richard and Sanchia.

Henry and Eleanor did not leave Gascony before late September 1243. Matthew Paris's taunt that Henry wasted the year 1242–3 in useless diplomacy and extravagant living at Bordeaux has rightly been questioned. He embarked on a serious attempt to pacify Gascony, both the feudatories and the urban factions. He not only attacked various rebel strongholds, but in a purposeful drive to compose the dissensions in the greater municipalities he visited the towns of Dax and Bayonne, as well as spending time in his base at Bordeaux.[81] Whether or not the queen accompanied him or stayed at Bordeaux, she would have begun to get the measure of this duchy. The physical character of the area, the political importance of the castles, held by unreliable local lords, the economic prosperity generated by the wine trade of Bordeaux and the carrying trade of Bayonne, the people and the places that mattered; all this she would have taken in, not systematically, but effectively, at the level of daily contacts and news. In one instance she was required to play a minor political role. Gaston de Béarn, Eleanor's first cousin through his mother Garsende, sister of Raymond-Berengar V, was lord of the largest and the most independent of the Gascon fiefs, situated on the southern border with Spain. He owed Henry the service of sixty knights, but he claimed that by custom he was not obliged to do homage to the duke/king except at the Béarnaise city of St Sever. It was at the queen's special request that he consented to come with his mother to Henry's court at Bordeaux and to perform the act of homage there.[82] This personal meet-

[78] *CM*, iv. 487.

[79] *CPR 1232–47*, 394; *Foedera*, i. 253.

[80] C 47/9/1; Ridgeway, 'The Lord Edward', 91; Wait, 'Household and Resources', 11.

[81] *CM*, iv. 236, 242–5; Marsh, *English Rule in Gascony 1199–1259*, 89–110.

[82] *Rôles Gascons*, i, no. 721; *CM*, iv. 236; Ellis, 'Gaston de Béarn', 101–2. For the relationship of Eleanor and Gaston see Ellis, 'Gaston de Béarn', 24 and *Receuil des Actes des Comtes de Provence*, table facing p. xxxvi.

ing of Eleanor and her cousin was to establish a bond which was later to prove politically significant for them both.

After a delay occasioned by an illness of Eleanor, she and Henry eventually set sail from Gascony in late September or early October 1243.[83] Their homecoming was dominated by arrangements for the marriage of Sanchia to Richard of Cornwall. Sanchia and her mother the Countess Beatrice arrived in England early in November and the marriage took place at Westminster on 23 November. The king's long-term settlement with Richard is dated 1 December.[84] Richard was granted the county of Cornwall and the honours of Wallingford and Eye in fee to himself and his heirs; in return for the all-important renunciation of his claim on Gascony, he was granted additional lands worth £500 a year. The wistful proviso 'unless the king confer Gascony upon him (Richard) again of his mere liberality' is a measure of Richard's disappointment and of the queen's success. Matthew Paris comments on public speculation when the marriage with Sanchia was first announced: 'At this the whole community in England, taking it ill, began to fear that the whole business of the kingdom would be disposed of at the will of the queen and her sister...who would be as it were a second queen.'[85] Although Sanchia was never overtly active politically, the chronicler was right in foreseeing an escalation of Savoyard influence on the king's return from Gascony.

In order to counter criticism of his military failure, Henry III on his return to England staged a series of magnificent receptions, first for the homecoming of himself and his queen, then for the arrival of Sanchia and her mother, and finally for the marriage celebrations of Sanchia and Richard.[86] Henry was already a master of what has been described as the theatricality of monarchy.[87] Matthew Paris strains after superlatives when he reaches the crescendo of the wedding festivities; the brilliant variety of the costumes, the elaborate entertainments by the minstrels and above all, the food. With pardonable exaggeration he insists that 30,000 dishes were prepared for those who sat down to the wedding banquet. Expensive presents around the time of the wedding and the Christmas and New Year festivities which followed them added to the pleasure and excitement. Thomas of Savoy presented the king with a fine length of scarlet cloth which was immediately made up into sets of robes trimmed with squirrel fur for the king and queen, and Henry gave

[83] CM, iv. 244, 254.
[84] CPR 1232–47, 437.
[85] CM, iv. 190.
[86] Ibid., 255–63.
[87] Clanchy, England and its Rulers, 282.

Beatrice of Savoy an equally fine set of robes and a magnificent gold eagle, set with jewels.[88] The high profile of the three ladies of Savoy on these occasions of royal pageantry was intentional, a point where the political and the social merged. In chivalric society the knight renowned for his prowess had a female counterpart. Good birth, good breeding and good looks combined to produce the chivalric ideal of the aristocratic woman, a powerful concept which had a prolonged influence on European culture. Henry III would have felt his own image enhanced by the beauty and elegance of his womenfolk.[89]

Eleanor's mother, Beatrice of Savoy, was an intelligent and persuasive woman, with considerable diplomatic skill. Henry III, who generously endowed her with an annual fee of £400 for six years, before she left England, was susceptible both to her charm and her reasoning.[90] Beatrice succeeded in two tasks on this visit. One was to promote goodwill between the king and Simon de Montfort. Simon's resentment over the inadequacy of his wife's dower from the Marshal estates was compounded by his anger that the king had given him no marriage portion when he married Henry's sister. Through Beatrice's intervention Henry granted Montfort the equivalent of a yearly fee of 500 marks to redress the lack of a marriage portion.[91] Although it failed to give Montfort full satisfaction, it was a just act and a prudent one, undoubtedly helping to initiate the period of greatly improved relations between Montfort and the king, which followed the return to England. It is also likely that Montfort's appreciation of Beatrice's intervention encouraged him in a favourable attitude to the queen.

Beatrice's second, and in her own view far more urgent object, was to secure money for her husband's military needs. Henry III agreed to advance a large loan of 4,000 marks to Raymond-Beregar on the security of five Provençal castles, chosen for their strategic value.[92] This is often dismissed as a typically bad bargain from Henry's point of view, but its political purpose was serious. Guy de Roussillon, an able Savoyard clerk, high in the favour of both king and queen, was one of two proctors sent by Henry to take formal possession of the castles, which were then handed over to the custody of the archbishop of Embrun and the distinguished canonist and friend of Henry III, Master Henry of Susa, both Savoyards. They were to take an oath to keep the castles 'to the use of the

---

[88] CM, iv. 263; CR 1242–47, 145; CLR 1240–45, 213.

[89] Note Pauline Stafford on the value of royal women as spectacle, *Queens, Concubines and Dowagers*, 109.

[90] CPR 1232–47, 414.

[91] Bémont, *Simon de Montfort* (1st edn), 335; Maddicott, *Montfort*, 32–3, 53–5.

[92] *Foedera*, i. 254.

king and the queen'.[93] Henry's likely motive was to strengthen his hand in Provence in view of the approaching death of Raymond-Berengar.[94] Eleanor, as the count's second daughter, could regard herself as having a claim on the inheritance, which both she and Henry would wish to press. This is surely the force of the specific mention of the queen in the direction for the custody of the castles. It is likely that Henry knew the contents of Raymond-Berengar's will, made as long ago as 1238, allocating 10,000 marks as the final marriage portions of both Margaret and Eleanor and 5,000 marks as that of Sanchia. The Countess Beatrice was to be given substantial properties in Forcalquier and Gap, several castles on the Durance and the usufruct of the county of Provence for life, as dower. It was the youngest daughter, also named Beatrice and unmarried, who was designated in her father's will as the heiress to Provence.[95] If Henry knew of these provisions, that did not mean that he accepted them. Acquiring the five Provençal castles might well seem the best way of staking a territorial claim in Provence in the name of his wife. Eleanor continued to press that claim even beyond her husband's death.[96]

The Countess Beatrice left England early in 1244, having provided her daughter Eleanor with a fine role-model in the practice of diplomacy. This came at a moment when the young queen was prompted by events to widen the scope of her own activities. So far, her role had been based primarily on her motherhood, defending Edward's interests when these were threatened and achieving a recognized position as supreme guardian of those interests in the event of the king's death. In addition to this she had facilitated Peter of Savoy's career by establishing various of his protégés in positions which were personally connected with herself and her children. Finally, she had no doubt been party to the plan for the marriage of Richard of Cornwall and her sister Sanchia. There is no evidence, however, that she had been substantially involved in purely English political issues; her intercession with the king in 1241 for Walter Marshal, whose inheritance had been withheld, being an isolated instance where the prompting came from others.[97] It was the arrival of her uncle Boniface of Savoy in the spring of 1244 which soon faced Eleanor with a wider range of matters, of a more public kind. Although the queen had actively furthered her uncle's promotion to the see of

[93] *CPR 1232–47*, 418; *CM*, iv. 505–6. Paris was confused as to the number of castles involved.
[94] Stacey, *Politics, Policy, and Finance*, 243–4.
[95] *Receuil des Actes des Comtes de Provence*, ii, no. 292A.
[96] Ch. 12, below.
[97] *CM*, iv. 135, 157–8.

Canterbury, neither she nor the king had presumably foreseen the implications of thrusting this independent-minded churchman into the distinctive role of primate of all England, where he stepped into the inheritance of Thomas Becket, Stephen Langton and Edmund of Abingdon. His novitiate in the austere and spiritually elite monastery of Grande Chartreuse made its mark, even though followed by very different experience as prior of Nantua and bishop-elect of Belley, which earned him a reputation as a militant ecclesiastic.[98] On past performance it should have been predictable that Boniface at Canterbury would defend the rights of his see and exercise the full measure of his metropolitan authority. It was less predictable, but not out of character, that he should have entered into a broader defence of ecclesiastical liberties, in England looking to men like Robert Grosseteste and Adam Marsh, who shared his ultramontane stance. This was not acceptable to a king who, despite his piety, guarded his patronal claims over the Church as vigorously as had his royal predecessors.

The queen too, like her husband and her uncle, had a potential role to play; but hers was less stereotyped. To be the wife of the king and niece of the archbishop posed a formidable challenge to a woman whose feeling for family ties was as strong as Eleanor's. Before Boniface actually arrived she had already experienced attempts to use her in connection with elections to bishoprics. In the vacancy at Bath and Wells in 1242 the king had evidently persuaded her to second his own request to the Bath chapter to elect his Poitevin clerk Peter Chaceporc. This had failed, thanks to the canny promptitude of the chapter in electing a candidate of their own choice.[99] On the other hand, it was from the side of the Church that Eleanor was urged to persuade the king to abandon his truculent opposition to William Raleigh, the bishop-elect of Winchester. Innocent IV wrote to Eleanor personally on the matter and Robert Grosseteste begged Boniface to enlist his niece's help. She should work on the mind of the king 'according to the prudence bestowed on her by God'.[100] However, although the king eventually yielded, there were many pressures on him apart from his wife's entreaties.

In the election to the bishopric of Chichester, in the very month of Boniface's arrival, the queen found herself in a far more difficult position than in the previous two cases. Quite suddenly she was caught in sharp crossfire between the king and the archbishop. In a piece of typical electoral manoeuvring the king had pressured the chapter into choosing his oppressive forest judge Robert Passelewe. But the elect had to be

[98] *CM*, iv. 259; Cox, *Eagles of Savoy*, 135.
[99] *Two Chartularies of the Priory of St Peter at Bath*, 45–6.
[100] *CM*, iv. 349; *Roberti Grosseteste, Epistolae*, no. 86.

examined for suitability by the archbishop. Boniface deputed the task to Grosseteste and four other bishops, who confidently declared Passelewe to be insufficiently learned and unsuited to the office. Boniface, accustomed to taking decisive action, accepted the verdict, rejected Passelewe and briskly proceeded to secure the willing approval of the assembled prelates to the choice of Richard Wych, a scholar of holy life who had served as chancellor to Archbishop Edmund and was now chancellor to Boniface.[101] Having confirmed the election of the new candidate, Boniface no doubt regarded the matter as satisfactorily concluded. He reckoned without the king. Furiously rejecting all that had been done, Henry forbade Richard Wych to act as bishop, seized the temporalities of the bishopric into his own hands and indignantly confronted Boniface with a charge of rank ingratitude.[102]

King and archbishop immediately looked to the queen for her reaction; she was caught. Young as she was, she did not lose her nerve; this was always to be one of her great political virtues. She knew that her uncle was within his rights in rejecting Passelewe, although it was less certain that he had the authority to appoint Wych, without reference to either king or pope. Her uncle's reputation and authority were at stake, but so was the king's trust in the loyalty of his wife. All these threads in the situation are brilliantly exposed by two pieces of evidence, which show Eleanor's mind intent on a difficult problem. First she wrote to the king, a submissive and affectionate letter, revealing that she had received letters from Boniface, in which the archbishop begged her not to be angry with him. She assured the king that Boniface had been told that he had no chance of recovering her goodwill until he had made his peace with the king. The archbishop had then come to her in person and had received the same stern message. This was what the king wanted to hear, that his wife ranged herself on his side in outrage at the affront to his wishes.[103]

But this was not the end of the story. According to Matthew Paris, it was the queen who then pointed out to the king that Passelewe was not indeed suited to be a bishop, but that he was excellent in his present position in accumulating money for the king's use.[104] The chronicler may well have been correct in giving weight to Eleanor's influence with the king in this case since there is independent evidence that, after the succession of Richard Wych to Chichester, he and the queen became

---

[101] *Ann. Waverley*, 333; Cox, *Eagles of Savoy*, 138, 140; Emden, *Register*, 2099–101.
[102] *CM*, iv. 359.
[103] *Royal Letters*, ii, no. 447.
[104] *CM*, iv. 509–10.

friends.[105] Boniface continued to rely on the queen's support and it was to her that he appealed when he met resistance to his rights of visitation in the diocese of London. His aggressive handling of that resistance further increased resentment against the Savoyards.[106] As a keen man of business, Boniface also determined to free the see of Canterbury from the debts of his predecessors. Late in 1244 Innocent IV granted him the first year's revenue from all benefices falling vacant within the province for a period of seven years, up to a sum of 10,000 marks. The appointment of Peter d'Aigueblanche to supervise the collection of these revenues confirmed the English clergy in seeing this as typical Savoyard collusion. Strong protest was made to the king, but despite Henry's initial anger, the exactions went ahead and Matthew Paris believed that it was the queen who had weakened the king's resolve.[107]

If these incidents are considered as a group, one can see that the queen's intervention was based partly on family loyalty to her uncle, partly perhaps on the traditional view of a queen as a peacemaker at court, but certainly not on a principled defence of the rights of the English Church in the face of oppressive practice. On issues of Church and State or issues of royal authority in secular government, the position of Eleanor of Provence was basically never in any doubt. Since her life was to be caught up in a constitutional revolution and its aftermath it is worth considering her likely viewpoint on broader issues of government even as early as this.

In the autumn of 1244 Henry III was in great need of money. The expenses of the Poitou campaign and of a recent expedition to Scotland, in which he had received notable but costly help from a Flemish force under Thomas of Savoy, had eaten into his dwindling reserves.[108] In addition, trouble was now escalating on the Welsh border. The king's recourse to a parliament failed to produce the grant of a subsidy. The laity resented recent government measures aimed at increasing Crown revenues, and they deplored the king's waste of his resources in his expedition to Poitou. The clergy, harassed by papal taxation, were also critical of the king's exploitation of vacant bishoprics and manipulation of episcopal elections in contravention of the royal promise made in Magna Carta to observe the freedom of the Church. By common assent a committee of twelve was set up, asking the king for the observance of Magna Carta and the Forest Charter, the appointment of a chancellor

[105] Ch. 4, below.
[106] *CM*, v. 124, 178, 217–18.
[107] *CM*, iv. 506–10.
[108] Stacey, *Politics, Policy, and Finance*, 245.

and justiciar and the supervision by the committee of twelve of the spending of any grant which they made to the king.[109] These demands related, as the king well knew, to the style of government which operated during his minority. During that period the key importance of the Charters had been established and ministers of state were appointed by great councils. This was a frame of reference shared between Henry and his subjects and it was to lie behind the more far-reaching demands of the reformers in 1258. For the present Henry would not yield.[110]

It would be wrong to assume that the queen was ignorant of the issues raised in this parliament. Both Peter and Boniface of Savoy were involved in different roles in the negotiations and it was about this time that Robert Grosseteste, a vigorous protagonist of reform in Church and State, wrote to Queen Eleanor with an impassioned plea that she would use her influence to alleviate the wrongs which the clergy and people of England suffered. The clerk who carried the letters had been instructed to explain to her in person the matters which the bishop had so urgently in mind.[111] But Eleanor had only come to England in 1236 and she could never take the long view of English politics that went back to her husband's minority. Her father's achievement in Provence had been to suppress resistance to his authority among feudatories and in the towns by reliance on clerks and lawyers obedient to his will; there had been no consultations with an organized baronage, and there had been no developing conception of a community of the realm. The bishops had been the willing supporters of the power of the count. Eleanor's political perspective was necessarily different from that of her husband and far more limited than that eventually achieved by her eldest son.

Meanwhile, Eleanor of Provence had not yet satisfactorily fulfilled all that was hoped of her as a mother. She had now borne the king a son and two daughters but both Henry and Eleanor knew that they had need of another son. The rate of infant and child mortality was high.[112] The Lord Edward himself became ill to our knowledge in 1245, when he was six years old, in 1246 and in 1251 and these childish illnesses could kill. One young son was no guarantee of the succession. In 1244 Eleanor was again pregnant. The king, deeply anxious, believed in keeping his needs

---

[109] *CM*, iv. 362–3. For the best recent discussion of this parliament, see Stacey, *Politics, Policy, and Finance*, 247–54.

[110] *CM*, iv. 365–8. For relevance of events of the Minority to later conflicts, see Carpenter, *Minority of Henry III*, 404, 407, 410–12.

[111] *Roberti Grosseteste, Epistolae*, no. 103. Boniface was a member of the committee of twelve (*CM*, iv. 362); Peter was one of those sent by king to entreat the bishops to make an aid (*CM*, iv. 365).

[112] Prestwich, *Edward I*, 6.

insistently before God. A thousand tapers burned before Becket's shrine at Canterbury and another thousand in the neighbouring church of St Augustine's. The purpose was made absolutely explicit; the preservation of the health of the queen and her safe delivery.[113] But it must be a son. Henry had promised the abbot of the prestigious royal abbey of Bury St Edmunds that if he had a second son the boy should be named after their patron saint, the Anglo-Saxon royal martyr Edmund. Henry left nothing to chance; when the queen was in labour and the delivery near, he arranged for the antiphon of St Edmund to be chanted. The king told it all to the abbot of Bury: 'when the following prayer was not yet finished, the bearer of the present letter, our valet Stephen de Salines, came to tell us the news that our aforesaid queen had borne us a son. So that you may have the greater joy from this news we have arranged for it to be told you by Stephen himself.'[114] The chronicler of Bury proudly recorded the royal letter. An embroidered chasuble was immediately offered at the great altar at Westminster; another fine chasuble was made from Edmund's baptismal robe;[115] the *Laudes* were sung in the queen's presence.[116] The rejoicing – and the relief – were tremendous.

The births of their first four children laid the foundation of the personal relationship of Henry III and Eleanor of Provence. The support which the king gave his wife, his joy in his children and the place which he allowed Eleanor and was to continue to give her, as a partner in their upbringing were the very substance of her experience as a young mother. The fruitfulness of these six years increases the slight mystery which hangs over the marital relations of Henry and Eleanor in the eight years that follow Edmund's birth. The queen was probably twenty one when Edmund was born in January 1245 and she did not conceive again successfully until 1253, when she was to give birth to her daughter Katharine, who died before the age of four. It may be that there were miscarriages or stillbirths in between, but the uncertainty about this interlude is tantalizing.[117] However that may be, Eleanor by 1245 had already produced a thriving family. The importance of that family to the

[113] *CLR 1240–45*, 275.

[114] *Memorials of St Edmund's Abbey*, iii. 28–9.

[115] *CLR 1240–45*, 288; *CR 1242–47*, 288.

[116] *CLR 1240–45*, 292; Howell, 'The Children of King Henry III and Eleanor of Provence', 63.

[117] Howell, 'The Children of King Henry III and Eleanor of Provence', 57–72. The absence of any contemporary evidence for the four children named as Richard, John, William and Henry in later insertions in the Chetham MS of the *Flores* makes their existence improbable, unless as miscarriages or stillbirths. Richard and John are the two names placed chronologically between Edmund and Katharine in Chetham Library MS 6712, ff. 203v, 202 (*Flores*, ii. 374, n. 2; 368, n. 1).

queen herself was the scope which it gave for her own emotional fulfilment and also for the realization of her personal ambition. Eleanor's
maternal feeling was by no means a wholly gentle emotion. Tenderness
and warmth were there in full measure, even when her children had
become adults, but so too was an element of hard, thrusting ambition.
In the end it was to bring her much anguish as well as satisfaction.

In August 1245, later in the year of Edmund's birth, Count Raymond-
Berengar V died. Henry III mourned the count with prayers and almsgiving and he protected Eleanor from the knowledge of her father's death
until his own return from a campaign in Wales.[118] But there was more
involved in this event than personal loss. The provisions of Raymond-
Berengar's will now became operative, with his youngest daughter Beatrice as heiress to Provence. The issue for Henry, as for others, was the
balance of power in the Midi. The young Beatrice became a glittering
prize and that prize was snatched from the teeth of three other powerful
suitors by Louis IX's brother Charles of Anjou.[119] This diplomatic coup
was the work of Louis IX himself, his brother Charles, his mother
Blanche and Pope Innocent IV in close and secret discussion at Cluny
in December 1245. Pope Innocent at this time was based in Lyon, a
refugee from the forces of his arch-enemy Frederick II, and in Lyon his
chief protector was Eleanor's uncle, Philip of Savoy, soon to be made
archbishop-elect of Lyon by a grateful pope. Already, before the end of
1244, Philip had been joined at the papal court in Lyon by his brother
Boniface, who was there consecrated to Canterbury by Innocent himself.
Philip and Boniface and their sister Countess Beatrice evidently facilitated the marriage of the younger Beatrice to Charles of Anjou. The
marriage was in the interests of Innocent IV, who thereby secured French
protection against the threat of attack by Frederick II, but above all it
was in the interests of Louis IX, who by this move had drawn Provence
into the orbit of the French Crown far more neatly than by pressing his
wife's claim to a share of Provence.

Henry III had reason to feel that his interests had been betrayed by
Eleanor's mother and by Boniface and Philip of Savoy.[120] Both Henry
and his brother Richard made a formal protest to Innocent IV against the
legality of Raymond-Berengar's will. Pope Innocent of course dismissed
their protests.[121] Eleanor was vulnerable. The diplomatic value of her
own marriage in her husband's eyes might now seem questionable, and a
breakdown of the special relationship between Henry III and the Savo-

---

[118] *CM*, iv. 485.

[119] Cox, *Eagles of Savoy*, 146–9.

[120] *CM*, iv. 505.

[121] *Reg. Innocent IV*, no. 1967; Denholm-Young, *Richard of Cornwall*, 52.

yards could have been disastrous for her. No breakdown was in fact permitted. Peter of Savoy and Peter d'Aigueblanche had not been overtly involved in the plan for the Anjou marriage. How early they knew of the plan is another matter. At the very time when the project was under way, Peter d'Aigueblanche was guiding the English king into a treaty with Amadeus count of Savoy, which reached its final form on 16 January 1246. Amadeus was to receive a grant of 1,000 marks and an annual pension of 200 marks in return for becoming the vassal of the English king in respect of four of his castles, which commanded the Mont Cenis and Great St Bernard passes through the Alps and also the passes themselves. In addition, one of the granddaughters of Amadeus was to marry a royal ward, either the future earl of Surrey or the future earl of Lincoln.[122] There has been much discussion as to the significance of this Anglo/Savoyard treaty and the advantages to each party, but part of its significance surely lies in its inspired timing. The Savoyard brothers were immensely skilled in pursuing seemingly independent policies while in fact giving each other quiet support. Henry III was being pulled into the closest association with Savoy itself and given a territorial presence in the Alps just at the time when he might be tempted to throw over the 'papal' brothers, Philip and Boniface, and when he was feeling that his stake in Provence was slipping away from him.

Amid the hazards of this situation Eleanor of Provence was absorbing a view of the complexities of the international scene which was partly independent of that of her husband. In the last resort she needed to think for herself. This particular storm did die down. In 1246 Boniface acted as Henry III's representative in receiving the personal homage of Count Amadeus.[123] The dowager Countess Beatrice visited Henry in 1248 in order to give him her personal assurance that she had not agreed to relinquish to Charles of Anjou the rights over the five Provençal castles to which Henry laid claim. In fact she did not relinquish those rights until permitted to do so by Henry III himself in 1257, and full compensation was then required, at least nominally.[124] Thomas of Savoy arrived in England at the same time as Beatrice, to enlist the king's support in extracting from the new countess of Flanders the pension due to him under his late wife's will.[125] Customary relationships between Henry III and Eleanor's family had clearly been established.

The years covered by this chapter were those in which the foundations of the queenship of Eleanor of Provence were established. They saw the

---

[122] *Foedera*, i. 264.

[123] *CM*, iv. 550.

[124] *CM*, v. 2–3; *CPR 1247–58*, 584; Cox, *Eagles of Savoy*, 161–2.

[125] *CM*, v. 2–3; *CPR 1247–58*, 7.

births of all but one of her children, securing for her an impregnable position at court and in the kingdom as the mother of the heirs to the English Crown. Beyond this she had further assets. The links of a wife with her natal family in the high Middle Ages could help to sustain her position after marriage and of this Eleanor of Provence provides a supreme example. The ambitions of her Savoyard uncles, their attitude to their womenfolk as collaborators in diplomacy, together with the deliberate patronage of the Savoyards by Henry III, and Eleanor's own growing political aptitude were mutually reinforcing factors in determining the future style of her queenship. Her influence on the course of events in England from this point to the end of her husband's reign stems from this situation.

3

Queen's Men and King's Men

The Savoyard dimension in the queenship of Eleanor of Provence began with her mother and uncles, but did not stop there. The story would have been different if it had. We have seen that there had been an appreciable influx of Savoyard clerks and knights in the wake of the queen's maternal uncles before 1246, but it was during the next decade that the queen became the figurehead of a substantial expatriate Savoyard community, which in the short term added to her political strength and increased her prominence but which ultimately threatened to distort her role as queen.

The scale, tempo and distribution of the Savoyard infiltration into England has been analysed by Huw Ridgeway in a series of studies on the aliens in the reign of Henry III which has been fundamental to all subsequent work.[1] Of the 170 or so Savoyards who tapped the springs of Henry's patronage, of whom fewer than half became resident in England, some two-thirds were clerks, many of them in the households of Boniface of Savoy or of Peter d'Aigueblanche, or in Aigueblanche's chapter at Hereford.[2] A few were employed in the royal households and among those prominent in the service of the queen herself were Guy de Palude, James d'Aigueblanche, Walter de Dya, Peter de Alpibus, Raymond de Bariomono and William de Salines; all of whom had functional tasks in the queen's household or those of her children. Some were in line for high preferment elsewhere, Guy de Palude becoming archdeacon of Lyon and

[1] For Dr Huw Ridgeway's published and unpublished work on this topic see ch. 2, n. 52, above; also 'Foreign Favourites', 590–610.
[2] Ridgeway, 'Henry III and the "Aliens"', 81.

William de Salines dean of Besançon.[3] Eleanor's own contacts regularly reached out beyond England to highly-placed Savoyard diplomats who were active for the king and queen at the papal court and elsewhere, such as Guy de Roussillon (an earlier archdeacon of Lyon), John d'Ambléon (papal chaplain, and richly beneficed in Savoy),[4] and, still more exalted, Rudolph Grossi (archbishop of Tarentaise and senior ecclesiastic of Savoy) and the canonist Henry of Susa (who rose to be archbishop of Embrun and then cardinal bishop of Ostia). The two last were later involved in royal business concerning Sicily.[5]

Some thirty nine Savoyards obtained grants of land from the king and most of these were laymen of knightly status. Others received annual fees at the exchequer.[6] Administrators, diplomats or fighting men, they reached the circle of royal patronage by various routes. For some, service of one of the great Savoyard lords might precede service of the king or queen. Imbert de Montferrand, diplomat, castellan, marshal of the king's household, emerged from the entourage of Peter d'Aigueblanche and finally entered the service of Eleanor when she was queen mother.[7] Bernard of Savoy, constable of Windsor and keeper of lands set aside for the Lord Edward, probably came to England with Thomas of Savoy in 1240.[8] Imbert Pugeys, steward of the king's household and keeper of the Tower of London, had arrived in England with the queen herself.[9] These men, and others like them, all moved within her orbit.

More distinctive in character was the arrival of high-ranking Savoyards who were bound by kindred or affinity to Peter of Savoy. Peter was working in close collusion with the queen but his keenest ambitions were focused on his lands and influence around the shores of Lake Geneva, his Savoyard homeland. An examination of the documents listed in the *Regeste Genevois*, recording Peter's acts in this area during the 1240s and 1250s, shows how neatly Henry III's patronage was made to play Peter's game. The young men who found fortunes in England were ready to repay Peter by supporting him in Savoy. Peter and Ebulo of Geneva, the

---

[3] For Palude and Aigueblanche see Tout, *Chapters*, v. 267 and Howell, 'The Resources of Eleanor of Provence', 388–9. For Dya see ch. 2, above; for Alpibus and Bariomono see Talbot and Hammond, *Medical Practitioners*, 244–5, 267; for Salines, *CPL*, i. 300, Delaborde, 'Un frère de Joinville', 339–40 and Wait, 'Household and Resources', 363.

[4] For Roussillon see Ridgeway, 'Politics', 187, and for references to his communication with the queen, E 101/308/1 m. 2; for d'Ambléon, *CPR 1247–58*, 197, 246, 269.

[5] Ch. 7, below.

[6] Ridgeway, 'Henry III and the "Aliens"', 81–2.

[7] Career summarized, Moor, *Knights of Edward I*, iii. 180–1; for link with the queen mother, *CPR 1272–81*, 75, *CChR 1252–1300*, 216–17.

[8] Ridgeway, 'Politics', 47; grant of a wardship by the queen in 1242, *CPR 1232–47*, 283.

[9] *CPR 1247–58*, 538, 547; *Book of Fees*, ii, no. 823.

dispossessed sons of Peter of Savoy's uncle, Count Humbert of Geneva, are a case in point. Peter of Savoy brought the young men to England and Henry III provided them with marriages to wealthy Anglo-Irish heiresses.[10] They showed their gratitude to their friend and patron from Savoy by making over to him all their claims on the county of Geneva. The documents recording Ebulo's renunciation of his claims happen to survive; they were drawn up in London but those who placed their seals to them belonged to the Savoyard families of Chauvent, Grandson, de Montibus and Joinville, all members of Peter's affinity and all privy to his ambitions in the Pays de Vaux.[11] He was their benefactor and this bound them to him and to each other. It also bound them to the queen, without whom none of their good fortune would have been possible.

It is, nevertheless, important to distinguish between the position of Peter of Savoy and the position of Queen Eleanor. Eleanor had no personal dynastic interests in Savoy and her attitude to Peter's protégés was therefore differently based from his own. She welcomed them as queen of England. Some of them were her own kinsfolk and the claims of kinship went deep with her; others she welcomed as Peter's dependents, but the relationships which she established with them were essentially personal to herself. This becomes clear in the case of the Joinville family, the brothers of John de Joinville, friend and biographer of Louis IX, and lord of the family patrimony in Champagne. These men were half-brothers of Peter of Savoy's wife, Agnes de Faucigny, and through Peter they were steered into careers in the service of Henry III and his family.[12] The youngest, William de Salines, was a clerk of the queen, as we have seen, and a member of the Lord Edward's household. A second, Simon, having been married, by Peter of Savoy's manipulation, to the heiress of the Lord of Gex (to the west of Lake Geneva), came to England to be knighted by Henry III in 1252 and was presented with a belt by the queen on that occasion.[13] Simon fought for the king in Gascony and was one of those who sealed Ebulo of Geneva's deed of renunciation to Peter of Savoy in 1259. It was also in 1259 that the queen put pressure on the justiciar, Hugh Bigod, to pay Simon's annual exchequer fee of 50 marks and the context suggests that he was the queen's political accomplice at this point.[14] She gave him a ring on 1 January 1259 and, by then

---

[10] Watson, 'Families of Lacy, Geneva, Joinville and La Marche', 1–11.

[11] *Regeste Genevois*, no. 912.

[12] Watson, 'Families of Lacy, Geneva, Joinville and La Marche', 12–14; Delaborde, 'Un frère de Joinville', 334–43.

[13] For Salines see above, n. 3. For Simon de Joinville: *Regeste Genevois*, nos 837, 843; CLR 1251–60, 77; E 101/349/13 m. 2.

[14] *CLR 1251–60*, 487.

a royal banneret, he was summoned to help the king in the political crisis of autumn 1261.[15] The third brother, Geoffrey, became a life-long friend of the queen. In 1252 Henry III granted him the marriage of Maud de Lacy, widow of the Savoyard Peter of Geneva and heiress to the vast county of Meath, north of Dublin, and extensive properties in the Welsh March, including Ludlow castle. The span of his landed interests stretched beyond his wife's fiefs in Ireland, Shropshire and Hereford to his native Vaucouleurs in Champagne, where one of his sons succeeded him. A knight of his household received a robe from the queen in 1252–3 and he was in Gascony with the Lord Edward in 1255, after Edward had come into his appanage, witnessing some of his loans, in association with Edward's chief counsellor John fitz Geoffrey and the prince's close companion Ebulo de Montibus.[16] Significantly, he did not follow Edward into opposition to the Crown in the late 1250s, and in April 1260 when Edward was defying his father, Geoffrey was with the king and queen at Boulogne.[17] The estrangement from Edward was not permanent and Joinville played a key role in Edward's eventual triumph over Montfort in 1265, when the queen is likely to have been in close communication with him; he was to accompany Edward on crusade in 1270 and served as Edward's justiciar in Ireland from 1273 to 1276. He kept up his contacts with Eleanor of Provence, even in her widowhood.[18]

Ebulo de Montibus, feudatory and protégé of Peter of Savoy, had a political career which partly and significantly mirrored that of Geoffrey de Joinville. He too married a wealthy widow, Joan de Somery, formerly wife of the king's steward, Godfrey de Craucombe. He too was placed in close personal contact with the Lord Edward and witnessed many of his acts, yet, like Joinville, he would have no truck with Edward's flirtation with rebellion; his political loyalty lay with the queen and with Peter of Savoy, to whom he was bound by feudal ties.[19] He was royal steward in 1262–3 when the king's assertive policy against the reformers was at its peak and the queen's influence over her husband was strong. When Ebulo died in 1268 Eleanor of Provence was an executrix of his will, alongside his wife.[20]

[15] E 101/349/26 m. 3; *CR 1259–61*, 319, 487.
[16] Delaborde, 'Un frère de Joinville', 334–43; E 101/349/18; *Rôles Gascons*, i (Supplement), nos 4538, 4636.
[17] *CR 1259–61*, 285.
[18] See chs 9 and 12, below.
[19] Ridgeway, 'Politics', 176; for the queen's contacts with Ebulo and his wife, E 101/308/1 m. 2, E 101/349/19; for Ebulo as witness, Studd, 'Acts of the Lord Edward', nos. 37, 123, 436, 529, 621, 677, 694, 695; for his loyalty to the Crown, *CPR 1258–66*, 8; *Regeste Genevois*, no. 881.
[20] Tout, *Chapters*, vi. 40; E 372/113 rot. 1d.

Clearly, issues of worldly advancement and political support entered into the relationships just described, but so too did warm personal friendship and mutual loyalty. What of the women whom these Savoyard adventurers married? Peter and Ebulo of Geneva, Geoffrey de Joinville and Ebulo de Montibus all married wealthy Englishwomen whose marriages were in the gift of Henry III; stereotype victims, one may say, of the feudal marriage market. Eleanor of Provence had no quarrel with that, but she viewed marriage as something more than the initial contract. She showed sympathy and support for Maud de Lacy, first married to Peter of Geneva, in the illness and death of her young son, and on the death of Peter, Maud herself became for a while keeper of Windsor castle, clearly with the queen's approval. In 1254 Maud, who was by then married to Geoffrey de Joinville, accompanied the queen to Gascony. Joan de Somery, wife of Ebulo de Montibus, received gifts and messengers from the queen in 1252–3, and again there was interest in the birth of her child; and Christiana de Marisco, married to Ebulo of Geneva, was one of the longest-serving ladies of Eleanor's household. The queen, by extending personal friendship to these women, showed a concern for making their marriages work in human terms.[21]

The Anglo/Savoyard treaty of 1246 set a pattern for yet another style of profitable Savoyard marriage. The targets in this case were the male heirs to English earldoms or other top-ranking fiefs. Girls related to the comital house of Savoy were brought to England to marry aristocratic wards of Henry III. In 1247, as provided by the treaty, Peter of Savoy arrived with Alice de Saluzzo, granddaughter of his brother Count Amadeus and daughter of the queen's first cousin, as wife for the young Edmund de Lacy, heir to the earldom of Lincoln. In the event, Peter brought another Alice too, whose parentage is unknown but who was probably of similar status, for marriage to Richard de Burgh, heir to the Irish lordship of Connacht.[22] The next Savoyard prey was the powerful northern lordship of the Vescy family, based on Alnwick. William de Vescy swore to the king, on the eve of Henry's departure for Gascony in 1253, that he would accept as the wife of his heir a Savoyard bride, as the queen and Peter of Savoy should provide. In the event they provided the sister of Alice de Saluzzo, Agnes.[23] Yet another such marriage was that of Eleanor of Geneva to Alexander Balliol, but the greatest match of all was the marriage of Thomas of Savoy's daughter Margaret in 1257 to Bald-

---

[21] For Joan de Somery, n. 19, above; for Maud de Lacy, E 101/349/17 and E 101/308/1 m. 1.

[22] *CM*, iv. 598, 628; Cockayne, *Peerage*, xii/ii. 171, n. e.

[23] *CPR 1247–58*, 217, 237–8; Cockayne, *Peerage*, xii/ii. 279.

win, heir to the great earldom of Devon.[24] Amice, mother of Baldwin, was the queen's friend, and the marriage is said by Matthew Paris to have been procured by the queen. It had already been granted in 1252 to Peter of Savoy, with the proviso that Baldwin should be married to a kinswoman of the queen.[25] There can be no doubt of the personal involvement of Eleanor of Provence in these various Anglo-Savoyard marriages, and in 1257 she persuaded the earl of Gloucester to allow the marriage of his eldest daughter to her kinsman, the marquis of Montferrat.[26] The queen watched such alliances closely, keeping in touch with the Savoyard women who came to England as brides and furthering their interests.[27]

This did not alter the fact that these marriages did harm to the queen's reputation. In the Petition of the Barons of 1258 it was asked that women whose marriages were in the king's gift, should not be disparaged by being married to those who were not true-born Englishmen; marriage to a foreigner was regarded as self-evident disparagement.[28] Matthew Paris makes it clear that imposing Savoyard girls on the heirs to English earldoms or greater baronies was another practice deeply resented. Such manoeuvring, even though technically within the king's feudal competence, frustrated the marriage strategies of the great English landholding families, and resentment at the king's policies was a significant factor in stiffening baronial opposition to the Crown by 1258.[29] The queen may have been seen as primarily responsible.

From this investigation of the 'queen's men', we must now turn to the 'king's men'. In 1247 Eleanor's position at court was placed under a new and significant strain, when Henry III invited his Poitevin half-brothers, William de Valence and Geoffrey, Guy and Aymer de Lusignan, together with his half-sister Alice, to avail themselves of his patronage in England. These were the children of Henry's mother Isabella of Angoulême and her second husband, Hugh count of La Marche. Their prospects in Poitou had been diminished by the terms of the surrender to Alphonse of Poitiers in 1242. They were welcomed to England with characteristic royal largesse and their achievements began to mirror those of the Savoyards. William de Valence was married to Joan de Munchensy, heiress to the lordship of Pembroke, and granted annual fees at the exchequer

---

[24] For Eleanor, Sanders, *English Baronies*, 25, n. 7; for Margaret, *CM*, v. 616.

[25] *CPR 1247–58*, 616; Cockayne, *Peerage*, iv. 320.

[26] Notarial instrument of 18 December 1257 drawn up in queen's chamber, *CChR, 1257–1300*, 3–5. For context see ch. 6, below.

[27] Queen's messengers to Alice de Burgh and Alice de Saluzzo, E 101/308/1 mm. 1, 2. See also ch. 7, below.

[28] *DBM*, 80–1.

[29] *CM*, iv. 598, 628; Waugh, *Lordship of England*, 245–6.

totalling over £800, with the promise of replacement by lands in due course. Aymer, the churchman of the family, was thrust by Henry upon the chapter of the wealthy monastic see of Winchester, of which the Poitevin became bishop-elect in 1252, while he was sent to complete his education at Oxford.[30] His sister Alice was married to John de Warenne, royal ward and heir to the earldom of Surrey, while Guy and Geoffrey were granted generous yearly revenues from the exchequer. Two of the king's Lusignan nieces were later married to the heirs to the earldoms of Gloucester and Derby.[31] The queen and Peter of Savoy were now faced with a newly-favoured group of aliens at a time when Henry III's reserves of patronage were increasingly restricted. The Poitevin community soon came to include other men who quickly rose to prominence, Elias de Rabayn and Guy de Rocheford, who became constables of Corfe and Colchester castles respectively, and William de St Ermine, who was appointed king's chamberlain; each was inevitably accompanied by men at arms, *valetti*, clerks and servants.[32]

The Poitevins soon realized that they were in effect in competition with the Savoyards for the available royal patronage and their hostility readily focused on the queen. She had unique access to the king as well as the loyal support of an increasingly numerous body of kinsfolk and protégés who ultimately looked to her for the protection of their present gains and for future benefits. The queen's household was a prominent and privileged institution within the royal court. It was particularly galling to the Lusignans that the queen, working in effective partnership with Peter of Savoy, was able to keep a firm controlling hand on the household and affairs of her eldest son, Edward, the heir to the throne. This gave Eleanor and her uncle an incalculable advantage over the Poitevins, which they maintained rigorously.[33]

The king was well pleased to encourage the Savoyard surveillance of his heir, permitting Peter to acquire an increasingly entrenched position. The former lands of the countess of Eu, set aside for Edward's sustenance, came under Peter's control in 1249, and during his absence in 1252 large sums from the issues were directed into the queen's wardrobe, a sign of the tight collaboration between the queen and her uncle.[34] Peter's

---

[30] The Lusignan acquisitions are summarized by Ridgeway, 'Foreign Favourites', 593–8. For more detailed treatment see Snellgrove, *The Lusignans in England*. For Aymer's election to Winchester, *CM*, v. 179–83, but also Ridgeway, 'The Ecclesiastical Career of Aymer de Lusignan', 150–1.

[31] Cockayne, *Peerage*, xii/i. 507; iv. 201, v. 707; *CM*, v. 364, 366–7.

[32] Ridgeway, 'Politics', 245–6.

[33] Ridgeway, 'The Lord Edward', 90–3.

[34] *CPR 1247–58*, 52; sums totalling £1,007 were received into the queen's wardrobe from these issues, E 372/96 rot. 18.

special responsibility towards Edward was conspicuously acknowledged when he was entrusted with the custody of the documents of 1249 and later of 1252 granting Gascony to Edward. This was the key component of Edward's future appanage. The grant included the Isle of Oléron, where Guy de Lusignan had ancestral claims. On the very day of the 1252 grant to Edward, Guy elicited from the king the restoration of the lands he claimed in Oléron, pending Edward's entry into actual seisin of Gascony. This was provocative. Peter of Savoy pounced immediately; Guy's personal written acknowledgement of the explicit limitation to his acquisition was lodged with the other documents in Peter's safe-keeping.[35] The clash between Savoyard policy and Lusignan ambition resounded unmistakably. As for the queen; she had fought off the designs of Richard of Cornwall on Gascony and she would not tolerate those of Guy de Lusignan.

At court Eleanor of Provence was strengthening her position. Her warm welcome to the Savoyards never precluded her businesslike and friendly relations with English men and women within her own household and beyond. She seems to have been on good terms with some of the people most frequently seen at court, Simon de Montfort and his wife Eleanor, Richard of Cornwall and Sanchia, Joan, wife of William de Valence, John de Plessis, earl of Warwick, Gilbert de Segrave and John fitz Geoffrey. She also had friendly contact with those doyens of the aristocratic establishment, Amice, dowager countess of Devon and Margaret de Lacy, dowager countess of Lincoln.[36] Still more important, the queen was already laying the foundations of a close working alliance with able royal administrators such as John Mansel, William of Kilkenny and Henry of Wingham. These were men of influence in the king's counsels, each serving in due course as keeper of the great seal and each having experience in diplomatic work. All three are known to have been cooperative with the Savoyards and there are also indications in each case of a personal association with the queen.[37] Her messenger list of 1252–3 shows that the queen sent messengers to John Mansel ten times, an indication of his importance to her, since she would also have had personal access to him when they were both at court.[38] His application to work, his supple mind, his discretion and even his courageous

---

[35] *CChR, 1226–57*, 386, 389; *CPR 1247–58*, 136.

[36] For contacts through messengers, E 101/308/1 mm.1, 2; for gifts to John fitz Geoffrey (E 372/97 rot. 9), to Richard of Cornwall and Sanchia (E 101/349/13), to the countess of Lincoln (E 101/349/14); gifts from the earl and countess of Cornwall and Gilbert de Segrave (E 101/349/13 m. 1), from John de Plessis (E 101/349/14).

[37] Ridgeway, 'Politics', 66.

[38] E 101/308/1 mm. 1, 2.

loyalty to his friends when they were threatened by the king's disgrace were all qualities which would have recommended him to Eleanor of Provence. In 1260, when she was commending him as a candidate for election to the see of Durham, she described him as admirably circumspect in things temporal and spiritual and 'special and beloved' as a counsellor to the king and to herself.[39] As a diplomat he was prominent in the negotiations for Edward's marriage and he helped to deal with the problems of the queen's daughter Margaret in Scotland.[40] William of Kilkenny, described by Matthew Paris as handsome in appearance and highly articulate in discussion, well-versed in civil and canon law and honourable in his professional life, was another man of a type to win the queen's trust. He had served in the household of Nicholas Farnham, the queen's early friend and mentor.[41] She was to work closely with him during the regency and later to show him rare favour, after he had become bishop of Ely, by granting him the manors of Upwell and Outwell in Cambridgeshire.[42] Henry of Wingham belonged to this same group; he gained the queen's confidence early in his career and later became a member of her council.[43] In 1252–3 Wingham not only received the usual New Year's gift from the queen but himself presented her with a goblet.[44] One of the clerks of her chapel in 1252 was Wingham's protégé Hugh de la Penne, who later became keeper of Eleanor's wardrobe.[45] Contacts such as these with highly-placed king's clerks, all of them Englishmen, were part of the power structure at court which the queen was steadily constructing and which provided her operational base. The Poitevins had nothing to match it and therefore became increasingly hostile to her, but they were not without their own distinctive assets.

In the welcome which he gave to the Poitevins, Henry III did not in any way jettison the Savoyards; that was far from his intention, but he began to establish deeply affectionate personal contacts with his half-brothers. Queen Eleanor was to learn painfully that they were far too deep for her to eradicate. The intensity of ties of kinship in medieval society is difficult to recapture, but there is no doubt that Henry's bond with his brothers was even stronger than with his wife's relatives. Moreover, this

---

[39] *CM*, v. 213–4 for Mansel's intercession for Henry of Bath, and *CM*, v. 261, 271 for his intervention on behalf of Philip Lovel; for the queen's letter of commendation, ch. 7, below.

[40] See chs 5 and 4, below.

[41] *CM*, v. 464; Meekings, 'Walter de Merton', lxix; Emden, *Register*, 1048–9.

[42] BL Cotton Charter XVII. 6.

[43] Ch. 11, below.

[44] E 101/349/13 m. 2; E 101/349/14.

[45] *CPR 1247–58*, 127, 241; accounts: E 372/109 rot. 11d, E 372/113 rot. 1.

was a tie backed by more prosaic political considerations. The defence of Gascony was of prime importance to him, and the Lusignans held possessions, although greatly reduced since 1243, strategically placed close to the border between Gascony and Poitou. Their territorial interest in this area was a counterpoise to the power of Louis IX's brother Alphonse, now in fully effective control as count of Poitou.[46]

Queen Eleanor's consciousness of her position as the ultimate figure-head of the Savoyard community in England was almost certainly sharp-ened by the presence of the Lusignans. That caused her to over-react when any Savoyard was attacked. In 1248 Stephen de Charron, Savoyard prior of the Cluniac house of Thetford, was murdered by a Welsh monk of the house, after a drunken orgy on the part of Stephen and two of his brothers. The queen, obviously greatly angered, apparently persuaded the king to take immediate punitive action and the wretched monk was chained, blinded and thrown into the deepest dungeon in Norwich castle.[47] In 1252, in a comparable incident, an agent of Peter d'Aigue-blanche, was murdered at mass in his own chapel. Suspicion fell on one John of Frome, who was handed first to Aigueblanche then to Stephen de Salines, closely connected with the queen and at that time constable of Hadleigh castle, and finally brought to London where he managed to escape his guards. It may again have been the anger of the queen which caused Henry III to take the step of deposing the sheriffs of London, who were regarded as having ultimate responsibility for the prisoner.[48] Cer-tainly the Savoyard network was involved in avenging the murder, and at the heart of that network was Eleanor of Provence.

The factors which bound Henry III and Eleanor of Provence together were still firmly in place, and in some respects their relationship contin-ued to be strengthened. In 1249 the king asked the pope to inquire into the matter of his matrimonial undertaking to Joan of Ponthieu in 1235. This may at first seem highly significant; in fact its significance is obscure. It does not seem likely that the Savoyards were as yet working for a marriage between Edward and Joan of Ponthieu's daughter, Eleanor of Castile, but the marriage of the king's daughter Margaret was soon to take place and a plan for the marriage of Edward into the ducal house of Brabant had been mooted, but had foundered, in 1247.[49] It was clearly

---

[46] Ridgeway, 'Henry III and the "Aliens" ', 83–4; Maddicott, *Montfort*, 127.

[47] *CM*, v. 31–3.

[48] *Ann. Worcester*, 441; *CR 1251–53*, 286; *CLR 1251–60*, 96; *Cron. Maiorum*, 22; Ridgeway, 'Politics', 51–2.

[49] Against Ridgeway's suggestion that the inquiry was linked to Savoyard plans for Edward's marriage ('The Lord Edward', 92), see Parsons, *Eleanor of Castile*, 10 and n. 13. For Brabant mission see *CM*, iv. 623–4.

important that there should be no doubts as to the legitimacy of the king's children. Innocent IV defined the purpose of the inquiry as being 'for the honour of the king and his children so that nothing can be imputed against them on this score in the future'.[50] This was the slant of the whole process, which was put into the hands of Peter d'Aigueblanche and the archbishop of York. The archbishop excused himself, under pressure of business, in 1251 and Aigueblanche conducted the inquiry to its wholly foreseeable conclusion. The king's earlier union with Joan of Ponthieu was pronounced to have no validity. Joan herself confirmed that she was related to Henry III within the prohibited degrees, and then declined to have anything further to do with the proceedings. Henry III and Eleanor were now entirely secure in the validity of their own marriage, and the adjudication was confirmed by Innocent IV in 1252.[51]

In mid-Lent 1250 Henry III, together with some of his magnates and some of the senior members of his household, took the Cross at the hands of Archbishop Boniface, who had been enthroned at Canterbury in the previous November in the presence of the king and queen and an impressive gathering of prelates.[52] Only the Waverley chronicler mentions that the queen also took the Cross, but this at least suggests that it was intended that Eleanor should accompany her husband to the Holy Land.[53] The fact that Henry never fulfilled his vow and that the revenues which he collected for the crusade were directed to other ends, with papal approval, has generated much debate as to his good faith in making his initial promise. That good faith should not be doubted, however, in view of the substantial preparations which he made for his departure.[54] His motives of course were mixed. Genuine religious enthusiasm, emulation of crusading predecessors such as Robert Curthose and Richard the Lionheart, the necessity to compete with the crusading fervour of Louis IX and to meet the expectations of the papacy and of his own subjects all helped to push him to the point of decision. Simon Lloyd has drawn attention to the deep religious devotion, caught up in a framework of fierce competition, which had already given an edge to the solemn ceremonies surrounding the king's presentation of the relic of the Holy Blood to the church at Westminster in 1247. This 'English' relic

[50] *Foedera*, i. 270–1.

[51] Ibid., 277–8, 284–5. David d'Avray kindly drew my attention to the fuller account of this case in BL Cotton MS Cleopatra E. I.

[52] *CM*, v. 101–2.

[53] *Ann. Waverley*, 342.

[54] Forey, 'The Crusading Vows of the English King Henry III', esp. 232–7; Lloyd, 'King Henry III, the Crusade and the Mediterranean', 97–101.

was seen as a powerful counter to the impressive collection of the relics of the Passion which Louis IX had acquired for his newly built Sainte-Chapelle. In March 1250 the French king was on his way to the Holy Land, redeeming his own crusading vow.[55] His wife Margaret was with him and probably already in correspondence with her sister Queen Eleanor; it may be that Eleanor, like her husband, felt moved to personal emulation.[56]

The prospect of taking part together in a military expedition to the Holy Land, with the sense of religious purpose and chivalric adventure which heightened the emotional appeal of crusading, appears to have had the immediate effect of creating a new bond between Henry and Eleanor. There is a sense of excitement and expectancy in the king's order on 17 May 1250 that a French book of romances in the care of the Master of the Temple shall be taken out for the queen to peruse. It contained the popular *Chanson d'Antioche* which apparently was what the queen was wanting, a romanticized account of the siege of Antioch at the time of the First Crusade.[57] The king then began to create a series of Antioch chambers by having these stirring deeds depicted on walls in the castle at Winchester and his palace at Clarendon, together with a chamber at Westminster which was perhaps for the use of the queen.[58] Eleanor, who had a great liking for romances, would have revelled in such displays. Many years later the exploits of crusaders and other famous knights were celebrated in verse after verse of the Anglo-Norman poem *Rossignos*, which her clerk John of Howden dedicated to her.[59]

In the following year another event was celebrated with equal excitement and also with fine visual imagery, the marriage of Margaret, the eldest daughter of Henry and Eleanor, to Alexander III of Scotland. This magnificent pageant, which is described in a later chapter, took place in York in December 1251.[60] It was in part an emphatic statement of English royal majesty, aimed at the Scots and with a clear political message, but it was also a family wedding and again emphasized the bond between Margaret's mother and father, who both loved her dearly; she was the first of their children to be married.

---

[55] Lloyd, 'King Henry III, the Crusade and the Mediterranean', 101–8; Lloyd, *English Society and the Crusade*, 204–5, for comment on CM, iv. 640–4.

[56] Queen Margaret wrote to Eleanor in 1252 'concerning the state of the Holy Land', E 101/308/1 m. 1.

[57] CR 1247–51, 283; Tyerman, *England and the Crusades, 1095–1588*, 117.

[58] CLR 1245–51, 358, 362; CR 1247–51, 464 and an order, later cancelled, for an Antioch painting in the Tower of London, CR 1247–51, 454. See also *King's Works*, i. 128–9 and Lloyd, *English Society and the Crusade*, 198–200.

[59] Ch. 4, below.

[60] Ibid.

Joint commitment to the crusade and the marriage of their eldest daughter were among the events which reinforced the relationship of Henry III and Eleanor of Provence in a marriage which had now lasted some fifteen years. They knew each other well, but no relationship is static and this one now became more complex and more hazardous. The queen was realizing capacities which had been of gradual and uneven development during her years of regular child-bearing. There had been early signs of interest in political issues, seen, as Eleanor of Provence would always tend to see such issues, in essentially personal terms, but now her keen appetite for active political participation and for an increase in her own real power began to emerge strongly. Finding an enemy in the Lusignans may have produced added anxiety, but also added zest. There are indications that the king did not welcome his wife's rapidly developing confidence and independence of judgement. She was establishing her own friendships and formulating her own views, and they were not always his friendships or his views. In the series of crises which punctuated Simon de Montfort's rule in Gascony between 1248 and 1252, in the quarrel between the king and queen over Eleanor's presentation to the living of Flamstead in 1251–2 and in the first open conflagration between Savoyards and Lusignans in 1252–3, the new image of Eleanor of Provence comes through unmistakably. These matters may be looked at in turn.

Since Gascony was to be the most prestigious component of the Lord Edward's future appanage, the king and queen were concerned that it should be secure and that it should be handed over in good order. In 1248 its fate was uncertain and its condition disturbed. The duchy was threatened by endemic disorder which might be given explosive force by hostile attacks from the Spanish kingdoms on its southern border. The royal houses of Castile and Aragon had claims to Gascony through descent from the English king Henry II, and the king of Navarre was actually making raids across the frontier. Gascony was also vulnerable from the north, since Poitou was now in the hands of Louis IX's brother Alphonse and the truce with France was soon due to expire.[61] The duchy needed the control of a man with exceptional ability and authority who could reduce it to order. It was Simon de Montfort who was chosen. Simon himself said later that he was begged to accept by the king and his counsellors and by 'my lady the queen'.[62] Evidently Queen Eleanor was keen that Montfort should undertake the task. The terms of the

---

[61] Maddicott, *Montfort*, 107–8; Powicke, *Henry III*, 208–16.
[62] Bémont, *Simon de Montfort* (1st edn), 335–6; Maddicott, *Montfort*, 108–9; Ridgeway, 'The Lord Edward', 92.

commission must be regarded as Simon's own. It was to last for seven years during which Montfort was to have control of Gascon revenues and to rule as the king's lieutenant. Expenditure on castles, a vital feature of the political and military organization of the duchy, was to be refunded to Montfort by the king and the king retained full responsibility for defence against external attack.[63]

Montfort's mission did not fulfil anyone's hopes. It roused bitter hostility among the Gascons, it soured relations between Montfort and the king and it was cut short two years before the expiry date, on Henry's decision to buy Montfort out and to go to Gascony himself. Montfort was the wrong man for the job, although perhaps no other could have done even what he did. He served the king loyally and vigorously but his methods were ruthless and high-handed and the Gascons hated him for his father's grim reputation as well as his own. He looked to his own advantage as well as the king's and so became involved in a complex dispute over the succession to the county of Bigorre where his claims were at odds with those of the formidable and politically unreliable Gaston de Béarn.[64]

For over a year Montfort seemed to be making good headway and to have retained the confidence of the king, but the first serious setback came in December 1249 and the queen played an important part in the incident. Montfort defeated and captured Gaston de Béarn himself, leader of the rebel group, but also cousin of the queen. Gaston was sent forthwith to England. It was a gratifying achievement from Montfort's point of view, but it went for nothing, as he saw it. He later made sardonic comment on what he felt to have been the king's folly.[65] Gaston was magnanimously pardoned, and by the queen's intercession his lands were restored to him. In return he was made to renew his homage to Henry and to do homage to Edward.[66] Since Gaston was soon to renew his rebellion and later to offer his fealty to Alfonso of Castile, the king's leniency does at first sight seem to have been a stupid misjudgement, and it is usually condemned as such. Yet this view is not quite unanimous.[67] The ultimate answer to a man such as Gaston was to win him over. To have retained him as a prisoner in England or to have confiscated his lands permanently could have worsened resentment in Gascony. Eleanor

[63] Maddicott, *Montfort*, 108–9.

[64] Ibid., 110–11, 134; Powicke, *Henry III*, 220–5, and for more detailed account, Ellis, 'Gaston de Béarn', ch. 8.

[65] Bémont, *Simon de Montfort* (1st edn), 342.

[66] *CM*, v. 103–4; *CPR 1247–58*, 57.

[67] Ellis, 'Gaston de Béarn', 114–17; for effect on relations between Montfort and the king, see Maddicott, *Montfort*, 111–12.

of Provence was undoubtedly prejudiced by her tie of kinship with Gaston, and relied on his loyalty much too readily, but she never ceased to work on him politically and eventually she had some success.

The next intervention of the queen in Gascon affairs was late in 1251, when Montfort returned to England and attended the marriage of Henry and Eleanor's daughter Margaret at York in December. The king was coming to distrust Montfort's harsh methods which had resulted in a flood of complaints from Gascony. Henry was also resentful at Montfort's increasing demands for money, one sharply contested matter being the king's earlier promise to meet the costs which Montfort incurred in the maintenance and defence of the castles which he had captured. Exasperated by the escalating costs of Montfort's mission and the outbreak of yet another rebellion in Gascony, the king said he would not pay. Montfort immediately countered this with a threat to alienate the castles. It was at this point that the queen intervened. She realized that such an act would imperil what had so far been achieved to secure ducal control over Edward's inheritance and she urged the king insistently (*ententivement*) to meet Montfort's demands.[68] The king yielded, but one suspects that he did not care to see his wife as Montfort's ally.

The alignment of loyalties at this point is further illuminated by the Franciscan Adam Marsh, who spent a hectic twelve days, between 25 February and 7 March 1252, assisting consultations between the Montforts, the queen and Peter of Savoy. He recorded his movements in a letter to Grosseteste. First he was summoned urgently by the queen to Reading to discuss matters 'touching the king and his heirs'; from there he made his way to the Montfort castle at Odiham, where he stayed over the weekend; then back to Reading and thence to Bromhall to meet both Montfort and his wife on the same day that Montfort and Peter of Savoy went to the queen at Windsor.[69] This provides a backstage view of the informal discussions and planning among this group of friends, to the exclusion of the king. We cannot be certain of their agenda, but it probably included the inquiry set up by the king to determine the costs of Montfort's operations in Gascony to date, and the proposed renewal of the grant of the duchy to Edward, which was effected on 27 April 1252.[70] The mention of the king's heirs betrays the consideration uppermost in the queen's mind, but by involving herself so closely in discussions with the Montforts she was in danger of undermining the king's

---

[68] Bémont, *Simon de Montfort* (1st edn), 336; Maddicott, *Montfort*, 114.
[69] Adam Marsh, 'Epistolae', no. 48.
[70] *CPR 1247–58*, 124, 132; *CR 1251–53*, 203–5; *CChR 1226–57*, 386; Ridgeway, 'The Lord Edward', 91.

trust in her. He naturally wished her to be absolutely at one with him over the handling of the issues in Gascony and he no doubt resented her more judicious and friendly approach to a man to whom he was becoming profoundly antagonistic.

The next event in the Gascon drama was the so-called trial of Simon de Montfort from May to June 1252, when he defended himself before an assembly of English magnates in parliament against the accusations of leading Gascon prelates and laymen.[71] The trial is described by both Matthew Paris and Adam Marsh, the latter praising Montfort's restraint.[72] Although the king had to accept the exoneration of Montfort by the magnates, he burst out against him very bitterly immediately afterwards. According to Adam Marsh, the three men on whose support Montfort could rely unfailingly were Peter de Montfort (not a relative), Walter Cantilupe bishop of Worcester, and Peter of Savoy. Peter de Montfort and Cantilupe were closely tied into Simon's affinity, which makes the inclusion of Peter of Savoy, who was not, the more interesting. The support of Peter of Savoy almost certainly implies the support of the queen, even if less publicly given.[73] This impression is confirmed by the assurance given by Marsh to Earl Simon in another letter (undated) that the queen had responded reasonably and kindly when he had discussed Simon's affairs with her.[74] In April 1252, as has been seen, the grant of Gascony to Edward had been renewed and after further recriminations between the king and Montfort and further fighting in Gascony the earl surrendered his involvement in the duchy to Edward in return for a sum of 7,000 marks to cover his debts.[75] Montfort's mission to Gascony was at an end.

The increasing assurance of Eleanor of Provence and the lack of full sympathy between herself and the king, makes the storm over the presentation to the church of Flamstead and flaring of tempers over the Lusignan raid on Maidstone and Lambeth entirely intelligible. The quarrel over Flamstead had begun before Montfort's trial and outlasted it. The quarrel was personal, not political, and Matthew Paris, who had contacts at court and who was interested in this case because it involved a St Albans clerk, told the story vividly.[76] In 1242 Henry III had granted

---

[71] For summoning of both parties to England, *CR 1251–53*, 207–9.

[72] *CM*, v. 287–96; Adam Marsh, 'Epistolae', no. 30; Maddicott, *Montfort*, 115–17; Bémont, *Simon de Montfort* (2nd edn), 104–9.

[73] Ridgeway describes her support of Montfort as 'open', 'Politics', 113–15, but how open it is difficult to judge.

[74] Adam Marsh, 'Epistolae', no. 140 (p. 268).

[75] Bémont, *Simon de Montfort* (1st edn), 321–4; Maddicott, *Montfort*, 119.

[76] *CM*, v. 298–9; Ridgeway, 'Politics', 112.

the queen the wardship of the lands and heir of Ralph de Tony and the grant included the right to wardships and escheats falling in during young Roger de Tony's minority.[77] When the church of Flamstead, in the Tony gift, fell vacant the queen promptly presented her chaplain, William of London. Paris describes the queen as 'confident in her right', and assumes throughout that she was acting correctly. In fact she had no reason to be confident, because she had overstepped the king's grant, which made no reference to advowsons. It is of course conceivable that the queen had misunderstood; it is also conceivable that she was trying it on. On 20 December 1251 the king presented his distinguished wardrobe clerk Artaud de St Romain to the living, with a mandate to Robert Grosseteste bishop of Lincoln to induct him.[78] Whether the king did this in ignorance of the queen's presentation or not, one cannot be sure. He soon became extremely angry. On 5 March he ordered the sheriff of Buckinghamshire to instruct Robert Grosseteste to admit Artaud to the church of Flamstead or to give pledges to appear in court to explain his refusal. Ten days later the sheriff of Hertford was summarily ordered to remove William of London, now significantly styled 'formerly chaplain of the queen', and all his effects from the church of Flamstead, which the king had conferred on Artaud de St Romain; the king's right of patronage was at issue.[79] Henry had evidently dismissed the unfortunate William of London from the queen's household and now stood aside while Artaud ejected William from the benefice. Meanwhile, 'glowing with anger', the king burst out upon the queen with what amounted to both a taunt and a threat: 'How high does the arrogance of woman rise if it is not restrained.'[80]

Queen Eleanor's reaction when this storm broke over her is of some significance. Matthew Paris reported that she was deeply chagrined because of the injustice and humiliation involved. This does not suggest that she was immediately overcome with remorse. What was even worse from the king's point of view was the support which she received from Robert Grosseteste as diocesan, who excommunicated Artaud and laid the church of Flamstead under an interdict.[81] That the queen should have managed to be put in the right by Grosseteste made her behaviour inexcusable. The king was forced to plead his case in the courts. On 28 May he notified Eustace de Lenn the official of Canterbury of the names of his proctors and on 16 August he appointed twenty-one men to

[77] *CPR 1232–47*, 283.
[78] *CPR 1247–58*, 121.
[79] *CR 1251–53*, 208, 202.
[80] *CM*, v. 298.
[81] Ibid., 298–9.

maintain and defend his right of advowson to Flamstead in the lay court.[82] The dispute was dragging on intolerably from the king's point of view. Moreover the incident was attracting attention. Adam Marsh wrote to Thomas of York, asking help for William, a priest, who was 'one of those presented to churches by the queen – about whom you heard'.[83] This letter suggests that there was possibly more than one presentation now in question. As for Flamstead, the queen's candidate apparently won, since William of London was rector of Flamstead in 1274.[84]

The king's anger was understandable. The young girl whom he had fashioned as his queen, the supportive wife, the mother of his children, in whose companionship he had such pleasure, were images familiar and dear to him. Now, in her late twenties, and without rejecting her established role, Eleanor of Provence was pressing beyond it to an image of her own making. Yet it would be mistaken to think that she was adopting an attitude of defiance. This was not Eleanor's way, and she knew that a queen should be seen to be a peacemaker. Again it is Adam Marsh who records that the queen and Eleanor de Montfort were trying hard at this time to pacify the king over the advowson dispute and over his anger with Earl Simon in relation to Gascony. Reconciliation was their aim.[85]

This perception that a queen should be at peace with her husband, a belief which separates Eleanor of Provence sharply from such queens as Eleanor of Aquitaine or Isabella of France, came under more severe strain at a point when the quarrel over Flamstead was perhaps still smouldering. The continuing tension between Henry and Eleanor may be reflected in the king's angry imprisonment of the queen's clerk, Robert del Ho, on a charge of corruption on 28 October 1252. One cannot determine whether or not Robert was guilty of misuse of the seal of the exchequer of Jews, where he was apparently attending to the queen's business; he was allowed bail on 2 November and was finally pardoned on 26 December.[86] Following very quickly on this acrimonious incident, was the far more serious open conflict which now broke out between the Savoyard and Lusignan factions at court, a sinister little prelude to the great political upheaval of 1258. The main contenders were Archbishop Boniface and Aymer, bishop-elect of Winchester, half-brother to the king. The question at issue was the appointment to the vacant post of prior of

---

[82] *CPR 1247–58*, 140, 160.

[83] Adam Marsh, 'Epistolae', no. 226.

[84] *Rotuli Ricardi Gravesend*, 180.

[85] Adam Marsh, 'Epistolae', no. 226.

[86] *CM*, v. 345; *Ann. Dunstable*, 186; *CR 1251–53*, 270; *CPR 1247–58*, 168; Ridgeway, 'Politics', 112.

the hospital of St Thomas at Southwark. Aymer claimed the presentation and installed his nominee. Boniface was out of the country at this point, but his official, Eustace de Lenn, took prompt action on his behalf. He pointed out that the archbishop's confirmation was necessary, and when Aymer ignored this, the official excommunicated the new prior. The prior defied him, whereupon Eustace had the man seized and incarcerated in the archbishop's prison at Maidstone. Aymer, abetted by his brothers, immediately resorted to the style of violence which was coming to be seen as typical of the Lusignans. He dispatched a band of armed men, most of them from the households of one or other of the Lusignan brothers, to Maidstone, to release the prior by force and to seize Eustace de Lenn. Having ransacked and fired the archbishop's manor at Maidstone, they rode off again, now hot on the scent of the unfortunate Eustace. They tracked him down at Lambeth, seized him, along with some of the archbishop's servants, thrust him on to a horse and dragged him off to Farnham where he was sent on his way on foot. Shaken and terribly humiliated, he made his way to the abbey of Waverley and there told his story.[87]

News of the raid, which took place on 3 November, rapidly reached the court at Windsor. The queen and Peter of Savoy, who were both at court at the time, appeared to have every justification for righteous anger against the Lusignans.[88] This would not have improved matters for the king. From his disciplinary actions against both sides, it is clear that he was furious that the incident had occurred at all, but he was not prepared to take sides against his half-brothers.[89] He turned on the queen; events had placed her seemingly in the right once too often. Next day, after taking in hand all her lands, and almost certainly suspending her control of queen's gold as well, he packed her off to Guildford, en route for Winchester, while he himself left for Reading.[90] He was in a very grim mood. Peter of Savoy left court on the same day. The king's harsh punitive action against the queen must have tried Peter's temper too.

The events of the next two months are difficult to disentangle. The return of Boniface to England in mid-November made the conflict more bitter and more personal. He was not a man to bear the insolence and

---

[87] *CM*, v. 348–51 should be compared with statement by Boniface in 1252 (*CM*, vi. 222–5) and his plea in 1258 (JUST 1/873 m. 8); also Ridgeway, 'The Ecclesiastical Career of Aymer de Lusignan', 165–6.

[88] The queen's presence at court is testified by her household alms account, E 101/349/24 m. 1. Huw Ridgeway mistakenly believed her to be already at Winchester, 'Politics', 120–2.

[89] Henry stopped or diverted monies payable to William de Valence and to Peter of Savoy's agent, Stephen de Feugères, *CR 1251–53*, 272, 273.

[90] Ibid., 273, 283; E 101/349/24 m. 1.

thuggery of the Lusignan raid with patience and he excommunicated those who had perpetrated the offence with the maximum publicity, first in London and then in Oxford, where Aymer had recently been a student.[91] The king's great fear was that the quarrel should develop into something on a bigger scale, and on 3 December he wrote a strongly worded letter to some of the leading magnates, forbidding them on pain of dispossession to take part in what he claimed was a purely ecclesiastical dispute.[92] It is therefore little wonder, if the chronicle of John of Wallingford is to be believed, that when Peter of Savoy in the week after Christmas was ordered by the king to stop the quarrel, and replied that this was impossible since it now affected the whole realm, he was ordered to leave the court.[93] Some of the English magnates were indeed taking sides. John de Warenne was married to the king's Lusignan sister Alice, and Richard de Clare's son was about to marry one of the king's Lusignan nieces; other magnates, however, were already antagonistic to the arrogant, aggressive behaviour of the Poitevins. Yet Matthew Paris perhaps rightly saw the quarrel as essentially one of Poitevins *versus* Savoyards, in fact a conflict of the two alien groups at court.[94] The friends of the king (*regines*) and the friends of the queen (*reginales*) were seen in open conflict.

The queen did not linger in disgrace at Winchester for very long, although her situation was presumably uncomfortable enough. She had to send twice to the court for money for her expenses and she evidently kept in urgent communication with both Boniface and Peter of Savoy, and sent messengers to Eustace de Lenn and to Boniface's clerk Henry of Ghent.[95] Henry, who had originally been a protégé of Thomas of Savoy, had apparently fled in terror from the tumult at Lambeth on 3 November – 'as a braver man than he might have done' – wrote Matthew Paris with quiet malice.[96] Yet Eleanor of Provence had sufficient grasp on the hard role of queenship to know that she could not afford to indulge either anger or wounded pride for long. She must be willing to work for reconciliation, although she did not for a moment yield her allegiance to her own side. She was back at court, now at Clarendon, on 18 November, although it was not until 27 November that control of her lands and queen's gold was restored to her, and she was presumably

---

[91] *CM*, v. 351–3, vi. 222–5.
[92] *CR 1251–53*, 431.
[93] BL Cotton MS Julius D. VII, f. 101v, printed by Vaughan, 'The Chronicle of John of Wallingford', 72.
[94] *CM*, v. 352.
[95] E 101/308/1 mm. 1, 2.
[96] *CM*, v. 350.

received once more into the king's favour.[97] The truth was that, for the reconciliation which he was determined to secure, he needed her help. Although she spent most of December at Marlborough away from the king, she was with him at Winchester for Christmas, although this was Aymer territory; they were together again at Westminster for the feast of St Edward on 5 January and by 12 January the king and queen were established at Windsor.[98] They both worked hard for peace, the king on Aymer and the queen on Boniface; Matthew Paris is quite specific on this, and the queen's efforts and her gestures of goodwill are seen too in the evidence of her jewel rolls. She made New Year presents of expensive belts to Geoffrey de Lusignan and William de Valence, comparable in price to those which she gave to her sister Sanchia and to Richard of Cornwall.[99] She also received a valuable present of plate from Aymer de Lusignan, who may at this point have valued her efforts for peace.[100] All these were made in connection with the traditional present-giving on 1 January, the feast of the Circumcision, although she was not in fact with the court on that particular day. To the king himself Eleanor gave a crystal goblet on a stand, and from him she received a present of a belt.[101] At a council of bishops held in London between 13 and 26 January Aymer, who swore that he had been no party to the raid, was absolved and given the kiss of peace by Boniface.[102] The king returned to Westminster and the whole incident was officially at an end.

In reality the bitterness between Savoyards and Lusignans persisted and was to reach a new crescendo five years later. For the moment the king's mind was concentrated on other issues. The bishops were prepared to concede the crusading tenth granted to the king by the pope, but only in return for a further solemn and public confirmation of Magna Carta and a promise to observe ecclesiastical liberties.[103] To go on crusade was probably still the king's serious intention, but his more immediate and pressing task was to deal with the problem of Gascony. Increasingly serious disorder had compelled him to resolve on a military campaign which he would lead in person.[104] This had naturally strengthened his

---

[97] E 101/349/24 m. 1; *CR 1251–53*, 283.

[98] Huw Ridgeway's view of the queen's participation in events 3 November 1252–12 January 1253 ('Politics', 120–7, *passim*), needs modification in the light of the continuous dating of her alms account, E 101/349/24 m. 1.

[99] *CM*, v. 359; E 101/349/13 m. 2.

[100] E 101/349/15 m. 1.

[101] E 101/349/14; E 101/349/13 m. 1.

[102] *CM*, v. 359. For the efforts of the bishops see also 'The Chronicle of John of Wallingford', as in n. 93, above, also printed in *Councils and Synods*, II, pt i. 468.

[103] *Councils and Synods*, II, pt i. 469–72, 477–8.

[104] Maddicott, *Montfort*, 120; Trabut-Cussac, *L'Administration Anglaise*, xxviii–xxx.

determination to close the rifts at court among the men who were his closest allies and friends and upon whom he would depend for diplomatic and military support. In this view the queen necessarily concurred. The protection of Gascony for Edward was her most pressing anxiety, and she too must have seen that Henry could not leave with his court openly divided. From the settlement of the factious quarrel at court in January to the departure of the king for Gascony in August there is plentiful evidence that the king had turned to Eleanor with renewed trust and that they were collaborating purposefully in diplomacy and in practical planning for the government of England during the approaching period of regency. The queen was now to find more scope for her abilities than ever before.

During the past eight years, whether Eleanor had conceived or not, there had been no successful births. We do not know why. In the spring of 1253 she was again pregnant and was to give birth to a daughter Katharine in the following November.[105] This perhaps underlines the warmth of the personal reconciliation which Henry and Eleanor had achieved.

---

[105] Katharine was born on 25 November 1253.

4

The Queen's Lifestyle

The physical setting for the life of Eleanor of Provence was richly varied. In England she spent most of her time in royal castles such as Windsor and Winchester, in the palaces of Clarendon, Woodstock, Havering, Guildford and Marlborough and the great palace of Westminster itself, and from time to time in many smaller establishments, either manors or hunting lodges, scattered across the southern and midland counties of England. These buildings and their surrounding gardens and parks were part of her cultural experience on a day-to-day basis. The character and style of the royal residences were partly determined by their individual setting and by the building work of previous kings, but Henry III had an absorbing interest in schemes for aesthetic improvement and practical modernization. His achievement was part of a development that was neither exclusively royal nor wholly insular, yet in his case it was strikingly individual. In striving for beauty he never lost sight of the fact that these domestic buildings were primarily functional. The Antioch Chamber at Clarendon or the Painted Chamber at Westminster, showpieces as they undoubtedly were, were intended for use as audience chambers. The many orders for wall fireplaces, tiled floors, covered ways and glazed windows were all conceived with the overriding aim of improving the quality of living in the king's court.

Eleanor of Provence was clearly a beneficiary of these building projects, and she was also a collaborator. The king who progressively allowed her more independence in the control of her own resources and the appointment of her own officials would hardly have held back from inviting her views on the restructuring and refurbishment of her own apartments. In provision for the queen immediately after her marriage the king of course relied on his own judgement, and as we have seen, his handling of the building and decoration of her apartments was sensitive and imaginative. In later schemes it would be entirely artificial to attempt any lines of demarcation between the ideas of the king and those of his wife. The creation of the various Antioch chambers soon after the queen had borrowed the book of romances containing the story of Antioch, and in the wake of the decision that they should both go to the Holy Land, points to companionable discussion of schemes of decoration.[1] The queen's share in planning shows quite explicitly in 1268, when the king orders the delivery of twenty glass windows decorated with forty heraldic shields to Havering, to be installed in the queen's chamber 'as more fully enjoined by her'.[2] Her impatience at the delays in directing money to the building works on her new apartments at Windsor in 1260 snaps through a peremptory order to the sheriff of Hampshire to produce £20 without delay; it is authorized 'by the king, at the queen's request'.[3]

Eleanor of Provence, like her husband, required artistic excellence in the adornment of her apartments, combined with comfort and convenience. The site of the royal palace at Clarendon, some two and a half miles east of Salisbury, has been the subject of a recent detailed archaeological investigation, which helps to create a lively impression of the queen's accommodation there in the early 1250s, shortly after a major programme of enlargement and refurbishment.[4] Many of the details come from the chancery rolls. By 1252 Eleanor had a compact suite of apartments at Clarendon, comprising a hall, a chapel, three chambers and a wardrobe. They were situated on two floors.[5] The rooms were spacious, two of them extending to a length of 40 feet, and the amenities of her chambers had been greatly improved by the adjacent construction of a two-storey building providing access to 'a fair privy chamber, well vaulted on both floors'.[6] The focal point of the queen's hall was an imposing new fireplace with double marble columns on each side and an overmantel carved with representations of the twelve months of the year.[7] The windows of her rooms were glazed, perhaps mainly in plain glass or the delicate silver-grey *grisaille* patterns, but also with some figured glass, which would be coloured. The windows of her hall over-

[1] Above, ch. 3, nn. 57, 58.
[2] *CLR 1267–72*, no. 109.
[3] *CLR 1251–60*, 515.
[4] James and Robinson, *Clarendon Palace*.
[5] Ibid., 17–22; also Eames, 'Royal apartments at Clarendon', esp. 73–9.
[6] *CLR 1240–45*, 224.
[7] *CLR 1245–51*, 362; James and Robinson, *Clarendon Palace*, 18–19.

looked a garden. The chapel, on the upper floor, had a marble altar, flanked by two windows, which could be opened and closed, and above the altar was a crucifix, with the figures of Mary and John.[8] Religious imagery was not confined to the chapel; in the window of one of the queen's chambers there was a representation of the Virgin and Child with the kneeling figure of an earthly queen, presumably Eleanor herself, with an *Ave Maria* scroll.[9] This would have been closely reminiscent of the iconography of the donor portraits in the contemporary illuminations of the Amesbury Psalter and the Missal of Henry of Chichester.[10] The walls of the chapel were initially painted with scenes from the life of St Katharine, but later redecorated 'with symbols and stories as arranged'.[11] One distinctively up-to-date feature of these rooms were the tiled floors and the remaining portion of one of these, lifted in the post-war excavations at Clarendon, can be seen on the far wall in the medieval ceramics room of the British Museum. The pavement dates from 1250–2 and was laid in one of Eleanor's ground-floor chambers. Divided into panels of patterned and figured tiles, glowing in muted shades of gold, grey and warm pink, its power to evoke is incomparable.[12]

In many of the residences the queen's chapels were richly furnished and each had individual touches. For her chapel at Havering the king ordered a painting of the Annunciation and a small image of the Virgin and Child.[13] The walls of her chapel at Winchester depicted St Christopher carrying the Christ Child, and St Edward giving his ring to a pilgrim, and at Windsor there was a wall painting of the Wise and Foolish Virgins.[14] Another feature here, and also in the chapel of the royal house at Kempton, was the placing of two detached paintings, one above and one in front of the altar.[15] The chapels at Kempton, Winchester and Windsor were also distinctive in their actual structure, having the additional feature of a gallery for the queen's personal use, with room for members of her household below.[16] The decorative themes for her

---

[8] *CLR 1245–51*, 239, 269, 296–7.

[9] Ibid., 324; Marks, *Stained Glass in England during the Middle Ages*, 10–11.

[10] For the Psalter see plate 10; for the Missal, Alexander and Binski, *Age of Chivalry*, no. 108.

[11] E 372/80 rot. 5; *CLR 1245–51*, 67.

[12] Plate 6; Eames, 'A tile pavement from the queen's chamber, Clarendon Palace, dated 1250–2', 95–106; also, Eames, in James and Robinson, *Clarendon Palace*, 143–7. For a coloured reproduction of the pavement see Eames, *English Tilers*, 41, where 'Queen Eleanor' should replace 'Queen Philippa'.

[13] *CLR 1245–51*, 372.

[14] Ibid., 177; *CR 1237–42*, 514.

[15] *CLR 1245–51*, 45, 83.

[16] *King's Works*, i. 125–6.

chambers, as distinct from the chapels, might be either religious or secular. Scenes from the Romance of Alexander brightened the queen's chamber in Nottingham castle, and one wall of her small chamber at Winchester was decorated with a painting of a city. On the other hand, the representation of the Four Evangelists on the chamber walls at Havering and a magnificent Christ in Majesty, surrounded by other figures, the whole effect heightened by gilding, on the walls of Eleanor's great chamber at Winchester reflect omnipresent religious imagery.[17]

Around the chapels and chambers, beneath windows, in the angles of buildings, or at the base of a flight of steps we find gardens. Eleanor of Provence loved gardens and there can be no doubt of her personal influence here. In 1245 a walled garden was made outside her new chamber at Clarendon and an enclosed lawn already separated her chambers from the king's chapel.[18] At Guildford the queen's wardrobe was situated above the garden steps, and there were herb gardens at Winchester, Kempton and Windsor, adjacent to the queen's apartments.[19] Windsor had particularly fine gardens and here one of the queen's apartments had windows with glass casements which overlooked a courtyard with a herber in the centre.[20] By 1268 there were two full-time gardeners at Windsor, one of them, significantly, a Provençal.[21] Some of the queen's gardens were small, but not all of them. It has been thought likely that the queen's gardens at Kempton may have covered two or three acres.[22] The best place of all for gardens was Woodstock. In 1245 the king created a special walled garden for Eleanor outside her chapel and later, what was evidently a spacious herb garden for her to walk in beside the king's fish-pond.[23] Within the park at Woodstock, but situated a little way from the palace, was Everswell, where chambers for the king and queen were set among pools and gardens, created originally by Henry II as the setting for his amours with Fair Rosamund. Everswell deliberately evoked the romance of Tristan and Isolde, and here again a beautiful garden for the queen was laid out around one of the pools.[24] Henry III had arranged for the

---

[17] *CLR 1251–60*, 18; *CLR 1245–51*, 30, 372; Tristram, *English Medieval Wall Painting*, ii. 553.

[18] *CLR 1240–45*, 291; *CLR 1226–40*, 402.

[19] *CLR 1226–40*, 319, 342, 365, 439; *CLR 1240–45*, 48; *CLR 1245–51*, 175. An imaginative reconstruction of a thirteenth-century queen's garden may be seen outside the great hall of Winchester Castle.

[20] *King's Works*, ii. 867.

[21] Harvey, *Medieval Gardens*, 156.

[22] Ibid., 11.

[23] *CLR 1240–45*, 307; *CLR 1245–51*, 292.

[24] *CLR 1226–40*, 412; *King's Works*, ii. 1014–16.

planting of 100 pear trees in another of the gardens at Everswell and the sight of the blossom in springtime must have made this place an idyllic retreat. So essential were gardens to Queen Eleanor's pleasure that on one occasion, rather than be deprived, she borrowed one. When resident at Gloucester, one of her dower castles, she persuaded the canons of Llanthony priory on the other side of the river to allow herself and members of her household to walk for their refreshment in the priory gardens, and a little bridge was built to make it possible.[25]

Castles and palaces provided a regal setting, and closely related to that setting were the queen's clothes and jewels. For the single year of 1252–3 there still exist the detailed accounts and inventories which lay behind the summaries of the queen's wardrobe finance, recorded on the exchequer pipe rolls. It is from these 'particulars', extant exceptionally and by chance for this year, that much of the subsequent material in this chapter is drawn. Two of the documents concern expenditure for the queen's chamber and so-called 'necessary expenses'.[26] To read these through is to enter with astonishing immediacy into a world of high fashion. These were no ordinary clothes; the colours, the textures and the workmanship were exquisite. Most of them were made for Eleanor of Provence and her ladies; gowns of russet, blue and green, trimmed with borders worked in gold or silver thread and decorated with dozens of minute pearl buttons; hoods and capes trimmed with fur, stout capes to keep off the rain, fine wool caps and hose, and then the more delicate items, chemises, veils, wimples and silk kerchiefs. There were shoes, too; little slippers, presumably for indoor wear, stouter boots for more protection, styles worn by both the queen and her ladies, and one pair of fine goatskin boots for the queen herself. To assemble such a wardrobe required more than local resources. Some silk was bought at the fairs of Winchester but there were coifs and hair tressures of Parisian work and one cloak was trimmed with Irish frieze. Several items came through the agency of the queen's Florentine merchant Deutatus Willelmi and others through the contacts of ladies around the queen; Lady Alice the nurse bought wimples; Margaret of Montpellier procured gold thread and the Lady Willelma had a sister in Paris who was evidently able to lay her hands on particularly attractive tressures in the French capital. It was Colin the tailor who masterminded the queen's clothes, who supervised the cutting out of the cloth and saw to its being stitched with thread of gold or silver or with black silk and to the sewing on of the innumerable buttons. He moved from one royal

[25] Cited from the Llanthony Cartulary, in *King's Works*, ii. 652, n. 4. The main priory had been moved from Llanthony (Monmouth) to Gloucester because of Welsh incursions.
[26] E 101/349/19, 18.

residence to another, but stayed for three weeks this year in London to make robes for the queen and her ladies. The contact between the queen and her tailor was necessarily close and Eleanor was paying for the son of another of her tailors, Richard, to go to the Oxford schools.[27]

The queen's jewels were the ultimate responsibility of the clerk who was keeper of her wardrobe, a professional administrator, but the queen would have needed easy access to the jewels which she wore herself, some of which were bought, some received as presents; brooches, rings and girdles, all of them worn by both men and women, and garlands for her hair, often decorated with pearls. The accounts are of interest, because Eleanor of Provence presumably spent many hours in making decisions about clothes for herself, for her ladies and for her children. There are gowns for Beatrice, robes for Edward and Edmund, a tabard of Ypres silk for Edward, bought at Oxford by Colin the tailor, doublets for Edmund and Beatrice, tunics of camlet for Edward and Edmund and innumerable pairs of children's shoes.[28] These accounts suggest that Eleanor of Provence knew a great deal about the importance of presentation. Her own appearance and royal style mattered socially and also politically; it was a facet of queenship.

Although she travelled less widely than the king, Eleanor would have been a familiar figure in any of the residences on the traditional royal circuit. Between July 1252 and July 1253, the time covered by these accounts, her main base was Windsor, where her children were, and where she spent some thirty weeks. For the rest she was mainly at Clarendon, Marlborough, Woodstock and Winchester, usually for about a fortnight at a time, with only two very brief visits to Westminster.[29] She probably spent longer than this at Westminster in other years. When she was resident in a place she might have specific local contacts, as with the Franciscans who acted as chaplains when she was at Clarendon.[30] The queen was to be seen on her journeys, too, as she passed through Reading, Wallingford, Oxford, Highworth, Ludgershall, Salisbury and Kempton, occasionally staying a night before she moved on. Usually she would have travelled in her carriage, its interior newly covered this year with 14 ells of canvas and 17 ells of blue cloth, with attendant horsemen.[31] This was part of the royal drama, and so too on other occasions was the sight of the queen on horseback, seated on her palfrey, with a splendid saddle ornamented with orphrey work and gold

[27] E 101/349/8.
[28] E 101/349/18, 19, *passim*.
[29] The queen's itinerary may be followed from her alms accounts, E 101/349/17, 24.
[30] *CLR 1267–72*, no. 409.
[31] E101/349/18.

studs, accompanied by her ladies, also finely mounted.[32] Whether she was receiving visitors in her own chamber, assisting at great court festivities, attending such outside events as the dedication of a major ecclesiastical foundation – Beaulieu in 1246, Hailes in 1251, Salisbury cathedral in 1258 – or taking part in state visits to the French court, as in 1254 and 1259, her profile was high.[33] Although her image was ultimately of her own making she had to meet the expectations of the king and of his subjects. In her role as queen her natural beauty and dignity had to be enhanced by fine clothes and jewels. Sartorial splendour was an attribute of royal state, part of the drama of power, and it had of course a significant aesthetic and emotional appeal; Eleanor of Provence, arrayed in queenly majesty was all of a piece with the Painted Chamber at Westminster.

Few state occasions in Henry III's reign could have equalled in splendour the celebrations for the marriage of his daughter Margaret to Alexander III of Scotland, held in York in December 1251, when Margaret was only eleven. The marriage had been arranged as part of an agreement between Henry III and Alexander II in 1244. Like all spectacle of the highest quality, it was underpinned by the concentrated effort of immaculate planning.[34] The setting itself was dramatic and York still retains the essential pattern of its medieval past, a city encircled by walls, the massive building of the Minster dominating the narrow streets that thread across the land to the south, Deangate, Goodramgate, High Petergate, Stonegate and Lendal. In 1251 the Minster was still substantially a Romanesque building, but the work that was to transform it into a masterpiece of Gothic elegance had already begun and the north and south transepts were probably nearing completion. The archbishop who had launched the rebuilding on such a magnificent scale was a prominent figure at Margaret's wedding. The king and queen were lodged in his palace, and he entertained all the more important guests for several days. Matthew Paris captures authentically Walter de Gray's skill and consideration as a gracious host. The archbishop was ready with help and advice whenever there was a need or a crisis; he provided lodgings for travellers, fodder for horses, household utensils, fuel for fires and even gifts of money.[35] The whole area around York was alive to the celebration of a royal occasion on the grand scale, and in the north porch of

[32] *CLR 1226–40*, 288; *CLR 1251–60*, 378.
[33] *Ann. Waverley*, 337, 343; *Ann. Tewkesbury*, 166; *CM*, iv. 562, v. 262; for visits to France see chs 6 and 7, below.
[34] For fully documented description of the York wedding see Staniland, 'The Nuptials of Alexander III of Scotland and Margaret Plantagenet', 20–45.
[35] *CM*, v. 269–70.

Bridlington priory are three carved corbels, an isolated group, almost certainly representing Henry III, Eleanor of Provence and Walter de Gray.[36]

Details of the visual splendour of the pageantry are plentiful. Henry III and Queen Eleanor had garments of samite (a heavy silk) trimmed with gold braid, and mantles furred with ermine. The Lord Edward and his companions Nicholas de Molis, Bartholomew Pecche and Ebulo de Montibus wore distinctive tabards of cloth of gold embroidered with the royal leopards. Although there was separation according to nationality, tensions were predictable among the English, Scots and French billeted in the various streets of York and excitement ran high. Fights broke out, punching at first, then fighting with staves, then with swords. In anticipation of the wedding itself, crowds pushed and jostled for good places. The glamour and the hazards of a great royal occasion are very well caught here, and the king prudently decided that the marriage ceremony should be performed secretly in the early morning, before anyone was expecting it.[37] Even so there were plenty of set-pieces to be watched, including the knighting of the young Scottish king by Henry III himself. The York marriage is an outstanding example of the significance Henry attached to elaborate, well controlled, but none the less stunning royal display.[38] Queen Eleanor had probably been trained by her husband to enter into that view with equal zest and discrimination.

Among the rolls of particulars drawn up by the controller of Eleanor of Provence's wardrobe for the year 1252–3 are eleven dealing exclusively with jewels and plate. Ten of these are inventories and the eleventh is a list of the jewels bought by the queen in that year.[39] She spent some £200 on jewels and among these were sixty-one rings, ninety-one brooches and thirty-three belts. Some shine out in their beauty; a brooch with emeralds and pearls, eight brooches with pearls and sapphires, thirty-two rings with rubies and emeralds, a very fine gold belt, made by Andrew the goldsmith, decorated with shields of small pearls, which cost the queen the large sum of £8–12s. She bought ten goblets of the work of Tours, all mounted, some fully gilded, others partly gilded. The descriptions of the items of repair work are equally detailed and even more evocative; a flower for a garland belonging to Beatrice, the lengthening of the silver chain on a cloak which the queen had given to her sister Sanchia, copper for repairing of one of the queen's lecterns.[40] The buying of jewellery on

[36] *Letters of the Queens of England*, 56.
[37] CM, v. 266–8.
[38] Clanchy, *England and its Rulers*, 282.
[39] E 101/349/6, 7, 11, 12, 13, 14, 15, 23, 25; E 101/684/56/1; E 101/349/21.
[40] E 101/349/21.

this scale related to a deep-rooted social convention in the life of the royal court. By far the greater number of these rings, brooches, belts and goblets were bought in order to be given away again. The descriptions indicate a sophisticated art of high aesthetic quality, partly inspired and financed by royal patronage, although the giving of jewels was by no means an exclusively royal prerogative.[41]

The custom of presenting jewels, especially by a king or prince, stemmed from a tradition reaching far back into the Germanic past. The imagery of Beowulf scintillates with 'ring-riches and jewel-brooches' given to followers.[42] Centuries later this giving of jewels retained a symbolic importance, which had been absorbed into the conventions of a very different society. It was now associated with that chivalric quality of *largesse* which played so significant a part in Henry III's image of kingship. Occasions for the giving of jewels could occur at any time. Some presentations were diplomatic, as with the goblets given by the queen to the papal nuncio and his two companions in January 1253 and to the nuncio of the king of Navarre in the following June.[43] Some gifts reflect normal social intercourse. Aristocratic ladies such as the countess of Devon and the countess of Lincoln would be accompanied by their own *domicellae* and knights when they visited the queen, and these attendants would receive presents too.[44] In the years immediately following Margaret's marriage to Alexander III the queen was lavish in her present-giving to those who were sent to Scotland to watch over Margaret's welfare and interest. The learned and honourable Matilda Cantilupe, who was given a pair of dishes by the queen in September 1252, was one of these and so was that unscrupulous careerist, also a favourite of the queen, Geoffrey de Langley, who received a valuable goblet in November of the same year.[45] But the special time for general present-giving to relatives and to members of the royal households was 1 January, the feast of the Circumcision. The queen gave over sixty such presents in January 1253.

It is interesting to note how the various nurses at Windsor feature in the inventory for brooches, many of them, but not all, given on 1 January 1253. The queen's daughter Beatrice, now aged ten, was given a brooch which she was then told to give to her nurse, Lady Agnes. Lady Agnes was also given a brooch by the queen herself and so was Lady Alice, nurse of the Lord Edward and always regarded with great affection by

---

[41] J. Cherry, 'Jewellery' in Alexander and Binski, *Age of Chivalry*, 176–7.
[42] *Beowulf*, lines 3008–9, 3163–8.
[43] E 101/349/7, 14.
[44] E.g. E 101/349/13 m. 2.
[45] E 101/349/15, 7.

Edward himself. More than this, Queen Eleanor gave a brooch to Lady Petronilla, nurse of Alice de Lusignan's little daughter by John de Warenne, and to the nurses of Sanchia's son Edmund and of Alice de Saluzzo's son Henry, later earl of Lincoln.[46] Most of these children were being brought up at Windsor, and one catches the feeling of an establishment where children and those who cared for them were part of the rhythm and interest of life.

Eleanor of Provence was open to the complex influences of a highly developed culture which was all the more stimulating for not being entirely cohesive and for containing inner tensions, especially between the secular and the religious. She had none of that systematic knowledge which characterized the men of learning with whom she came into contact and whom she respected. If we begin with her possible view of the world in the figurative sense we should speculate on her probable acquaintance with those maps of the world which were a feature of contemporary manuscript illumination and mural decoration. Unfortunately Matthew Paris's copy of the *Mappa Mundi* on the wall of the king's chamber at Westminster (later the Painted Chamber) no longer exists, but the queen would presumably have seen this and also the *Mappa Mundi* on one wall of the great hall in the castle at Winchester.[47] In the absence of more exact knowledge of these maps, the famous *Mappa Mundi* still in existence at Hereford and usually dated to the 1280s is perhaps as good a guide as any to her likely visual and intellectual conception of the world.[48] Geographically it comprised only three continents, Asia, Africa and Europe. The queen would have been personally familiar with a few of the rivers and the cities depicted on such a map, but the Hereford *Mappa Mundi* is also a treasure-house of knowledge, snippets of learning culled from books of the ancient world and conveyed in small lively pictures. It is packed full of biblical, historical and legendary references, such as the figure of Moses receiving the tables of the covenant, St Augustine presiding over Hippo or Jason's golden fleece lying by the Black Sea; the Minotaur is not far away from Noah's ark. If Eleanor did have the chance of examining a *Mappa Mundi* like this one she would have absorbed a wealth of disconnected stories, facts and marvels, without much differentiation of cultures or categories of information or distinction between fact and myth. At the physical and spiritual centre of that world was Jerusalem and there was no escape

[46] E 101/349/12.

[47] *CLR 1226–40*, 405; Lewis, *The Art of Matthew Paris in the Chronica Majora*, 372–4; Binski, *The Painted Chamber at Westminster*, 44; Alexander and Binski, *Age of Chivalry*, no. 36.

[48] Harvey, *Mappa Mundi: The Hereford World Map*.

from God and God's judgement. For many incidents in everyday life scientific explanation was neither available nor sought for; miracles and wonders took its place. Contemporaries distinguished carefully between the two.[49] Eleanor of Provence was deeply impressed by miracles and she perhaps tended to credulity even by contemporary standards. On one occasion, later in her life, she was convinced that a miracle had been performed at her husband's tomb, on evidence that Edward I dismissed out of hand.[50] Natural prodigies were distinct from miracles and Matthew Paris records the discovery in the Isle of Wight of a small boy, not deformed, but who at the age of eighteen was hardly three feet high. When he was brought to the queen's notice she arranged for him to be taken about with her 'to excite astonishment as a natural prodigy'.[51] We receive a sudden sharp insight into Eleanor's mind.

The conventional social life of the court partly conditioned the range of Eleanor's daily experience. We do not know whether she hunted, as Eleanor of Castile certainly did, but there is evidence that she practised falconry. In her 1252–3 accounts there is mention of a mewed hawk belonging to the queen, and gloves for falconry were bought for Edmund and Beatrice by their mother.[52] Minstrelsy, dancing and games of chess were routine indoor entertainment, and it was perhaps the queen who suggested that Richard the Harper should be retained for the comfort of the royal children when the parents were in Gascony in 1242.[53] Many years later it was a former minstrel of Queen Eleanor who delivered a book of romance to her grandson, the future Edward II, originally bequeathed on her death to his father, Edward I.[54]

All this seems sedate; the elegant diversions so familiar from manuscript illumination. But Henry III's court was not uniformly decorous; the tone was lively and could be harsh. One foreign jester was thrown into the water and another had his clothes ripped up by the king, although both were later compensated.[55] Versifying and witty repartee took place in an atmosphere where violent temper and coarse vituperation were commonplace. Perhaps this very lack of inhibition promoted the ease with which divers talents could be brought together quickly in an individual project. An instance which involved the queen was the solemn translation of a relic of St Thomas the Apostle to a new reliquary

[49] Le Goff, *The Medieval Imagination*, 35–6.
[50] Ch. 12, below.
[51] *CM*, v. 82.
[52] E 101/349/18; Parsons, *Eleanor of Castile*, 55.
[53] *CR 1237–42*, 523.
[54] Bullock-Davies, *Register of Royal and Baronial Minstrels, 1272–1327*, 117.
[55] Salter, *English and International*, 82.

on 21 December 1244, at which she was representing the king himself.[56] Henry had ordered his royal goldsmith to fashion a fine gold and sapphire ring, which was to be placed on a finger of the new arm-shaped reliquary. On the inner surface of the ring certain verses were to be engraved, composed by the court poet Henry of Avranches.[57] The ready combining of the written word, the work of art and the religious act reflects the spontaneous cultural creativity of Henry III's court. But always there was a seedier underside and Henry of Avranches happens to lead us there too. His rival and enemy, Michael of Cornwall, alleged that after Henry was given a fine robe by the queen, he demeaned the queen's gracious act by passing it on to his red-headed whore. It could well be; the prostitutes of Charing were notorious in the mid-thirteenth century and some were no doubt frequented by members of the court.[58]

Henry of Avranches, a prolific writer, whose professional career had made him familiar with the papal court and most of the royal courts of Europe, including that of England, was representative of a supranational tradition which already existed at the court of Henry III in literature and the visual arts before its cultural apogee was reached. From the late 1240s onwards the opportunities for the reception of artistic forms from the Continent multiplied. The stimulus which came from the French court has long been recognized, but stress is now being laid on the multiplicity of sources of patronage and the rich diversity of ideas which contributed to the full artistic achievements of England in the second half of the thirteenth century. In this, the debt to the households of the Savoyard and Lusignan incomers was probably substantial. The factors forming the taste of Eleanor of Provence were intricately cosmopolitan.[59]

One powerful influence in shaping Eleanor's *mentalité* was obviously the chivalric code and the chivalric lifestyle. She bought and read romances. Within the space of six months, between 24 June and 28 October 1252, she bought two romances, one from Peter of Paris for 10s and one 'done by the hand of William of Paris at Oxford' for £1 15s. There was also a payment for binding one of the queen's romances.[60] It may be said that the evidence is only for purchase, but romances were bought for the pleasure and excitement of reading, or, more precisely, of listening to them being read aloud. The mention of Paris and Oxford is

---

[56] CR 1242–47, 276.

[57] Ibid., 270.

[58] Russell and Heironimus, *The Shorter Latin Poems of Master Henry of Avranches*, 153 and n. 32; Rosser, *Medieval Westminster*, 143.

[59] Salter, *English and International*, 80–9; Binski, *Westminster Abbey*, 44–5.

[60] E 101/349/19, 18.

what one would expect. Oxford was already a main centre of book production in England; Paris was the great production centre for romances, written in continental French, not the Anglo-Norman ancestral romances that were popular with the English baronage. Eleanor apparently relished both the romances based on classical themes and the Arthurian romances, the so-called 'matter of Britain'. This is evident from the list of heroes introduced by her chaplain John of Howden into his Anglo-Norman version of his Latin poem, *Rossignos*, a version which was composed specifically for Eleanor; he would know what allusions the queen would understand. Hector, Troilus, Alexander and Caesar are there as well as Gawain, Iwain, Perceval, Lancelot and Arthur.[61] The purchase of at least two romances in a matter of six months implies that unless the year 1252 was exceptional, and there is no reason to think that it was, the queen was in the process of acquiring a substantial collection of such books. The significance is clear. These books not only fed her imagination with their tales of prowess and of sexual passion, with their marvels and magic, they were also powerfully didactic in inculcating the values of the chivalric ethic. The view that these values were merely an artificial veneer, superficially imposed upon a much nastier and more brutish real world has been convincingly rejected by Maurice Keen.[62] Neither Eleanor of Provence nor any other contemporary reader of these romances had any illusions about the harsh, bloody realities of much medieval warfare. Eleanor was inescapably near to such realities; men to whom she was most closely connected, including her own husband and son, were involved in such fighting in Gascony, in Wales, and later in England, during the baronial wars, and especially in the two battles of Lewes and Evesham, and in Edward's case, in the Holy Land. At court it was mainly the young *valetti* and the clerks who had not known fighting. Yet Eleanor's uncle Boniface of Savoy and her adviser, John Mansel, both ecclesiastics, had experience of armed conflict. The quality of *prouesse*, so much prasied in the romances, was pre-eminently a quality which was universally respected and admired in real combat – physical courage and the capacity for hard fighting. Eleanor's appetite for deeds of *prouesse* is beyond question. Interspersed with tales of heroes of the ancient world and of romance, John of Howden recounted the valiant deeds of more recent knights and princes, from the early crusaders to the thirteenth century, citing many whom the queen knew personally, her own father and her uncle Peter of Savoy, Raymond of Toulouse, Charles of Anjou, the French knight Erard de Valery and the Marcher lord Roger Clifford,

---

[61] Salter, *English and International*, 76–7, 90; Stone, 'Jean de Howden', 509–13.
[62] Keen, *Chivalry*, 3, 249–51.

as well as Louis IX and Edward I himself; all were depicted as men of valour, fit to be mentioned in the company of the heroes of old.[63]

The chivalric ethic enshrined other values. The *loyauté* of a knight to his lord was not in practice limited to that one relationship. The loyalty of a wife to her husband, who was also her lord, was a striking attribute of many aristocratic Englishwomen and tenacious loyalty was one of Queen Eleanor's finest qualities. She valued it in others and practised it herself in respect of her husband, her children, her wider family, her friends and those who had served her. In 1264, when almost overcome with anguish at the news of the disastrous defeat at Lewes and the surrender of her husband and her eldest son, it was loyalty which triumphed over her despair.[64] In 1257, to help in the release of her uncle Thomas of Savoy, imprisoned in Turin, she exerted herself ceaselessly and over-stretched her resources.[65] The demands were not always so dramatic, but they still required effort, in defending her protégé Geoffrey de Langley against the anger of the king or in the quiet kindness through which she showed her gratitude to her ladies, Margaret Biset and Willelma.[66]

The author of *La Estoire de Seint Aedward le Rei* praised Eleanor's *bonté* and *franchise*, denoting a much prized warmth and openness of manner.[67] The quality of *débonaireté* has been seen by Malcolm Vale as a striking feature of social and diplomatic intercourse within that cosmopolitan society of which the English and French courts formed the core and where magnates, knights or clerks from either side of the Channel moved with ease.[68] Among the figures of the Virtues which decorated the window embrasures of the Painted Chamber at Westminister, *Débonaireté* is seen whipping the cowering figure of Anger. The man or woman who was *débonaire* was kindly disposed towards others, courteous and with a temper well under control. It was a quality which Henry III valued highly, since the figure of *Débonaireté* is represented bearing the royal arms, but it was perhaps more characteristic of his wife than of himself.[69]

In the cultural ambience of Eleanor of Provence the chivalric ethic was held in combination with, and in tension with, the Christian ethic. These were not two rigid systems setting up a ceaseless conflict for men's allegiance. The best chivalric literature was a learned literature, and

---

[63] Stone, 'Jean de Howden', 509–13.
[64] Ch. 9, below.
[65] Ch. 6, below.
[66] Ch. 2, above and ch. 4, below.
[67] *Estoire* (ed. Wallace), 2.
[68] Vale, *Angevin Legacy*, 22–3.
[69] Binski, *The Painted Chamber at Westminster*, 41–4.

already in the twelfth century Chrétien de Troyes had been insistent on the interdependence of *chevalerie* and *clergie*.[70] Eleanor's clerk John of Gatesden became a knight, and the *prouesse* of the clerks Boniface of Savoy and John Mansel has already been mentioned. John of Howden, learned and holy as he was, showed complete familiarity with chivalric romances. Yet the tension was there. Chivalry was secular in its origins and could show itself anti-sacerdotal; chivalric romances made little reference to priests; hermits were preferred. The Church deplored the theme of courtly love, either in troubadour lyrics or romances, and it made sustained efforts to direct the martial energies of knights exclusively towards 'Holy War'. Yet in practice there was of course much give and take. In the thirteenth century the Church was still firmly opposed to the holding of tournaments, that highly popular and colourful ludic element in chivalric culture. Edward I himself was sternly rebuked by Gregory X for participation in tournaments, but early in the next century this completely ineffective opposition to the sport was abandoned.[71] Meanwhile the increasingly elaborate rites attending admission to knighthood were clothed more and more in religious symbolism.

Religion was as vital a force as chivalry in shaping the thought and actions of Eleanor of Provence. The term 'conventional piety' in this context is meaningless. Henry III was by temperament a deeply pious man, and his devotion, it goes without saying, was expressed in 'conventional' ways. His devotion to relics, his lavish almsgiving, his patronage of the Dominican and Franciscan friars, his rebuilding of Westminster Abbey were the outlets which stood open to him. These were also manifestations of religious faith which were expected of him; conspicuous piety was an attribute of royalty. This immediately suggests a mixture of motives. Henry's devotion to the Confessor was compounded with his sense of the exalted character of his own office as king; his presentation of the relic of the Holy Blood to Westminster and his rebuilding of the abbey church were given added urgency from Louis IX's possession of the Crown of Thorns and building of the Sainte-Chapelle; emulation was a great spur. None of this negates the ultimate sincerity of Henry III's religious devotion.

This reflection holds good, transposed into a slightly different key, for Eleanor of Provence. In piety Henry III was Eleanor's chief mentor. She loved what her lord loved.[72] In respect of Edward the Confessor, Eleanor made the effort to identify herself with her husband's intensity of feeling, and the Confessor came to hold a special place in her own religious

[70] Keen, *Chivalry*, 5–6, 31–2.
[71] Barker, *The Tournament in England*, 82–3.
[72] *Estoire* (ed. Wallace), 3.

devotion. As regent during the king's absence in Gascony in 1253, she celebrated the feast of St Edward with great magnificence at the king's special request.[73] She never failed to treat the feast with the reverence that her husband wished. In October 1259 she refused to let either her own illness or the bad weather prevent her from getting back from St Albans to Westminster by St Edward's Day.[74] Henry also taught her to love beautiful settings and beautiful objects as aids to devotion. The furnishing of her chapels, where she would have attended mass daily, has been described. Apart from wall paintings, there were many sculptured representations of the Virgin and Child and of the Crucifixion, focusing the mind on the two dominant themes in the religious devotion of the laity. Not everything was bought by her husband or dictated by his taste. In her 'necessary expenses' account of June to October 1252 there is an entry for the purchase of three and a half pounds of ivory; this was evidently to be worked into images for her chapels or chambers by one Richard the sculptor, who was paid £2 for his wages for the period covered by the account and given a robe costing 17*s*. He may have been resident in her household on a long-term basis.[75] The entries evoke the rare but exquisite English ivories which have survived from the thirteenth century.[76] The number of images of the Virgin and Child, although entirely to be expected, must raise the question of what this type of representation meant to Eleanor of Provence. The style of portrayal is perfectly captured in the beautiful manuscript illumination in the Amesbury Psalter which dates from the mid-thirteenth century. The figure of the Virgin, as always in this period, conforms to the ideal of courtly feminine grace and the relationship of mother and child is endued with a moving warmth and delicacy.[77] It has been stressed that medieval women, and especially medieval queens, were expected to distance themselves from such an image of the Virgin, while being exhorted to reach out for her qualities of chastity and obedience. The link of image and imagination is much debated, but it is surely easy to see, at the simplest level, and perhaps mainly subconsciously, how a young queen and mother such as Eleanor of Provence might treat this gentle, aristocratic image of the Virgin, made more accessible and human by her tender relationship with the young Child, as her enduring ideal of womanhood.

[73] *CR 1251–53*, 503–4.

[74] *Flores*, ii. 435.

[75] E 101/349/18.

[76] N. Stratford, 'Gothic Ivory Carving in England' in Alexander and Binski, *Age of Chivalry*, 107–13, and no. 248.

[77] Plate 10; Morgan, *Early Gothic Manuscripts*, ii. 59–61.

Another resource for the religious life of Eleanor of Provence would have been devotional books.[78] There is no book now extant of which we can say with absolute certainty that it belonged to Eleanor of Provence, but there are several books which may have belonged to her and there are several which certainly lead us to her. This can prove more important than specific ownership attribution. In her 'necessary expenses' for June to October 1252 the queen paid Robert *le copitre* in two instalments, implying by the wording that he was continuously employed. Immediately following the first entry for his wages is a payment for a dozen sheets of parchment, at a price which suggests that this was high-quality material, for copying books rather than for financial accounts or letter writing.[79] There is no reference to a *pictor* such as Eleanor of Castile was later to employ in her scriptorium, but it seems likely in any case that both queens would have commissioned high-class illuminated manuscripts from centres outside their households. However, it is interesting to know that the facility for more mundane copying was there.

Fashions in book ownership were changing during the long course of Eleanor's life, as the devotional habits of the laity, and especially of lay women took shape, particularly under the direction of the Dominican and Franciscan friars. From her earliest years in England one might have expected her to have a psalter. Margaret Biset, the heroine of the assassination attempt of 1238, was reciting her psalter by candlelight when the assailant broke into the king's apartment. The queen would not have been less well equipped in devotional books than Margaret Biset. The psalter would have been written in Latin, but a knowledge of liturgical Latin must be assumed in aristocratic women of this period. The richly illuminated Rutland Psalter of about 1260 has a special interest in connection with Eleanor of Provence since there are figures of a king and queen within the initial of Psalm 101, the usual place for donor figures.[80] However, there is no other evidence suggesting royal ownership, and at an early stage the book appears to have been in the possession of the Lacy family, earls of Lincoln, with the obit of Edmund de Lacy, who died in 1258, entered on the calendar.[81] What has not been remarked is the fact that Edmund de Lacy's wife was Alice de Saluzzo, Queen Eleanor's cousin. Margaret, dowager countess of Lincoln, and mother of Edmund de Lacy, was also a friend of the queen, who corresponded with her in 1252–3. Henry de Lacy, the son of Edmund and Alice de Saluzzo,

---

[78] Bell, 'Medieval Women Book Owners', 152.

[79] E 101/349/18.

[80] Plate 7.

[81] Millar, *The Rutland Psalter*; Morgan, *Early Gothic Manuscripts*, ii. 78–82; Lewis, *Reading Images*, 14–15.

married Queen Eleanor's ward, Margaret Longespee, and it is among Lacys and Longespees that Eleanor features alongside other patrons of the priory of Bicester, on a shrine from that house, now in Stanton Harcourt church.[82] None of this reveals the provenance of the Rutland Psalter but it places this fine manuscript within a family grouping which had many intimate links with Queen Eleanor. Another psalter, dated about 1270, now in the New York Metropolitan Museum, has apparent links with Amesbury, and it has been thought that this manuscript may possibly have been made for Eleanor of Provence. The calendar includes, as an added entry, the feast of St Melor, whose relics were at Amesbury, where Eleanor spent the last years of her life, and there is a half-legible inscription on the first page of the psalter which may refer to Fontevrault, the mother-house of Amesbury.[83] Again, this is not in the nature of proof that it was a personal possession of Eleanor of Provence, but it raises the possibility. What matters much more than clear attribution of specific manuscripts is the fact that Eleanor's mind, like that of Margaret Biset and countless others, was nourished by the Psalms of David.

A type of devotional book, which came by the fourteenth century to outstrip even the psalter as a guide to the devotions of the laity, was the book of hours. The lavish fifteenth-century Hours of the Duc de Berri can mislead as to the more modest prototypes which date from the thirteenth century.[84] These earlier books, designed for use, not for display, although some were illuminated, reflected the increasing attention given to lay devotion by the Church and especially by the friars. The liturgical day was divided into the eight hours, long familiar in the pattern of clerical devotions. Different books contained different sets of hours, appropriate for use on different occasions, but each was based primarily on the hours of the Virgin. The text and the illustrations of these books concentrated the mind of the reader on the life and Passion of Christ and on scenes from the life of the Virgin.[85] It is pertinent to note that this was equally the subject matter of John of Howden's *Rossignos*. We have no proof that Eleanor of Provence, in the 1250s or 1260s, came to possess a book of hours, but it would be very surprising if she did not. Eleanor followed fashion, she was attended by friars and her spiritual devotions would have formed one of the most basic parts of her daily

---

[82] *Rotuli Hundredorum*, i. 315; CPR 1247–58, 534, 536; Waugh, *Lordship of England*, 57–8, 200. For the Bicester shrine see Kennett, *Parochial Antiquities*, i. 304, 340–87 *passim*, and Greening Lamborn, 'The Shrine of St Edburg', 43–52.

[83] Morgan, *Early Gothic Manuscripts*, ii. 140–1.

[84] Backhouse, *Books of Hours*, 3–4; Donovan, *The de Brailes Hours*, 183–200.

[85] Donovan, *The de Braites Hours*, 25–6.

routine. Moreover, there is still extant a book of hours belonging to her daughter Beatrice.[86] Recent work on women as transmitters of books to their daughters raises the possibility – far from certainty – that this book may have been a gift from Eleanor to her daughter. The approximate date given for the book is 1260–70 and it was in 1261 that Beatrice left England for her new home in Brittany.[87]

Beatrice's book of hours would have been designed with her requirements specifically in mind; this was a characteristic of the genre. It is small, easy to hold, its Latin text clearly written, with delicately illuminated initials and rubrics in French written in red. The text included several sets of hours, the Litany of the Saints and the Penitential Psalms and in several blank spaces there are personal prayers, written later and much more informally, for the soul of Beatrice, 'daughter of the king', that she may be raised to heaven, having been purged of the venial sins which she may have committed through worldly contacts.[88] She died in 1275 at the age of thirty-two and was buried in the Franciscan church in London, where her mother's heart was later to be buried. In one respect the book is highly distinctive. Following the Gradual Psalms are a prayer, verse and anthem for St Roger.[89] This brings us not just to England but to the diocese of London. When Bishop Roger Niger died in 1241 his cult within his diocese grew steadily and was even recognized in Rome, although he never reached the calendar of the universal Church. Matthew Paris describes him as a learned man, a good preacher and a good host.[90] Although he was buried in St Paul's, where Henry III provided a gold cloth to be placed over his tomb, Roger's heart-shrine was at the priory of Beeleigh in the Essex village which was probably his birthplace.[91] Beatrice herself had never known Roger Niger, but her mother had known him. He assisted Edmund of Abingdon at Eleanor's coronation and he had received the Lord Edward from the font after baptism. One of the main benefactors of Beeleigh was Henry of Wingham, later bishop of London himself, and also a trusted member of the queen's council. Wingham left the large sum of 360 marks to Beeleigh in return for the provision of two chaplains to celebrate masses for his own soul in St Paul's church in London.[92] It was Henry of Wingham who was

---

[86] BL Add. MS 33385.

[87] Bell, 'Medieval Women Book Owners', 155–7; Parsons, 'Mothers, Daughters, Marriage, Power', 74; Donovan, *The de Brailes Hours*, 190.

[88] BL Add. MS 33385, f. 124; see also ff. 23v, 26, 41v, 53v, 83v, 96v, 123v, 140v.

[89] Ibid., ff. 168v–169v; plate 8.

[90] Kemp, *Canonization and Authority in the Western Church*, 116–17; CM, iii. 169–70.

[91] CLR 1240–45, 86; Round, 'The Heart of St Roger', 1–4.

[92] VCH, Essex, ii. 173.

initially entrusted with the responsibility of conducting the Lady Beatrice to Brittany in 1261.[93] These various associations linking Beatrice's book of hours with her mother and those in close contact with her mother are not in the nature of proof of a gift on Eleanor's part, but they are in the nature of evidence suggesting a close community of religious devotion between mother and daughter.

A very different category among thirteenth-century privately owned religious books was the illuminated apocalypse. This of course was much more dramatic and exciting stuff; quite as vivid and packed with action as a romance. Again, it seems almost certain that Eleanor of Provence would have had one. It is just possible that we still have it. The brilliantly illuminated Trinity Apocalypse is an exceptionally fine manuscript. It bears no certain marks of ownership. Art historians are inclined to the view that it was produced for a high-born lady, possibly for either Eleanor of Castile or Eleanor of Provence. It has been dated stylistically to the 1250s or 1260s. The illuminators have introduced women into several of the illustrations and one of the women wears a crowned head-dress. In the scenes where the women appear there are also monks and friars, both Dominican and Franciscan. It is the Franciscans who predominate, and from other evidence it is apparent that it was to the Franciscans above all that Eleanor of Provence turned for guidance in her spiritual life, whereas Eleanor of Castile was a special patron of the Dominican order. In one particularly dramatic encounter, the woman with the crowned head-dress, confidently brandishing a sword, attacks the seven-headed beast, to the evident admiration of those around her and the excitement of the beast. The other assailants are doing brave work with an axe and a dagger; this indeed was female *prouesse*, if only figurative.[94] The 'Spiritual' Franciscans were powerfully influenced by the apocalyptic teachings of Joachim of Fiore. Eminent among them was the French Franciscan Hugh de Digne (or Berions), who preached before Louis IX and was particularly influential in Provence. Hugh de Digne was a friend of Grosseteste and Adam Marsh, the latter a keen mentor of the queen. Adam's proposal that Grosseteste should use the queen's physician Peter de Alpibus to take a copy of his translation of Aristotle's *Ethics* to Hugh, implies a transmission of ideas

[93] *CLR 1260–67*, 51.

[94] Alexander and Binski, *Age of Chivalry*, no. 349. Peter Brieger considered Eleanor of Provence was the likely owner (*The Trinity College Apocalypse*, 14–15) and Nigel Morgan thought her 'a plausible candidate' (*Early Gothic Manuscripts*, ii. 74). Suzanne Lewis, however, believes the book was probably made for Eleanor of Castile (*Reading Images*, 240).

and lines of communication which would make Eleanor's interest in possessing an illuminated apocalypse seem very natural.[95]

The two works which are actually known to have been written for Eleanor of Provence, very different from each other, are both 'religious'. Both have been touched on. *La Estoire de Seint Aedward le Rei* may have been written and presented to Eleanor around 1245 when Henry III embarked on the rebuilding of Westminster Abbey; John of Howden's *Rossignos* was probably written in 1274, shortly after Henry III's death.[96] If the copy of the *Estoire* presented to Eleanor was indeed written and illustrated by Matthew Paris, as seems most likely, then this is not the grand copy now held by Cambridge University Library, which has been dated between 1255 and 1260. The Cambridge manuscript may well have been one which was presented to Eleanor of Castile, who was equally bound to absorb the details of the Confessor's life.[97] The text of the *Estoire* imparted a very distinctive image of kingship. Edward was represented as just, generous, *débonaire* and endowed with outstanding humility; he combined kingship with sanctity, not with martial prowess, and the depiction of the meek Queen Edith may have been intended for Eleanor's own edification.[98] Hagiography was very popular and Eleanor of Provence would have had access to other saints' lives. In addition to the *Estoire*, Matthew Paris wrote Anglo-Norman lives of St Alban, Thomas Becket and Edmund of Abingdon. From a well-known note on a flyleaf to the Life of Alban, in Matthew Paris's own handwriting is a request that the countess of Arundel be asked to return 'the book about St Thomas the Martyr and St Edward, which I translated and illustrated, and which the Lady Countess of Cornwall may keep until Whitsuntide'.[99] This is Sanchia. He then goes on to mention the arrangement of illustrations in 'the countess of Winchester's book'. What we see here is the passing to and from St Albans of saints' lives which are circulating among a group of very high-born women, Sanchia, the queen's sister, being one of them. The queen herself may well have read a Life of St Alban. When she was so ill in 1257 that her life was thought to be in danger, she vowed to make a pilgrimage to St Albans if she recovered. Later in the same year she

---

[95] Adam Marsh, 'Epistolae', no. 26 (p. 114); Southern, *Robert Grosseteste*, 283, n. 17, 290 and n. 30; Moorman, *A History of the Franciscan Order*, 118, 189. Also see Brieger, as in previous note.

[96] For Matthew Paris's likely authorship of the text and a date of around 1245, see Binski, 'Reflections on La Estoire', 338–9 and *Westminster Abbey*, 57–60. For dissentient views on authorship see Morgan, *Early Gothic Manuscripts*, ii. 94–8, and on date, *Estoire* (ed. Wallace), xxi–xxiii.

[97] Binski, 'Reflections on La Estoire', 340; Parsons, 'Ritual and Symbol', 61.

[98] Binski, 'Reflections on La Estoire', 343–8.

[99] Vaughan, *Matthew Paris*, 168–70.

fulfilled her vow, visiting the abbey in the company of Eleanor of Castile and many other ladies, to present a fine baudekin at St Alban's shrine.[100] We shall need to return to this glimpse of a 'community of devotion' existing among a group of aristocratic women.

Books were greatly valued, but Eleanor of Provence would always receive her most lasting impressions from contacts with people. It has already been suggested that the queen's openness to the lyrical tones of early Franciscanism may have originated with her childhood in Provence. In England, by the mid-century the character of the order was changing; learning was a threat to poverty and the simplicity of life so movingly described by Thomas of Eccleston was under heavy and distracting pressures. Yet the original idealism and vigour were far from dead.[101] Both Franciscans and Dominicans were bent on the shaping of lay piety, a development which was to bring some corruption in its wake, but not at first and not universally. Patronage of both orders was enthusiastic, in the royal family, among reforming bishops, among the secular aristocracy and townspeople. Eleanor of Provence, like her husband, was a generous patron of the friars. During the year 1252–3 she gave special alms to the Dominicans at Winchester and Oxford and to the Franciscans at Salisbury, Reading, Oxford, London and Winchester. It is worth noting that she never made donations to the Dominicans apart from the Franciscans, whereas she frequently gave to the Franciscans alone.[102] She also paid for the vesting of two Poor Clares and gave £10 for the making of an altar to Thomas the Apostle for the Grey Friars of Oxford.[103] The Franciscans were her clear favourites.

It was to the Franciscans that she turned for spiritual direction. Around 1252 three Franciscan friars were prominent in contacts with the queen.[104] Thomas of Hales was a member of the London house and is twice mentioned by, or in association with, Adam Marsh, who may have introduced him to the queen. He was a scholar who moved with ease from English to French to Latin, and from poetry to prose. His *Luve Ron* was a poem written in English, in praise of the cloistered and dedicated life, probably for a young nun. It was intended to be sung and has passing references to the heroes and heroines of French romances.[105] More surprisingly it has two graceful references to

---

[100] *CM*, v. 653–4.
[101] Thomas of Eccleston, *The Coming of the Franciscans*.
[102] E 101/349/16, 22; E 101/349/8.
[103] Ibid.
[104] Adam Marsh, 'Epistolae', nos. 75, 227 (p. 395).
[105] Hill, 'The Luve-Ron and Thomas de Hales', 321–30.

Henry III. His best known and very popular Latin work is a *Vita Beate Marie*, where he introduces a long aside on the founding of the Order of Fontevrault, in whose mother-house Henry II, Eleanor of Aquitaine, Richard I and Henry III's mother, Isabella of Angoulême, were all buried.[106] A third extant work is a sermon which is in the nature of a meditation on the Life of Christ, mingling passages in Latin with short prayers in French. Again there are chivalric overtones, in praise of Christ's *courtoisie* and *franchise*, and an interesting comment that Christ preached 'simply and intelligibly to the people and wisely and profoundly to masters and princes'.[107] It has been noted that Thomas seems to have combined a great respect for monarchy with a tendency to address himself to aristocratic women. His style of writing, whatever the form and whatever the language, is infused with a characteristically Franciscan affective piety, aiming at an emotional response to the verbal images which he presents.[108] This is the same tradition in which John of Howden was later to write, again touched with the language of chivalry, although John himself was not a friar. It is evident that Eleanor of Provence was deeply attuned to this style of piety; that she found its fervour and its lyricism satisfying. This is bound to surprise in a woman who in many respects was so tough, but one cannot disregard it. The fact that Thomas of Hales had contacts with the queen has not previously been noticed, although this obviously strengthens all that has been surmised about him. In her secret alms account of 1252–3 there are references to three gifts which the queen made at Thomas's request. One is to a nun, one to a certain Ralph Crispin 'to acquit himself of Judaism', and one to Crispin's wife. The gifts are substantial and there is no other person mentioned in the account who prompted as many as three.[109]

A further interesting and important extension of the connection of Thomas of Hales with the queen would be possible if he might be identified with the 'Brother Thomas of the Order of Friars Minor' who witnessed her charter of 1246, in which she stated that she wished, like her husband, to be buried in Westminster Abbey.[110] Brother Thomas appears as the first witness and the other three are senior members of the queen's household. Earlier in the same year the king had made a gift of plate to the Franciscans of Chester through 'Brother Thomas the queen's chaplain'.[111] If this was already Thomas of Hales, then he had a close

[106] Horrall, 'Thomas of Hales OFM', 293, 296–7.
[107] Legge, 'The Anglo-Norman Sermon of Thomas of Hales', 212–18.
[108] Horrall, 'Thomas of Hales OFM', 296, 298.
[109] E 101/349/8.
[110] WAM Domesday, f. 62v.
[111] *CLR 1245–51*, 19.

link with the queen over at least six years, when she was in her twenties, an impressionable age in her religious development. This must remain speculation.

The second Franciscan close to the queen at about the same time is Brother William Batale (or Bellum). Adam Marsh is certainly the link in this case. Writing to the Provincial William of Nottingham to request him to allow the queen to have Batale with her at court, he praises him as dignified, prudent and unlikely to give way to pressures.[112] Adam Marsh knew the court well, but in fact he himself applied his own pressures to Brother William, once the latter had been installed, commending a succession of people to his notice and in one letter asking Batale to thank the queen for her inexhaustible liberality.[113]

This brings us to Adam Marsh himself. His relationship to Eleanor of Provence is particularly interesting in that it bridges the gap between spiritual adviser and practical counsellor. She made relentless demands on his time. She enlisted his help over specific problems, such as her wish to retain in England some of the men whom the king was presumably about to take to Gascony in 1253 or her clash with the citizens of London over queen's gold in 1255, and also over major political issues.[114] When she asked him to go to her at Reading to discuss business 'touching the king and his heirs' he speaks of the vehemence of her request.[115] Richard of Cornwall was presumably resentful of the renewed grant of Gascony to Edward in 1252 and on one occasion he is said to have spoken sharply in the queen's presence. It was Adam Marsh who was entrusted with reasoning with him afterwards and he reported to the queen with assurances of the earl's loyalty.[116] The friendship between Adam Marsh and Simon de Montfort is well known. It has been seen that Marsh spoke to the queen about Simon's affairs at the time of his trial and the friar's letters imply a particular closeness between the queen and Eleanor de Montfort.[117] A personal and unusually informal note is struck in a simple postscript written in French at the end of one of his letters to the queen at this time. For once discarding his usually highly elaborate forms of address, he writes to her simply as Lady (Dame), and suggests that she and the countess of Leicester come together at the

---

[112] Adam Marsh, 'Epistolae', no. 185. William Batale was attached to the Northampton friary, ibid., no. 156, and E 101/308/1.

[113] Adam Marsh, 'Epistolae', no. 235; also nos 228–34, 236.

[114] This seems the probable interpretation of Letter 152; on queen's gold see Prynne, *Aurum Reginae*, 106.

[115] Adam Marsh, 'Epistolae', no. 48.

[116] Ibid., no. 155.

[117] Ibid., no. 140.

approaching Easter-tide 'to treat earnestly of the salvation of souls, as far as in you lies'.[118] This exhortation to a purely spiritual exercise shows the range of his counsels to both women and associates them in his thoughts.

Assiduous as Adam felt himself to be in responding to the urgent summonses of the queen, she would have made heavier demands still. On one occasion he admits that she has had to write to him twice to get a reply, and in a letter to his Provincial he deplores the persistence of the queen and the countess of Leicester, although he says that the queen has written him 'an earnest and moving letter'.[119] In reply to another request he tells her straightly that he cannot come.[120] Nor would he yield to her persuasion or that of Boniface himself to become a member of the archbishop's household.[121] Even so, he was a firm friend; Eleanor of Provence had great confidence in Adam Marsh's judgement, and her reliance on his advice in secular as well as spiritual matters shows her own belief that there was a significant connection between the two.

Adam Marsh was a distinguished scholar, a pupil of Grosseteste and a reader to the Franciscans in Oxford. One might suppose that this aspect of his life, to which he yearned to give more time, would have been beyond the queen's understanding, since her own piety was in no way grounded in learning of an academic kind. In one sense that was true, yet repeatedly Eleanor of Provence stretched out for guidance and friendship towards men who combined their spirituality with a high degree of learning. For the most part, of course, scant evidence of the nature of these relationships is left. Adam Marsh testified to her friendship for Grosseteste, who has left his own proof that he treated her queenly role as a high calling.[122] For early contacts with Edmund of Abingdon or Roger Niger we are left groping. Together they took part in her coronation after she had been married by Edmund at Canterbury. These official occasions, formal as they were, were moments of great solemnity in the young queen's life and Eleanor continued after Edmund's death to show a special protective concern for the small Cistercian house of Catesby, where his cult was cherished and where his sisters Margery and Alice were nuns.[123] It is purely by chance that we do catch a glimpse of the queen's friendship with Richard Wych, chancellor to archbishops Edmund and Boniface. Wych was a scholar of repute, versed in theology

---

[118] Ibid., no. 153 (p. 290).
[119] Ibid., nos 154, 172.
[120] Ibid., no. 155.
[121] Ibid., no. 188 (p. 336).
[122] Ibid., no. 17; ch. 11, below.
[123] Lawrence, *St Edmund of Abingdon*, 107–8; CPR 1247–58, 599; SC 1/16/193.

and canon law, and a chancellor of the Oxford schools. From the particulars of the queen's wardrobe, drawn up in what was the last year of Richard Wych's life, it emerges that he had prompted her to make the substantial gift of £9 to one John of Cornhill to free his property from a mortgage to Florentine merchants.[124] Wych fell mortally ill while preaching the crusade in the south of England in the spring of 1253 and he died at Dover in April. The queen sent a messenger to him there 'quando laborabat in extremis' (in his last illness); the added phrase suggests that she was aware that he was dying. When the news of his death reached her at Windsor she made a special offering for his soul.[125] In his will he made a fitting response to the queen's kindnesses towards him, from the point where she had eased his accession to the see of Chichester; he left 'to my lady the queen a ring, with Henry the clerk'.[126] This half-humorous bequest has puzzled editors of the will, but the meaning was perfectly clear to the queen, and also to the king. On 19 April, still within a month of the bishop's death, the king appointed Henry of London, formerly clerk of Richard bishop of Chichester, to his own service and settled him in the queen's chapel with wages of $4\frac{1}{2}$ d a day.[127] Richard Wych was canonized in 1262, and in 1276, some twenty-three years after his death, the ceremony of the translation of St Richard of Chichester to his shrine behind the high altar took place in the cathedral church. From an aside in the Canterbury/Dover chronicle we find that Eleanor of Provence made a special journey to Chichester to do honour to her friend.[128]

Eleanor of Provence not only cherished the memory of this distinguished group of reforming bishops, linked in friendship with each other and linked with the Oxford schools; she cherished the image, the ideal of spirituality and learning. In the late 1260s and early 1270s she enjoyed the services of a future cardinal and a future saint, both men of learning. She certainly preened herself on the cardinal, Hugh of Evesham. It is possible that he was attached to Eleanor's household, since Edward I in 1275 refers to him as a king's clerk 'who has long served the king and his mother'.[129] She promoted his career, presenting him to the living of Benefield in the diocese of Lincoln, and to the church of Spofforth in the diocese of York, but he also held several other prestigious benefices, including the archdeaconry of Worcester and prebends in York and in

[124] E 101/349/8.
[125] E 101/308/1 m. 2; E 101/349/24.
[126] *English Historical Documents, 1189–1327*, 778.
[127] CR 1251–53, 344–5.
[128] *Gervase of Canterbury*, ii. 284.
[129] CCR 1272–79, 158.

the newly formed collegiate church of Howden.[130] He became a cardinal in March 1281, after an earlier appointment as physician to Pope Martin IV. His academic and professional distinction is beyond doubt and he had studied at both Oxford and Cambridge as well as France and Italy.[131] It was almost certainly at Eleanor's request that Hugh had attended her ailing grandson Henry when the boy was in her care, in the last months of his life.[132] After Hugh was elevated to the rank of cardinal Eleanor loses no opportunity of mentioning his new status. When she intercedes with the king for the prior of Great Malvern she says she does so more readily because he is a nephew of the cardinal.[133] In a plea for the new bishop of Caithness she points out to Edward I that the bishop is a clerk of Hugh of Evesham, 'who is our cardinal and yours, and by you came to this dignity'.[134] The proprietary note is wholly characteristic of the queen.

The future saint in her service was John of Howden, whose poem *Rossignos* has already been cited for its insights into Eleanor's *mentalité*. John was almost certainly a Yorkshireman, to be identified with the Master John of Melton who held the prebend of Howden in that church.[135] Hugh of Evesham, a fellow prebendary in the same church, may have introduced him to the queen, and from the later years of Henry III's reign he is to be found as one of her more senior clerks, already referred to as 'a clerk of the queen' in 1268, witnessing one of her charters in 1274 and receiving money for her at the exchequer together with her gold keeper John de Whatley in 1275.[136] On two occasions he prompted Henry III to grant pardons to fellow Yorkshiremen in trouble with the law.[137] The style of his religious writing, touched with romance and troubadour imagery, has already been seen in that poem which he wrote 'in a fair orchard in flower where the nightingales were singing'.[138] He was a cultured man rather than a scholar but with a remarkable literary facility in both French and Latin, and surely, like Thomas of

---

[130] *Rotuli Ricardi Gravesend*, 133 (for presentation on Hugh's resignation); *Reg. William Wickwane*, 32; *DNB* entry; Brown, 'The Institution of the Prebendal Church of Howden', 171.

[131] *DNB*; Emden, *Register.*

[132] Johnstone, 'Wardrobe and Household of Henry, son of Edward I', Appendix (printed from E 101/350/18), 409, 412.

[133] SC 1/16/166 (printed in *Reg. Johannis Peckham*, ii. 749).

[134] SC 1/16/154.

[135] A.J. Taylor, in appendix to *Poems of John of Hoveden*, ed. Raby, 270–4.

[136] *CPR 1266–72*, 189; *CChR 1257–1300*, 189; E 403/30 m. 3 (here called 'Master' John de Hoveden).

[137] *CPR 1266–72*, 189, 338.

[138] Salter, *English and International*, 90.

Hales, with whom he seems to have so much in common, he would have been articulate in English too. A spontaneous local cult would be difficult to explain otherwise. He had a considerable grasp of astrology, which is mentioned by the Lanercost chronicler, who praises John's compassion, his hospitality and the simplicity of his lifestyle.[139] Yet he was evidently a man of some wealth since he began the rebuilding of the church of Howden at his own expense. It was completed after his death by the offerings of pilgrims at his tomb, which stood in the middle of the choir. The church built on those pilgrim offerings still stands.[140] Despite the partly ruined state of its choir it bears comparison architecturally with neighbouring Beverley Minster, although the setting at Howden makes a sharp contrast with the affluent elegance of the town of Beverley. Inside Howden Minster there is some fine thirteenth- and fourteenth-century sculpture, including a life-size figure of a priest in mass vestments. It may or may not represent John of Howden, but in its quiet distinction and grace it evokes a certain style of thirteenth-century spirituality which made a powerful appeal to Eleanor of Provence.

John of Howden should not, I feel sure, be identified with another member of the queen's household in the 1260s, her chaplain John de Sancta Maria.[141] The latter is interesting as a particularly eminent member of the group of men who serviced the queen's chapels. Very few of them emerge as individuals, and their status and level of contact with the queen varied greatly. Henry III's orders to various sheriffs to secure a chaplain to celebrate divine service in one of the queen's chapels, at the standard wage of 50*s* a year, leave the impression, probably correct, that the king was not concerned with the personal qualities of these men but simply with their professional competence for the work required.[142] Some chaplains evidently ranked considerably higher than this and acquired benefices through royal patronage. Among these was Thomas, who became archdeacon of Llandaff; William of London, later rector of Flamstead, who was given a prebend in Pontefract castle in 1241; Hugh de Akeford, presented to the Devonshire church of South Tawton in 1256; and Henry of London, presented to the vicarage of Kelloe in the Durham diocese in 1260.[143] Brother Richard de Tellisford, the queen's almoner, was vigorously and successfully pushed by Eleanor for election

---

[139] *Chron. Lanercost*, 93.

[140] *Poems of John of Hoveden*, ed. Raby, xii.

[141] A.J. Taylor discusses this possibility, but John de Sancta Maria outlived John of Howden.

[142] For example: *CLR 1245–51*, 30, 33, 166, 212, 345.

[143] *CPR 1232–47*, 370 (here called king's chaplain, but see *CPR 1281–92*, 393), 258; *CPR 1247–58*, 496; *CPR 1258–66*, 94.

as prior of Kenilworth in 1275.[144] John de Sancta Maria, her almoner in the 1260s, was evidently high in her favour and in the favour of other members of the court too. In 1259 he accompanied the queen to France and in 1260 he was excused from jury service 'because he was so constantly employed in attending to divine service for the queen'.[145] He acted as attorney for the Lord Edmund in 1261 and went abroad with Edward in 1262; in 1266 he was one of the keepers of the vacant bishopric of Norwich when the issues of the vacancy were committed to Edmund by the king.[146] He held many benefices, but the greatest sign of the queen's favour was his appointment as warden of her greatly cherished hospital of St Katharine by the Tower of London. Before February 1275 he had acquired a prebend in St Paul's and probably died in 1284 or 1285.[147] John de Sancta Maria was no hack; nor was he an alien, but almost certainly belonged to an Anglo-Norman family with a record of royal service.[148] Indeed, one striking fact about these men who either influenced the queen or served her in matters touching on religion is that they were Englishmen. No doubt they all spoke Latin and French and all were heirs to a cosmopolitan culture, but there is also a sense in which they were men of the vernacular. It is a point worth remembering in relation to this foreign queen.

The advancement and well-being of her family formed the core of Queen Eleanor's political creed and gave her the weapons to cut through problems which seemed more complex to others than to herself. This did not make her actions wise but it tended to make them decisive. Her instinctive protectiveness towards her children and her deep affection for them was mingled with an acute awareness that in her motherhood lay the ultimate strength of her queenship, a belief that was sedulously fostered by Peter of Savoy. From both angles the children were her constant preoccupation.

For two-thirds of the year 1252–3 Eleanor resided in her apartments at Windsor, close by the children. The pattern of the royal households at Windsor defies precise analysis. Apart from that of the queen, the household of the heir to the throne is obviously clearest. Money was frequently allotted by the king for the expenses of Edward's household and the provision was sometimes extended to 'the household of the king's son and the other children dwelling with him at Windsor' or 'the expenses of

[144] SC 1/8/42.
[145] *CPR 1258–66*, 47; *CR 1259–61*, 348.
[146] *CR 1259–61*, 339; *CPR 1258–66*, 222, 528.
[147] *CPR 1258–66*, 385, *CChR 1257–1300*, 409–10; Le Neve, *Fasti*, ed. Greenway, i. 87.
[148] The family of Sainte-Mère-Eglise.

Edward and the king's other children'.[149] Convenience might dictate separate provision for an individual child or a group of children. Silver plate was ordered for Edward in October 1242, but not until four years later for Edmund and the king's other children dwelling at Windsor, 'as was done for Edward the king's son'.[150] When Edward left with the queen for Gascony in 1254 provision was again made jointly for Edmund, Beatrice and Katharine under the overall custody of the queen's clerk Simon of Wycombe, and in 1256 joint provision was made for the king's daughter Katharine and a young niece of the king living with her at Windsor.[151] Although the children's establishments were manned by people in whom the queen had great trust, such as the Savoyards Walter de Dya and later Ebulo de Montibus, or Englishmen such as Simon of Wycombe and Bartholomew Pecche, both of whom had close contacts with her, it is too much to say that the children's households were simply an extension of her own. She did not have overall financial responsibility for these establishments. On the death of Edward's first keeper, Hugh Giffard, Hugh's widow Sybil rendered the accounts on behalf of her late husband before the keeper of the king's wardrobe and the king made frequent grants from his own wardrobe, or more often from the exchequer, direct to the children's keepers.[152] As has been seen, however, Peter of Savoy's custody of the lands of the countess of Eu, set aside specifically to meet Edward's needs, brought finance more within the Savoyard orbit, and this money did flow into the queen's wardrobe in Peter's absence; even so, these households were not under the sole control of the queen.[153]

Her personal contacts with her children seem to have been unrestricted. Health loomed large. The death of either of her sons would have been a political as well as a personal disaster, especially as it seems likely that Eleanor bore no other sons and that the fertility of the marriage had perhaps all but exhausted itself after 1245. She reacted decisively over the illness of Edward when he and his parents were present at a large gathering for the rededication of the royal Cistercian foundation at Beaulieu in 1246. Edward suddenly became very ill, as children can, and Beaulieu was a great distance from Windsor. In the queen's view,

---

[149] *CLR 1240–45*, 31, 60, 90, 323. For discussion see Wait, 'Household and Resources', 1–8, 203–6 and Ridgeway, 'The Lord Edward', 91.

[150] *CLR 1240–45*, 148; *CLR 1245–51*, 83.

[151] *CR 1253–54*, 74–5; *CLR 1251–60*, 183–4 (where Margaret is an error for Beatrice); *CR 1256–59*, 7.

[152] For example: *CLR 1240–45*, 19, 31, 38, 127, 148, 293, 323; for Sybil Giffard's account in 1246, *CPR 1232–47*, 487.

[153] Ch. 2, above.

and presumably in the view of the doctors always readily available to the queen and the children, Edward was not fit to be moved. To his mother the solution was clear; he must stay where he was and she must stay with him, which she did for a further three weeks. The king made special provision for her expenses at Beaulieu. For a woman to stay within the abbey precincts was a serious contravention of Cistercian rules, and the prior and cellarer of Beaulieu were summarily deposed at the next visitation of the house.[154] One can only say that they would have been men of exceptional resolution to have withstood Eleanor of Provence when her son's health was at stake. She was not prepared to leave him in the care of nurses, doctors or the monks; she would stay with him herself.

In the accounts of 1252–3 it is Edmund's health which emerges as the queen's chief anxiety. He is attended at different times by three of the queen's doctors, Master Peter de Alpibus, Master Ralph de Neketon and Master Raymond de Bariomono. They seem to have prescribed various syrups and electuaries. In one case Edmund is said specifically to be 'ill, at Windsor' but perhaps the purchase of *penides*, a kind of barley sugar and not prescribed by anyone, was just because he liked it.[155] That the queen called in her own doctors to Edmund and that she paid for his medicines indicates close personal concern for him.

Katharine, the last of Eleanor's children, was born when her mother was thirty. She was a pretty child and it may be that she seemed perfectly normal to begin with, but at the time of her death, less than four years later, she was described by Matthew Paris as *muta et inutilis*.[156] This has been taken to mean that she was deaf and dumb, but he does not say she was deaf and she may have been suffering from a degenerative disorder which only developed gradually. When she became seriously ill, both parents were deeply distressed. On 24 March 1256 Henry ordered a silver image of his daughter to be placed on the shrine of St Edward and three days later he gave a robe to a messenger sent by the queen to give news of an improvement in Katharine's condition.[157] This was surely disinterested love and concern on the part of both parents, when virtually no political interests were at stake. After Katharine's death on 3 May 1257, the queen became dangerously ill and the king succumbed to a fever shortly afterwards, with Katharine much in his mind.[158] He appointed a

---

[154] *Ann. Waverley*, 337; *CLR 1245–51*, 65.

[155] E 101/349/10, printed by Trease, 'The Spicers and Apothecaries of the Royal Household', 38–9.

[156] *CM*, v. 632.

[157] *CR 1254–56*, 287, 288.

[158] *CM*, v. 632, 643.

chaplain to celebrate daily for her soul and he arranged for a fine tomb with a silver effigy to be placed in the church in Westminster. Characteristically, he gave presents to the nurses who had cared for Katharine.[159] This sense of overwhelming domestic grief points to a family life in which the children were valued individually for their own sakes.

The years which Henry III's children spent in the frequent company of their mother at Windsor affected them for life, but they reacted to her strong personality and protective love in different ways. She never let go of them. The case of Margaret is particularly revealing. In the year after Margaret's marriage we find messengers plying their way between Queen Eleanor and her daughter in Scotland.[160] Matilda Cantilupe, who accompanied Margaret to Scotland, was with Eleanor at Windsor in the following September; Geoffrey de Langley was with the queen two months later before he in turn set off for Scotland, and in the same month Eleanor sent her sergeant Robert Russell to Scotland to stay with the queen.[161] In the next year Henry III wrote to Alexander III to ask that Margaret should be allowed to come to visit her mother, but the Scottish lords would have none of it.[162] In 1255, on her return from France, Eleanor was so eagerly concerned for the safety and well-being of her daughter and her daughter's husband, 'whom she loved like an adopted son', according to Matthew Paris, that she sent the physician Reginald of Bath to investigate the situation. Finding Queen Margaret wretchedly unhappy, Reginald rounded on her custodians and reported back to the English king and queen, shortly before his own sudden death, allegedly through poisoning.[163] Henry and Eleanor promptly set off north accompanied by an armed force. Earl Richard de Clare and John Mansel were sent ahead of the royal party to secure an interview with Margaret, who complained bitterly of her own lack of freedom and her husband's lack of access to her. Quietening her distress, they promised that matters would be put right. While Henry dealt with the difficult political situation, Margaret was able to stay for a while with her mother at Wark in Northumberland.[164] She enjoyed another, happier reunion with her parents in 1256 when she and her husband visited Woodstock and London before being lavishly entertained by John Mansel in his house at Tothill in Westminster.[165] They came south again in 1260.

[159] *CLR 1251–60*, 375, 376, 385, 398.
[160] E 101/308/1.
[161] Above, n. 45; E 101/308/1 m. 2.
[162] *Royal Letters*, ii, no. 497.
[163] *CM*, v. 501–2.
[164] *CM*, v. 504–7; *Chron. Melrose*, 112.
[165] *CM*, v. 575.

This time Margaret was pregnant, and determined to have her baby in England. To this end she may have deceived her husband as well as the suspicious Scottish lords as to when the child was due, and in this way contrived to give birth to her daughter in the comforting atmosphere of Windsor, with her understanding and affectionate mother at hand.[166]

Margaret was evidently ready to flee to her loving mother for protection in all her troubles. Certainly there is no backing here for the view that daughters were marginal members of their father's lineage, in whom little interest was shown or expected after marriage. That simply was not true of the daughters of Eleanor of Provence. It is true that the Scottish marriage was of political importance to Henry III, but Eleanor's involvement is clearly that of an anxious mother. Eleanor's daughter Beatrice had the great advantage of not marrying until she was seventeen and therefore much more mature than her sister. She had a loving husband, John of Brittany, who did not remarry after her own death and cherished her memory.[167] Yet the pull of her parents' court was strong for Beatrice too. When she went with her husband on crusade in 1270 she left some of her children in the care of her own mother in England.[168] Like Margaret, she had been present with her husband at her brother's coronation at Westminster in 1274, when the beauty of the two sisters was a matter of comment by the Westminster chronicler.[169] Like Margaret, she died in the following year, both young women being in their early thirties. Beatrice expressed her wish to be buried in the church of the Franciscan friary in London, which was to become the place of her mother's heart-burial and which received many benefactions from John of Brittany in memory of his wife.[170] Beatrice's youngest daughter Eleanor, at the wish of her grandmother and namesake, entered the convent of Amesbury, where Eleanor of Provence had decided that she would spend the last years of her own life and where she arranged that Edward I's daughter Mary should also take the veil. Evidently the managing maternal style of Eleanor of Provence extended to her relationship with her grandchildren, and in one case at least perhaps her capacity and confidence were inherited, since the young Eleanor of Brittany, after leaving Amesbury, was to become a distinguished and successful abbess of Fontevrault.[171]

[166] *Flores*, ii. 459–60, 461, 463.
[167] For Beatrice see Green, *Princesses*, ii. 225–68.
[168] *CLR 1267–72*, nos. 556, 1320, 1464.
[169] *Flores*, iii. 44–5.
[170] BL Harleian MS 3674, ff. 70, 71; Kingsford, *The Grey Friars of London*, 71, 163.
[171] Ch. 12, below.

Enough has been said to establish what kind of a mother Eleanor of Provence was. Her relations with her sons, and especially with her eldest son, must form part of the main narrative of this book. It is sufficient at this point to note that the protective and directive love which made Margaret so dependent was to breed a rebel in Eleanor's eldest son.

Apart from her family there was another small group within the household ambience of Eleanor of Provence who were in very close contact with her in a social setting where complete privacy was almost unknown.[172] These were her ladies. This term may be used for convenience to denote all such women of rank who were in attendance on the queen, but in fact two words were used; *domina* and *domicella*. The distinction seems to have been mainly one of seniority, and these were the precursors of the 'ladies of the bedchamber' and 'maids of honour' of later centuries. Attendance was not necessarily continuous, and the number with the queen at any one time seems to have varied. In 1237 the king paid for five saddles and five sets of harness for the use of the queen's damsels at Easter, an occasion when Eleanor might have appeared publicly on horseback accompanied by her ladies.[173] This seems comparable to the number of ladies incidentally mentioned in the wardrobe accounts of 1252–3. Even when their names only flit briefly through the rolls, there seems to be evidence of the queen's concern for them. When Emma Biset was taken ill at Worcester in 1237 and then lost her sight, the king, presumably in consultation with the queen, made considerate arrangements that she should be brought back to court and he then provided her with a pension.[174] In 1252 the queen paid the expenses of her former damsel Roberga when she stayed with the queen at Clarendon for a few nights, and later gave a present of £1 to the messenger who brought the good news of the birth of Roberga's child.[175] The picture given by Christine de Pisan of a rather arid relationship between a royal mistress and her ladies does not seem to fit the case of Eleanor of Provence.[176]

From the early years of Eleanor's queenship three names among her ladies stand out. The first was Margaret Biset, whose courage and the evidence for the queen's warm regard for her have already been mentioned.[177] A woman of a different background, who probably accompanied Eleanor to England and served her devotedly until her retirement in

---

[172] Régnier-Bohler, 'Imagining the Self', 344–8.
[173] *CLR 1226–40*, 288.
[174] Ibid., 295, 315; *CLR 1245–51*, 85.
[175] E 101/349/18; E 101/308/1 m. 2.
[176] Christine de Pisan, *The Treasure of the City of Ladies*, 74–6; 109–23.
[177] Ch. 2, above.

1258, was Willelma d'Attalens. Willelma came from Savoy and was perhaps chosen by the Countess Beatrice as a companion for her daughter.[178] The queen's warm affection for Willelma and all her family cannot be doubted. In 1244, surely through the queen's influence, the king granted Willelma the marriage of the heir of John fitz Philip, the king's former steward, and the custody of his lands, to the use of her daughter Isabel.[179] Isabel also lived in the queen's household, and even after her mother's death she is found going abroad with the queen in 1262.[180] In 1242 Isabel's brother Peter d'Oron was promised a benefice of up to £50 by Henry III because 'the king is bound to him by special affection for his constant, faithful and devoted service to the queen', and in a smaller way, in 1252, we find Eleanor herself giving a present of a horse to Willelma's nephew when he joined the Order of the Templars.[181] The wardrobe accounts of that year show that Willema seems always to have travelled with the queen, and in 1254 she undertook the rigorous journey to Gascony with her mistress.[182] She may have been forcing herself in doing this, for Willelma was growing old. By 1258 she could manage no more. The king's tribute reflected the queen's own feeling and perhaps even her actual words. He granted £48 a year for the remainder of her life to this devoted lady, 'who from the childhood of the queen has served her and now, wearied in that service and worn out by old age and sickness, does not wish to follow the queen, but proposes for her better quiet to dwell in the abbey of Lacock or some other religious house'. Two years later Willelma was dead.[183]

A third of the queen's ladies who emerges as more than a name was, like Margaret Biset, an Englishwoman, Sybil Giffard. Sybil has already been mentioned as the wife of Hugh Giffard, first custodian of the Lord Edward, and as the woman who had given Queen Eleanor greatly appreciated help and support on the occasion of Edward's birth.[184] Although Sybil was said by Matthew Paris to reside with the queen, she was not invariably at court.[185] In December 1249 Sybil's skill in helping mothers over their confinements had required her attendance on Joan de Valence, the king's sister-in-law. Perhaps it was the absence of the

---

[178] For the Savoyard family surnamed 'd'Oron' and 'd'Attalens', see W.C.H. von Isenburg-Budingen, *Stammtafeln zur Geschichte der Europaischen Staaten*, ed. D. Schwennicke, xv, table 32. I owe this reference to the kindness of John Parsons.

[179] *CPR 1232–47*, 423.

[180] *CPR 1258–66*, 222–3.

[181] *CPR 1232–47*, 290; E 101/349/18.

[182] *CPR 1247–58*, 368.

[183] Ibid., 613–14; *CR 1259–61*, 397–8; *CLR 1251–60*, 502.

[184] Ch. 2, above.

[185] *CM*, v. 156.

king and queen from Windsor at the time that prompted the king's
anxious message to the Lady Willelma, asking her to stay with the king's
children at Windsor until Sybil Giffard was able to return.[186] Henry and
Eleanor evidently thought it important to ensure that a responsible and
experienced woman should be with the royal children. For part of the
year 1252–3 Sybil Giffard was at Witham near Oxford and in the year
1256–7 she and her son Walter had been allowed lodgings in Oxford
castle, perhaps while Walter was studying at Oxford, for two of Sybil's
sons rose to the episcopate and a daughter became abbess of Shaftesbury.[187] The queen, who corresponded with Sybil in the latter's absence,
gave her valuable presents of jewellery and plate and there is reference to
a garland which Sybil gave to the queen.[188] This was a relationship of
regard and affection on both sides. The last time we hear of Sybil she was
again at Windsor, in the spring of 1261, when she and the queen together
interceded with the king to allow the men of Windsor a respite of their
assessed tallage of 20 marks, in view of their poverty.[189] The king
granted their request.

Of other ladies of the queen we know much less. Eleanor outlived Sybil
Giffard as she outlived Margaret Biset and Willelma, and her relationship with a younger generation of attendants, who had only known her
when she had become a dominant figure in the royal court, was bound to
be different. Sybil, Margaret and Willelma were irreplaceable in every
sense. While they lived they played their own unobtrusive roles in fash-
ioning a queen of England.

Range and style of communication can be a useful pointer to mental
horizons. This gives special value as evidence to the two membranes
which comprise the messenger account of Eleanor of Provence for
1252–3.[190] It is the most complete of its kind to survive from Henry
III's reign, and until recently it was thought to be the king's own messenger list for this year.[191] There are no others at all for the queen herself.
The document gives a sharply focused photographic view of the dispatch
and reception of messengers, not systematically grouped, but in simple

---

[186] CR 1247–51, 247.
[187] CPR 1247–58, 479; Walter Giffard archbishop of York 1266–79; Godfrey Giffard
bishop of Worcester 1268–1302; Mabel Giffard elected abbess of Shaftesbury 1291.
[188] E 101/308/1 m. 2; E 101/349/7; E 101/349/13; E 372/93 rot. 1.
[189] CR 1259–61, 343.
[190] E 101/308/1.
[191] Mary Hill has treated E 101/308/1 as an account for messengers of the king rather
than of the queen, *The King's Messengers 1199–1377* (1961) and similarly in her list of *The
King's Messengers* (1994) covering the same period.

chronological order of their coming and going. Apart from sumpter-men sent to collect wines from Southampton or wax, nuts and fruit from London, the regular messengers would almost always have carried letters. This was the normal function of royal messengers and Eleanor of Provence was a prolific and skilled letter writer, as her extant letters, particularly from the time of her widowhood, make clear.

The letters were carried either by messengers travelling on foot (*cokini*) or by the more highly regarded *nuncii*, who were mounted.[192] The queen used fourteen *cokini* in this year, two of whom were employed more often than the others, and four *nuncii*. She also frequently used one or other of her *valetti* to act as her messengers, especially to highly placed persons.[193] Since it was quite customary for trusted envoys to amplify the contents of letters which they delivered, she may have trained her *valetti* in this role. The geographical range covered by incoming and outgoing messengers reflects the wide span of the queen's contacts, and therefore the span of her planning and thinking. During this one year she sent to her uncle Archbishop Boniface in Savoy, to her cousin Gaston de Béarn in Gascony, to her sister Margaret at Acre and frequently to her daughter Margaret in Scotland. She welcomed messengers from her mother, possibly writing from her dowager-castle of Brignoles in Provence, from her uncle Thomas of Savoy, now normally resident in Piedmont, from Philip of Savoy, bishop-elect of Lyon, from her sister Margaret, writing 'about the state of the Holy Land', and from the duchess of Brabant. Eleanor's view was effortlessly international.

The great majority of the messengers sent by the queen in this year were of course bound for destinations within England, and from these entries certain patterns emerge. The person to whom she sent more often than to anyone else was Peter of Savoy, on sixteen occasions. To Boniface she sent on six occasions and received his own *nuncii* on three. One needs to note here that a messenger taking letters may also have brought back a reply, which would have gone unrecorded, and also, most importantly, that *viva-voce* contacts could temporarily eliminate the need for letters; the messenger list must be used with many caveats. Among the king's ministers and counsellors John Mansel already stands out as the closest contact, but Gilbert de Segrave, Robert Walerand, William of Kilkenny and Peter d'Aigueblanche also appear. It is predictable from what has been said earlier in this chapter that one would find Franciscans in this list, and they are there: Adam Marsh, William Batale, William of

---

[192] Hill, *The King's Messengers* (1961), 11–19.

[193] William de Valers, who later took the news of the birth of Katharine to Henry III (*CPR 1247–58*, 267), was sent on one occasion to Peter of Savoy; William de Gardinis to the countesses of Leicester and Pembroke; Herbert Pecche to the king.

Nottingham, who was the Franciscan Provincial Minister in England, and the Grey Friars of Reading. Aristocratic women feature too, but only an exclusive group. Apart from the king's sister, Eleanor de Montfort, and his sister-in-law, Joan de Valence, the queen's correspondents almost all have Savoyard connections. Maud de Lacy was wife of Geoffrey de Joinville; Alice de Burgh and Alice de Lacy were Savoyards themselves. Two important English dowagers, Margaret countess of Lincoln and Amice countess of Devon, had sons married to or about to marry Savoyard kinswomen of the queen. The only exceptions to the all too obvious picture of a Savoyard social network are the two occasions on which a messenger is sent to the ageing Clemence countess of Chester, who was near to her death, and the single dispatch of a messenger to the widowed countess of Arundel. One must conclude that Eleanor of Provence had made no attempt to cultivate a wider range of English aristocratic contacts.

The evidence for the daily life of Eleanor of Provence in the early 1250s reflects the cultural diversity of the environment in which she moved. This was at one with the range of her habitual political thinking; she was impatient of insularity. From the assured base of her position at the royal court she could develop personal relationships selectively and virtually on her own terms. For the preoccupations and prejudices of her husband's disgruntled English subjects she had little time or imagination.

5

Queen Regent

The sharp confrontation between Savoyards and Lusignans in 1252, which had set the king against the queen, seems lost to view in the firm accord between Henry III and Eleanor of Provence in the first half of the year 1253. In fact the same contentious issue was to recur, with even more dramatic force, in 1258. This might suggest that the apparent trust and mutual commitment of Henry and Eleanor in 1253 was no more than a patching-up. This was far from the truth. In 1253 circumstances thrust to the fore one of the deepest and most enduring aspects of their relationship, their joint commitment as parents. Eleanor's political prominence in 1253–4 is partly explained by what is currently referred to as a queen's 'familial' role, that role as mother which Peter of Savoy had so steadily seen as Eleanor's ultimate strength.[1] The need for a regency, the plans for Edward's Castilian marriage, the assembly and handing over of his appanage, and the contingency provisions for control of the realm in the event of the king's own death, all firmly underlined Eleanor's role and potential role as Edward's mother. The political crisis which erupted in Gascony in April 1253 was the catalyst of events which gave all these matters a new urgency.

It is now uncertain whether Alfonso X, who succeeded to the throne of Castile in 1252, acted spontaneously or at the instigation of Gaston de Béarn when he made a sudden intervention in Gascon affairs in March or April 1253 by asserting his own claims to the duchy, derived from Henry II's daughter Eleanor, who had married Alfonso VIII of Castile. Alfonso X proceeded to receive the homage of Gaston de Béarn and his followers among the Gascon nobility, and probably promised them financial

---

[1] Parsons, 'Family, Sex and Power', 6–7.

assistance.[2] This transformed the bitter resentment of the Gascons against the harsh rule of Simon de Montfort into an all-out rebellion against the rule of the English king/duke. When the news reached England towards the end of April, Henry III saw that he was threatened with permanent loss of the last of his continental dominions. His only chance of averting the catastrophe was to go to Gascony in person with a sufficiently strong military force to bring Gaston and his allies to heel and re-establish his own control of the duchy.

A parliament was called in May 1253, but the magnates refused to grant the king the national aid for which he had asked; they simply agreed to support his levy of a feudal aid for the knighting of his eldest son, which was in fact used to help to defray the expenses of the coming campaign in Gascony.[3] Even this concession, and a levy on the clergy, was conditional on a solemn republication of Magna Carta. His feudal tenants could not of course refuse the king military service, or fines in lieu of service, but there was little enthusiasm for Henry's urgent efforts to assemble money, men, provisions and ships at Portsmouth to sail for Gascony in July 1253. In the event the king was delayed until the following month by unfavourable winds.

Henry's military response to Alfonso X and the Gascon rebels was balanced by a diplomatic initiative which may have been the brainchild of John Mansel, who was certainly its chief executant.[4] Mansel saw the permanent solution of the Gascon problem in an Anglo/Castilian alliance, backed by a marriage between Alfonso's half-sister Eleanor of Castile and the Lord Edward, in return for which Alfonso would renounce his claim to Gascony and help to bring the Gascon rebels to submission. Henry III, who had never deluded himself into believing that brute force alone would achieve peace in Gascony, was persuaded of the worth of a diplomatic venture which might lead to the permanent pacification of the duchy and stabilize its position with its neighbours. Having made formal overtures to Alfonso, Henry appointed Mansel on 24 May 1253, together with the bishop of Bath and Wells, to treat for a marriage between Edward and Eleanor of Castile.[5] This was the hoped-for solution, but meanwhile Gascony was in the grip of a full-scale rebellion, with several of the towns, including La Réole and St Emilion, now rallying to Gaston de Béarn, who already had formidable support

[2] *CM*, v. 368, 370; Trabut-Cussac, *L'Administration Anglaise*, xxix–xxx; Parsons, *Eleanor of Castile*, 12 and n. 16; Ellis suggests that the initiative came from Gascony, 'Gaston de Béarn', 158.

[3] *CM*, v. 373–8; Harriss, *Public Finance*, 36.

[4] Baylen, 'John Maunsell and the Castilian Treaty of 1254', 486–91.

[5] *Foedera*, i. 290; *CPR 1247–58*, 230; *CR 1251–53*, 475–6.

among the Gascon nobility.[6] Alfonso's initially favourable response to Henry's overtures slackened ominously for a while. Mansel had indeed progressed as far as a draft treaty before Alfonso spent the summer months of 1253 pursuing an alternative matrimonial project for his sister with the king of Navarre.[7]

John Mansel was not the man to embark on this venture without having assured himself of the firm support of those who stood closest to the Lord Edward; the queen and Peter of Savoy. Later, when the marriage proposals were once again firmly in train, in February 1254, Mansel was accompanied to Spain by the Savoyard diplomat Peter d'Aigueblanche.[8] A peaceful Gascony, in which her son could exercise his lordship in security, the conversion of her belligerent cousin Gaston de Béarn into a loyal subject of the English king/duke and the marriage of Edward to a girl of royal lineage, prospective heiress, by right of her mother, to the county of Ponthieu, would have engaged the eager support of the queen. Yet in the summer of 1253 these plans must have seemed difficult to realize, and the immediate task was her husband's military expedition to quell the Gascon rebellion.

It was the imminent absence of Henry from his kingdom which prompted the sudden enhancement of the status of Eleanor of Provence. On 1 July 1253, before the formal arrangements for a regency were announced, Henry III drew up his will; he is not known to have made another. Its terms make clear that in the event of his death his unreserved trust was placed in the queen. She was given not only the custody of the heir to the throne and their other children but of all the king's territories in Wales, Ireland and Gascony as well as the realm of England, until Edward came of age. It was Eleanor, and Henry's other executors, who were to fulfil the king's crusading intentions by arranging for the transport of his gold treasure and his Cross to the Holy Land. The queen was to pay his debts from the issues of his lands, as far as she was able, and his faithful servants were to be rewarded; the completion of the rebuilding of the abbey church at Westminster being entrusted in the long term to his son Edward. The executors of his will were the queen herself, Archbishop Boniface, Aymer de Lusignan, Richard of Cornwall, Peter of Savoy, John Mansel, Peter Chaceporc, John prior of Newburgh, John de Grey and Henry of Wingham; all would have been completely acceptable to the queen with the single exception of Aymer, the king's favourite half-brother.[9]

[6] Trabut-Cussac, *L'Administration Anglaise*, xxx.
[7] CPR 1247–58, 291; Parsons, *Eleanor of Castile*, 13–14.
[8] *Foedera*, i. 295.
[9] Ibid., i. 496 (misdated).

The arrangements for the regency were fully in line with the purport of Henry III's will. If Eleanor of Provence could be entrusted with supreme power on a long-term basis, in the event of the king's death, then she could certainly be trusted with more limited power in the short term. Henry appointed his wife as regent during his absence in Gascony. Although some historians persist in describing Eleanor and Richard of Cornwall as joint regents, the terms of Henry's instrument are quite specific. Eleanor was appointed 'to keep and govern the realm of England and the lands of Wales and Ireland, with the counsel of Richard earl of Cornwall'.[10] All were to be submissive to her as 'keeper and governor' of the said kingdom. The appointment of a queen as regent in the absence of the king was not automatic. In England one must reach back as far as the early years of Eleanor of Aquitaine for a precedent.[11] In France Louis IX, during his first absence on crusade, took his wife with him and appointed his experienced and capable mother Blanche of Castile as regent. When absent on his next crusade, however, after his mother's death, he made a deliberate decision not to place the regency in the hands of his wife Margaret. Her judgement had given him cause for unease on several occasions, and one imagines that he quite simply did not think she was up to it.[12] Henry III by now knew his wife well. He had assessed not only her loyalty but the scope of her thinking, the strength of her will and her courage and vigour in action. He judged her capable, and Henry III's standards were high in this respect; few kings have had more able ministers and servants. What then of Richard of Cornwall? Denholm-Young's comment that since the queen was pregnant, 'the brunt of the regency fell on Richard' simply is not true.[13] Trabut-Cussac far more perceptively writes that the queen was 'ably seconded' by Richard.[14] This strikes the right note. Richard's role was important, for he had a better knowledge of England, of English ways and of Englishmen than the queen; he was respected as the king's brother and for his own shrewd political judgement. But Henry never intended that the queen should merely be a figurehead, and Eleanor herself certainly did not intend it. Her opportunity had come.

---

[10] Ibid., i. 291; *CPR 1247–58*, 209; for imprecise use of the term 'regents' see Powicke, *Henry III*, 234 and Bémont, *Simon de Montfort* (2nd edn), 146–7.

[11] Richardson and Sayles, *Governance*, 152–3; Eleanor of Aquitaine's role in Richard I's absence was exceptional, ibid., and Parsons, *Eleanor of Castile*, 72–3.

[12] Barry, *Les Droits de la Reine sous la Monarchie Française jusqu'en 1789*, 42–4; Sivéry, *Marguerite de Provence*, 209–12.

[13] Denholm-Young, *Richard of Cornwall*, 77.

[14] Trabut-Cussac, *L'Administration Anglaise*, xxxvii.

As the regency approached the queen was granted two major privileges, both concerned with property. On 16 July 1253 she was given power to make a will to the sum of 3,000 marks, over and above her own personal possessions, and on 23 July, in a little noticed deed, she was granted a new and greatly increased dower assignment.[15] This second document anticipated the possibility of the king's imminent death in the Gascon campaign, and it marked even further the queen's increased consequence. Apart from the grant of a more substantial dower in England she was now to be endowed with lands in Ireland. One notable change from the assignment of 1243 was the omission of Chester, obviously now earmarked as a component of the Lord Edward's future appanage.[16] The queen recovered the whole of the original 1236 dower assignment, except for the towns of Cheltenham and Lothingland, which were replaced by Alton and Middleton. She retained Newcastle under Lyme from the 1243 assignment, but she was now additionally assigned eleven other towns, including the prestigious Wiltshire group of Marlborough, Ludgershall and Devizes, together with the Lincolnshire manors of Stamford and Grantham, and all the lands which had belonged to the late Geoffrey de Craucombe. This new grant of dower was to include several forests attached to the towns specified, one being the extensive forest of Savernake, near Marlborough, and she was to have the counties as well as the towns of Cambridge and Huntingdon. In Ireland she was assigned the whole of Ulster, the castle of Carrickfergus and three other lordships. Moreover, there was detailed specification of her comprehensive judicial and fiscal rights over all the lands mentioned, both in England and Ireland. In what seems an appendix to the assignment, on 30 July, the queen was further granted in dower the Irish manor of Any, a grant which was soon to cause a political skirmish with the Lusignans.[17] Stamford and Grantham, on the other hand, were shortly to be included in Edward's appanage, presumably a change of plan.[18] More puzzling is the witness clause to the new dower assignment. Where one might have expected the names of Peter d'Aigueblanche and Peter and Boniface of Savoy in a major grant so closely touching the queen, the Savoyards are conspicuously absent, and the only witnesses recorded are Roger Bigod, earl of Norfolk and

---

[15] *CPR 1247–58*, 213; E 163/1/9 m. 2, calendared in respect of Irish provisions in *Calendar of Documents relating to Ireland*, ii, no. 255.

[16] For 1243 assignment see ch. 2, above.

[17] E 163/1/9 m. 2 (*Calendar of Documents relating to Ireland*, ii, no. 271). Any (or Knockany) was in Limerick.

[18] *CPR 1247–58*, 270.

John de Plessis, the curial earl of Warwick. It is difficult to suggest any explanation.[19]

The grants to the queen were accompanied by more favours for Peter of Savoy; a large grant of the value of 5,500 marks in view of Peter's promise to accompany Henry to the Holy Land, a further payment of 10,000 marks to be made after the beginning of the crusade, and concessions concerning the wardship and marriage of Peter's heir, if he should have a son.[20] In addition, the queen and Peter jointly received the right to marry the prospective heir to the valuable Vescy lordship to a daughter of either the lord of Chambre or the viscount of Aosta, both Savoyard allies.[21] Eleanor of Provence and Peter of Savoy clearly stood high in the king's favour.

The arrangements for the regency administration of England had been well thought out. For his own use in Gascony, Henry III had a special seal made, leaving behind in England the great seal and the exchequer seal. On 22 June the king had demised his great seal to the keeping of the queen, but not for her use, simply to be kept against his own return.[22] The seal to be used in its place was the seal of the exchequer, and on 8 July the queen was ordered to deliver this to William of Kilkenny 'when he comes to her'.[23] Kilkenny was head of the chancery, and his receiving the seal in person from the queen was a token of her ultimate authority, beneath the king, for the government of the kingdom during Henry's absence. The king's wardrobe went with him to Gascony. How the queen dealt with the resulting gap in the royal financial administration in England will be seen in a moment.

The authority of the queen and her chief counsellor Earl Richard was restricted. Since the king did not necessarily envisage a prolonged absence and since he could still give some attention to English affairs from his base in Gascony, he determined to retain certain matters in his personal control. Elections to major bishoprics and abbeys were to be referred to him, although in the case of lesser prelacies the licence to elect was to be sought from the queen, and in these cases it was she who gave assent to the election, in consultation with the earl.[24] It was perhaps a sharp recollection of the Flamstead incident which caused the king to entrust the conferring of all other ecclesiastical benefices to Richard of

---

[19] Peter of Savoy was in Portsmouth with the king on 22 July, ibid., 237–8.
[20] Ibid., 188, 220.
[21] Ibid., 217, 237–8.
[22] Ibid., 200; Tout, *Chapters*, i. 292–3.
[23] CPR 1247–58, 210.
[24] Ibid., 206.

Cornwall and the chancellor.[25] Keepers of castles were not to be removed without the king's permission, although the queen and the earl might dismiss sheriffs or bailiffs at their own discretion. Castles, of course, were a particularly sensitive issue, since they touched national security. On 20 July 1253 Bertram de Crioil, constable of Dover, perhaps the most strategic castle of all, was instructed by the king that in the event of Henry's death he was not to hand over the castle to the Lord Edward during the latter's minority without the consent of the queen, another sign of Henry's reliance on Eleanor's judgement.[26] More immediately, on 27 July the king ordered the queen to superintend the transfer of Bamburgh castle to John de Lexinton, after Henry himself had sailed. Three days after her husband's embarkation Eleanor forbade Lexinton to meddle with the custody of the castle until he had shown her the letters patent which had been sent to him by the king.[27] She was clearly determined to tolerate no slackness in the observance of protocol.

To assist her in the governing of the kingdom the king provided the queen with a sworn council. He himself decided on its composition and as late as 1 August he was discussing with Earl Richard the inclusion of the bishop of Salisbury, who did not wish to be a member, but who might be called upon if tricky legal matters arose.[28] The only specific mention of membership apart from this is the mandate that the queen should admit the abbot of Westminster, the king's friend Richard de Crokesley.[29] The nature of her support team, whether all were councillors or not, was of prime importance to the queen, who would inevitably have missed the advice of her uncle Peter of Savoy and that of Peter d'Aigueblanche, John Mansel and Henry of Wingham, although Archbishop Boniface remained in England until her own eventual departure. Nevertheless she was working with men whom she already knew. William of Kilkenny at the chancery was a firm friend of the Savoyards, and it may have been partly in gratitude for his support during the regency that Eleanor made him the land grant in Cambridgeshire, already mentioned.[30] The treasurer Philip Lovel and the justiciar of Ireland, John fitz Geoffrey, were also well disposed to the queen and she needed to work closely with them both.

A name which calls for particular comment is that of Geoffrey de Langley. Energetic, unscrupulous and acquisitive, but with a knowledge of how to please, Langley had found his way into the queen's favour as

[25] Ibid., 214.
[26] Ibid.
[27] Ibid., 217; *CR 1251–53*, 408.
[28] Ibid., 497.
[29] Ibid., 480.
[30] Ch. 3, n. 42, above; Ridgeway, 'Henry III and the "Aliens"', 89.

well as the king's. In 1252 he was transferred from his office as justice of
the forests, where he had proved harsh but effective, to become one of
the custodians of Queen Margaret of Scotland. On the eve of his departure, as we have seen, Eleanor gave him a handsome present of a goblet,
but Matthew Paris comments tartly that the Scots could not long stand
his arrogance and soon got rid of him.[31] More dubiously and more
deviously, the queen had recently assisted Langley in at least one of his
bids to increase his landed property by taking on debts to the Jews,
incurred by needy gentry. In this case she had initially acted through
her wardrobe keeper Walter de Bradley, but her personal involvement
was to become absolutely clear in November 1256, when she acknowledged receipt into her wardrobe 'of the full payment of £213 6s 8d in
which Sir Geoffrey de Langley was bound to her for the marriage of
Robert de Willoughby, son and heir of Sir Robert de Willoughby and for
twenty years custody of the manor of Ashover'. The elder Robert had in
return been relieved of his own heavy debt in Jewry.[32] Such trafficking in
Jewish debts at court was bitterly resented among the landed classes and
later became an issue of importance for the baronial opposition.[33] During the regency Langley was employed on commissions, to which he had
already been appointed by the king, concerning the partitioning of the
estates of Clemence countess of Chester and in making extents of
the Vescy estates, but the clearest evidence of the queen's confidence
lies in the appointment, which she undoubtedly approved, by which
Langley became the steward of the English and Welsh lands of the Lord
Edward's appanage in 1254.[34] When Langley was disgraced in 1257,
because affairs in Wales had gone badly wrong, it was through the queen's
intercession that he was eventually restored to royal favour in 1258.[35]
The various contacts of Langley with the queen tell us something about
Eleanor of Provence. She was not so naive as to be duped as to his real
character. She liked his enterprise, his thrust, his firm, clear-cut approach
to problems. Her own stewards William of Tarrant and Richard of
Pevensey were men of the same style. There was a hard streak in Eleanor's
own nature and she was persistent in disregarding administrative mal-
practice and oppression.[36] Her lack of sensitivity in this respect would

---

[31] *CPR 1247–58*, 162; *CM*, v. 340; E 101/349/7; ch. 4, above.

[32] Coss, 'Sir Geoffrey de Langley and the Crisis of the Knightly Class in Thirteenth-
Century England', 9–10; *The Langley Cartulary*, nos 329, 336, 522.

[33] *DBM*, 86–7 (Petition of the Barons, May 1258).

[34] *CR 1251–53*, 495; *CPR 1247–58*, 238, 361; *CLR 1251–60*, 153; C 61/1 m. 4 (Studd,
'Acts of the Lord Edward', no. 11).

[35] *CPR 1247–58*, 616.

[36] Ch. 11, below.

have precluded sympathy with some of the main aims of the reformers in 1258. It also invites close comparison with the harsh administrative style later practised by her daughter-in-law Eleanor of Castile.[37]

It was intended that in due course the queen should follow the king to Gascony, but for a period of almost ten months, from 6 August 1253, when the king embarked for Gascony, to 29 May 1254, the date of her own departure, Eleanor of Provence directed the government of England, and that experience shaped her political judgement thereafter. In working with her council and with the departments of government, in attending two parliaments and above all in directing the large-scale financial operations necessary for servicing her husband's military campaign and diplomatic initiatives, she gained that personal experience of the different aspects of central administration for which there is no substitute. The death of Clemence, dowager countess of Chester, creating a need to avoid a further scramble for land among the co-parceners of her late husband Earl Ranulf's great earldom, the deaths of the Vescy lord of Alnwick and the Ferrers earl of Derby, both leaving heirs under age, brought into focus that 'lordship of England' which was at once the king's trust and his field for exploitation.[38] The decisions over the disposal of patronage were not the queen's, but it was she, together with her council, who dealt with the administrative implications.[39]

The queen's personal involvement in these matters is clear from a study of those writs which are issued *per reginam*, and therefore by her personal authorization. Throughout her pregnancy and her lying-in she seems to have kept her finger on government. Her daughter Katharine was born on 25 November 1253 and Matthew Paris comments that the queen 'rose well from her childbed'.[40] At the time she was watching closely over the Vescy lordship, which had recently come into the king's hand. The marriage of the young heir had already been promised, as has been seen, to herself and Peter of Savoy, but they hoped to lay their hands on the lands as well as the boy.[41] This was in fact achieved in the following February, when the king granted the wardship of the lands and heirs to Peter.[42] Meanwhile a writ was issued for the assignment of her marriage portion to the widowed Agnes de Vescy, authorized *per reginam* in the presence of John fitz Geoffrey and Henry of Bath on the very day of Katharine's birth. Two days later, not surprisingly, it was

[37] Parsons, *Eleanor of Castile*, 102–17.
[38] CPR 1247–58, 238; Waugh, *Lordship of England*, 232.
[39] CPR 1247–58, 361; CR 1253–54, 7.
[40] CM, v. 415, 421.
[41] See n. 21, above.
[42] CPR 1247–58, 268.

the justice Roger de Thurkelby who authorized a writ allowing the goods and chattels of William de Vescy to his executors.[43] However, as early as 5 December, when the queen would still have been lying in, the order for making an extent of the Vescy lands was again authorized *per reginam*, and on the following day the expenses of Gilbert de Preston, travelling north to make the extent, were authorized by Geoffrey de Langley 'on behalf of the queen'.[44] It may be impossible to discern exactly where lines of authorization began and ended during this period immediately after Katharine's birth, but one can say with confidence that the queen was not out of touch.

This is not to diminish the importance to Eleanor of the birth of another child. The queen's *valettus*, William de Valers, was dispatched to the king in Gascony with the happy report that the queen had given birth to a fair daughter (*filiam speciosam*). Valers was rewarded by the king with a fee of £15 a year.[45] The queen celebrated her purification with a great banquet at Westminster which she arranged for the January feast of St Edward, to which large numbers of prelates and lay magnates were invited.[46] She understood the importance of maintaining all the magnificence of royal state in her husband's absence.

One of the most arduous and exacting of the queen's tasks as regent was the handling of finance. But she was good at this. In October 1253 Alphonse of Poitiers made formal complaint to Henry III of the incidental damages done to his own men and their property in violation of the truce existing between the English and French kings. Aware that the maintenance of the truce was essential to his own subjugation of Gascony, Henry knew that the claims of Alphonse must be met. The agreed compensation sum of £14,516 5s 8d of Bordeaux (c.£3,226 sterling) was to be delivered to Alphonse in Paris in two instalments, the first at mid-Lent and the second at Pentecost 1254.[47] It was an unwelcome drain on Henry's restricted resources, but Eleanor would have been fully alive to the political importance of prompt payment and personally eager for good relations with France. In England the Templar Alan de Kancia was made responsible for receiving the two instalments of money from the exchequer and making the first payment to the representatives of Alphonse in Paris in the presence of Peter de Montfort, whom the king was dispatching from Gascony for this purpose. On this first occasion

[43] *CR 1253–54*, 7 (writs of 25 and 27 November).
[44] *CPR 1247–58*, 361; *CLR 1251–60*, 153.
[45] *CPR 1247–58*, 267.
[46] *CR 1253–54*, 105–6.
[47] *Rôles Gascons*, i, nos 2175, 2176; Trabut-Cussac, *L'Administration Anglaise*, xxxiv–xxxv.

Alan de Kancia received £1,500 sterling from the exchequer although the exact amount due to Alphonse turned out to be only £1,451, thus leaving a small balance. This happens to provide the clue for the queen's personal handling of the deal.[48] It was the type of transaction which would normally have been dealt with by the king's wardrobe, but the king's wardrobe was in Gascony. The queen therefore used her own. Not only was the cash balance paid into her wardrobe, but all the relevant documentation, the queen's letters ordering the procedure to be followed, her husband's bond to Alphonse, and Peter de Montfort's letters testifying to the actual payment were all lodged with the keeper of the queen's wardrobe, Walter de Bradley.[49] No one but the queen herself would have been in a position to have organized this. The issue of the second instalment to Alan de Kancia, again on the queen's authorization, was ordered on 17 May 1254 and the outpayment was duly recorded at the exchequer.[50]

Another financial transaction with political overtones fell to the queen's lot to implement. Of the 7,000 marks by which the king had agreed to buy out Simon de Montfort's interest in Gascony, only 2,000 marks had been paid by the start of the regency. Since the king was then on the brink of yet another expensive settlement with Earl Simon it was imperative that the full 7,000 marks should be paid off quickly. Again the queen realized the priority of this commitment and her arrangements were crisply businesslike. On 14 December 1253 a payment to Montfort of 3,000 marks was made on the queen's authorization in the presence of the treasurer Philip Lovel and Henry de la Mare.[51] On 11 May 1254 the queen authorized the payment of the balance, but stipulated that the king's letters obligatory for the full 7,000 marks must be received at the exchequer before payment was made, and there is a final emphatic note that the earl had now been satisfied of the whole sum by writs of *liberate*. It seems, however, that the exchequer was unable to implement this final order immediately.[52]

For the queen and for her advisers the financial obligation which undoubtedly overrode all others was the supply of the king in Gascony. For this, specie and treasure had to be shipped from England. On 30 October 1253 the exchequer was ordered to deliver 13,060 marks to three royal servants to take to Gascony, on the authorization of queen,

[48] CPR 1247–58, 364, 369; E 403/9 mm. 1–2.
[49] CPR 1247–58, 367 (Mid Lent 1253 should read Mid Lent 1254).
[50] CLR 1251–60, 168; E 403/10 m. 1 (the sum is £1,460).
[51] CLR 1251–60, 154. This sum is entered on E 403/10 m. 1.
[52] CLR 1251–60, 167; Maddicott, *Montfort*, 133.

earl and council.[53] A well-armed ship had been requisitioned for transporting the treasure.[54] More cash was needed, and the exchequer issue roll of Easter term 1254 records a payment of 4,672 marks to Alan de Kancia, who had ultimate responsibility for conveying this money to the king in Gascony.[55] It appears that the task of actually handling the treasure had been given to Brother Luke de Marisco and the experienced royal clerk John of Stratford, but the queen evidently decided that while this very large amount of money was being held in Portchester castle ready for transportation it should be in the hands of one of her own most senior financial officials. To this end her clerk Robert de Chaury was made responsible for its immediate safe-keeping, and its subsequent delivery to Luke de Marisco and John of Stratford when the Channel winds became favourable for sailing.[56] Chaury was controller of the queen's wardrobe and in this year was transferred by the queen to become keeper of her gold at the exchequer.[57] Again Eleanor was using her own senior men.

The resources of Ireland had to be tapped as well as those of England. On the strength of 1,000 marks that were on their way from Ireland to Westminster via Chester, the queen negotiated a loan to that amount from a firm of Florentine merchants.[58] On 3 February 1254 the queen and John fitz Geoffrey, the justiciar of Ireland, in their pressing anxiety to meet the king's needs, ordered the papal custodian of the crusading money which had been collected there, to deliver all the money in his care to fitz Geoffrey himself. This was going too far, and on 11 April the queen more prudently advised fitz Geoffrey not to take the crusading money against the will of its custodian.[59]

Throughout the regency the queen was pursued by her own problems of liquidity. Her expenses were naturally greater than usual, and between 24 June 1253 and 3 May 1254 £2,784 15s was paid into her wardrobe by the treasurer of the exchequer.[60] On one occasion she had to borrow £400 from Boniface of Savoy's clerk, Henry of Ghent, to see her through.[61] Yet she showed a high order of competence and the capacity to think in large sums without sacrificing attention to detail. She worked

[53] *CLR 1251–60*, 150.
[54] *CR 1251–53*, 508–9.
[55] E 403/10 m. 1.
[56] *CR 1253–54*, 36.
[57] E 159/28 m. 7 (printed in Prynne, *Aurum Reginae*, 17).
[58] *CLR 1251–60*, 157; E 403/9 m. 2.
[59] *CR 1253–54*, 20, 46–7.
[60] E 372/97 rot. 9.
[61] *CLR 1251–60*, 152, 157.

extremely hard. Matthew Paris records that she sent Henry a New Year's gift of 500 marks. If so, the king was no doubt grateful, but he had more to thank her for than that.[62]

The supreme task of 1253–4 for the king and his advisers in Gascony and for the queen and her regency council in England was to save Gascony for the English Crown. Although the situation in the duchy began to turn in Henry's favour soon after his arrival, in response to a judicious mixture of severity towards the rebels combined with encouragement for those who defected from Gaston de Béarn, the swing towards success was still recent and uncertain.[63] Henry could take no chances and he needed further experienced help. In October 1253, brought to a halt before the stolid resistance of the key town of Benauges, Henry summoned Simon de Montfort, willing once more to accept the rigorous terms which Simon stipulated as the price of his assistance.[64]

In England the queen and Earl Richard were faced with a difficult task of political management at a parliament of magnates, lay and ecclesiastical, called to Westminster, at the king's request, for 27 January 1254. It was common knowledge by now that the king was making vigorous efforts to conclude a lasting peace with Alfonso of Castile, to be cemented by a marriage between the Lord Edward and Alfonso's half-sister, Eleanor. At the same time Henry was demanding a national effort to help him to wage war on Alfonso's allies in Gascony in a situation which he claimed to be critical.[65] To rouse support for a strong military initiative when a diplomatic solution was rumoured to be well on the way was a very tricky wicket to play. That the queen and Richard did not meet with a flat refusal to their urgent appeal is a tribute to their own drive and evident personal loyalty. The letter which they wrote to the king on 14 February reporting the outcome of the January parliament is well known.[66] In the face of a direct attack by Alfonso on the English king the prelates would provide an aid and the lay magnates would come personally to the king's help, but Eleanor and Richard warned Henry that the lower clergy would only grant money if the exaction of the current crusading subsidy was substantially relaxed, while they believed that the lesser lay tenants in the counties would only respond if Magna Carta was again publicly reaffirmed, since there was complaint that the king's sheriffs and bailiffs were failing to abide by it.

---

[62] *CM*, v. 421.
[63] Trabut-Cussac, *L'Administration Anglaise*, xxxiii–xxxiv.
[64] Maddicott, *Montfort*, 121–3.
[65] *CM*, v. 423–5; *CR 1253–54*, 107; Denholm-Young, *Richard of Cornwall*, 78–9.
[66] *Royal Letters*, ii. 101–2.

Throughout the three months following the January parliament summonses were issued for the assembly of a large fighting force in London three weeks after Easter. This was to include tenants-in-chief, bound by feudal obligation, and lesser men who would fight for pay.[67] Orders for the supply of food, horses and fully manned ships went alongside continued financial pressure on clergy, laity and Jews. Yet the queen and Earl Richard were aware that the diplomatic initiative, being pursued with fresh vigour in Castile, might in the end make their strenuous efforts seem excessive. Alfonso X, now strongly inclined to an Anglo/Castilian alliance, but also aware of Henry III's pressing need for his co-operation, applied himself to exacting the best possible terms from the English envoys.[68]

From the English side the keen Savoyard interest in the proposed Castilian alliance is underlined by the active part which Peter d'Aigueblanche now took in the negotiations. On 8 February he was ordered to join John Mansel in a further embassy to Castile, for the conclusion of a definitive peace. In a writ of 11 February Aigueblanche was pardoned £300 in consideration of the embassy to Castile 'which he undertook of his own free will', a wording which possibly suggests his own enthusiasm for the mission.[69] Mansel and Aigueblanche were now armed with the evidence which Alfonso required, that Henry III was prepared to endow his son with a very large appanage worth 15,000 marks a year and that Edward's wife would be suitably dowered. The endowment for Edward was dated 14 February.[70] On 31 March the Castilian envoys announced that peace was made and that Alfonso would abandon his claims to rule in Gascony. Henry III undertook to seek commutation of his crusading vow in order to join Alfonso in a projected expedition against the Moors in North Africa and agreed that his daughter Beatrice should in due course marry one of Alfonso's brothers.[71] On 1 April Alfonso sent a safe conduct for the Lord Edward to come to Spain, and Mansel and Aigueblanche confirmed that the treaty had been concluded.[72]

On 24 March, when these negotiations were already well advanced, Henry III had written a letter to his English subjects which Trabut-Cussac describes as 'surprising enough'.[73] The king thanked his subjects

---

[67] *CR 1253–54*, 111–12, 114–15, 119; Powicke, *Thirteenth Century*, 116–17.

[68] Trabut-Cussac, *L'Administration Anglaise*, xxxv–xxxvi and n. 72; Parsons, *Eleanor of Castile*, 14.

[69] *Foedera*, i. 295; *CM*, vi. 284–6; *CPR 1247–58*, 267.

[70] *Foedera*, i. 296, 297.

[71] Ibid., 297, 298.

[72] Ibid., 298; Parsons, *Eleanor of Castile*, 15.

[73] Trabut-Cussac, *L'Administration Anglaise*, xxxvi; *CPR 1247–58*, 279–80.

for their support, alluded to his continuing negotiations with Castile, but announced that he had good reason to believe that Alfonso intended to launch a full-scale attack against him, planning to gather troops at Burgos by Easter (12 April). The view of Matthew Paris, followed by several later historians, that Henry's letter was downright deceitful fails in the light of fuller investigation. Henry was needlessly alarmed but his alarm was almost certainly genuine. He probably believed that the military preparations which Alfonso was making for an attack on Navarre were in fact directed against himself. The queen and Earl Richard held a parliament a fortnight after Easter as they had planned, but the political purpose of the assembly was to be vitiated by Simon de Montfort, recently returned from France, who gave assurances that the king was in no danger from attack. Although this was by now true, Simon evidently encouraged a disillusioned reaction to the king's appeal for support.[74]

The Easter parliament of 1254 is rightly regarded as politically and constitutionally important. Two representatives elected by each shire, fully empowered to make an aid to the king, were to come before the regency council. The plea to be put before them was that of a national necessity.[75] The plea of necessity as justifying extraordinary measures in defence of the king and kingdom was later used by Eleanor herself in the crisis of 1264.[76] She had evidently grasped the concept, which ultimately derived from Roman law. This raises the more general question of the influence of her experience as regent on Eleanor's subsequent stance on the major issues of English politics. As head of the regency she had been present at meetings of her council, composed of knowledgeable officials and men of affairs. She was present at the parliament of 27 January 1254, attended by magnates and greater barons, where she would have been able to hear discussion and to sense the mood of that gathering in its response to the king's request.[77] It was she as well as Richard who sent the letter of 14 February to the king, reporting on the outcome of that parliament. Even if we suppose that she had no hand in the actual composition of the letter (and that cannot be assumed), she knew its contents. She knew that the lesser clergy deeply resented the king's crusading tax; she knew that the men of the shires were restive under the behaviour of the king's sheriffs and bailiffs and that they would not co-operate without a further formal royal commitment to the Charters.

[74] CM, v. 440, 445; Powicke, *Henry III*, 234–5; Trabut-Cussac, *L'Administration Anglaise*, xxxvii–xxxviii; Maddicott, *Montfort*, 139.
[75] *Select Charters*, 365–6; Harriss, *Public Finance*, 38–9.
[76] Ch. 9, n. 11, below.
[77] *CR 1253–54*, 111–12.

Finally, she had been present at the parliament which met after Easter, and she had previously been party to the decision to call two representatives from each shire to come before the council at that time, empowered to grant an aid, an indication of the political weight now attached to this group in society.[78] In the light of all this it becomes impossible to regard the queen as remote from knowledge of opinion beyond the court. Although Eleanor of Provence could not share in the 'long view' of the English political scene she certainly knew enough to be fully aware when the storm broke in 1258 that she was involved in something more than a palace revolution.

The queen's vigour and sense of urgency in responding to the king's incessant appeals for men and money could not have been faulted by her husband. In March 1254 she was faced with a further exacting task in the actual transfer to Edward's lordship of the lands which his father had bestowed on him, partly in response to the stipulations of Alfonso X, who wished his future brother-in-law to have a truly princely endowment. The charter which Henry III promulgated at Bazas on 14 February 1254 was witnessed by Peter of Savoy, Peter d'Aigueblanche, William de Valence and Geoffrey de Lusignan, among others.[79] Much preliminary planning had of course taken place, some of it presumably of long standing. The final endowment comprised Gascony and the Isle of Oléron, both of which had been confirmed to Edward in 1252, together with Ireland (with certain reservations, which included lands promised to Geoffrey de Lusignan and Robert Walerand), the Channel Islands, the county of Chester with the conquered Welsh lands between the Dee and the Conwy, the royal castles in Wales, and in England the castle and town of Bristol, the towns of Stamford and Grantham, the honour of the Peak, the lands formerly belonging to the count of Eu and the manor of Freemantle. It was stipulated that none of these was ever to be separated from the Crown of England.

The significance of this huge transfer of lordship has been variously interpreted. The view that Henry impoverished himself to endow his son has been greatly modified in recent writing.[80] The king reserved his own superior lordship over every part of the appanage, retaining also his titles of Lord of Ireland and Duke of Aquitaine. The reversion of the lands to the Crown was guaranteed, as we have seen, and none had previously formed a part of the ancient demesne of the Crown. In this sense the king was consolidating his authority. Yet, for all this, the granting of this large

[78] *CPR 1247–58*, 370; *CR 1253–4*, 114–15.
[79] *CPR 1247–58*, 270.
[80] Studd, 'The Lord Edward and Henry III', 4–19; Prestwich, *Edward I*, 11–14.

appanage to Edward did mark a turning-point in Henry III's reign. There had been a shift in the body politic. When the heir to the throne became a man of substance, his future destiny became part of men's thinking, especially the thinking of courtiers, and his personal favour became a matter of moment even though for the time being his authority and patronage were restricted. In the course of the year 1254, in which he attained the age of fifteen, Edward became a major landowner, a knight and a married man. He sprang to the status of an adult prince.[81]

It was probably a moment of maternal triumph for Eleanor of Provence, on Edward's behalf and on her own. Edward's affairs had so far been kept pretty well within the queen's ambit, partly through the initiatives of Peter of Savoy and through the ready compliance of the king. Now, by the chance of regency, it was his mother who supervised the transfer of the English, Welsh and Irish lands of Edward's appanage to his own officials. Of the six men who took initial seisin of his possessions, four had close contacts with the queen: Geoffrey de Langley, Ralph Dunion, Bartholomew Pecche and Stephen Bauzan.[82] The arrangements had to be speedy and were evidently co-ordinated by the regency administration. On 16 March all the constables of Edward's castles were summoned to attend at Westminster three weeks after Easter 'to speak with the queen, Richard the earl, and the rest of the king's council, touching certain business affecting the said Edward'.[83] Of the appointments made in Edward's name the most striking was that of chief steward in charge of all Edward's English and Welsh lands apart from the county of Chester and North Wales. The man chosen was Geoffrey de Langley, the queen's protégé and collaborator.[84] Her influence in this appointment can hardly be doubted and it is the extent of her own confidence that is probably reflected in the remarkable series of writs relating to the appointment, issued by Edward on 24 May at Winchester.[85] All constables, foresters and bailiffs on Edward's lands were to be intendant to Langley, but Langley was specifically exempted from blame for any wrongs of theirs which were done without his orders. He was to visit in person all the lands in his charge, ordering improvements wherever he thought necessary and, even more remarkable, he was to take such measures against potential enemies of the king and the Lord

---

[81] Wait, 'Household and Resources', 10–23.

[82] For Langley see above; Dunion and Pecche had held posts in charge of the royal children; Bauzan was a knight of Edward and was given a brooch by the queen in January 1253 (E 101/349/12 m. 1).

[83] *CPR 1247–58*, 365.

[84] For his possible administrative initiatives see Wait, 'Household and Resources', 22.

[85] C 61/1 mm. 3 and 4 (itemized by Studd, 'Acts of the Lord Edward', nos 11–21).

Edward as he might think fit. For these responsibilities he was to be given the substantial annual fee of £80.[86] When the queen placed her trust in a man she gave him scope. There can be little doubt that in Eleanor's view Edward's new status, far from terminating her own authority in his affairs, would have seemed to open up new vistas of patronage and influence.

Queen Eleanor's present anxieties did not relate to the remoter implications of Edward's greatly enhanced status but to the immediate preparations for their departure for Gascony. Earl Richard was to be left in control in England and the queen's younger children were to remain at Windsor, while the queen herself, Edward and Archbishop Boniface, together with a large company of magnates, knights, royal officials and courtiers, embarked for Gascony in readiness for Edward's own journey to Castile to be knighted and married at Alfonso's court.[87] They finally left on 29 May, but as early as 18 February bridges and hurdles were ordered for 300 ships.[88] Certain named ships were to be specially requisitioned, although some later escaped 'by night'.[89] The city of London was to provide all ships in the port capable of carrying sixteen horses, and the issuing of writs for the huge quantities of victuals and fuel to be assembled and stacked on board the ships already at Portsmouth became faster and more insistent as the time of departure approached.[90]

The most urgent need of all in the queen's mind was to get together all the money and other treasure that she could possibly lay hands on, to take with her to the king. Pressure was brought to bear on the Jews to pay a 5,000 mark tallage, although only a fraction of that was available by 29 May.[91] The queen ordered the abbot of Westminster and the treasurer, with two other colleagues, to go in person to the New Temple and to Westminster to value the king's jewels, plate and his treasure in gold.[92] Part of this was taken to her at Portsmouth as she awaited embarkation, but part she had already pledged to Earl Richard in return for a heavy loan of 10,000 marks.[93] The king needed it all.[94]

---

[86] Studd, 'Acts of the Lord Edward', no. 14 (C 61/1 m. 4).

[87] Paris (*CM*, v. 447) states that Edmund went too, but the chancery rolls prove this mistaken (*CR 1253–54*, 74–5; 156).

[88] *CLR 1251–60*, 158.

[89] *CR 1253–54*, 121.

[90] *CLR 1251–60*, 162–70, *passim*.

[91] *CR 1253–54*, 62–3; *CLR 1251–60*, 169; *CM*, v. 441.

[92] *CR 1253–54*, 62.

[93] *CPR 1247–58*, 528.

[94] *Rôles Gascons*, i, no. 3874 for an itemized record of the money and treasure received by the king in Gascony up to 21 July 1254.

At this crucial point the queen was almost thwarted on two counts, both vividly recorded by Matthew Paris. The first incident, with its own comic twist, arose from the perennial jealousies and rivalries of the men of the Cinque Ports. The men of Winchelsea, who had prepared the queen's own ship, on seeing the far finer ship which the men of Yarmouth had prepared for the Lord Edward, 'a large and handsome vessel, manned by thirty skilful and well armed sailors', were so overcome by fury that they fell upon the Yarmouth ship, tearing it apart, injuring some of the mariners and slaying others. They finally seized the mast, and with typical bravado fitted it to the queen's own vessel, in the hope of avoiding her displeasure. The queen's reaction drew unaccustomed praise from the chronicler. She wrote to Earl Richard 'to endeavour to calm discreetly the discord and excitement which had arisen among the people of the Cinque Ports, as it was fraught with peril to the kingdom'.[95] The final setback was a last-minute message from the king, ordering her not to set out. The reason is obscure but may have been connected with a new crisis in Gascony. The queen, fully prepared for embarkation, determined to sail, 'concealing her annoyance at these circumstances'.[96] Matthew Paris may have dramatized the details in both cases, but his portrayal of the queen carries conviction. We see her here in a familiar human situation, not of danger but of multiple frustration. She acted in character. She was firm in making the decision to embark, even though she risked her husband's displeasure; it was a situation in which she trusted her own judgement. In the second place she was capable of exercising self-command, 'concealing her annoyance'. The capacity to act decisively and to exercise restraint were signs of her increasing political maturity.

[95] *CM*, v. 446–7.
[96] *CM*, v. 447. For crisis over Bergerac see Trabut-Cussac, *L'Administration Anglaise*, xxxviii–xxxix.

6

Faction

The queen and the Lord Edward disembarked at Bordeaux shortly before 11 June 1254.[1] Eleanor's steward Matthias Bezill had made ready the house where she stayed when she was last in Gascony, possibly the house where her daughter Beatrice had been born.[2] Edward was housed separately. The king provided three gold cloths for the queen and three for Edward to present on their arrival at Bordeaux in the churches of St Andrew, St Sever and Holy Cross.[3] Henry III made such details his concern although he was pressed by the now urgent need for the reduction of the stronghold of La Réole, and by the eruption of a potentially dangerous dispute over the succession to the lordship of Bergerac, which may have prompted his sudden order to the queen to delay her departure from England.

On her arrival in Gascony the queen was faced with the need for a major readjustment. She had worked extemely hard and performed well during the regency and she must have known it. She had experienced the excitement and the profound satisfaction of exercising authority, working alongside an able team. Now she had to put all this behind her. Her importance was for the moment diminished and she would have had the disturbing experience of coming cold to a situation where a sense of shared danger, physical hardship, uncertainty and eventual success bound together those who had been with the king during the previous nine months. Among them of course were many Savoyards; the king had relied throughout on the continuing political counsel of Peter of Savoy,

---

[1] Trabut-Cussac, *L'Administration Anglaise*, 3, n. 1.
[2] *Rôles Gascons*, i, no. 3658.
[3] *CR 1253–54*, 247.

while Peter d'Aigueblanche and John Mansel were concluding with Alfonso X the arrangements for Edward's marriage, for Henry's reconciliation with the Gascon nobility and for Alfonso's all-important renunciation of his own claim to Gascony. Yet the men who had rendered Henry the most energetic and notable service in the field on this occasion were the king's Lusignan half-brothers, backed by their affinity and the Poitevin knights of the king's household. It has been estimated that over a hundred Poitevin knights, together with their numerous men at arms, fought with Henry III in what was his one successful continental campaign.[4] The king, always deeply sensitive on the issue of personal loyalty, felt an urgent obligation to reward these men, whose vigorous support contrasted sharply with the reluctant response of many English barons. Moreover, the Lusignan brothers were beginning to edge into the field of diplomacy, where the king was using them in situations where their knowledge of local political relationships could be of use.[5] This enhancement of Lusignan participation in the king's affairs and his ever-deepening affection for his half-brothers must have caused the queen considerable unease.

A Savoyard/Lusignan skirmish over lands in Ireland shows the two rival groups at court once more bracing themselves for conflict. On 11 February 1254, four days before the assignment of Ireland to Edward, Henry III had granted 500 librates of Irish lands to Geoffrey de Lusignan.[6] The queen and Peter of Savoy would have seen this as the thin end of a wedge which could be driven further and further into Edward's appanage. There is no proof of their collusion with the justiciar of Ireland, John fitz Geoffrey, but collusion does seem almost certain. John fitz Geoffrey stalled over giving effect to the grant on two counts, first that the lordship of Ireland had been granted to the Lord Edward and second, that the land in question included the manor of Any, in Limerick, which had been allocated to the queen in dower.[7] The implication was that the grant to Geoffrey de Lusignan would have constituted alienation of royal demesne. There was evidently a stiff tussle. In July the king ordered the Irish justiciar to assign alternative lands, in Connacht, to Geoffrey de Lusignan, but it is clear that the stalling continued, from a sternly reproachful letter from the king to Edward himself in the following December requiring that the grant be effected without delay. Geoffrey de Lusignan never got his Irish lands but he was eventually compensated by Edward with lands in England.[8]

[4] Ridgeway, 'Politics', 141–3.
[5] Ibid., 145–6.
[6] *CPR 1247–58*, 271.
[7] Ibid., 308 and ch. 5, above.

Neither Henry nor Eleanor was present at their son's marriage. Accompanied by a fairly modest retinue, Edward and several of his companions were knighted by Alfonso X, and on 1 November 1254 in the great abbey church of Las Huelgas he was married to Alfonso's half-sister Eleanor; by 21 November Edward was back in Gascony with his bride.[9] She was a girl of thirteen, an exile to a foreign court, as Eleanor of Provence herself had been at a similar age, but the younger Eleanor was not required for many years ahead to assume the role of queen. It is likely that Eleanor of Provence would have welcomed the young girl warmly, as she welcomed the marriage partners of her other children. Eager though she was to retain control of Edward's affairs, she never as far as we know showed personal jealousy or hostility to her daughter-in-law, as Queen Blanche showed to Margaret of Provence. Queen Eleanor's knowledge of the culture of the Midi and interest in books and gardens may even have made her a congenial companion for the younger woman. In 1255 the younger Eleanor's wardrobe was set up under a former clerk of the queen, John of London.[10] On the rare occasions when Eleanor of Castile flits through chronicles or archives in the next few years she often appears in close proximity to her mother-in-law, on a pilgrimage to St Albans in 1257, at the consecration of Salisbury Cathedral in 1258, and more significantly, on 1 January 1259 with the court at Mortlake.[11]

Some months before Edward's marriage took place, Eleanor of Provence had become involved in plans to secure a crown for her younger son, Edmund. 'The business of Sicily', as it came to be known in England, was an ambitious and risky scheme to place Edmund on the throne of the Regno, that famously rich and culturally diverse kingdom comprising southern Italy and Sicily which had been at the core of Frederick II's empire. In 1250 the Emperor Frederick, *stupor mundi*, had died, but his son Conrad IV proved as ruthless an enemy of the papacy as had his father. Innocent IV had determined to supplant him in the Regno with a candidate of his own choosing.

The pope, wanting a prince of royal blood, had approached Richard of Cornwall.[12] They could not agree upon terms but the matter was still sufficiently open in December 1252 for Innocent to send his nuncio Albert of Parma to England to press Richard further, with Henry III's

---

[8] *CPR 1247–58*, 384; *CChR 1226–57*, 453–4; Ridgeway, 'Foreign Favourites', 599.

[9] Trabut-Cussac, *L'Administration Anglaise*, 7.

[10] *Rôles Gascons*, i (Supplement), no. 4555.

[11] *CM*, v. 653–4; *Ann. Tewkesbury*, 166; E 101/349/26 m. 4; Parsons, *Eleanor of Castile*, 17.

[12] *Foedera*, i. 284.

support.[13] Richard still declined. While Albert of Parma was in England he met the queen, who gave costly New Year's gifts of goblets to Albert and his two companions.[14] Whether there was any discussion at court about possible alternative candidates to Richard is not known, but the pope obviously wanted an adult prince who was capable and experienced and, having failed with Richard of Cornwall, he approached Louis IX's brother Charles of Anjou. Charles, failing to get the support of the French king, also declined. The next step came quickly. On 11 April 1253 Innocent IV was in correspondence with Albert of Parma proposing a commutation of Henry III's crusading vow to support for the pope in Sicily, if Henry was prepared to accept that kingdom either in his own name or that of his son, Edmund.[15] For the proposal to be made so soon after Albert's visit to England at the turn of the year 1252/3 does suggest the possibility that Edmund's candidature may at least have been mooted during that visit. Whatever the point at which it was discussed in England, one may be certain that the queen would have been privy to it, but nearly nine months passed before a further move from the papacy.

The papal offer of the Sicilian Crown for Edmund was revived on 20 December 1253, when Henry III was in Gascony, and on 12 February 1254 it was accepted in principle by the king, with momentous implications for the future.[16] Eleanor of Provence was in England at the time but there can be no doubt of her active approbation. John d'Ambléon, papal chaplain and clerk of Henry III, was the intermediary between the king and the papal nuncio Albert of Parma.[17] John d'Ambléon was a Savoyard, close in the counsels of both Philip of Savoy and Peter d'Aigueblanche. In the margin of a later patent roll entry, whether or not by scribal error, Ambléon is identified as 'queen's proctor', although in the main entry he is designated king's proctor in Rome.[18] In addition to Henry's two special proctors in the Sicilian business, John d'Ambléon and a canon of Hereford, the king nominated seven further proctors on 12 February 1254 to negotiate terms with the papacy. Of these, three were Eleanor's uncles, Philip, Peter and Thomas of Savoy, and a fourth was Peter d'Aigueblanche.[19] In short, the commitment had the weightiest

[13] *CM*, v. 346–7; Henry III's response to the pope, *CR 1251–53*, 449.

[14] E 101/349/7 m. 2.

[15] *Reg. Alexandre IV*, no. 3036 (p. 89).

[16] Ibid., no. 3036 (pp. 89–90); for best recent account of the negotiations see Lloyd, *English Society and the Crusade*, 222–4.

[17] For Savoyard involvement see Cox, *Eagles of Savoy*, 242–5.

[18] *CPR 1258–66*, 570.

[19] *Reg. Alexandre IV*, no. 3036 (pp. 89–90, letter of 12 February 1254).

possible Savoyard backing. At first the matter moved swiftly. On 6 March 1254 Albert of Parma signified the pope's consent and on 14 May Innocent himself confirmed the grant of the kingdom of Sicily to Edmund.[20] But on 21 May Frederick II's legitimate son and heir Conrad IV died suddenly. The political scene immediately changed. Innocent IV found himself with alternative solutions to the problem of Sicily and for a few months it seemed possible that he would conclude a deal with Frederick II's illegitimate son Manfred, who now put himself forward as the successor to Conrad. But Innocent's hopes were doomed; by November Manfred had turned against the pope and seized effective control of the Regno for himself. In the following month Innocent IV died, a bitterly disappointed man, and Edmund's candidature for the throne of Sicily appeared to depend on the policy of Innocent's successor.[21] Alexander IV, elected to the papal throne within a month of Innocent IV's death, seemed in fact to have little option but to look again to the support of Henry III. By April 1255 an agreement on terms was reached and in October Edmund was officially invested as king of Sicily, at Westminster.[22] He was of course a king without a kingdom.

The importance of the Sicilian business in the political history of Henry III's reign, and especially as a factor in bringing about the crisis of 1258, has always been recognized. Until recently it was common form to dismiss the venture as a chimerical scheme, indicative of Henry III's folly and his bondage to the interests of the papacy. That judgement has been challenged by several scholars. Even Henry III's vision of a Mediterranean empire, with the conquest of Sicily as a first step, is now treated more seriously.[23] It is the crippling cost of the business of Sicily which is still roundly condemned, as it has always been; the commitment made by Henry to meet the papal debts so far incurred in the war, estimated at 135,541 marks, in addition to providing a fighting force to wrest possession of the Regno from Manfred.

Yet the question of the essential practicability of the scheme still needs further discussion and has rarely been looked at in terms of ways and means. It is important in any estimate of the political competence of Eleanor of Provence since it was a project to which she was deeply committed. It was Huw Ridgeway who first emphasized the extent to which the negotiations throughout were in the hands of Savoyard diplo-

---

[20] *Reg. Alexandre IV*, no. 3036 (pp. 90–2).

[21] Cox, *Eagles of Savoy*, 244–5.

[22] *Foedera*, i. 316; *CM*, v. 515; *Ann. Burton*, 349.

[23] Lloyd, 'King Henry III, the Crusade and the Mediterranean', 97–119; Clanchy, *England and its Rulers*, 235–40; Maddicott, *Montfort*, 128–9.

mats; it was indeed a Savoyard ploy.[24] In that case it needs to be asked whether these hard-headed royal uncles, so experienced in diplomacy and fighting, did themselves regard the scheme as practicable. Perhaps the answer depends partly on what strategy was envisaged. In 1255 Henry III, according to Matthew Paris, was thinking in terms of taking an army across France, although he did see this as a problem.[25] But this may not have been the main direction of Henry's thinking, nor that of the Savoyards. This is perhaps better seen in an interesting series of writs issued at Woodstock on 20 July 1255, appointing Thomas of Savoy, with the advice of his brothers Peter and Philip and Henry's own mercenary captain Drew de Barentyn to retain knights to the king's use. These knights were to go on the king's service 'to those parts which the said Thomas will let them know'.[26] There can be little doubt that if a military campaign to place Edmund on the throne of Sicily had in fact come about, it would have been the Savoyard brothers with their Italian base, their skill in fighting, their intimate knowledge of Italian princely, communal and curial politics, who would have been its effective commanders.[27] But one cannot escape a further question. Did the Savoyards ever seriously intend that there should be a campaign, or were they merely supporting a plan which they knew to be of such vital concern to the papacy that they could hope to use it indefinitely as a lever to extract concessions from the pope for matters which touched them more nearly? For the pope too knew that they were the men who mattered.[28]

Whatever the motives of her uncles, Eleanor of Provence envisaged and worked for an expedition to place her youngest son on the throne of the Regno. She was far from being indifferent to her uncles' immediate interests but it was Edmund's future which mattered to her supremely. In fact, the family loyalty of the house of Savoy was such that it is very unlikely that the uncles were deliberately misleading Eleanor. But they were supple politicians, ready to venture, ready to exploit inviting situations. Thomas in particular was well aware of the incidental personal benefits to be reaped by himself from the papacy.[29] One need not assume that the Savoyards necessarily thought in terms of fighting every inch of the way. They were aware of the growing strength of Manfred of

[24] Ridgeway, 'Politics', 163–6.
[25] *CM*, v. 515–16.
[26] *CPR 1247–58*, 413.
[27] The appointment of Henry of Castile as captain of a projected force for Sicily in 1257, after the capture of Thomas of Savoy, was an unlikely gambit, *Foedera*, i. 359–60; Carpenter, 'What Happened in 1258?', 184.
[28] Huw Ridgeway inclines to this view, 'Politics', 163, 165.
[29] Cox, *Eagles of Savoy*, 251–3.

Hohenstaufen within the Regno, but to them Manfred did not appear as the implacable enemy that he appeared to the pope. Manfred was recently married to one of their nieces, Beatrice, daughter of the late Count Amadeus. In the summer of 1256 they evidently floated the suggestion, taken up by Henry III, that Edmund should marry Manfred's daughter, after which Manfred would grant the kingdom to Edmund but retain the province of Taranto. The Savoyard archbishop of Tarentaise, Peter of Savoy and the papal nuncio Rostand were involved in the discussions; such solutions were not out of the question, but Alexander IV himself continued to press for vigorous military action against Manfred, and above all he wanted Henry's money to promote the papal campaign.[30]

The dominant figure in the Sicilian scheme was Thomas of Savoy, who had swung from the imperial side to that of the pope after the death of Frederick II in 1250. In 1251 Thomas had married a niece of Innocent IV, Beatrice de Fieschi.[31] If any man knew his way in the complexities of Italian politics it was Thomas. In October 1254 Henry III confirmed the grant to Thomas, made in Edmund's name, of the principality of Capua, north of Naples, a province of Edmund's new kingdom.[32] This obviously marked Thomas's special association with the project and it is noticeable that from this time onwards Eleanor of Provence is found working in particularly close collaboration with Thomas. She trusted him to exert himself strenuously for Edmund, and she in her turn was ready to do her utmost to strengthen his influence in northern Italy and his connections in England by the promotion of matrimonial alliances, an area of diplomacy in which she was a consummate performer. Between 1253 and 1255 Thomas's standing in northern Italy had been enhanced. He became guardian not only of his nephew Boniface, heir to the county of Savoy in succession to his father Count Amadeus, but also to the heirs to the marquisates of Montferrat and Saluzzo.[33] Both young marquises were his great-nephews and their lordships came within Thomas's territorial sphere of influence. From now on Eleanor of Provence had the young Montferrats and Saluzzos very much in her mind; they were of course her own cousins. In 1253 the Vescy heir to the northern lordship of Alnwick was to be married, as we have seen, 'as Peter of Savoy and the queen should decide'. In due course he was married to Agnes de Saluzzo, said by one chronicler to have been 'nurtured in the household of the

---

[30] *Diplomatic Documents*, i, nos. 282, 283; *Foedera*, i. 360; Lloyd, *English Society and the Crusade*, 226–7.

[31] Cox, *Eagles of Savoy*, 210.

[32] *Foedera*, 1. 308.

[33] Cox, *Eagles of Savoy*, 251, and table, 462–3. See also figure 6.

queen of England'.[34] Agnes's sister Alice was already married to Henry de Lacy, heir to the earldom of Lincoln, and the two girls were sisters of the marquis of Saluzzo, Thomas's ward. In 1257 Eleanor was to draw Richard de Clare earl of Gloucester into her schemes by arranging a marriage between one of Gloucester's daughters and the young marquis of Montferrat,[35] and in the same year, according to Matthew Paris, the queen procured the marriage of Baldwin, heir to the earldom of Devon, to Margaret, almost certainly the daughter of Thomas himself.[36] Baldwin's marriage had been granted to Peter of Savoy in 1252 with the express provision that the boy was to be married to a relative of the queen.[37] Finally, the queen was bringing up in her own household the marquis of Montferrat's sister, whom she eventually succeeded in marrying to Albert of Brunswick.[38]

The Savoyards believed that security for Edward in Gascony and the promotion of Edmund's candidacy for the Sicilian throne both required peace between England and France. In 1254 Henry III was prepared to move in that direction and had asked Louis IX to allow himself and his queen to travel back from Gascony to England by way of France. As a result of Louis's warm response, Henry and Eleanor set out from Gascony in October 1254 on a French visit which was to bring them much pleasure at the time and vital supportive friendship in the long run. Matthew Paris listed the considerations which had prompted Henry's request as the hope of a safer journey, a keen interest in French architecture, a desire to visit both Fontevrault and Pontigny and 'an ardent desire to visit the French kingdom, his brother-in-law the king of France and the queen, who was sister to the queen of England'.[39] It is likely of course that Eleanor had played a part in encouraging the French visit. Politically the time was propitious for the first step towards a more relaxed relationship between the two kingdoms. Recent contacts had been constructive on both sides. The truce between the two had been renewed with Louis's full approbation when he was still on crusade in 1253, and Henry had made an honest effort to meet the grievances of Alphonse of Poitiers over infringements of that truce. There were other matters calling for discussion. When Louis landed in Provence at the end of his crusading expedition he thought it wise to bring back to Paris his mother-in-law, the dowager countess of Provence. The elder Beatrice

[34] Cockayne, *Peerage*, xii/ii. 279.
[35] *CChR 1257–1300*, 3–5.
[36] *CM*, v. 616; Cockayne, *Peerage*, iv. 320; Powicke, *Henry III*, 707.
[37] *CPR 1247–58*, 148.
[38] *CR 1261–64*, 176, 259; *CR 1268–72*, 49.
[39] *CM*, v. 467, 475–6.

claimed that her son-in-law Charles of Anjou had failed in his obligations to her and with typical Savoyard acumen she refused to yield her military strongholds in Forqualcier and Gap until she had got better terms.[40] Louis's wife, Queen Margaret, nursed her own grievances over the Provençal succession and mother and daughter were in agreement in their hearty dislike of the arrogant Charles of Anjou. Henry III in his own wife's name still claimed the Provençal fortresses handed over to their proxies in 1244. Apart from unsolved problems in Provence, Henry III knew, as did Eleanor and her Savoyard uncles, that peaceful relations with France were a prerequisite for the success of Edmund's claims in Sicily. This alone would have accounted for Thomas of Savoy's presence in Paris in December 1254, but he also had desperate need of immediate financial help from the kings of France and England for his activities in the Piedmont. From Louis he hoped for pressure for the payment of his pension from Flanders and from Henry III the payment of his English pension and that of his nephew, son of Count Amadeus. Henry ordered Thomas's claims to be met from lands in royal wardship.[41]

Henry and Eleanor travelled by way of Fontevrault where Henry insisted that his mother's tomb should be moved from the cemetery into the church, to receive honour equal to that given to Henry II, Eleanor of Aquitaine and Richard I.[42] Their visit cast a long shadow towards the future. Eleanor of Provence was to end her life as a Fontevrauldine nun in the English daughter-house at Amesbury; Henry's heart was eventually buried at Fontevrault itself, as he apparently promised on this occasion, and their granddaughter Eleanor, not yet born at this point, was to become one of Fontevrault's most eminent abbesses.[43] From Fontevrault they moved on to Pontigny, to offer prayers and gifts at the shrine of Edmund of Abingdon who had celebrated their marriage over eighteen years earlier. From Pontigny they travelled to Chartres, where the glories of the cathedral were the first high point in a visit which provided one of the great aesthetic experiences of Henry III's life. It was at Chartres that the first personal contact was made with the French royal family, when King Louis rode out to meet his guests, soon joined by Queen Margaret, her younger sister Beatrice and the dowager countess of Provence. Sanchia, coming separately from England, joined them too. From Chartres the stately double royal cortège proceeded on its way to Paris, where the students turned out to greet them, cheerfully singing and

[40] Cox, *Eagles of Savoy*, 246.
[41] *CPR 1247–58*, 386.
[42] *CM*, v. 475.
[43] Ch. 12, below.

playing on their instruments, carrying their festivities far on into the night.[44]

Through the courtesy of the French king, Henry III and his entourage were based first in the vast buildings of the Old Temple and on the following night in the royal palace. As an attentive and urbane host Louis showed his brother-in-law the finest buildings in Paris, culminating in the most beautiful of all, in Henry's eyes, the Sainte-Chapelle. The English king impressed the Parisians, as he always impressed, by his lavish generosity, feeding large numbers of the poor in the great halls of the Old Temple, making costly gifts of jewels and plate to the French magnates and entertaining his host and all the other guests to a sumptuous banquet. In a hall where the walls were hung with shields, in the continental fashion, the kings of England, France and Navarre presided over this magnificent feast, where the dukes, barons, bishops and knights sat separately from the ladies. According to Matthew Paris there were no fewer than eighteen ladies of the rank of countess or above.[45] For Eleanor of Provence it was probably her first sight of the splendours of Paris and the French court and she was seeing the city in gala mood. This was spectacle of a high order.

The spectacle was deliberate and was not entirely competitive; it was in essence celebratory. Matthew Paris, who could react as sardonically as any modern critic to royal spectacle, felt that on this occasion the money had been well spent. He wrote, 'The honour of the king of England, and of all the English, was much exalted and increased.'[46] The significance of the occasion lay in that blend of the personal and the political which underlay all contemporary European diplomacy. Louis IX was deeply impressed by the occasion as a family gathering. The family was essentially that of the dowager Countess Beatrice of Provence, his difficult mother-in-law. All four of her daughters, three of their husbands and at least two of her brothers were present. Matthew Paris attributes words to the French king, used in addressing Henry III, which are much quoted because they capture the tone of Louis's thinking. 'Have we not married two sisters, and our brothers the other two? All that shall be born of them, both sons and daughters, shall be like brothers and sisters.'[47] The mutual loyalty of the family of Provence/Savoy came near to being Louis's ideal of what kinship should mean.

The prime importance of the meeting in Paris in 1254 lay quite simply in the establishment of personal contacts between Louis IX and Queen

---

[44] CM, v. 475–7.
[45] Ibid., 478–82.
[46] Ibid., 482.
[47] Ibid., 481; Richard, *Saint Louis*, 68.

Margaret on the one hand and Henry III and Queen Eleanor on the other. Eleanor and Margaret, of course, were already bound by childhood intimacy. They all four drew on this personal knowledge and friendship repeatedly in the troubled years that followed. The great concordat achieved between England and France in the Treaty of Paris in 1259, Queen Margaret's part in promoting the marriage of Henry and Eleanor's daughter Beatrice to the duke of Brittany's son, the loyalty of Margaret and Louis to Eleanor when she became the victim of Lusignan slander in 1258, their financial and diplomatic help during the period of baronial strife – all this stemmed from the relationships which began to be established in December 1254. Thereafter the king and queen of England and the king and queen of France could not only visualize one another; they possessed that immediacy of understanding which came from recent personal association.

It is incidentally interesting that the family structure which underlay the 1254 meeting depended on a group of five women. Of these, we know little of Sanchia or of the younger Beatrice of Provence, but the elder Beatrice and her two elder daughters were keenly aware politically. In informal discussion they no doubt knew how to play their part. They were not in a position to direct policy, but they were not pawns either. Their potential influence lay partly in the solidarity of their mutual understanding.

Eleanor of Provence may have felt some understandable sense of elation at the success of the visit to France. Admittedly, Louis IX had made it clear to Henry III that the peers of France would never agree to any restoration of the forfeited Angevin lands to the kings of England, but a great improvement in relations between the two countries now seemed possible.[48] This would have been of substantial comfort to Queen Eleanor. Apart from this, however, there was very little comfort for her in the three years which followed her return to England and which preceded the political revolution of 1258. It was a time of deep personal anxieties about her children and growing antagonism towards the king's Lusignan half-brothers who were soon to begin to threaten her relationships with her husband and with her eldest son.

The personal problems of the queen need to be seen in the context of the troubled state of the country. The 1250s were a time of intensifying discontent with Henry III's government among both clergy and laity. It was from the English clergy that the pope hoped to extract the money for the Sicilian enterprise and for the payment of the crippling debts he had already incurred in the struggle against Manfred. Already the crusading

[48] *CM*, v. 482–3.

tax, which had now been diverted to the business of Sicily, had been extended from three to five years, but the pope pressed for further payments through a mission of his nuncio Rostand, who attempted to bully and cajole the English prelates. It was probably in May 1257 that the prelates offered a round sum of £52,000 provided that the pope withdrew his demand for further monies, and subject to the remedy of grievances.[49] The depth of the clergy's disillusion with Henry III's government can be measured by the massive support which they were later to give to the reform programme and to Simon de Montfort's administration. Their resentment was not only against Henry's manipulation of episcopal elections, his exploitation of vacant bishoprics and abbeys and encroachment on the judicial liberties of the Church courts; they deeply resented his co-operation with the papacy in the fleecing of the English Church for the Sicilian project. Eleanor of Provence was completely committed to the business of Sicily and for this reason her political influence would have been deplored by the clergy.

Archbishop Boniface, bound by family loyalty and by obedience to the pope to support the payment of clerical subsidies for the Sicilian project, was nevertheless prepared to fight for the liberties of the English Church against the Crown on all other counts, with the energy and professionalism which characterized him. When Boniface called a council to formulate grievances in August 1257, Henry III forbade the prelates to attend, giving the Welsh war as his reason.[50] In defiance of the king the council met and pursued its business. The outcome was the initial work on a notable set of constitutions which took shape in the council of Merton in June 1258 and were put into their final form in May 1261.[51] In the king's view they embodied an aggressive antagonism to the established rights of the Crown and the responsibility for the defiance was fastened on Boniface. The queen could hardly have escaped the results of this ill will between king and archbishop.

Discontent thrust as deep among the laity as among the clergy, and again the complaint was of royal misgovernment. From the viewpoint of the lesser baronage, the knights and the country gentry, the widespread oppression in the administration of justice and the government of the shires had become almost intolerable. Two factors were mainly responsible. The first was the heavy load of debt incurred by Henry as a result of the Gascon campaign, and the sense of near-panic created by his huge commitment to the pope. Financial extortion through the exchequer, the

---

[49] *Councils and Synods*, II, pt i. 524–30; Powicke, *Henry III*, 374–5; Lunt, *Financial Relations*, 274–8.
[50] *Councils and Synods*, II, pt i. 530–2.
[51] Ibid., 532–48; 568–86; 660–85; Storey, 'The First Convocation, 1257?', 156–9.

eyre and forest visitations resulted from the king's awareness of his drastically mounting debts.[52] The second factor was the king's deliberate protection of favoured courtiers and magnates in the face of all complaints against them. One notorious example of this is the order which he is said to have given that no writs should be issued from chancery against the interests of Richard of Cornwall, the earl of Gloucester, Peter of Savoy or the king's half-brothers.[53] The queen, by her status, enjoyed similar protection. When the sheriff of Buckinghamshire and Bedfordshire explained to the exchequer that there were certain estates where the power of the lords who owned them prevented his levy of dues, the names he cited were those of the earls of Cornwall and Gloucester, Sanchia of Provence, William de Valence and the queen herself.[54] The conduct of her estates steward Brother William of Tarrant at this time was notorious. When Eleanor was made aware of his oppressive administration, according to Matthew Paris, she cleverly excused it.[55] Despite her experience at the time of the regency of the strength of resentment against oppressive administration she evidently did not take that discontent seriously. Nor, one may say, did men like Richard de Clare or Simon de Montfort himself as yet.[56] But by the summer of 1258 these men and other magnates had been compelled to view that discontent very differently, partly because they needed the political support of those below them socially and, in the case of some individuals, out of a more disinterested desire for the reform of local as well as central administration.[57] There is no evidence at all that Eleanor of Provence shared in that concern.

In respect of central government, the remedy for which the baronage in parliament asked repeatedly was the appointment of a justiciar, chancellor and treasurer in accordance with its advice. They were pleading for more responsible government in which there should be an element of consent.[58] In parallel with this demand was the reiterated call for the observance of Magna Carta, that great political symbol which had come to stand for rule according to the law. Again, there is no evidence that Eleanor of Provence showed any sensitivity to these demands.

In part, therefore, '1258' was a reform movement with its roots in the grievances of the community of the realm, but it was also a palace

[52] Maddicott, 'Magna Carta', 44–8.
[53] *CM*, v. 594.
[54] E 101/505/9; Maddicott, 'Magna Carta', 50–1.
[55] *CM*, v. 621, 716.
[56] Carpenter, 'King, Magnates and Society', 100–1; Maddicott, 'Magna Carta', 51, 55–6.
[57] Maddicott, *Montfort*, 157–9; Treharne, *Baronial Plan*, 70–2; Carpenter, 'Simon de Montfort', 221.
[58] Carpenter, *Minority of Henry III*, 411.

revolution and the relationship between the two has been a vexed question in recent historical writing.[59] The Savoyard and Poitevin groups, with their respective allies at court had clashed, as has been seen, in 1252. In the three years before 1258 the enmity deepened. The Savoyard group, which conspicuously included Peter of Savoy and Peter d'Aigueblanche, had always looked to the queen as its figurehead. The Poitevins clustered round the king's Lusignan half-brothers. In the wake of the Gascon expedition of 1253–4 the Poitevins were in the ascendant. The king squeezed his dwindling patronage resources to reward them for their loyal military support in Gascony, and he drew nearer to them personally, unwisely protecting them even in their most unlawful acts.[60] His patronage and protection extended to eminent Poitevins such as Elias de Rabayn, castellan of Corfe, Guy de Rocheford, castellan of Colchester and William de St Ermine, the king's chamberlain, but the Lusignans themselves were closest to him. Since they were his own blood relations they were even dearer to him than his relatives by marriage, already richly rewarded by patronage earlier in the reign. Factional rivalries were complicated by the presence of other politically weighty members of the court who did not belong to either group of aliens, notably the king's brother Richard of Cornwall and Richard de Clare earl of Gloucester, two of the wealthiest and most influential men in the country, and by one who was neither fully alien nor yet English-born, Simon de Montfort.[61] Less involved in faction, but perhaps more in touch with the community were men such as the earls of Norfolk and Hereford, Roger Bigod and Humphrey de Bohun. Among royal servants who were of magnate status, John fitz Geoffrey, Robert Walerand and Peter de Montfort stand out, and among politically indispensable royal clerks, John Mansel and Henry of Wingham. All these men could pull strings and their alignment in the increasingly factious atmosphere of the court was of great moment. The king did not jettison any of them.

Unlike her husband, Eleanor of Provence was all too clearly the figurehead of one faction and deeply hostile to the other. It was, however, open to her to strengthen her contacts with the more or less unaligned. When Richard of Cornwall made a bid for the throne of Germany, and succeeded in having himself crowned king in 1257, with the full support of Henry III, the queen had reason to rejoice in so far as this potentially strengthened Edmund's claim to Sicily, also part of the former

[59] Carpenter, 'What Happened in 1258?', 183–97; Ridgeway, 'The Lord Edward', 90–1; Maddicott, *Montfort*, 156–9.

[60] Ridgeway, 'Henry III and the "Aliens"', 600–3; 'Politics', 104–7; Carpenter, 'What Happened in 1258?', 191–2.

[61] Maddicott, *Montfort*, 145–6.

Hohenstaufen empire, but she must have viewed with reservation the friendly part now being played in Richard's affairs by the Lusignans, who were of course Richard's half-brothers as well as Henry's.[62] Simon de Montfort and his wife were traditional political allies of the Savoyards, and by 1257 the strong personal antagonism which had developed between Montfort and William de Valence may have strengthened that bond. John fitz Geoffrey, Robert Walerand and Peter de Montfort were also friendly towards the queen and her associates, but the allegiance of the far more important and unpredictable earl of Gloucester was much more problematic. The queen was evidently determined to draw him into alliance with the Savoyard group. By 1249 Gloucester had aligned himself with the Lusignans as a tourneying comrade, and in 1253 he agreed to a financially profitable match for his son and heir Gilbert with the king's niece Alice de La Marche.[63] In 1257 the queen set about enticing Gloucester into her own orbit. This was certainly one factor in her promotion of the marriage of his daughter Isabel with Eleanor's young cousin, the marquis of Montferrat.[64] That marriage may possibly have been part of a more broadly based political understanding between the queen and the earl. It is only the well-informed Dunstable annalist who has recorded their meeting at Tutbury in the spring of 1257. The earl, we are told, suddenly left the section of the army which he was leading in south Wales, 'secretly and accompanied by only one armed follower', to talk with the queen at the castle of Tutbury. This was not a meeting arranged by the king. Henry had sent the queen to stay at Nottingham, but Eleanor had sought refuge from the smoky atmosphere of Nottingham in the Ferrers castle of Tutbury, which was in her wardship at the time.[65] Although the substance of their talks may have been confined to the Montferrat marriage, the chronicler's hint that the meeting was in some way clandestine suggests that they may have talked on a broader range of issues. We do not know. What is certain is that the queen recognized the prime importance of the earl as a political ally, as she was to do again in 1261.[66]

Apart from her antagonism towards the Lusignans, it was through her self-perceived role as a mother that one finds the threads to unravel the policies which Eleanor of Provence pursued in the three years leading up

---

[62] *CM*, v. 601–2; Denholm-Young, *Richard of Cornwall*, 86–90; Hilpert, 'Richard of Cornwall's candidature for the German throne and the Christmas 1256 Parliament at Westminster', 185–92; Ridgeway, 'Politics', 156–7; Richard, *Saint Louis*, 119–200.

[63] *CM*, v. 83; Barker, *The Tournament in England*, 49; *CM*, v. 363–4.

[64] Above, n. 35.

[65] *Ann. Dunstable*, 203–4.

[66] Ch. 8, below.

to 1258. The queen's anxiety at this time about the troubles of her daughter Margaret in Scotland have already been mentioned, but Margaret was at least a real queen.[67] Edmund's kingship was for ever to elude him. This of course was not apparent on 9 April 1255 when Alexander IV spelt out the dauntingly oppressive terms which were imposed on Henry III as the price of his son's entitlement to the Regno.[68] In September the bishop of Bologna arrived in England to invest Edmund by papal authority with the kingdom of Sicily, placing a ring upon his finger. The Burton annalist remarks that the king and queen were delighted.[69] The general reaction was very different. The magnates in parliament refused the king a subsidy for a project which they considered ill advised and on which they had not been consulted. The complaint about this lack of consultation was reiterated explicitly by the clergy in 1257.[70] The truth was that Henry III had undertaken this huge commitment almost exclusively on papal and Savoyard advice, although he had taken the precaution of securing the formal approval of the Lusignans and of John Mansel in November 1255.[71]

The disastrous sequel is well known. In England the resulting financial oppression has been seen to have added powerfully to the mounting pressure for reform. In practical terms the project was fatally maimed almost from the start by events in the valley of the Po. In November 1255 Thomas of Savoy, campaigning against the city of Asti, which was resisting his aggressive territorial policies, was captured and imprisoned by his enemies in Turin, whose citizen body had now rebelled against him.[72] For the next two years the whole attention of the Savoyard brothers was engaged in securing the release of Thomas. It was a magnificent family effort and it succeeded, but the whole business was a fatal blow to any chances that Edmund might have had of gaining Sicily. Eleanor of Provence was sufficiently intelligent and well informed to realize the serious implications of Thomas's misfortune for the prospects of her son. But she would also have felt keenly the plight of Thomas himself, who had provided her with support and friendship in the early stages of her queenship. Her immediate task must be to raise money for his ransom. It was this which pulled Eleanor remorselessly into a trap of financial commitment which was to leave her without funds when her eldest son came to her in urgent need of help.

[67] Ch. 4, above.
[68] *Foedera*, i. 316–18.
[69] *Ann. Burton*, 349.
[70] Ibid., 390–1; *CM*, v. 520–1.
[71] *CR 1254–56*, 240.
[72] Cox, *Eagles of Savoy*, 255.

Henry III, eager to help Thomas of Savoy, but desperately pressed for money himself, granted to Peter of Savoy the 4,000 marks which the king regarded as still owing to him on account of the Provençal castles allocated to him in 1244. It was a gesture of goodwill, but in practice no more. Richard of Cornwall provided £1,000.[73] Matthew Paris bemoaned that the city of London was tallaged 'now for the needs of the king, now for those of the queen'.[74] Eleanor had no resources comparable to those of her husband or Earl Richard, but she had a good reputation with the Florentine merchants and she now used this to indulge in some dubious financial devices. On 4 June 1257 the king confirmed letters obligatory of the queen and Peter of Savoy made out to several English religious houses, Cirencester, Chertsey, Abingdon, Hyde and Pershore, to a total of 4,500 marks as backing for the loans made to the queen by the Florentine firm of Maynettus Spine.[75] It was less than a fortnight later, this time in connection with the money owed to the papacy, that the king, the queen and the Lord Edward bound themselves to the same merchants for a sum of 10,000 marks to be repaid by midsummer 1258, with the stiffest ecclesiastical penalties for non-payment.[76] One member of the merchant group used for these transactions was Deutatus Willelmi, who often acted as a merchant for the queen.[77] Eleanor of Provence was implicated up to the hilt.

The damage which the Sicilian business did to her reputation is difficult to assess. Her enthusiasm was entirely open and the scheme was deeply unpopular. The theatrical step of presenting Edmund before Parliament, decked out in Sicilian dress, in October 1257 was regarded with contempt and anger by the magnates. Perhaps neither the king nor the queen saw the political seriousness of the disillusion of their subjects with the Sicilian scheme as a parody of crusading. The ideal of the crusade to the Holy Land, to which Henry III had pledged himself in 1250, still touched men's minds with some sense of religious exaltation in the thirteenth century, almost irrespective of the worldly motives of many of those who actually went on crusade. The diversion of a crusade against the infidel to a war against fellow Christians invariably provoked disgust.[78] The force of such disgust in this case was to be made remark-

---

[73] *CPR 1247–58*, 540–1, 559; 469.
[74] *CM*, v. 568.
[75] *CPR 1247–58*, 557–8.
[76] Ibid., 562–3.
[77] Ibid., 423; *CPR 1266–72*, 519; E 101/349/18.
[78] Powicke, *Thirteenth Century*, 80; Houseley, *The Italian Crusades*, 50; Tyerman, *England and the Crusades, 1095–1588*, 92–5.

ably explicit in the barons' statement of their case against Henry III at Amiens in 1264.[79]

When Eleanor of Provence returned to England from France at the end of 1254 she may have imagined that at least the affairs of her elder son had by now entered a phase of settled prosperity. The need for vigilance over his interests was still there and she no doubt assumed that such vigilance would continue to be exercised in large measure by herself and Peter of Savoy. Indeed the evidence suggests that this was her firm intention. Until Edward's return from Gascony in 1255 and to a lesser extent even after that, the queen, through her estates steward William of Tarrant, played some part in the management of various of Edward's English and Welsh lands.[80] At a higher level, the king himself continued to regard Peter of Savoy as the appropriate man to play a guiding role in the conduct of Edward's affairs. In August 1255 Henry III wrote to Edward, then in Gascony, that Peter of Savoy thought it advisable, since the truce with France had now been extended, that Edward should leave Gascony in the hands of a seneschal and proceed to Ireland to attend to his affairs there. The king added that he felt that the peace of Gascony would best be provided for by the appointment of Stephen Longespee to the seneschalcy and that he had already approached Stephen on this matter.[81] In short, this was a command. Longespee was on good terms with the Savoyards and the king concluded his letter by telling Edward to be guided by Peter on the whole matter, if Peter himself came to Edward in Gascony, as Henry had asked him to do. Nothing here was left to Edward's decision.

Edward's entourage showed other signs of the hands of the queen and Peter of Savoy.[82] John fitz Geoffrey, Edward's chief councillor, was one of their curial allies and Michael de Fiennes, Edward's first chancellor, was a kinsman of the Savoyards.[83] Stephen de Salines, Ebulo de Montibus and Edward's wardrobe keeper Ralph Dunion were all Savoyards with intimate connections with the queen. The evidence is not confined to personnel. When the king wrote to urge upon Edward the claims of Geoffrey de Lusignan in Ireland in 1255 he thought it useful to mention that he was conveying the wish of Edward's mother, the queen, as well as his own.[84] Geoffrey de Langley, appointed by the king and queen to be

---

[79] *DBM*, 278–9; Stacey, 'Baronial *Gravamina*', esp. 143–4.
[80] *Rôles Gascons*, i (Supplement), no. 4431; SC 6/1094/11 mm. 5d-7, 17–18; C 61/3 m. 1; Ridgeway, 'The Lord Edward', 92–3; Wait, 'Household and Resources', 22.
[81] *CR 1254–56*, 219.
[82] For fully documented analysis see Ridgeway, 'Politics', 170–6.
[83] *Reg. Innocent IV*, no. 7693.
[84] *CR 1254–56*, 204–5.

supreme seneschal of Edward's English and Welsh lands, apart from
Chester and the Perfeddwlad, is said to have boasted before them in
1256 that he had the Welsh in the palm of his hand.[85] When that boast
was followed by the disastrous Welsh rising of that year and some of the
responsibility was pinned on Langley, it was, as has been seen, at the
instance of the queen that he was pardoned by the king in February
1258.[86]

It was of course the king who had ultimate control of Edward's affairs
and his close surveillance was frequently unacceptable to his son. That
surveillance was the more determined in that it was based on what had
become a fundamental principle of English kingship – the inalienability
of the lands and prerogatives of the Crown. Edward's rights over his
appanage were limited to those of lordship. Sovereignty belonged to the
king alone. Edward resented the stringent limitations which this view
imposed on his ability to dispense patronage from the resources apparently at his disposal.[87] But the personal influence of the queen and her
political associates at court over Edward's household and administration
was particularly contentious. The sphere of her influence was being
extended in a way that was viewed with jealousy by those who were
excluded, and those conspicuously excluded were the Poitevins. If the
queen was to retain her present share of influence over her son's affairs
indefinitely this could restrict the fortunes of those outside her circle.

The key to this situation was Edward himself. His relationship with his
mother and with those who were ranged with his mother and had guided
his steps so far, held together this whole power bloc. By 1255 Edward
had tasted authority in Gascony, and Trabut-Cussac has assessed his
performance there favourably, but there were other traits in his character,
which asserted themselves after his return to England.[88] Stories of his
violent and disorderly behaviour and his disreputable retinue were soon
current.[89] The temperament which bred his keen enthusiasm for the
tournament began to have free rein. He was ready for an opportunity
to break free, to choose his own friends and his own lifestyle, and his
chance, paradoxically, came with the Welsh rising of 1256, so galling to
his pride in some respects. This drew Edward into the politics and
personnel of the Welsh March. His entourage obviously needed to be
increased and he let go some men and drew in others. By August 1257,
for example, the Savoyard Imbert de Montferrand had been replaced as

[85] *Ann. Dunstable*, 200.
[86] Ibid., 200–1; *CPR 1247–58*, 616.
[87] Studd, 'The Lord Edward and Henry III', 4–19.
[88] Trabut-Cussac, *L'Administration Anglaise*, 9.
[89] *CM*, v. 593–4; 598; Prestwich, *Edward I*, 23.

constable of Montgomery by Hamo Lestrange, one of the more violent of Edward's new Marcher friends.[90] Roger Clifford and Roger Leybourne were now to be found fighting with him in the Welsh campaign, both tough aggressive men, who were to play a significant part in Edward's fortunes in the next few years. All these men were young, energetic and unconnected with the main court establishment. They began to form the nucleus of his own set. It was about the same time that Edward began to team up with two young magnates who arrived fresh from Richard of Cornwall's coronation as king of Germany, which took place in May 1257. These were Henry of Almain, Richard's son by his first wife, and John de Warenne, the young earl of Surrey, both of them restless and unbiddable and both of them in the Lusignan rather than the Savoyard camp.[91] Nevertheless, Edward widened his contacts without at first setting aside most of those who had been placed about him by his parents. In a witness list of December 1257 Roger Clifford and Hamo Lestrange have crept in alongside John fitz Geoffrey, Ebulo de Montibus and Geoffrey de Langley, but a grant from Edward to Roger Mortimer on 8 February 1258 has none of the 'new' names among the witnesses.[92] The queen must have felt considerable unease at some of these developments, but not as yet complete dismay.

The Welsh war effected a profound change in Edward's outlook in another way. Matthew Paris perceptively notes that Edward was shamed as well as injured by the Welsh rebellion 'because although he was called lord of Wales, he could not restrain the rebels'.[93] In this first call to defend the lands of his appanage he was hamstrung by lack of money for troops and supplies. His family did help him. Richard of Cornwall lent him 4,000 marks and Boniface of Savoy advanced £1,000 on a five-year mortgage of the manor of Elham in Kent, while the queen and Peter of Savoy bought the Ferrers wardship from him for 6,000 marks.[94] Edward needed more than this, and there was no more to give. It was not until the decisive Welsh victory in which Edward's knight Stephen Bauzan was killed that the king decided that he must launch an expedition himself against the Welsh, to contain the worsening situation.[95] This was not necessarily what Edward wanted, and he may even have resented the way in which money flowed so freely for the affairs of his brother Edmund

---

[90] CR 1256–59, 147; Ridgeway, 'The Lord Edward', 97; Wait, 'Household and Resources', 287–9.

[91] Ridgeway, 'The Lord Edward', 97.

[92] CChR 1257–1300, 2, 7.

[93] CM, v. 597.

[94] CM, v. 593; CPR 1247–58, 569, 572; 554.

[95] CR 1256–59, 139–41; Prestwich, Edward I, 18–19.

and for Thomas of Savoy, when his own need was just as great. Matthew Paris says specifically that because of the money which the queen had spent in helping Thomas of Savoy, she now had nothing to give to Edward.[96] But Edward had other uncles and to them he now turned. By the spring of 1258 at the latest, Edward had mortgaged his towns of Stamford and Grantham to William de Valence and Tickhill to Aymer.[97] He had also incurred a large debt to Geoffrey de Lusignan.[98] Some of the men to whom he was moving closer also had Lusignan links. John de Warenne was married to the king's half-sister Alice de Lusignan and Roger Leybourne had been in the household of William de Valence.

For the queen this was a threatening development. She had every reason to fear the Lusignans. The King's fond partiality towards them would obviously have disturbed her, and there had been several sharp tussles for patronage between the Poitevin and Savoyard groups.[99] If Edward himself was to be drawn within the Lusignan circle then the queen's authority at court might be about to suffer a serious eclipse. Besides this, there was surely the quite straightforward feeling of anger and resentment at seeing the son whose interests she had watched over so carefully, pulling away from her. But the queen had strong potential allies in the forthcoming struggle. By their violent and arrogant behaviour both within and beyond the court the Poitevins, and particularly the Lusignans themselves, had made dangerous enemies. There was an angry interchange between William de Valence and Simon de Montfort in parliament in 1257, and again in April 1258, in relation to the Welsh war, when Valence accused both Montfort and Gloucester of treasonable collusion with the Welsh.[100] On a wider front, men were finding it impossible to get redress in the ordinary course of law against the aggressions of the Poitevins, who were so imprudently and flagrantly favoured by the king.[101] A climax was reached when Aymer de Lusignan dispatched an armed band to make a violent swoop on John fitz Geoffrey's manor of Shere, injuring several of his servants, one of them fatally.[102] The style of the attack recalled vividly the raid Aymer's men made on Lambeth in 1252. When parliament opened, about a week after this incident, probably on 9 April 1258, John fitz Geoffrey laid his complaint before the king. The royal response was outrageous, but by

[96] *CM*, v. 597.
[97] Ibid., v. 679; *CPR 1247–58*, 644.
[98] *CCR 1279–88*, 180.
[99] Ridgeway, 'Foreign Favourites', 602–3.
[100] *CM*, v. 634; 676–7; Maddicott, *Montfort*, 145–6.
[101] Carpenter, 'What Happened in 1258?', 191–2.
[102] JUST 1/1187 m. 1; *CM*, v. 708; Carpenter, 'What Happened in 1258?', 192–3.

now all too predictable; Henry excused the crime, making light of it, and asked that no more should be said.[103]

This parliament had been called by the king in great urgency to seek financial help from the magnates for the huge sums of money still owing to the pope in respect of the agreement over Sicily. There was by now an overwhelming urge among the baronage in parliament, and beyond that, stretching down through the whole community, to which the barons and even the greater magnates were bound by multiple social, feudal and political ties, to block any grant to the king unless it were accompanied by a serious commitment on Henry's part to a thoroughgoing reform of government. The denial of justice to John fitz Geoffrey was symbolic. It brought together the anti-Lusignan party at court with the broader community in angry reaction to a failure in kingship which had become a threat to all. Henry's act was seen as a violation of Magna Carta and it stood for many earlier, similar incidents.

On 12 April 1258, just a few days after the opening of this parliament, seven magnates entered a sworn association of mutual aid, which was in fact, though not in name, directed against the Lusignans and the Poitevins who were grouped with them. The seven comprised John fitz Geoffrey himself, the earls of Gloucester, Leicester and Norfolk, Hugh Bigod, who was Norfolk's brother, Peter de Montfort, the close friend and ally of Simon de Montfort, and the queen's uncle, Peter of Savoy.[104] The brink of revolution had been reached and what followed must be considered in the next chapter, but in order to assess the queen's role in the swift-moving events which followed, two features of her position at this crucial point must be investigated: her enmity with the Lusignans, and her relations with the king.

The increasing tension between the queen and the Lusignans between the Lambeth raid of 1252 and the beginning of the reform movement in April 1258 has already been noted, culminating in her reaction, not recorded but hardly admitting of doubt, to the recent move of her eldest son into friendship with his Lusignan uncles and with others who had ties with them. Several chroniclers mention that in 1258 the queen was eager to be rid of the Lusignans, but there are two more specific pieces of evidence for the actively malevolent feelings of the half-brothers themselves towards the queen.[105] When they were evicted from England in July 1258, they sought, but were denied, permission to stay within the

---

[103] *CM*, v. 708–9. For the raid on Lambeth in 1252 see ch. 3, above.

[104] Bémont, *Simon de Montfort* (1st edn), 327–8; Carpenter, 'What Happened in 1258?', 194–5; Maddicott, *Montfort*, 153–4.

[105] *Ann. Waverley*, 355; Battle Chronicle in Bémont, *Simon de Montfort* (1st edn), 373; Ridgeway, 'Politics', 279.

lands of Louis IX, because Queen Margaret urged upon the French king that these men had 'outrageously scandalized and defamed' her sister, the queen of England. These are strong words, used by Matthew Paris.[106] The second piece of evidence is a letter written from France by Henry III to the pope in January 1260, at a point where he was once more under the influence of his wife and the anti-Lusignan lobby. The king asked Alexander IV not to allow the return of his half-brother Aymer to his see of Winchester because, among other offences, he had tried to provoke the king in many ways against the queen and had encouraged the disobedience of the Lord Edward.[107] What is not clear in either case is the timing of these malicious attempts by the Lusignans to suborn Henry from the queen. They may relate to the whole period from the first outbreak of trouble in 1252 to 1258, or they may possibly relate especially to the short but crucial stretch from April to July 1258, the point at which the Lusignans were expelled. The events of those three months have yet to be examined. What is certain is that the Lusignans reckoned that the queen was their enemy and that they did all in their power to weaken her position with the king. Most frustrating of all is the entire lack of evidence as to what accusations against the queen the Lusignans were making.

Obviously it is pertinent then to ask whether there was any apparent breakdown of relations between king and queen before April 1258. As far as public acts are concerned there seems to be no evidence for such a rupture. There was no angry seizure of the queen's assets, such as had taken place in 1252.[108] On the contrary, in June 1257 the king supported the queen in her order that the exchequer should accept on her authority the account drawn up by James d'Aigueblanche, her wardrobe keeper and Savoyard protégé.[109] Although the queen lost the wardship of Baldwin de Reviers earl of Devon on his attaining his majority, she received in that year the very prestigious and valuable wardship of William Longespee's estates, including the castle of Lincoln, and in January 1258 she was given the wardship of the lands and castles of Reginald de Mohun.[110] The king was amply fulfilling his obligation to support the queen financially. In political terms he was assiduous in promoting the business of Sicily and was moving steadily towards the conclusion of a lasting peace with France, both schemes very dear to her. He had also provided the queen's uncle Thomas of Savoy with what help he could.

---

[106] *CM*, v. 703.
[107] *Royal Letters*, ii, no. 533 (p. 152).
[108] Ch. 3, above.
[109] *CPR 1247–58*, 558.
[110] Ibid., 536, 614.

Thomas had now been freed and came to England on a brief visit in April/May 1258. When he left, the king gave him 1,000 marks for the arrears of his own fee and that of his nephew, money which he could ill spare, as Matthew Paris pointed out.[111]

These were public matters, although ones with a strong personal dimension. Evidence for the private relations of the king and queen is of course more difficult to discover, except for their anxiety and eventual grief over the illness and death of their three-year-old daughter Katharine, described earlier. It is difficult to believe that their shared grief over the loss of Katharine was other than a bond between Henry and Eleanor. She was a child of their middle years and it is likely that she was the only one of their children to die in infancy. Matthew Paris's explicit observation that the queen became seriously ill through grieving for Katharine, and that the king succumbed to a fever partly caused by his distress over Katharine's death and also by his anxiety over the queen's illness, implies a continuing closeness between Henry and Eleanor in their love for their children.[112] They were at one in their concern for Margaret's welfare in Scotland and in their continued hopes, despite great anxieties, for a brilliant future for their son Edmund. Alone among their children, it was the Lord Edward who began to pull them apart, by his move towards greater intimacy with the Lusignans. The king, bound to his brothers by deep affection and blind to their faults, could not view Edward's choice of new friends as in any way deplorable. To the queen it seemed an unmitigated evil.

[111] *CLR 1251–60*, 432; *CM*, v. 678.
[112] *CM*, v. 632, 643.

7

Revolution

'Eleanor of Provence, queen of England...was believed to be the root, the fomenter and disseminator of all the discord which was sown between her husband, King Henry and the barons of his kingdom.'[1] This entry under the year 1263 in the Scottish chronicle of Melrose makes startling reading as a study in causality. To attribute the great constitutional upheaval of 1258–63 to the machinations of Eleanor of Provence makes a nonsense, and yet this is evidence which deserves close scrutiny. The Melrose chronicler goes on to condemn the susceptibility of the king and queen to the influence of foreigners, and describes the queen as the foremost of the king's evil counsellors.[2] Clearly the writer had absorbed a full dose of the anti-alien passions which swept England in 1263.

This climax to the story must be considered in the next chapter, but even when one looks at the start of the revolution in 1258, the simplistic rhetoric of the Melrose chronicle is not irrelevant. Eleanor of Provence was already distrusted and disliked by some within and many outside the court circle for securing promotion and marriages for Savoyards within the highest ranks of society at the expense of native-born Englishmen. She was further perceived as politically active and influential, a factor to be reckoned with. These are threads to be held firmly as one attempts to disentangle her actual role and the image she projected in one of the most close-textured and controversial periods of English political history.

[1] *Chron. Melrose*, 125.
[2] Ibid., 125, 146.

It has already been seen that in the spring of 1258 hatred and fear of the Poitevins, especially among the magnates, combined with a more widespread determination within the broader political community to call a halt to Henry III's mismanagement of his government, both at the centre, where he was prey to court factions, and in the localities where his financial bankruptcy had led him to encourage heavily oppressive practices. The financial crisis was sharply intensified by the increasingly insistent demands of the papacy in relation to the business of Sicily and the more recent threat of full-scale warfare on the Welsh border. Henry III's subjects appreciated that their opportunity had come. The king's need for a parliamentary subsidy had never been more urgent. Eleanor of Provence was not unaware of the pressure for reform or the complexities of the situation in which she found herself. She was intelligent and politically experienced, but her absorbing concern at this point was not with reform, for which she cared little, but with plucking the Lusignans from their influence over her husband and over her son. She pushed her way through a great constitutional revolution, and later through civil war, guided by her remarkably consistent personal aims. These were not for self-aggrandizement. Her supreme concern was for the success and well-being of her family, but that of course included the preservation of her own influence and power. If she was untouched by the political idealism which moved some men, both laymen and clergy, who were involved in the reform movement, she held fast to a role in which she felt herself justified. It ultimately led to a heroic climax.

Peter of Savoy, as has been seen, was one of the seven magnates who, on 12 April 1258, had bound themselves into a sworn confederacy which was in reality aimed against the Lusignans. Towards the end of that month, when the king asked the magnates in parliament to grant him a subsidy, they promised to give him their reply within three days. When the reply came it was a threat of force, and in retrospect the beginning of a revolution. According to what was probably an eyewitness account, Roger Bigod, earl of Norfolk and marshal of England, led a group of 'noble and vigorous men, earls, barons and knights', all armed, to the king's palace at Westminster. They left their weapons at the door of the king's hall and entered to face him with their ultimatum. The earl called upon the king 'to let the wretched and intolerable Poitevins and all aliens flee from your face'.[3] This placed the demand for the expulsion of the Poitevins in the closest conjunction with Bigod's second demand, that the king should swear to abide by the counsel of a body of twenty-four prudent men, bishops, earls and barons, to whom he

[3] *Ann. Tewkesbury*, 164; Carpenter, 'What Happened in 1258?', 187–90.

should give authority. This was to be the first step in a major transfer of power from the king to a corporate body. It was not until the seventeenth century that constitutional innovation on this scale was mooted again in England.

Obviously one searches around for the queen and Peter of Savoy. The queen may possibly have been in the palace of Westminster at the point when Bigod confronted the king in the great hall; she was certainly there on 5 May when she presented a fine ruby ring to the brother-in-law of Thomas of Savoy, Cardinal Ottobuono, a man who was later to play a major role in English affairs.[4] Peter of Savoy was already at Westminster by 2 May, when he appears among the list of witnesses to the king's formal agreement to the setting-up of the committee of twenty-four and the re-ordering of the realm, in return for the barons' promise to try to secure an aid for the Sicilian business from the community.[5] But was Peter with Roger Bigod in the group which challenged the king on 30 April? There is no evidence, and it may be doubted, for Peter was a prudent man. Yet he had been party to the confederacy of 12 April and in some way he had evidently forfeited a measure of the king's trust, as will be seen. That did not bode well for the queen.

Eleanor of Provence at this moment had cause for great anxiety. The reforming committee of twenty-four was to comprise twelve men chosen by the king and twelve chosen by the barons. Already by 2 May the king's men had been chosen and we know who they were. The most striking fact is that Roger Bigod's plea that the Poitevins (and therefore the Lusignans) should flee the king's face, if he really did make it as specific as that, had met with no response whatever from Henry, and as yet the measure had not been forced on him. William de Valence and Aymer and Guy de Lusignan figure as three of the king's chosen twelve. Equally significant and astonishing is the absence of Peter of Savoy and Boniface of Savoy from the king's list.[6] Henry III clearly considered that he had grounds for distrusting them. The Lusignans themselves presumably regarded the Savoyards at court as associated with a move to displace them. One can see that the queen could now feel no safety until the half-brothers were expelled and that she would work urgently for that end.

Eleanor had further grounds for disquiet. Her son Edward had only consented reluctantly to the setting up of the committee of twenty-four.[7] His move towards the Lusignans has already been noted and the king had

---

[4] E 101/349/26 m. 1.

[5] *DBM*, 72–5.

[6] Ibid., 74–5, 100–1. Treharne's surmise that the king's unnamed 'twelfth man' was Boniface of Savoy is unfounded, Ridgeway, 'Politics', 276.

[7] *Ann. Tewkesbury*, 164.

further strengthened the Lusignan faction on the new committee by selecting two of Edward's young friends among the magnates, Henry of Almain and John de Warenne, both Lusignan sympathisers.[8] It seems that the court was no less factious than before and that the Lusignans still had the upper hand with the king and with Edward. Although there is no direct evidence for the king's attitude towards his wife at this point, this indirect evidence indicates that it would have been less than cordial. Yet there were policies which did still bind them together. Both were eager for the continued prosecution of the business of Sicily and for the conclusion of peace with France. Negotiations over Sicily, not materially assisted by the barons, remained substantially in the hands of the Savoyard archbishops of Tarentaise and Embrun, with continuing interest on the part of Thomas of Savoy.[9] The queen and Peter of Savoy may have felt that Henry's submission to the demands of the magnates was the only chance of getting the necessary parliamentary subsidy.[10] Although in December of that year the pope set aside Edmund's special claim to Sicily he did not refuse to consider Edmund as one candidate among others, and both Henry and Eleanor remained hopeful at this stage.[11]

Peace with France was far less chimerical. The queen eagerly desired it, both as a necessary preliminary to the prosecution of the Sicilian business and as an end in itself. It would be a mistake to regard the final conclusion of that peace in December 1259 as a purely baronial achievement.[12] The reformers favoured it, but when the baronial party attempted to substitute their own envoys for Henry III himself at a projected meeting at Cambrai in November 1258, Louis IX declined to meet them.[13] He regarded the peace as a personal treaty between himself and the king of England.

However, peace with France lay some way ahead in the spring of 1258. A new parliament had been called to meet in Oxford in early June, to coincide with a muster of tenants-in-chief preparatory to a campaign against the Welsh. This meant a large gathering in Oxford in which excitement ran high both inside and outside parliament. The miscellaneous but far-reaching list of desired reforms put together in a document known as the Petition of the Barons may have been circulated at this time.[14] The queen had little interest in this, and she would certainly have

[8] *DBM*, 100–1.

[9] *CPR 1258–66*, 51.

[10] Treharne, *Baronial Plan*, 103–4; Ridgeway, 'Politics', 319.

[11] *Foedera*, i. 379–80.

[12] For a full account of negotiations see Chaplais, 'The Making of the Treaty of Paris', 238–47.

[13] *CM*, v. 720–1.

[14] *DBM*, 76–91; Maddicott, *Montfort*, 156–7.

resented the criticism in the first clause of that document of her levy of queen's gold on feudal reliefs. Her insensitivity to current criticism of the king's disposal of his patronage and of the marriages of English royal wards to aliens is marked by a small but significant incident. On 29 May 1258, a few days before the death of Edmund de Lacy earl of Lincoln, the queen was looking ahead to the future interests of Edmund's wife, her Savoyard kinswoman, Alice de Saluzzo. The king's promise that Edmund de Lacy's debts should not be claimed from his executors but from his heirs, effectively putting the claims into the future, was secured 'at the instance of the queen'.[15] It is likely that it was again at Eleanor's prompting that the king promised within the same week that he would sell the wardship of Edmund de Lacy's lands to his widow Alice 'before all others'. If so, the queen here met with a slight rebuff since a proviso was added 'on condition that this go forth from the king's council about to meet at Oxford'.[16] In the event, the wardship was vested jointly in Edmund's English mother and the young Savoyard widow.[17]

What concerned the queen was not constitutional and administrative reform but the expulsion of the Lusignans from England. In fact the parliament at Oxford was to achieve both, and both were to affect the queen profoundly. By the so-called Provisions of Oxford the kingdom was virtually given a new form of government.[18] The committee of twenty-four was replaced by a council of fifteen, chosen by a complex system of election. This council, much more strongly baronial in composition than the committee which it replaced, was entrusted by the reformers with a quite unprecedented measure of central control. The three great ministers of state, justiciar, chancellor and treasurer, were to be fully responsible to the council and all but routine writs issued by the chancery and all major grants were to be approved by the council. Parliaments were to meet three times a year and co-operation between the council and the wider baronial community was ensured by the election of twelve representatives from the whole baronage to consult with the council on these occasions. The newly appointed justiciar Hugh Bigod, brother of the earl of Norfolk, was to travel round the counties hearing complaints against officials, while sheriffs were henceforth to be local men appointed for one year only. This represented reform root and branch, at the centre and in the shires. As John Maddicott has said, the new measures came near to putting the Crown into commission.[19] The

[15] *CPR 1247–58*, 631.
[16] Ibid., 632.
[17] Ibid., 649.
[18] *DBM*, 96–113; Treharne, *Baronial Plan*, 82–101.
[19] Maddicott, *Montfort*, 158.

queen was surely uneasy at this assault on the power of the monarchy, for it was intended to be long-term, although not permanent. Yet, from her point of view, there were weighty compensations in this revolutionary package, especially in the composition of the new royal council in which so much power was vested. This time the Lusignans were dropped and her uncles Boniface and Peter of Savoy were included; this was a most significant shift in power and foreshadowed the demise of the Poitevin faction.[20]

Towards the end of the Oxford parliament two further significant reforms were carried. All royal castles were in future to be in the hands of Englishmen, and all lands and castles alienated by Henry III were to be restored to the Crown.[21] It was these provisions which finally caught the Poitevins. They knew that they were directed against themselves and that it would be they who would suffer. Throughout the Oxford parliament the Lusignan brothers had been obstructive over the Provisions, and they had encouraged a rebellious attitude in the Lord Edward, Henry of Almain and John de Warenne. Now, at the end of June, they refused to take the required oath to abide by the Provisions, escaped from Oxford and made a dash for Aymer's episcopal castle at Wolvesey, with Simon de Montfort's curt challenge to William of Valence, 'yield your castles or lose your head' no doubt ringing in their ears.[22] It was a moment of high drama, creating a sense of danger which helped to bind together the supporters of the Provisions even more closely. The barons rode off in pursuit, tracked the royal half-brothers down and completed the work of the Oxford parliament at Winchester, expelling all four of the Lusignans from the country. Other leading Poitevins accompanied them, or in some cases were expelled shortly after.[23]

If this outcome was one for which the queen had desperately hoped, she had yet to learn that a political coup may do little to change men's deeper affections. The loyalties of her husband and her eldest son were already engaged by the Lusignans and they would both work hard to reverse this act. The king had consented under compulsion. At Winchester, when the fate of his brothers hung in the balance, he was eager to give a pledge that if they were allowed to remain 'they would not plot any hindrance or harm to the barons'.[24] The barons then offered to allow William and Aymer, who both held lands in England, and in Aymer's case office too, to remain in the country in custody, but they chose exile with

[20] *DBM*, 104–5.
[21] Ibid., 90–3.
[22] Ibid., 92–3; *CM*, v. 697–8.
[23] *CM*, v., 702, 725.
[24] *DBM*, 92–5.

their brothers. Queen Margaret's allegations to Louis IX at this point, of their scandalizing and defaming her sister possibly indicate that they had recent cause to suspect Eleanor of acting against them. This may have been so, and this may be hinted at in the Battle abbey chronicle, which refers to the queen's 'intervention'.[25]

The expulsion of the Lusignans signally failed to change the attitude of the Lord Edward. He had already drawn closer to his Poitevin uncles by appointing Geoffrey de Lusignan as seneschal of Gascony and making a life grant of the Isle of Oléron to Guy, probably in July 1258, acts which were quickly reversed by the reformers, who compelled Edward to revoke his grants.[26] Edward's own submission to the work of the Oxford parliament was sullen and reluctant in the extreme. His alienation from the group of advisers who had previously guided his affairs went deep, and friends of the queen such as Ebulo de Montibus and Michael de Fiennes were leaving his service at this time.[27]

Meanwhile great store was set by the magnates and the barons on the oath to uphold the Provisions of Oxford, required not only from the king and his heir but from all those of the community of the realm present in the Oxford parliament. The queen's uncles Peter and Boniface both took the oath, and indeed, Archbishop Boniface conducted the impressive ceremony in the Dominican church in Oxford where the king and magnates cast down their lighted tapers at the end of the archbishop's solemn excommunication of all who opposed the Provisions.[28] But was the queen herself required to swear? This is a point of great interest. Unlike the king, a queen did not take any oath at her coronation, which would have bound her in an official relationship with the community of the realm. The reformers of 1258 could not have been unaware of this, but they were pragmatic men. The queen had acted as her husband's regent in 1253–4 and, apart from this, her political influence was patently obvious. At some point the queen did take the oath. It is significant that no chronicler mentions it and the evidence comes from the papal bulls of absolution of 1261 and 1262. The pope would not have needed

---

[25] Battle Chronicle in Bémont, *Simon de Montfort* (1st edn), 373; discussed by Ridgeway, 'Politics', 279.

[26] *CPR 1247–58*, 639, 641; *Foedera*, i. 374, 378; *Gascon Register A*, ii, nos 168, 170. For the attitude of Henry III see Trabut-Cussac, *L'Administration Anglaise*, 16–17 and Studd, 'The Lord Edward and Henry III', 8; but for a different view, to which I incline, see Prestwich, *Edward I*, 25–6.

[27] Huw Ridgeway, 'Politics', 338–9, is more convincing on significance of changes than Hilary Wait, 'Household and Resources', 287–9. For Fiennes see Cuttino, 'A Chancellor of the Lord Edward', 231.

[28] *Flores*, iii. 253–4; *Robert of Gloucester*, ii. 734; *Chron. Guisborough*, 185–6; *DBM*, 258–9.

to absolve the queen from an oath she had never sworn. The occasion is unknown to us, but the fact seems certain.[29]

In 1258 the antipathy to aliens, which became an increasingly marked feature of the reform movement, was pointed in political terms at the Poitevins, while the Savoyards, who were less personally unpopular, were in the main absorbed into the new regime. Yet the situation in 1258 was not quite as comfortable for the queen and her friends as that may sound. According to the account incorporated in the Tewkesbury chronicle, mentioned earlier, Roger Bigod had asked for the expulsion of 'all aliens'. Below the rank of the magnate courtiers there was already a push within the community against many different aspects of foreign infiltration, including alien clergy and Cahorsin moneylenders, as well as aliens in the service of the king.[30] The demand at the Oxford parliament that castles should be entrusted only to 'the king's faithful subjects born in the kingdom of England' resulted in the removal of the Poitevins Elias de Rabayn and Guy de Rocheford from Corfe and Colchester, but also of the Savoyards Imbert Pugeys and Ebulo of Geneva from the Tower of London and the castle of Hadleigh respectively, although the queen's steward Matthias Bezill retained Gloucester.[31] Sharp hostility towards one of the queen's prime Savoyard allies in diplomacy, Peter d'Aigueblanche, led to a charge of his misappropriating funds in relation to the business of Sicily, but on this occasion the wily bishop managed to come through pretty well unscathed.[32]

Queen Eleanor's attention was now claimed by three other matters which touched her closely, the negotiations for peace with France, the proposed marriage of her daughter Beatrice to the son of the duke of Brittany and the deepening disaffection of the Lord Edward. At various points the themes intertwined. The course of negotiations with France, so central to Eleanor's plans, helped to lay bare a rift between two of the most prominent of the magnates, Simon de Montfort and Richard de Clare, earl of Gloucester. They were already at odds over the pace and direction of the reform movement. Montfort ranged himself with those who wanted radical change, with investigation of grievances against baronial as well as royal officials. The more conservative Gloucester held back; for him the pace of reform threatened to become too quick and the scope too wide. In the spring of 1259 the two magnates clashed openly over the publication of a further far-reaching scheme of reform,

---

[29] *DBM*, 240–3, 248–51.
[30] Carpenter, '"Statute" against Aliens', 261–2, 268–9. Compare Ridgeway, 'Henry III and the "Aliens"', 86.
[31] *DBM*, 80–1; *CPR 1247–58*, 638; *CM*, v. 725.
[32] *CR 1256–59*, 321–2, 462; Ridgeway, 'Politics', 319–20.

the so-called Ordinance of the Barons, when Montfort accused Gloucester of going back on his oath to the Provisions.[33] The reforming impulse
won, and the October parliament of 1259 saw the publication of
the Provisions of Westminster, introducing a large package of beneficial changes in law and administration at the level of the localities. It
proved to be one of the most lasting achievements of the whole movement.[34]

It is against this background of personal feuding and the quickening
pace of reform that the slow progress of the negotiations with France in
1258–9 must be charted. Here again Montfort and Gloucester were at
odds, with Gloucester in this case the critic of Montfort.[35] The peace was
to entail Henry III's renunciation of the bulk of the former Angevin
possessions in France, apart from Gascony, a renunciation which was
also to be required of Henry III's sons, of his brother Richard of Cornwall and of his sister Eleanor de Montfort.[36] It was this last requirement
which Montfort attempted to use as a lever to exact from Henry the most
advantageous settlement of his own claims against the king in respect of
his wife's dower. The Montforts withheld Eleanor's renunciation until
the last possible moment, 4 December 1259, the actual day of the
publication of the Treaty of Paris, and it was then given only on
the condition that Louis IX held back 15,000 marks of the money due
to Henry III under the treaty, until the personal disputes between the
Montforts and the English king had been settled.[37]

The rift between Montfort and Gloucester marks an important political realignment in England. Eleanor of Provence, together with Peter of
Savoy, had been a friend and political ally of Montfort in the fifties. They
now began to pull away from him and he from them. On the issue of
reform and on that of the French negotiations the queen evidently now
judged Gloucester much the sounder man. Indeed Montfort was apparently deliberately destroying his alliance with the Savoyards. On 16
March 1259 he declined to become a surety for a bond for 3,000
marks contracted to pay arrears of exchequer fees due to certain members of the comital house of Savoy.[38] Again, he had used the reform
movement to press for the satisfaction of other claims of his own against
the king and had now elicited from the council the promised conversion
of his £400 annual fee into lands; this had involved the displacement

---

[33] *CM*, v. 744.
[34] *DBM*, 136–65; Treharne, *Baronial Plan*, 157–212. See below, p. 191.
[35] *CM*, v. 745; Maddicott, *Montfort*, 181–2.
[36] Chaplais, 'The Making of the Treaty of Paris', 240–1.
[37] Ibid., 247.
[38] *CPR 1258–66*, 16–17.

of some Savoyards from property previously granted to them by the king.[39]

It was the proposed marriage of the Lady Beatrice to the son of the duke of Brittany which further revealed the erosion of the Savoyards' earlier friendship with Montfort and the strengthening of their new links with Gloucester. The evidence that Eleanor of Provence's sister Queen Margaret initiated the proposals for the Breton marriage comes from a letter of Henry III himself, written in March 1260.[40] It would clearly have been a matter of collaboration between the two queens, for Margaret would never have acted on this without the full agreement of Beatrice's mother. It therefore occasions no surprise to come across the chief Breton negotiator, the bishop of Brienne, at St Albans in October 1259, in the company of Queen Eleanor and John Mansel.[41] On the English side the negotiators for the marriage were Gloucester, Peter of Savoy and John Mansel, who were all closely involved as well in the negotiations for the Treaty of Paris.[42] Montfort himself was prominent in relation to the treaty, but conspicuously not involved in negotiations for the marriage. In fact, with characteristic quickness, Montfort spotted a weakness in the whole scheme, and exploited it politically. The duke of Brittany had an ancestral claim to the English earldom of Richmond and saw his son's marriage as the opportunity to prosecute this. Richmond would in effect make an admirable *maritagium* for Beatrice and her future husband. This was difficult. Henry III was prepared to accept the duke's claim in principle, but he made it clear that the concession of Richmond could only be effected with the consent of its holder at the time, Peter of Savoy. Predictably, Peter of Savoy intended to stand by his rights.[43] The English negotiators therefore proposed that for the present Beatrice and her husband should be endowed instead with financial compensation for the earldom: the equivalent of the revenues of the county of Agenais on the borders of Gascony, since this sum was to be made over to Henry III in the forthcoming Treaty of Paris.[44] As Huw Ridgeway points out, this arrangement was apparently one on which the consent of the full council of fifteen was never obtained.[45] It would have been viewed by many of the reformers as an unsanctioned alienation of

[39] Ridgeway, 'Politics', 330–1.
[40] *Diplomatic Documents*, i, no. 313.
[41] *Flores*, ii. 435–6.
[42] *CPR 1258–66*, 25.
[43] *Foedera*, i. 391.
[44] *Diplomatic Documents*, i, nos. 307, 308.
[45] 'Politics', 357. The duke's letter and Henry's response (dated 18 October 1259) were entrusted to John Mansel 'in the presence of the king and of his council in the chapel of the queen at Westminster', *Foedera*, i. 391.

royal revenues for the purpose of protecting the interests of an 'alien' Savoyard landholder. Montfort made all this clear in his dry comment to the duke of Brittany that the English king could give no land with his daughter, without the assent of the council. Of the king's anger over this remark we have explicit evidence in the charges which he brought against Montfort in July 1260.[46] For the queen's anger we hardly need any evidence.

Peter's public declaration on 3 November 1259 that in default of male heirs of his own he would demise his honour of Pevensey to the queen, giving her power to assign it as she wished, may have been a bid for popularity. In fact it failed to deflect the distrust aroused on the council by his machinations to retain Richmond.[47] This was to be put to the test when Montfort engineered the removal of Peter of Savoy from the council early in 1260.[48] Montfort and the Savoyards were fast pulling apart.

The queen's third preoccupation, the Lord Edward, probably caused her the greatest heaviness of heart. This problem too became entwined with the new pattern of court factions. In sympathy with the queen one discerns a pretty coherent and powerful pressure group consisting of Peter of Savoy, the earl of Gloucester, John Mansel, and fully cooperative with them, Henry of Wingham, the chancellor, soon to become bishop of London, and the royal steward Robert Walerand. These men were supportive of the French treaty, firmly opposed to the Lusignans and ready to hold back the pace of reform. Increasingly they were wary of Simon de Montfort. The king was for the most part inclined to them, although very reluctantly so on the issue of the Lusignans. The Lord Edward viewed them with unconcealed hostility. A pact of goodwill between Edward and Gloucester in March 1259 quickly lapsed, as Edward found it did nothing to restore his personal control over his possessions, his only possible motive for entering into it, as he hated Gloucester.[49] Gloucester was active in forwarding the French treaty, which Edward resented, and the earl never ceased to cherish hopes of regaining his ancestral hold on Bristol, which was now the headquarters of the Lord Edward's administration. These circumstances were certainly enough to keep Edward and Gloucester mutually and sharply opposed.[50] Gloucester stood opposed

[46] *DBM*, 204–5.

[47] C 47/9/1; for an earlier demise of Peter's English lands to Eleanor see Wurstemberger, *Peter der Zweite*, iv, no. 407; Ridgeway, 'Politics', 334–5.

[48] *DBM*, 206–7.

[49] HMC, *Middleton MSS*, 67–9; Carpenter, 'The Lord Edward's Oath', 243; Ridgeway, 'Politics', 341–4.

[50] Altschul, *A Baronial Family*, 77, 82–3; Maddicott, *Montfort*, 194; Ridgeway, 'Politics', 336.

to the Lusignans, opposed to further reform, and increasingly opposed to Montfort. In retrospect it seems almost inevitable that Edward, as an enemy of Gloucester, should now have begun to embrace reform and to make common cause with Montfort. In the important October parliament of 1259 the Lord Edward backed the reforming demands of the 'bachelors of England'.[51] Two days later he entered into a private contract with Montfort, pledging himself to the furtherance of reform and to support of Montfort in relation to a certain judgement which was pending in the king's court. This was probably an award about to be made on Montfort's claims over his wife's dower, a judgement which, if it satisfied Montfort, would win him enemies.[52] He could need Edward's help. The men who witnessed the pact between Edward and Montfort, on Edward's side, were Henry of Almain, John de Warenne and Roger Leybourne. They represented the group in Edward's entourage which also included the Marcher lords Roger Clifford, Hamo Lestrange and John de Vaux. It was a group deeply distrusted and disliked by the queen.

Whether or not Eleanor of Provence knew of Edward's pact with Montfort before she left for France on 14 November 1259 to be present at the finalizing of the French treaty and the marriage of her daughter Beatrice, she would have been increasingly angry about his attitude and the company he kept. Leybourne was typical of them, an aggressive man, keen on the tournament, with some allegiance to the Lusignans and none whatever to herself. He was now Edward's steward and Edward planned to place Leybourne in control of Bristol castle, which had been entrusted, with the sanction of the council, to the reliable Robert Walerand.[53] The queen's personal favour towards Walerand is clear from her gifts of rings to his wife and wife's mother, shortly before she left for France.[54] The king, evidently uneasy, ordered Walerand to deliver Bristol castle to no one without the assent of the king and council; but Edward was ready to spring. He had too many grievances to exercise the 'patience' which his father enjoined on him.[55] Once the royal party had embarked for France, he removed Walerand from Bristol on 7 December and replaced him by Leybourne.[56] He had already ousted John Mansel from Tickhill on 4 November, and on 13 November, the day before his parents left, he

---

[51] *Ann. Burton*, 471; Treharne, *Baronial Plan*, 160–4.
[52] Text printed in Carpenter, 'The Lord Edward's Oath', 251; for discussion see ibid., 241–50; Maddicott, *Montfort*, 186; Prestwich, *Edward I*, 28–9.
[53] *CPR 1258–66*, 29, 32.
[54] E 101/349/26 m. 2.
[55] *CPR 1258–66*, 63–4.
[56] C 61/4 m. 4 (Studd, 'Acts of the Lord Edward', no. 742).

removed Peter of Savoy's own bailiff from Hastings.[57] If the queen now began to understand that the expulsion of the Lusignans had failed entirely to bring her rebellious son to order, she could do very little at the moment, as she travelled towards Paris. Yet the knowledge was very bitter. Edward had clearly ranged himself against his mother's set. With his father he at least shared a regard for the Lusignans; his mother had become an out-and-out political adversary.

The queen's views were hardening on another matter in the autumn of 1259, the reform movement itself. The resolutions of the October parliament, embodied in the Provisions of Westminster, touched her personally. The sale of wardships falling to the king was to be placed in the hands of a committee of five, the justiciar, treasurer and three others, and the same men were to 'determine and decree in what matters queen's gold shall be paid'.[58] Queen's gold represented a substantial part of Eleanor's income, over which she now enjoyed a full measure of control; interference here appeared as an intrusion into revenue levied by her prerogative right.[59] This she would not readily tolerate. On the issue of the king's personal control of the disposal of wardships Henry himself felt very bitterly. The queen perhaps resented it almost as much. She was largely dependent on such grants for the funding of her household and through her influence with the king she had been able to secure grants for some of those whom she wished to favour. Her clear-cut reaction to the new measure came on the day before she left with the king for France. In return for his long service to the queen, 'as also to the king', Eleanor's steward Matthias Bezill was to be granted the first available wardship of £40 or £50 or £60 a year, with the marriage of heirs and no reservations. There is an indication that this royal mandate caused a constitutional flutter. It was noted on the patent roll that the writ was authorized by Hugh Bigod and John Mansel 'at the instance of the queen'; the official committee of five had apparently been bypassed.[60]

Henry and Eleanor left for France on 14 November, reaching Paris twelve days later. King Louis treated Henry with the greatest honour and there was nothing demeaning in the ceremony in the garden of the royal palace on 4 December when Henry knelt to do homage to the French king for all the possessions that he still held in France.[61] In return for his renunciation of his claims to Anjou, Maine, Touraine and Poitou and the

---

[57] C 61/4 m. 5 (Studd, 'Acts of the Lord Edward', nos. 715, 733, 734).

[58] *DBM*, 152–3; for exaction of queen's gold on reliefs see 'Petition of the Barons', ibid., 78–9.

[59] Howell, 'The Resources of Eleanor of Provence', 374–9.

[60] *CPR 1258–66*, 63.

[61] Gavrilovitch, *Traité de Paris*, 36–7.

receiving of Gascony as a fief, Henry was granted the fiefs and domains of the French Crown in the three dioceses of Limoges, Cahors and Périgueux; finally his claim to the Agenais was to be met; either by the ceding of the territory to the English Crown when it ceased to be in the possession of Joan, wife of Alphonse of Poitiers or by the yielding of its equivalent value in perpetuity. During Joan of Poitiers's lifetime, Henry was to receive the equivalence of its value once that had been determined, and as has been seen, Henry had agreed to settle this on the young John of Brittany and the Lady Beatrice. In addition, Henry III was to receive sufficient money to maintain a force of 500 knights for two years, to be used in the service of God and the Church or to the profit of the kingdom of England.[62] These provisions bristled with difficulties in the long term and few historians can say much in their favour, but in the lifetime of Eleanor of Provence the immediate effects, in the view of the parties concerned, were beneficial. The deepening personal relationships between the two royal families had profound political consequences in the decade following the treaty.

Henry III and Eleanor celebrated Christmas 1259 in Paris at Louis IX's court.[63] Eleanor's account for her gifts of rings, though not of other jewels, during this period happens to survive, and in her presents to the queens of France and Navarre, the countesses of Provence, Brittany, Guisnes and Eu and other high-ranking ladies, together with the damsels and knights who 'stood with' them and their numerous clerks, *valetti* and officials, one senses the force of Malcolm Vale's description of the Anglo/French aristocracy as being in effect one family.[64] The social festivities which were arranged to celebrate the visit of the English king and queen, who were accompanied by their own very large and impressive retinues, reveal only one facet of the intimacy that was developing between the two royal families. Henry and Eleanor spent most of the month of January in the abbey of St Denis and it was here that they received the sad news of the death of the eldest son and heir of Louis IX, the fifteen-year-old Prince Louis, 'most dear and lovable to us', as his father wrote of him.[65] Arrangements for the prince's funeral now took precedence over all other matters. He was to be buried at Royaumont on 13 January and the funeral cortège was to spend the previous night at St Denis. On the next day Henry himself acted as one of the bearers who carried the prince's coffin on their shoulders on the first stage of the journey to

---

[62] *Layettes*, iii, no. 4554; *Diplomatic Documents*, i, no. 305; Gavrilovitch, *Traité de Paris*, 23–5; Vale, *Angevin Legacy*, 53–4.

[63] *Flores*, ii. 440–1; Guillaume de Nangis, 'Vie de Saint Louis', 410.

[64] E 101/349/26, *passim*; Vale, *Angevin Legacy*, 47.

[65] *The Register of Eudes of Rouen*, 404.

Royaumont.[66] The very day of Prince Louis's burial had previously been intended as the day of the marriage of the Lady Beatrice to John of Brittany. The reaction of both royal families in this situation showed a warmth of feeling, a mutual respect and restraint that was significant for the future. Beatrice's marriage was postponed until 22 January and the French king and queen made the effort to attend the ceremony, little more than a week after their son's burial.[67]

Eleanor of Provence and her husband remained abroad until 23 April 1260. They repeatedly delayed their return home and their five months of absence saw a change in tone in the reform movement in England. It began its steady descent into faction. The unceremonious departure from France of Simon de Montfort, probably accompanied by his political allies Peter de Montfort and Richard de Grey, in late December 1259 or in January 1260, left a cluster of royalist councillors around the king, the earl of Gloucester, William de Forz earl of Aumale, Peter of Savoy and John Mansel.[68] Aumale was nearing the end of his life and was perhaps not very assertive. Peter of Savoy remained with the court long enough to have been a witness to the famous letter in which the king had been persuaded to plead with the pope against the return of Aymer de Lusignan to Winchester, citing Aymer's attempts to turn the king against the queen and Edward against his father.[69] Once Peter of Savoy had left for his Alpine territories, before the end of January, it seems likely that the king's most active advisers were Gloucester, Mansel, and surely the queen herself. Another strong-minded royalist now with the court, although not a member of the council of fifteen, was Robert Walerand, ejected from Bristol by the Lord Edward. The signs are that this group of advisers had things their own way.

The king and those around him seem to have worked deliberately and cleverly to play on the loyalty of the more moderate reformers on the council left in England, the justiciar Hugh Bigod, his brother Roger Bigod earl of Norfolk and Philip Basset, in order to drive a wedge between these men and the militant supporters of Montfort and the Lord Edward, who continued dangerously close allies. Edward was supported in his defiant stance by his Marcher companions Clifford, Leybourne, Lestrange and Vaux.[70] Roger Leybourne's prominence is suggested by the king's order to Hugh Bigod on 11 April to prevent Roger from strengthening the fortifications of his ancestral castle of

---

[66] Guillaume de Nangis, 'Vie de Saint Louis', 412; compare *Flores*, ii. 442.
[67] *CR 1259–61*, 267.
[68] Maddicott, *Montfort*, 192–3.
[69] *Royal Letters*, ii, no. 533.
[70] Treharne, *Baronial Plan*, 223–4; Ridgeway, 'Politics', 345–6.

Leybourne in Kent, where he was a major landholder.[71] When Henry prohibited the holding of a parliament in his absence, Montfort came to London with an armed following, hoping to force the issue, but Hugh Bigod held to the king's order.[72] The tension continued to rise, the alliance between Montfort and Edward no doubt making the former more bold in his opposition to the king and the king's councillors over the water. It seems to have been at this point that Montfort manoeuvred the removal of Peter of Savoy from the council; he peremptorily told Bigod not to send funds to the king and to order the king not to return with foreign troops.[73] Meanwhile Edward and Montfort seem to have been enlarging their own military following, and Montfort may have attempted to hold the parliament.[74] It was an explosive situation.

At the end of January Henry and Eleanor had moved from St Denis to St Omer, near the Channel coast. This denoted much more than one stage on the way home. St Omer was a base from which the king could assemble a military force of his own. He did indeed intend to depend primarily on his return to England on the loyalty and support of his own baronage, and in a letter of 27 March he ordered the justiciar Hugh Bigod to summon the tenants-in-chief and their knights, ready for service, to assemble in London on 25 April, explaining his intention of holding a parliament.[75] Significantly omitted from those summoned were Simon de Montfort himself and Edward's Marcher companions.

From early April 1260 the man who played a key role in calming anger and in avoiding armed conflict in London was that seasoned arbiter Richard of Cornwall. As the barons began to arrive in London in response to the king's summons, Richard of Cornwall, together with Hugh Bigod and Philip Basset, took steps with the Londoners themselves to exclude Montfort and Edward, with their armed followers, from taking up residence inside the city.[76] They also decided to exclude Gloucester, who had returned to England in March and who, in his personal antagonism to Edward and Montfort, may have been responsible for encouraging rumours that Edward was prepared to wage war against his father.[77] These rumours reached the king, as they were no doubt intended to, and alarmed him exceedingly, strengthening his conviction that he must ensure his own military position by arriving in England only

---

[71] CR 1259–61, 283–4.
[72] DBM, 206–7.
[73] Ibid., 208–11.
[74] Ibid., 206–7; CR 1259–61, 253–4, 277, 283.
[75] CR 1259–61, 157–8; Treharne, *Baronial Plan*, 226–7.
[76] *Cron. Maiorum*, 44–5; *Ann. London*, 54–5; Treharne, *Baronial Plan*, 230.
[77] *Ann. Dunstable*, 214; *Flores*, ii. 448–9.

when he was in a position to do so accompanied by a force of foreign knights. This was the force which he now assembled.

It is here that the role of Eleanor of Provence may have been particularly important. She was by nature perhaps more combative than her husband, ready to resort to force at an earlier stage than he was. Force had already played its part in the revolution. There was an implied threat of force in Roger Bigod's entry into the king's hall at Westminster on 30 April 1258, and it was by force that the Lusignans had been overcome at Wolvesey. It may be that the queen, by the autumn of 1259, with the obstructionism of Montfort over the Treaty of Paris at its peak and her son Edward increasingly disaffected and unruly, had already foreseen the likely need for the use of force on a larger scale. If so, she may have foreseen the means as well as the end. When Isabella de Fiennes, wife of the Anglo-Flemish knight Ingram de Fiennes, left England during the year ending October 1259, she took with her a quantity of rings, given her by the queen for redistribution to the lords and ladies of Flanders.[78] The Fiennes family were favourites with the queen and distantly related to her.[79] Michael de Fiennes had been Edward's first chancellor but, significantly, had left his service by 1258, later rising to become bishop of Thérouanne.[80] His brother Ingram, cast in a different mould, was a military man, with powers of organization and a capacity for decisive action which the queen approved. Ingram's sister Katharine received a ring from the queen at St Omer in February 1260, and Baldwin, a third brother, was one of the force of knights which crossed the Channel with Henry and Eleanor in April.[81] It is in the light of the queen's further contacts with Flemish and French knights in 1261, her encouragement of foreign knights in Edward's household in 1262 and 1263, and finally her assembling of a mercenary army near St Omer in 1264 that the full political significance of the contacts which she was establishing in the spring of 1260 becomes clear. It is likely to have been a factor in the escalation of her unpopularity in England. Hatred of foreigners was easy to rouse; hatred of foreign military men had a special edge, and Eleanor of Provence may have been regarded as closely connected with the king's use of foreign mercenaries in these years.

[78] E 101/349/26 mm. 1, 2 (noted by Ridgeway, 'Politics', 355).
[79] Isabella de Fiennes is described as *cognata regine* (E 101/349/26 mm. 1–2); For Michael de Fiennes see ch. 6, n. 83, above.
[80] Cuttino, 'A Chancellor of the Lord Edward', 229–32; Studd, 'Chancellors of the Lord Edward: a Supplementary Note', 181–3; Ridgeway, 'Politics', 338.
[81] E 101/349/26 mm. 1, 4.

The head of a queen, probably Eleanor of Provence, in the Muniment Room of Westminster Abbey, early 1250s: *by courtesy of the Dean and Chapter of Westminster*

The gilded bronze effigy of Henry III, Westminster Abbey, 1292: *by courtesy of the Dean and Chapter of Westminster*

The head of a young prince, probably the Lord Edward, above the Great North Door of Westminster Abbey, early 1250s: *by courtesy of the Dean and Chapter of Westminster*

Drawing by Matthew Paris (1250s) of the marriage of Henry III and Eleanor of Provence in 1236, miniature, *Historia Anglorum*, British Library, Royal MS 14. C. VII, f. 124v: *by permission of the British Library*

Drawing by Matthew Paris (1250s) of the return voyage of Henry III and Eleanor of Provence from Gascony to England in 1243, miniature, *Historia Anglorum*, British Library, Royal MS 14. C. VII, f. 134v: *by permission of the British Library*

Tiled pavement from the queen's apartments in Clarendon Palace, 1250–52, British Museum: *copyright British Museum*

Rutland Psalter (*c.* 1260): initial to Psalm 101, the usual place for donor figures, showing a king and queen, British Library, Additional MS 62925, f. 99v: *by permission of the British Library*

Beatrice Book of Hours (1260–70): a prayer to St Roger (Roger Niger, bishop of London), who assisted at the coronation of Eleanor of Provence, British Library, Additional MS 33385, f. 169: *by permission of the British Library*

Engraving on the underside of the plate beneath the effigy of Henry III (see Plate 2), 1292, Westminster Abbey. The veiled queen and the young nun probably represent Eleanor of Provence and her granddaughter Mary: *by courtesy of the Dean and Chapter of Westminster*

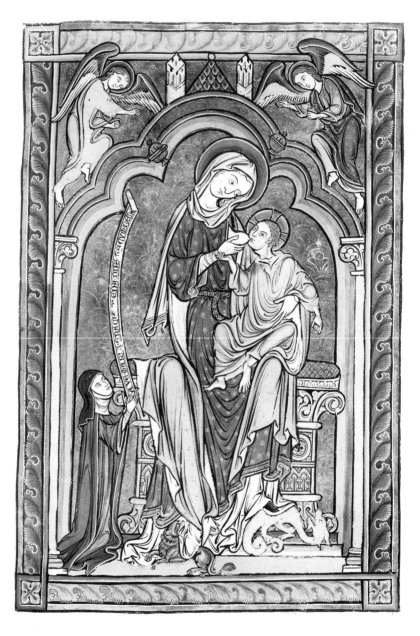

Amesbury Psalter (1250–5): a nun of Amesbury kneeling before the Virgin and Child, All Souls College MS 6, f. 2 (formerly f. 4): *by courtesy of the Warden and Fellows of All Souls College, Oxford*

The nature of Eleanor's contacts needs closer definition. Henry III's hiring of mercenaries was not in this case an impersonal transaction. The foreign knights coming to England in the 1260s were not faceless. An outstanding example is the count of St Pol, a landed magnate who figured significantly in the politics of northern France.[82] He was prominent among the knights coming to England both in April 1260 and in May 1261 and was holding himself in readiness for a similar expedition in November that year.[83] He was to give the queen support throughout her military efforts of 1264–5 and was to come to England again in 1267 for the suppression of the 'disinherited'.[84] St Pol was a man who revelled in military life, be it tournament, crusade or other warfare, and he had many friends in high places. He fought for Charles of Anjou in Sicily and was a prominent crusader in Louis IX's army in 1270.[85] There is no doubt at all that this man came to be on terms of trust and friendship with Queen Eleanor.

The other leaders of the forces of alien knights who came to England in the 1260s were not all of comparable standing to the count of St Pol, but they were men of substance. Baldwin d'Avesnes, Peter of Amiens, Gerard de Rodes and Alenard de Seningham all belonged to the landed aristocracy of Northern France and Flanders.[86] Some had property interests on both sides of the Channel, like Alenard de Seningham and Ingram de Fiennes.[87] Alenard de Seningham's wife became a member of Queen Eleanor's household in 1261.[88] This touch of social acceptance echoes the gifts of rings in 1258–9 to the ladies as well as the lords of Flanders.

If the leaders of these foreign military contingents were known personally to the queen and belonged to the aristocracy, there remains the question of the men whom they led. Some were no doubt mercenaries in the usual sense of the term, recruited for pay by a leader for a particular enterprise, but there were also many lesser knights attached to the service of the greater men, who were neither faceless or nameless from the queen's point of view. Only the queen's ring list remains for the period 1258–63; we do not have her other jewel accounts and so we have no information about the presentation of brooches, belts or other jewels or plate, but we know that some fifteen Picard knights who crossed with Henry and Eleanor to England in April 1260 received rings from the

---

[82] Richard, *Saint Louis*, 44–5.

[83] CR 1259–61, 282; CPR 1258–66, 152; *Flores*, ii. 467–70; CR 1259–61, 487.

[84] CPR 1258–66, 402, 516; ch. 10, below.

[85] Le Nain de Tillemont, *Vie de Saint Louis*, v. 16.

[86] CR 1259–61, 282; E 101/349/26 m. 5; CPR 1258–66, 152; CLR 1260–67, 40, 74, 100.

[87] CR 1261–64, 42; CPR 1258–66, 251, 436.

[88] CR 1261–64, 13–14.

queen before returning home.[89] The evidence of the ring list shows that Eleanor of Provence took trouble to nurture in these military men some feeling of personal commitment to her husband's interests and her own. She was also involved with this enterprise at another level, that of finance. King Louis was willing to advance money on the sums due to Henry under the Treaty of Paris. On 16 March 1260 Henry acknowledged receipt of £12,500 of Tours (c.£2,778 sterling), but the French king evidently required letters patent from Eleanor as well as from Henry, sealed with the queen's seal.[90] Henry further received a loan of £2,800 of Tours (c.£622 sterling) from the Temple in Paris, arranged through the mediation of Eleanor's sister Margaret.[91] Finally on 20 April it was Eleanor who was instrumental in securing a loan of £500 (sterling) from the *échevins* and merchants of Ypres.[92]

Henry and his advisers managed his return to England well. There was in the end no open conflict with Montfort and Edward. At first Henry refused to allow Edward into his presence, since he said he could not trust himself not to embrace him, but in due course the necessary reconciliation was effected by the mediation of Richard of Cornwall and Boniface of Savoy.[93] Edward swore before the assembled baronage that he had intended no injury to his father. The chroniclers specifically state that Edward's reconciliation was with the queen as well as with the king, and the Dunstable annalist suggests that the queen was the cause of all the ill feeling which had been generated.[94] The aside may well indicate that the antagonism between Eleanor and her son at this stage went very deep. The causes of that estrangement were not removed by the formal reconciliation.

On 18 May 1260 three of Edward's close companions, and perhaps in his mother's view the most objectionable, Roger Leybourne, Roger Clifford and Hamo Lestrange, were removed from their respective castellanies of Bristol, the Three Castles and Montgomery, a measure carried out in Edward's name but no doubt resented by him and by the men themselves.[95] They were not, however, removed from Edward's household and the men who replaced them did not have specific links either with the queen or with the earl of Gloucester.[96] At Bristol Leybourne was replaced

[89] E 101/349/26 m. 4.
[90] *CPR 1258–66*, 123.
[91] Ibid., 119.
[92] Ibid., 121.
[93] *Ann. Dunstable*, 215; *Ann. London*, 55.
[94] *Flores*, ii. 448–9; *Ann. Dunstable*, 215.
[95] C 61/4 m. 3; (Studd, 'Acts of the Lord Edward', nos 790, 792, 795).
[96] Ridgeway, 'Politics', 363.

by the steady and moderate Philip Basset, perhaps an indication of a wish
not to provoke Edward unnecessarily. At the insistence of the king, the
conduct of Simon de Montfort was to be a subject of investigation before
the council, although the heat was taken out of this too by the decision to
have an initial review by a group of six bishops.[97] Montfort's position
was further stengthened by the personal assistance of his friend Eudes
Rigaud, archbishop of Rouen, one of the negotiators of the Treaty of
Paris, and the Norman lord John de Harcourt. These men represented
Louis IX's personal desire to reconcile Henry III and Montfort, whom
the French king continued to esteem highly.[98] The two Frenchmen were
treated courteously by Henry III and by Queen Eleanor also. On 25 July
at Westminster, after the departure of Eudes Rigaud, Eleanor presented
rings to two of Harcourt's knights and on 1 August a ring to Harcourt
himself.[99] At Montfort's preliminary trial the king's charges against
Simon were answered by the earl with his usual easy contempt and the
repeated assertion that in all he had done he had acted with the rest of
the council and in accordance with the Provisions of Oxford and 'had
done no wrong'.[100] Proceedings in the July parliament were overshadowed by the war in Wales, where Builth castle had fallen to the Welsh
and where Montfort's military skill was thought to be urgently needed
for the intended campaign of retaliation. The projected campaign was in
the end abandoned in favour of a renewal of a truce with the Welsh,
concluded on 22 August. The continuation of Montfort's trial was still
pending when the next parliament met in October 1260, but at this point
the king was prevented from pursuing it by a new and unexpected
alliance between Montfort and the earl of Gloucester, formerly so bitterly opposed to each other.[101] The explanation for this very important
political realignment, which was presumably in the making in the summer of 1260, remains elusive. The St Albans chronicler, in noting an
earlier move on Gloucester's part for the postponement of Montfort's
trial, suggests that Gloucester was afraid of revelations of his own
attempts to discredit the Lord Edward in the eyes of the king.[102] One
wonders how the queen viewed the matter, since she had undoubtedly
been instrumental in securing Gloucester's support in 1257–8 and he had

---

[97] Jacob, 'A Proposal for Arbitration between Simon de Montfort and Henry III in 1260', 80–2.

[98] Powicke, 'The Archbishop of Rouen, John de Harcourt and Simon de Montfort in 1260', 108–13; Maddicott, *Montfort*, 197–9.

[99] E 101/349/26 m. 5.

[100] *DBM*, 194–211.

[101] Ridgeway, 'Henry III's Grievances', 231–2.

[102] *Flores*, ii. 446–9.

apparently remained a firm ally up to the point of his departure from France to England in March 1260; in the summer of 1260 he was still much in evidence at court and on the council.

The queen, having taken a gracious farewell of the Flemish knights in May and June, enjoyed the king's favour. One of her senior clerks, John de Whatley, was presented to the Somerset church of Bleadon; her wardrobe keeper Hugh de la Penne was given stone to build the chancel of his church at Stanton Harcourt in Oxfordshire, an elegant structure which still survives, closed by its original thirteenth-century screen, and the Lady Willelma's executors were given control of her revenues for five years.[103] In June the works on the queen's apartments at Windsor castle, her main place of residence, were forwarded.[104] Such evidence of the king's kindness towards her would have been very acceptable to Eleanor, but she had as much as ever to disquiet her in Edward's behaviour. Several incidents show his determination to take a dissident line. He backed away from his father's attempt to pressure him into exonerating Roger Mortimer from all blame over the capture of Builth castle by the Welsh on 17 July.[105] In the complicated struggle over Bigorre in Gascony, where Gaston de Béarn was acting in concert with the claimant Esquivat de Chabbanais and in opposition to Simon de Montfort, the Lord Edward decided to help Montfort. To this end, in August 1260, he dispatched three of his Lusignan uncles to assist in fortifying the strongholds of Lourdes and Tarbes on Montfort's behalf against the other claimants. In the truce in the Bigorre conflict, concluded on 2 October 1260, Montfort was represented by William de Valence and Geoffrey de Lusignan.[106] This open association of Edward with both Montfort and the Lusignans must have brought home to Eleanor the hollowness of the recent reconciliation with her son.

The third incident has an interest beyond its connection with the Lord Edward. On 9 August 1260 Walter Kirkham bishop of Durham died. The ensuing tussle between Crown and chapter over the election of a successor occasioned the writing of a report, clearly contemporary, by a monk of Durham, perhaps one of the two who travelled south to seek from the king at Winchester the licence to elect a new bishop.[107] The report, whose significance was first recognized by David Carpenter, presents a remarkably vivid and convincing picture of Eleanor of Prov-

---

[103] *CPR 1258–66*, 71; *CR 1259–61*, 50.

[104] *CR 1259–61*, 57.

[105] *CPR 1258–66*, 85.

[106] C 61/4 m. 1, printed in *Rôles Gascons*, i (Supplement), xcii–xciii; Maddicott, *Montfort*, 200.

[107] Muniments of the Dean and Chapter of Durham, Loc. 1. 60 m. 3d.

ence in the summer of 1260. Her style of influence with her husband, the high value which she placed on the abilities of John Mansel and her close collusive relationship with him, the almost automatic dissent of the Lord Edward from the political stance of his mother and father are all facets of the situation which thrust through the restrained, slightly informal style of the report. The events are best told in their natural story sequence.

At the time of Kirkham's death on 9 August 1260 the king and queen were almost certainly already together at Windsor.[108] Informal news of the vacancy would have reached them quickly, so they would have been able to discuss their strategy for the filling of this very wealthy bishopric, situated in a politically sensitive position on the Scottish border. It was evidently determined by the king and queen that their clerk John Mansel should be put forward for Durham. In the last month at St Omer, Mansel would have been their chief counsellor and it is possible that this very clever man masterminded the king's political manoeuvres while abroad and the impressive style of his return to England. The first step towards thrusting Mansel into Durham must be the selection of the right keeper for the vacant bishopric, and for this the king chose Mansel's nephew and namesake Master John Mansel. Here the king was chancing his arm, for according to the Provisions of Oxford the appointment of a keeper of a vacant bishopric was a matter for the council. The St Albans chronicler noted that the king's initiative was out of order and a memorandum on the patent roll stated that this appointment was made 'by order of the king by the mandate of John Mansel'.[109] Mansel himself presumably had the whole matter in hand and the queen's eager support may be deduced from what comes next.

When the two monks from the Durham chapter arrived at Winchester to request the licence to elect, the queen was at Marlborough. The monks were kindly received by the king and invited to dine with him, but immediately after the meal a messenger arrived from the queen with letters asking the king to request that John Mansel should be elected. The king then listened to the letters from the chapter and granted the licence to elect, 'adding that it was fitting that he should urge the chapter on behalf of John Mansel'. The licence to elect was dated 28 August and two days later the king and queen wrote separately from Winchester and Marlborough respectively, to urge the chapter to elect John Mansel.[110] The queen's letter is persuasive, fluent and gracious, written in a style wholly characteristic of the many extant letters of her dowagership. The

---

[108] The queen was at Windsor on 7 August (E 101/345/26 m. 5) and the king by 8 August (*CPR 1258–66*, 87).

[109] *Flores*, ii. 455; *CPR 1258–66*, 90.

[110] Issue of licence, *CPR 1258–66*, 91.

king's letter is shorter and may have been based on the queen's. Eleanor explains to the monks that because of the pre-eminence of the church of Durham she has been pondering all the more seriously on how its prestige could be even further enhanced and she then commends Mansel as a man circumspect in things temporal and spiritual. With serene disregard for the political turmoil of 1258–60, she assures the monks that the kingdom has long been happily governed by the counsel of John Mansel, who is 'specially and deeply regarded' by both the king and herself and who is a man of moral probity.

It is clear that Eleanor assumes that the Durham chapter will regard her intervention as 'acceptable' in conventional terms. Yet the two Durham monks were shrewd men, alert to current political tensions. By a swift messenger they sent back to Durham transcripts of the licence to elect and of the king's own letter in favour of Mansel and they also described to their brethren 'the state of the court as far as they were able to perceive it'. It is pretty clear that their observations encouraged them to think in terms of an independent choice on the part of the chapter, and they may not have been too surprised when another letter arrived at Durham, written little more than a week after the letters of his parents, from the Lord Edward. Edward had no liking for Mansel, who was much too close to his mother's policies, and he decided to sport a rival. He decided on Hugh Cantilupe, archdeacon of Gloucester, a nephew of Walter Cantilupe, Montfort's unfailing friend and ally. Edward's letter has some entertaining and some interesting touches. Among Hugh's eminent qualities Edward mentions his high birth, no doubt well aware that John Mansel was the illegitimate son of a country priest. Significant politically is his statement that the appointment of Hugh would be pleasing not only to himself but 'to the whole people'. Edward was by now well schooled in the importance of looking beyond the baronage. Perhaps with tongue in cheek he urges the chapter not to be moved by undue pressures, while assuring them that they will earn his own assistance and goodwill by following his advice. In the end the monks of Durham on 30 September elected one of their own number, Robert Stichill prior of Coldingham.[111] They had judged the situation at court with considerable acumen. The king was not in a strong enough position to reject their candidate. Robert Stichill wisely timed his arrival in London to coincide with the sitting of the October parliament and the king was fairly soon reconciled to his election. John Mansel had lost his last chance of a great English bishopric and the queen's hopes were dashed.[112]

[111] *Flores*, ii. 455.
[112] Ibid., ii. 456.

At this point there can be little doubt that the queen was losing ground politically. Peter of Savoy had been absent abroad for nearly the whole year, only returning in late November 1260, and it is likely that his absence weakened the queen's position. Montfort and Edward, still in close alliance, evidently determined to use the popularity of their cause, still regarded as the cause of reform, to beguile the October parliament into forwarding their own men and their own interests. This was the kind of manipulation in which Montfort already showed great skill. With open disrespect for the king he deliberately risked an arrogant gesture by appointing Henry of Almain to deputize for him as steward in the St Edward's Day ceremonies, not troubling to wait for the king's summons.[113] The king resented it. On the initiative of Montfort and Edward the offices of justiciar, chancellor and treasurer were now filled by men connected with themselves and unacceptable to the king. All this was grievous to the queen as well as to the king.[114] Perhaps equally unsettling for Eleanor was the new alliance between Montfort and Gloucester, so recently her own ally. As has been seen, Gloucester and Montfort together prevented the resumption of Montfort's trial while, to accommodate Gloucester's conservative views, the provision for reform in relation to the great baronies was modified.[115]

There was much more than parliamentary politics to grieve the queen. In the ceremonies of St Edward's Day Henry III knighted his son-in-law, John of Brittany. The young man, now much in Edward's company, can hardly have taken a favourable view of Peter of Savoy's tenacious grasp on the earldom of Richmond, and behind Peter of Savoy stood the queen, whose loyalties in the matter were perhaps divided. The knighting of the young Breton was followed by the knighting of the two eldest sons of Simon de Montfort, carried out by the Lord Edward himself.[116] It is clear from the king's complaints against his council in March 1261 that Henry believed that for some time Montfort had been deliberately seducing Edward from 'his father's friendship and obedience'.[117] When Edward left in October 1260 to try his luck in the continental tournament circuit his company included his friends Henry of Almain and John de Warenne, John of Brittany and the two young Montforts, and the three men who

---

[113] *CPR 1258–66*, 96; Ridgeway, 'Henry III's Grievances', 230, 241 (clause 29); Maddicott, *Montfort*, 200.

[114] For significant revision of Treharne's view of appointments (*Baronial Plan*, 245) see Ridgeway, 'Politics', 370–2, also 'Henry III's Grievances', 230–1.

[115] Ridgeway, 'Henry III's Grievances', 231 and 241 (clause 31); Treharne, *Baronial Plan*, 246–7; Maddicott, *Montfort*, 201–2.

[116] *Flores*, ii. 456.

[117] *DBM*, 216–17 (clause 21).

had been removed from their castellanies after Edward's 'reconciliation' with his parents in May, Roger Clifford, Roger Leybourne and Hamo Lestrange; it was a grouping to rouse the queen's foreboding.[118] Edward's behaviour abroad would have increased her anger. On 27 November in Paris he conferred his Kentish manor of Elham on his steward Roger Leybourne, an act witnessed by all four of Edward's exiled Lusignan uncles.[119] In 1257 Edward had mortgaged Elham to Archbishop Boniface for five years; that term was not up, adding a final touch of impertinent defiance to an act which again placed Edward alongside the Lusignans and against his mother's Savoyard connections.[120] The queen would have felt that defiance and the implied threat to her own influence much more sharply than the king, who was still hoping for Aymer de Lusignan's reinstatement as bishop of Winchester and was looking forward to the eventual return of his other half-brothers to England.

For Edward, friendship with the Lusignans, who encouraged his bid for more independent control of his appanage, had powerful attractions, both personal and political. He associated his former Savoyard mentors with the policy of restriction of his power to appoint officials or to make any alienations from his lands. Early in 1261 he evidently appointed Guy de Lusignan as his 'lieutenant' in Gascony and possibly confirmed him in possession of ancestral lands in the Isle of Oléron. This was done without reference to the king, who complained of it in his list of grievances against the council in March 1261, holding the council responsible for Edward's rebelliousness.[121] Edward's behaviour continued to defy what he knew to be the policies of the queen and Peter of Savoy. This mutual hostility represented a rift within the royal family which might vitiate any attempt to restore the king's power. The question was, could that rift be healed?

[118] Wait, 'Household and Resources', 258–9.

[119] E 368/94 m. 47 (Studd, 'Acts of the Lord Edward', no. 862).

[120] Ch. 6, above.

[121] *Gascon Register A*, ii, no. 99 (pp. 419–20); Ridgeway, 'Henry III's Grievances', 240 (clause 20); CPR 1258–66, 141; *Foedera*, i. 404.

8

Reaction

Eleanor of Provence had no mind to give way under the problems which pressed upon herself and her husband towards the end of the year 1260. The worsening situation hardened her resolution to enter into a scheme to overthrow the whole programme of the Provisions of Oxford, which she now hated as interfering with her own prerogatives, severely restricting the power of the king and demeaning his position. This plan probably began to take shape over the turn of the year. By December 1260 Edward and his young tourneying fraternity were for the time being out of the way; Montfort left for France early in December and Gloucester ceased to frequent the court at about the same time. In short, the king was rid for a while of his most troublesome opponents, and he had more friendly men about him. Richard of Cornwall had returned to England in October, a seasoned statesman, still loyal to his brother and prepared to help him recover royal power; Richard too was a king.[1] Richard's return was seen by the chronicler of Battle abbey as a main factor in the king's political recovery, but Richard was only intermittently at court, preserving a certain customary detachment from day-to-day planning.[2] The return of Peter of Savoy, probably in late November, must certainly have been of much greater immediate support to the queen. A close-knit group of advisers now formed round the king, consisting of the queen herself, Peter of Savoy, John Mansel and Robert Walerand, further backed by the Savoyards Ebulo de Montibus and Imbert de Montferrand.[3] It is

---

[1] Ridgeway, 'Politics', 377–9.
[2] Battle Chronicle in Bémont, *Simon de Montfort* (1st edn), 374; Denholm-Young, *Richard of Cornwall*, 106–7.
[3] Ridgeway, 'Politics', 378; Treharne, *Baronial Plan*, 250–1.

probably to this group rather than to any one individual that one should look for the devising and execution of the plan which was put into action in 1261. It was precisely because of their success as a deeply committed team that they were identified as such when the angry surge of opposition came in the early summer of 1261 and they were to be the chief victims of the lawless vengeance that was to be wreaked two years later.[4]

Action on a plan of royal recovery had begun before the end of January 1261, when John Mansel's nephew and namesake, Master John Mansel, was dispatched to Rome.[5] Here the papal agents, Arlotus and Rostand, long in Henry III's confidence, used their influence with Alexander IV to secure the bull which would release the king from his oath to observe the Provisions of Oxford.[6] It was not of course the king alone who needed to be absolved, but the queen and the royal princes and beyond them the prelates, magnates and others who had been 'forced' to swear to the Provisions. To secure these bulls of absolution was vital to any plan for the restoration of the king's authority; without them, any move which implied reversal of the Provisions would be vitiated by that most serious of moral charges, perjury. The chroniclers of Bury St Edmunds, Waverley and Tewkesbury specifically blamed the queen for turning the king against the Provisions and for reneging on them herself.[7] Robert of Gloucester claimed that this was always her intention 'with counsel or with message or with woman's trick'.[8] In fact, of course, no chronicler had inside information of the planning that went on among those close to the king at Windsor in the early months of 1261, but it cannot be doubted that the queen wholeheartedly concurred in this move and that she may have been among the most active in promoting it. It was she who was generally blamed for it.

Pending the return of John Mansel junior from Rome, the king, guided by his advisers, made vigorous efforts to overturn the authority of the council and to seize the political initiative. He nevertheless proceeded warily, attempting to gather supporters, to give an appearance of reason and moderation and to outwit his opponents. On 9 February he had moved from Windsor to the Tower, taking his advisers with him.[9] He was determined that the approaching Candlemas parliament should not follow the humiliating example of the parliament of the previous Octo-

---

[4] *Flores*, ii. 467, and below.
[5] *CR 1259–61*, 340, 377.
[6] *Royal Letters*, ii, no. 571 (p. 209).
[7] *Ann. Waverley*, 355; *Chron. Bury St Edmunds*, 26–7; *Ann. Tewkesbury*, 175.
[8] *Robert of Gloucester*, ii. 735.
[9] *Flores*, ii. 467; Carpenter, 'Henry III and the Tower of London', 205.

ber. Henry's present assertive mood was clear from his summons of twenty-seven barons, mostly minor ones, to come armed to the parliament.[10] In his speech to the assembled magnates he then made his first statement of his grievances against the council; these were put in writing on 9 March and a second, harsher version, including new charges, was drawn up shortly afterwards. This in turn was followed by a third and more conciliatory version, evidently intended to be used as the basis for arbitration.[11] All these statements comprised an important justification of Henry's own position and his present actions. The king claimed with some justice that the council had encroached on royal authority beyond what had been authorized by the original Provisions, that royal revenues had been allowed to decline and that the council had failed him in important matters of diplomacy. About 14 March the king agreed to submit his complaints to arbitration, while at the same time he agreed to an arbitration by Louis IX on his personal differences with Simon de Montfort.[12] Both arbitrations failed.

The queen and Henry's other advisers were well aware of the king's real aim, the strengthening of the royal position in both political and military terms so that he might destroy the power of his opponents once he had the papal bulls of absolution in his hands. Meanwhile there were other political issues to be addressed, alongside preparations for the presence of an armed force of foreign knights which could ensure the success of the final coup.

The resolution of personal and political issues within the royal family itself was now of high priority and this was going to be a grave problem for the queen. Aymer de Lusignan had died abroad in December 1260, to the king's great grief, but Henry was now determined to admit his other half-brothers and other exiled Poitevins back into England. Not only was Henry's affection for the Lusignans undiminished, but he felt a natural dependence on their political and military support.[13] He would no longer tolerate this division in his family, and he was well aware of course that the Lord Edward had made the Lusignans his friends and allies. The queen had no power to prevent their return, yet these men had injured her deeply; on whatever grounds, they had defamed her, and she had felt the triumph of seeing them expelled from England in 1258. There can be little doubt that Eleanor experienced a sense of failure and of humiliation

---

[10] *CR 1259–61*, 457.

[11] For first and third versions see *DBM*, 210–19 and 218–39, and for the intermediate (Durham) version see Ridgeway, 'Henry III's Grievances', Appendix, 239–42; for comment on the three versions, ibid., 227–38.

[12] *CPR 1258–66*, 145–6; Maddicott, *Montfort*, 207.

[13] Treharne, *Baronial Plan*, 256–7; Ridgeway, 'Politics', 393.

over the king's insistence on their return. Those feelings were not ignored by her husband. Whether the initiative came from Peter of Savoy, from her sister Margaret or from the queen herself, we do not know, but she was able to secure her husband's co-operation in laying down that any of the Lusignans about to be readmitted to England must first make a personal undertaking to the queen of France. There is no record of what that undertaking was, but it is not hard to deduce. The Lusignans were evidently to foreswear any repetition of their former machinations against the queen. William de Valence apparently jibbed at this requirement, but the king made the terms of readmittance clear.[14] He was loyal to his wife as well as to his half-brothers.

William de Valence arrived in England in the company of the Lord Edward towards the end of April and was officially received into the king's favour on 30 April.[15] Whether or not Edward initially persisted in opposition to his father, as the St Albans chronicler believed, by the end of May his support for the king had been secured.[16] The possible role of the queen in this is not easy to determine. According to the St Albans *Flores*, she had already played a part in winning over some of the king's opponents, and a letter of Peter of Savoy, which almost certainly dates from this time, shows that he too was urging the king to make grants to various named knights, several in Edward's service, in order to encourage others to the king's side.[17] The reasons for Edward's submission to his father's policy at this point have been much debated, and it has recently been pointed out that the greatest single factor was probably Edward's state of near-bankruptcy.[18] The king was prepared to bail him out and Edward's desperate need of financial help perhaps left him no other political option than loyalty to his father. In June 1261 Henry made grants to Edward from judicial profits and from the Jewry and in August the king repaid a large loan of £4,000 of Tours (c.£1,000 sterling) from Louis IX to Edward, on security of certain of Edward's lands.[19] The author of the *Annals of London*, however, claims that Edward was won over by the flattery of his mother. The context of this statement is interesting: 'From that time Edward the king's son, flattered by his

---

[14] *CR 1259–61*, 467 and *Diplomatic Documents*, i, no. 325. Treharne fails to grasp the significance of this (*Baronial Plan*, 257) but it is elucidated by Ridgeway, 'Politics', 393.

[15] *CPR 1258–66*, 150; *Cron. Maiorum*, 49.

[16] *Flores*, ii. 466. Treharne dismisses this account as without foundation (*Baronial Plan*, 258, n. 1), but Michael Prestwich (*Edward I*, 35–6) and Huw Ridgeway ('Politics', 385) treat it more cautiously.

[17] *Flores*, ii. 467; SC 1/5/26, cited by Ridgeway, 'Politics', 392.

[18] As strongly argued by Ridgeway, 'Politics', 385–7.

[19] *CR 1259–61*, 396–7; *CPR 1258–66*, 170.

mother, held to his father's side and favoured aliens as kinsfolk.'[20] Edward was too clever and too disaffected to accede to his mother's 'flattery', but he may have been influenced by her persuasion, especially in view of her recent, however reluctant, acceptance of the return of the Lusignans. He was also sharp enough to realize that a struggle on behalf of royal authority was one that touched him nearly. The further comment that from this time onwards he favoured aliens may certainly reflect his mother's influence. Two French knights, Erard de Valery and John Britaud, had been in Edward's entourage as early as November 1260, and when he went abroad again in July 1261, having broken with a group of his former English friends, he began to draw into his entourage other distinguished foreign knights from Flanders and Champagne; these were areas where his mother and Savoyard uncles had contacts.[21] They were men of standing and there can be no doubt that Edward's former friends, and especially the Marcher contingent, Clifford, Leybourne, Lestrange and their allies, would have blamed the queen for driving a wedge between themselves and Edward.[22] They were soon to feel her keen resentment against them even more sharply.

In May 1261 the reuniting of the king's family was only one of the preconditions of a successful royal coup. The other was a show of armed strength. This had been some little while in preparation. Huw Ridgeway has pointed out that as early as December 1260 knights of the Savoyard connection and with military experience, such as Simon de Joinville, Baldwin de Villa and Baldwin de Fiennes were receiving robes from the king.[23] The invaluable Ingram de Fiennes, who was a regular contact for the English Crown with knights of northern France and Flanders, received a ring from the queen at Windsor on 13 January 1261.[24] Since the king was elsewhere at the time, Ingram had clearly come to talk with Queen Eleanor. The queen had, as we have seen, established contacts with various foreign knights who had accompanied the king and herself to England from St Omer in April 1260. She foresaw that such men would be needed again.[25]

At the end of April 1261 Henry ventured to leave the Tower of London, making his way to Dover, where he placed the castle in the

---

[20] *Ann. London*, 57.

[21] E 368/94 m. 47 (see ch. 7 n. 119, above); Wait, 'Household and Resources', 290–2.

[22] *Flores*, iii. 256; see analysis of Edward's knightly entourage by Hilary Wait, 'Household and Resources', 258–68; Carpenter, '"Statute" against Aliens', 271; Maddicott, *Montfort*, 223.

[23] *CR 1259–61*, 319; Ridgeway, 'Politics', 378.

[24] E 101/349/26 m. 5.

[25] Ingram de Fiennes was organizing foreign knights for the king later in this year, *CR 1261–4*, 3.

hands of Robert Walerand, who was also made warden of the Cinque Ports.[26] This secured the means of entry for the foreign knights, whom Henry now summoned to his assistance. On 4 May he wrote to the bailiffs of the French Channel ports requesting passage for the count of St Pol, Gerard de Rodes and Alenard de Seningham, 'together with their knights, horses and arms'.[27] The queen, accounting these men as friends, welcomed them warmly when they arrived later in the month to strengthen the king's presence in Winchester. This was the place he had chosen for the dramatic climax of his recent moves to reassert his sovereignty: the publication of the papal bulls of absolution, which were now in his hands. Travelling with her own entourage towards Winchester, apparently some distance behind the king, Queen Eleanor paused at Sutton on her way through Hampshire. Here on 4 June she received the count of St Pol and gave rings to the count and eight of his companions.[28] This open association with the highly unpopular foreign military contingents, at a time when she was not actually with the king, would have been noticed. It was easy to infer that it was the queen who was encouraging the king to bring in alien knights to intimidate his own subjects. At Winchester, a few days later, the papal bulls were published in the course of the Whitsuntide celebrations, and the king regarded himself as henceforth unshackled. With his new freedom now legitimate in his own eyes, Henry quickly proceeded to further initiatives, replacing two of the great officers of state, appointed in the October parliament, by men loyal to himself, Philip Basset as justiciar and Walter Merton as chancellor.[29] The queen would have been well satisfied with the outcome of the plot which she had almost certainly helped to devise.

Yet the sequel was by no means reassuring. The reform movement was far from being a spent force. In some respects it had made an indelible mark on English political life. More immediately, there was a powerful reaction to the king's royalist coup and his rejection of the Provisions of Oxford, and an attempt was made by the reformers to rally the barons to assemble in arms at Winchester without delay. Henry, being warned of this by John Mansel, was able to withdraw with his queen to the safety of the Tower of London on 22 June.[30] The widespread surge of opposition to the king acquired a new injection of anger when he took the step on 8/9 July of dismissing many baronial castellans and twenty-two sheriffs appointed according to the Provisions, replacing them with his

---

[26] *CPR 1258–66*, 151; *Gervase of Canterbury*, ii. 212.
[27] *CPR 1258–66*, 152; Treharne, *Baronial Plan*, 257.
[28] E 101/349/26 mm. 5, 8.
[29] *Flores*, ii. 469–70; *CPR 1258–66*, 165, 172.
[30] *Flores*, ii. 470–1; Carpenter, 'Henry III and the Tower of London', 205.

own nominees.[31] This touched the men of the shires on the aspect of the reform movement which had mattered most to them. In response, the baronial party, under Montfort's direction, appointed their own 'keepers of the peace' in many counties, a move which rallied active support to their cause in the localities.[32] In Gloucester it led to a dramatic incident in which the queen's steward Matthias Bezill played a violent part. Bezill, who was sheriff of Gloucester and also castellan, determined to take action against the baronial keeper of the peace, William de Tracy, when the latter attempted to hold a session of the shire court. Forcing his way into the court, followed by his own men with their swords drawn, Bezill made for the dais, dragged Tracy out of the hall and hurled him into the mire. There Bezill's men ran their horses at him and finally took him off to prison. This is the account given by Robert of Gloucester, who had local knowledge.[33] Although the incident evidently caused a stir, the king gave unfaltering support to Bezill.[34] Matthias Bezill's close link with the queen was well known and he was to be an early victim of the baronial rising of 1263. Despite his valour, he harmed the queen's reputation.

In the summer of 1261 widespread anger at the king's treachery strengthened baronial resistance. At magnate level, Montfort and the earl of Gloucester were backed by John de Warenne and Hugh Despenser and also by the moderate Roger Bigod, earl of Norfolk and Hugh Bigod, formerly justiciar.[35] They had many baronial supporters and in September a defiant attempt was made to rally opposition to the Crown much more widely, by the issue of a summons to three knights from each shire to attend a parliament to be held at St Albans on 21 September, without the king's authority. Henry countered swiftly by summoning the knights to Windsor on the same day; apparently no parliament was held in either place.[36] The king and queen by now expected and actively prepared for an armed conflict. Henry planned help from abroad, on a far bigger scale than he had judged necessary in the previous May. In August he was summoning help not only from the French and Flemish knights who had come to his aid before, and from many other named knights from lands across the Channel, but also from the countess of Flanders and the duchess of Brabant, from the countess of Provence, from Gaston de

[31] *CPR 1258–66*, 162–4; Treharne, *Baronial Plan*, 263; Maddicott, *Montfort*, 212.

[32] *Flores*, ii. 473–4; *Cron. Maiorum*, 49; *Gervase of Canterbury*, ii. 211; *Ann. Dunstable*, 217; Treharne, *Baronial Plan*, 267–8.

[33] *Robert of Gloucester*, ii. 736–7.

[34] *CPR 1258–66*, 220.

[35] *Gervase of Canterbury*, ii. 211.

[36] Treharne, *Baronial Plan*, 266.

Béarn in Gascony, from Philip of Savoy in Lyon, and from the faithful Savoyard archbishops of Embrun and Tarentaise. It is significant that in writing to the count of Boulogne, Henry refers to the foreign knights as his friends (*amicos*). Many were asked to bring substantial contingents with them. Henry III did not underestimate the strength of the potential opposition which he faced in England. He made preparations for the crossing of most of the foreign knights to Dover in the first week in November, and meanwhile summoned his own tenants-in-chief to come to London, fully equipped with horses and arms, by 29 October.[37]

The queen's personal contacts with many of those abroad to whom the king turned are evident. More surprising is the part with which she is credited in some chronicles in the negotiations with the rebellious barons in England, which in the end made these huge military preparations unnecessary. The critical point was reached in mid-October when the earl of Gloucester suddenly ended his year-old alliance with Montfort and agreed to parley with the king. The effect was dramatic. The baronial opposition broke up in confusion, Simon de Montfort left England in disgust, and through consultations between Gloucester and Richard of Cornwall the Treaty of Kingston was agreed on 21 November. Victory lay with the king, since the treaty provided for further stages of arbitration by Richard of Cornwall, which ensured decisions in the interest of the Crown.[38] What part, if any, did Eleanor of Provence play in the all-important defection of Gloucester from the opposition and perhaps that of other magnates? The Waverley chronicler, in a passage which probably refers to 1261, states that the queen and John Mansel, 'who would do his utmost for the queen', won over some of the waverers among the barons.[39] The Battle chronicle states more specifically that Gloucester was moved 'by promises or by the favour of the queen'.[40] There is little here to be sure about, but it seems likely that the queen was known to have been active in approaching some of the baronial supporters in the course of 1261, and it is just possible that she made a decisive appeal to Gloucester in the autumn. For the moment an armed confrontation between the king and his opponents had been averted.

Eleanor of Provence was deeply occupied by political events, but not to the exclusion of other more personal concerns which touched her just as closely. In July her daughter Beatrice left for Brittany, taking with her some seventy rings given her by her mother, obviously for redistribution,

---

[37] CR 1259–61, 487–8, 495–6, 496–9.

[38] *Foedera*, i. 415; CR 1261–64, 126; *Ann. Osney*, 128–9; Maddicott, *Montfort*, 214.

[39] *Ann. Waverley*, 355.

[40] Battle Chronicle in Bémont, *Simon de Montfort* (1st edn), 374; see Ridgeway, 'Politics', 390.

like those given to Isabella de Fiennes.[41] The princess was accompanied by the queen's protégé Ebulo de Montibus, and on reaching Nantes they were entertained by Geoffrey de Lusignan, the Lusignans having close contacts with the ducal house of Brittany. Geoffrey wrote to Henry III of the safe arrival of the travellers.[42] The letter is interesting for its courtly *débonaireté* in treating delicate matters. Geoffrey discreetly accepts the need to give certain personal assurances to the queen of France before he visits England; he makes no difficulties. In light vein he mentions ruefully that he has caught Ebulo de Montibus's tertian fever, but one senses that there is a relaxing of tensions between Savoyards and Lusignans. Although Ebulo de Montibus was a member of the Savoyard faction at the English court he was now a welcome guest at Nantes; except for his tiresome fever. Following hard upon the departure of Beatrice came the death of Eleanor's sister Sanchia, on 9 November 1261. This broke what was probably one of Eleanor's closest personal relationships, judging by earlier evidence.[43] Sanchia was buried in Hailes abbey in the presence of her Savoyard uncles, Archbishop Boniface and Peter of Savoy, and the arms of Provence still mark the walls of the little parish church at Hailes with their striking vertical design. Sanchia's stepson Henry of Almain had little love of the Savoyards, but Sanchia remembered him in her will. When he visited the queen on 2 February 1262 she gave him a ring on her own account, and also a belt 'which the queen of Almain had bequeathed to him'.[44] Within the decade Henry had been brutally murdered in Viterbo and his body too was laid to rest at Hailes.

The last month of 1261 and the first half of 1262 was a period stiff with diplomatic activity. Alexander IV had died in May 1261 and there was a vital need to secure from his successor, Urban IV, a confirmation of Pope Alexander's absolution of the king, the queen and their children, together with various great men of the realm, from their oaths to the Provisions of Oxford. The bull was secured, but only in the teeth of strong opposition from certain cardinals who were working in the interests of Montfort and the reformers for a reversal of Alexander IV's policy.[45] The new pope proved less ready to listen to Henry's request for the renewal of Edmund's candidature for the crown of Sicily. Although Henry sought backing from the king and queen of France

---

[41] E 101/349/26 mm. 5, 6.

[42] *Diplomatic Documents*, i, no. 325. It was intended as late as 21 July 1261 that Henry of Wingham should accompany Beatrice, ch. 4, n. 93, above.

[43] *Ann. Osney*, 128. The queen's messenger list for 1252–3 showed frequent contact at that time.

[44] E 101/349/26 m. 8.

[45] *DBM*, 248–51; *Royal Letters*, ii, no. 571.

and the king and queen of Navarre, it was to no effect; the pope had decided to place his hopes on Charles of Anjou, who now seemed a far more promising candidate.[46] A more immediate matter was Henry's need for a settlement with the Montforts. The king was now acutely aware of Montfort's capacity to cause trouble in England and he felt the urgency both of reaching a settlement and of discrediting Montfort in the eyes of the French court, where the earl's reputation still stood high. Simon and his wife had indicated their willingness to agree to the arbitration of Queen Margaret and this was now put in hand.[47]

Meanwhile, the political success of the king in restoring his authority, begun in 1261 and continued in 1262, had the effect of consolidating the influence of the queen's set at court. This was not exclusively a Savoyard grouping, since John Mansel and Robert Walerand were key participants, but the Savoyard element was so noticeable that it could readily be dubbed 'alien' by its enemies.[48] Peter of Savoy was a dominant member, and his bond with the queen was as strong as ever. When Peter went abroad in June 1262 to deal with political developments in Savoy it was the queen, together with his Savoyard steward Guichard de Charron, who took charge of his affairs in England.[49] At the same time he was permitted to make a most advantageous exchange of land with the Lord Edward, by which Peter acquired the honour of Hastings in exchange for a group of less prestigious manors in his Richmond earldom.[50] It was clearly the interests of Edward which were being sacrificed but Edward was evidently powerless to prevent it. Further favours for Peter followed, including allowance of the issues of the honour of Richmond to his executors for seven years after his death.[51] The king set the highest value on Peter's diplomatic assistance, urging him at the end of June to go quickly to France, 'where we shall be in the greatest need of your presence'.[52] Although Peter's personal ascendancy at court was unique, there were other Savoyards influential in the royal counsels.[53] Among those most intimate with the queen were Ebulo de Montibus, a frequent witness to royal charters throughout 1261 and steward of the king's household from February 1262, and Henry of Ghent, long in Savoyard service and keeper of the king's wardrobe from July 1261.[54]

---

[46] *CR 1261–64*, 112–14, 121.
[47] Maddicott, *Montfort*, 217–18.
[48] Ridgeway, 'Politics', 390, 394–8.
[49] *CPR 1258–66*, 214.
[50] *CChR 1257–1300*, 42.
[51] *CPR 1258–66*, 161.
[52] *CR 1261–64*, 131.
[53] Ridgeway, 'Politics', 390–3.
[54] Tout, *Chapters*, vi. 38, 25.

Imbert de Montferrand, one of the king's marshals, was another of this group, acting with Robert Walerand as a keeper of the king's seal during John Mansel's illness in France in 1262; Montferrand later became a member of Queen Eleanor's household.[55] The queen herself was central to this powerful clique. In the summer of 1262 the king was well satisfied to follow their counsel, for they were dedicated to forwarding his interests. By outsiders they were increasingly seen as an all-powerful alien faction, responsible for the overthrow of the Provisions and all that the reform movement stood for. They had come to be as unpopular as the Lusignans had been in 1258.

One group of men hated the court establishment more keenly than most. These were the young Marcher lords who had followed Edward's fortunes in 1259 and 1260, had tourneyed with him in France in 1260–1, but who had broken with him and he with them in the summer of 1261, around the time of Edward's second reconciliation with his parents. Some of Edward's followers, as we have seen, had been won over to the king at that time as a matter of deliberate policy, a policy pushed by Peter of Savoy, and no doubt by the queen. But there was still a group who resisted, or were not even wooed, the most prominent being Leybourne, Clifford and Lestrange. These were the men who had lost their castellanies in May 1260 and who rightly believed that the present establishment at court was thoroughly hostile to them. Their resentment was soon to become dangerous.

At Michaelmas 1261 Henry III had ordered a general audit of the accounts of Edward's bailiffs. This was held in London rather than in Bristol and specific mention was made of Roger Leybourne, Roger Clifford and Roger de Stoke.[56] Roger Leybourne had ceased to be Edward's steward by July 1261 and had been replaced by John le Breton, who was now closely associated with the inquiry, which was extended and intensified in Hilary term 1262. Debtors were identified, Leybourne and Clifford among them, and Leybourne was charged with a particularly heavy debt.[57] Scholars differ on the extent to which the motive for the inquiry was the king's genuine concern about maladministration of his son's affairs. There is also disagreement as to how far Edward himself supported the inquiry.[58] Yet there can be little doubt that as the investigation gathered momentum there was an element of victimization of

---

[55] *CPR 1266–72* (Appendix), 734; *CPR 1273–81*, 75; *CChR 1257–1300*, 217.

[56] E 159/36 m. 8d. In November 1259 it was Roger de Stoke who had replaced John Mansel as Edward's constable at Tickhill, C 61/4 m. 5.

[57] For the fullest discussion of the audit see Wait, 'Household and Resources', 320–31.

[58] Studd, 'The Lord Edward and Henry III', 12; Ridgeway, 'Politics', 389; Maddicott, *Montfort*, 220.

Roger Leybourne, and to a lesser extent of Roger Clifford. Independently of the inquiry, Leybourne was deprived in April 1262 of the manor of Elham, granted to him by Edward, on the grounds that it was a demense manor and should not have been alienated from the Crown.[59] Leybourne was angry, angry with Edward and angry with the court establishment which he believed to be deliberately hunting him down. By the summer of 1262 he was in open revolt.[60] Moreover, he had friends. In August 1262, by which time the king and Eleanor were in France, the justiciar, in the king's name, ordered Leybourne, Clifford, John Giffard and Hamo Lestrange, among others, not to tourney or go about in arms.[61] These men were already in a mood to threaten the peace of the realm. Excluded from favour and patronage, they may have felt they had little to lose.

One chronicler, and only one, gives a prominent role in this story to the queen, but since this is the Canterbury/Dover chronicler, usually reliable and in this case dealing with events in his own county and the fortunes of a leading Kentish landholder, his version of the story carries weight. According to this, it was the queen, moved by malice, who incited Edward against Leybourne.[62] Certainly there are other slight corroborative wisps of evidence. The two men appointed on 25 July 1262 to investigate the dispersal of Leybourne's goods and to act as receivers, John Weston and William de Salines, were members of Edward's household who also had strong links with the queen, and Geoffrey de Langley, her favoured agent in the fifties, was one of the auditors appointed to investigate the accounts of Edward's bailiffs.[63] The Canterbury/Dover chronicler further asserts that it was 'by instigation of the queen' that the king disseised Leybourne of his lands and goods when he was alleged to have been guilty of peculation.[64] If this chronicler knew at least something of the truth, then the queen for a second time allowed her bitter animosity against a group of men whom she believed to have undermined her son's loyalty, to push her into vindictive action.[65] On this occasion it produced its own violent backlash and the queen's intervention may have brought England a step nearer to civil war. But that outcome lay a year ahead, as the king and queen prepared for their departure for France in July 1262.

---

[59] *CR 1261–64*, 117.
[60] Wait, 'Household and Resources', 327–8.
[61] *CR 1261–64*, 133.
[62] *Gervase of Canterbury*, ii. 220–1.
[63] *CPR 1266–72* (Appendix), 727; *Reg. Thomas Cantilupe*, i. 174.
[64] *Gervase of Canterbury*, ii. 221.
[65] Carpenter, '"Statute" against Aliens', 270–1.

Both Henry and Eleanor at this time made constructive efforts to improve the Lord Edward's liquidity. This was the more positive side of their determination to reassert control over his affairs. He was granted the revenues of the Jewry for three years, during which time the king was to recoup himself from Edward's lands.[66] When Edward traded the first instalment of these revenues to Florentine merchants for a loan of 1,110 marks it was the queen who arranged the deal, confirmed by the king on 1 July 1262.[67] Edward also got 4,000 marks of the 7,000 marks remaining from a Jewish fine with the Crown.[68] Already, in June 1262, the queen and Edward had together sealed a bond with another company of Florentine merchants for a loan of 1,700 marks. The names of those who stood surety for the loan make clear who were the men working with the queen; John Mansel, Philip Basset and Robert Walerand. Edward is referred to in the bond as the first-born son of the queen, rather than the more usual first-born son of the king.[69] The queen may have been giving her son some authoritative guidance in finance. This is the first evidence of the queen's involvement in Edward's affairs since the rupture between them in the late 1250s.

After the king and queen had crossed to France in July, the virtually exclusive influence of Eleanor and her support-group on the king's counsels was underlined even more starkly. The witness lists bear testimony to this. The pro-Savoyard *curiales*, including Ebulo de Montibus, Henry of Ghent, Imbert de Montferrand, Imbert Pugeys and the queen's steward Matthias Bezill, together with John Mansel, Robert Walerand and Ingram de Fiennes, dominated the court.[70] William de Valence and Henry of Almain were among the very few outsiders to this coterie, but after their ineffective attempt to ease the path of Gilbert de Clare to his entry into the earldom of Gloucester, his father Richard having died in July 1262, they both returned to England.[71] The Savoyard group had access to generous patronage from the king. The confirmation of Peter of Savoy's acquisition of Hastings, provision for the marriage of the heiress of Simon de Beauchamp to one of the sons of Thomas of Savoy and the making over of the annual fees of the late Count Amadeus and Thomas to their brother Philip, bishop-elect of Lyon, recall the lavish royal patronage of the 1240s and 1250s. There were also grants to lesser men, Henry of Ghent, Imbert de Montferrand and William de

---

[66] *CPR 1258–66*, 233.
[67] Ibid., 219.
[68] *CR 1261–64*, 84–5.
[69] BL Harleian Charter 43. C. 42.
[70] *CPR 1266–72* (Appendix), 726–40 *passim*.
[71] *Gervase of Canterbury*, ii. 216; Altschul, *A Baronial Family*, 95–6.

Chauvent.[72] The queen herself received the most significant grant of all in a more explicit and generous dower settlement. This should not be seen as a document hastily concocted in response to the king's serious illness, although that may have been the immediate occasion for its publication; it bears all the marks of careful preparation and practical foresight on the part of the queen and her friends.

The outline of this important settlement was broadly and very boldly conceived.[73] The enhanced dower allocation of 1253 is not referred to. Instead, the original settlement of 1236 is rehearsed and confirmed but it is now treated as specifying the dower provision intended to relate to the king's possessions in England alone.[74] Next comes the new section, which perhaps echoes the king's general promise of 1242 that, in the event of Henry's death, Eleanor shall have 'reasonable dower from all the king's lands, castles, rents and tenements, acquired or hereafter to be acquired'.[75] This promise was presumably made to act in 1262 as justification for the huge enhancement of Eleanor's dower provision to the handsome sum of £4,000. The additional £3,000 was officially specified as her dowager's third of the king's lands in Gascony, Ireland and elsewhere. One-third of this additional sum was in fact to be allocated to her in possessions in England and the remaining two-thirds in Gascon lands and revenues. The sources of income are carefully specified. The boldness of Eleanor's dower bid becomes apparent by contrast with the economical allowance of £1,333 6s 8d which had been agreed as the dower settlement for the Lord Edward's wife, once she had become queen.[76] As Edward put his seal 'for greater security' to his mother's dower instrument, knowing that every penny of it represented a temporary deduction from his own inheritance, he may have pondered wryly on the figure considered sufficient for his own wife. Peter of Savoy himself stood as the first witness, backed by a solid phalanx of curialist Savoyards and the faithful John Mansel and Robert Walerand, together with a sprinkling of other names. The Savoyard archbishop of Tarentaise acted as proxy in appending the seal of the Lord Edmund to the charter. Eleanor of Provence had done well for herself.

Queen Eleanor seems to have escaped the disastrous epidemic which struck the English court in France in early September 1262, but her husband, her son Edmund and John Mansel all succumbed, and the

---

[72] *CPR 1266–72* (Appendix), 726–35 *passim*; Ridgeway, 'Politics', 395.

[73] *CPR 1266–72* (Appendix), 736–7.

[74] For provision of 1253 see ch. 5, n. 15, above; for original provision see *CChR 1226–57*, 218.

[75] *CChR 1226–57*, 268.

[76] Parsons, *Eleanor of Castile*, 76.

illness killed more than sixty people, including the queen's ward Baldwin de Reviers. Baldwin was husband of the queen's first cousin, Margaret of Savoy, and son of Eleanor's friend Amice, dowager countess of Devon.[77] Although Henry III slowly regained his physical strength, his diplomacy was by now in tatters, and on 8 October he wrote to England to inform the justiciar Philip Basset that the negotiations over the points at issue between himself and Simon de Montfort had collapsed.[78] Montfort's own response to that situation was a lightning visit to England, so that he might produce in the Michaelmas parliament a papal letter actually enjoining observance of the Provisions of Oxford. This was a fine piece of drama. He had evidently contrived to extract this bull from the Roman *curia*, through the mediation of cardinals friendly to his cause, and the incident helped to foment unrest and to keep him in men's minds.[79]

By November the king and queen, who were still in France, were receiving alarming news from the Welsh March, where Llywelyn ap Gruffudd had already followed up a Welsh revolt on the lands of Roger Mortimer and was poised for a more general offensive.[80] On 20 December the king and queen disembarked at Dover, celebrating Christmas at Canterbury in sombre mood. Among the New Year's gifts exchanged in a depleted court at Rochester was a ring given by the queen to William de Valence.[81] It was perhaps a small token of the gradual healing of one rift in the royal family. In January the king judged it prudent to reissue the Provisions of Westminster, enshrining the popular legal and administrative reforms of 1259, 'of his own free will'.[82] The king never proved deeply opposed to this facet of the reform movement, and much was incorporated in the Statute of Marlborough in 1267. Although news from the Welsh March was very bad, much was hoped by the king and queen from the return of Edward in February. The hopes proved false. Prominent among Edward's following on his return were the foreign knights, many of them distinguished names, who now formed a substantial element in his military household. Nothing was more certain to inflame the jealous resentment of the group of disaffected Marchers formerly in Edward's entourage, now incited to direct their anger even more forcibly against aliens, both the Savoyards around the queen, whom they blamed for their disgrace, and the Frenchmen who had

---

[77] CPR 1266–72 (Appendix), 736.
[78] *Diplomatic Documents*, i, no. 369.
[79] *Gervase of Canterbury*, ii. 217; Maddicott, *Montfort*, 219.
[80] Davies, *Conquest, Coexistence and Change*, 312–13.
[81] E 101/349/26 m. 9.
[82] *Flores*, ii. 477; *Ann. Osney*, 130–1.

displaced them in Edward's service and affections.[83] Edward failed to contain the Welsh revolt, which now gathered fierce momentum, with extensive raids penetrating into Marcher territories, and he blamed the Marcher lords for failing to give him adequate support.

The group of former Edwardians, together with Henry of Almain and John de Warenne, saw the advantages of opposing the queen's party at court in the name of the Provisions. This gave their cause a wider appeal and a moral justification, if in their case a specious one. All that they lacked was an experienced military leader, and for this they recalled Simon de Montfort. Simon's return took place about 25 April 1263 and was followed by a meeting at Oxford which brought together various leading malcontents including the former friends of Edward, notably Henry of Almain, John de Warenne and the Marchers Roger Clifford, Leybourne, Lestrange, Vaux and others, together with Gilbert de Clare, who had been deeply alienated from the court by the king's unfriendly attitude to his claims as his father's heir.[84] According to the Dunstable annalist, Richard of Cornwall also met Simon at Oxford, but with what intention is not known for certain.[85] Oaths to the Provisions were renewed and before 20 May an ultimatum was sent to the king under the seal of Roger Clifford, demanding not only renewed commitment to the Provisions but the proscription as mortal enemies of all who opposed them.[86] This of course was closely directed at the group presently advising the king, who had worked for the overthrow of those Provisions. Naturally, the demand was rejected, providing the signal for a violent eruption on the part of Edward's former companions who now unleashed all their pent-up resentment against the queen and her supporters at court; she had pulled Edward away from his chosen affinity and had then tried to ruin them.[87] There is no evidence that Simon de Montfort himself took part in the violence at this stage, but it is almost certain that he orchestrated it and extended its appeal by drawing upon widespread opposition in the shires to Henry's oppressive administration, upon hopes once raised by the reform movement and now, in a more sinister way, upon the endemic hatred of all aliens, whether non-

---

[83] (Merton) *Flores*, iii. 256; (St Albans) *Flores* ii. 478; *Ann. Burton*, 500; Carpenter, '"Statute" against Aliens', 271; Maddicott, *Montfort*, 223.

[84] *Ann. Dunstable*, 221–2; Maddicott, *Montfort*, 225–6. For Leybourne's Marcher associations and identification with this group see Powicke, *Henry III*, 435.

[85] *Ann. Dunstable*, 221; Denholm-Young, *Richard of Cornwall*, 119, 122. Urban IV's reproach to Richard on disloyalty must bear some weight, *Reg. Urbain IV*, no. 724 (*CPL*, i. 402).

[86] *Cron. Maiorum*, 53.

[87] Maddicott, *Montfort*, 226–9; Carpenter, '"Statute" against Aliens', 270–3; Ridgeway, 'Politics', 397.

resident foreign clergy, Cahorsin moneylenders, Flemish and French mercenaries, or aliens at court. An alien queen was a particularly easy focus, someone who could be suspected of being at the root of most of these evils. And that was how the chronicler of Melrose writing in 1263 saw her, the cause of all the troubles.

The queen's party was marked down with a considerable degree of precision, although the destruction soon spread further and there were many innocent victims as well.[88] Roger Clifford, Roger Leybourne, John Giffard and John de Vaux raided Hereford early in June, seized the Savoyard bishop Peter d'Aigueblanche in his cathedral together with several of his compatriot canons and thrust them into prison in Roger Clifford's castle of Eardisley.[89] The rebels ravaged Aigueblanche's lands and then swept on, by way of Robert Walerand's castle of Kilpeck, which they paused to plunder, to Gloucester where the valiant Matthias Bezill was ready to defend the castle in person. For several days Bezill fought them off, winning a reluctant tribute from the chronicler Robert of Gloucester, but eventually he too was seized and dispatched, like Aigueblanche, to Eardisley.[90] Bristol, Worcester, Bridgnorth and Shrewsbury all surrendered to the rebels, who were now assisted by an alliance between Montfort and the Welsh. Llywelyn's men were reaching out to Edward's castles of Diserth and Deganwy in the north.[91] What started as an attack on the Savoyards and their political allies in the west was soon directed against the lands and goods of the queen's party in other areas. John de Vaux plundered the East Anglian estates of Peter of Savoy; the lands of Ebulo de Montibus in Cambridgeshire were ravaged, as were the estates of Ingram de Fiennes in five counties, the extensive possessions of Robert Walerand, scattered over fifteen counties, and the midland estates of Geoffrey de Langley and Gilbert Talbot, both auditors in the financial investigation of the accounts of Edward's bailiffs in 1261–2.[92] John Mansel and the royalist bishop of Norwich, appointed together with Archbishop Boniface to give effect to the papal bulls against the Provisions of Oxford, were obvious victims of attack.[93] According to the chronicler Wykes, the possessions of the queen herself were also a prime target for the rebels 'because they saw that she had turned openly against the Provisions of Oxford'.[94] This was their

[88] *Chron. Wykes*, 134–5; *Chron. Bury St Edmunds*, 26–7.
[89] *Gervase of Canterbury*, ii. 221–2; *Ann. Dunstable*, 221–2; *Flores*, ii. 479–80.
[90] *Flores*, ii. 480; *Robert of Gloucester*, ii. 737–8.
[91] *Flores*, iii. 256; Davies, *Conquest, Coexistence and Change*, 312.
[92] *CR 1261–64*, 369–70, 245, 249–52; *Ann. Dunstable*, 222; Ridgeway, 'Politics', 397–9.
[93] *CR 1261–64*, 369; *Chron. Bury St Edmunds*, 27.
[94] *Chron. Wykes*, 135; Ridgeway, 'Politics', 396.

overt political stand, but the motives of the Marcher group were private, not public.

In truth the rebellion of 1263 was a rebellion focused on the queen and her policies. Such a forceful woman was a satisfactory target for blame. By genuine reformers she was held responsible for the policy of destroying the Provisions; by the native baronage and magnates she was blamed for insinuating aliens into official positions and lucrative marriages and into the counsels of the king; by the group of tough Marchers who had been the first to take to open violence she was blamed for persuading Edward to break with them and to hound them, especially Leybourne, into a state of disgrace and deprivation, and it is likely that many opponents saw her, probably with reason, as partly, if not largely responsible for the repeated calls upon foreign mercenary knights to strengthen the king's most unpopular repressive acts. In the general view, it was high time to call her to account.

The swift-moving events of June to July 1263 show Eleanor for the first time at bay. She was shocked and greatly angered by the June rebellion, but worse was to come. With rare political skill, Simon de Montfort had discerned and exploited the opportunity to gather the diverse threads of discontent and to head a military campaign which would paralyse Henry III's resistance. On 19 June the king and queen withdrew to the Tower of London and it was there that an anxious deputation of leading London citizens sought out the king about 24 June to show him a letter bearing the seal of Simon de Montfort, demanding an assurance that they would stand loyal to their oaths to the Provisions of Oxford.[95] Apart from the members of the deputation only five people were present at that meeting in the Tower, the king and the queen, the Lord Edward, Richard of Cornwall and Robert Walerand. They were not of one mind. Richard of Cornwall, whose attitude during the rebellion had been equivocal, was evidently inclining the king towards a settlement with the barons.[96] The queen and the Lord Edward were far more defiant, and perhaps Walerand too, since he was soon to join Edward's raid on the New Temple.[97] The Londoners wished to reaffirm their oath to the Provisions, which they believed to be 'to the honour of God, to the interest of the king and the benefit of the realm', and they were eager to rid the city of Edward's foreign knights. The king yielded; he allowed a delegation of citizens to go to make their peace with the barons.[98]

[95] *Cron. Maiorum*, 53–4.
[96] See n. 85, above.
[97] *CPR 1258–66*, 279.
[98] *Cron. Maiorum*, 54.

The response of the hawks in Henry's family was very different. On 29 June Edward raided the Temple, stole considerable treasure and made off for Windsor with his followers, including the unpopular foreign knights.[99] There he entrenched himself and raided the countryside for supplies. His brother Edmund was dispatched to Dover, accompanied by Gerard de Rodes and also by John Mansel, who was in charge of a cluster of frightened women.[100] It was presumably the queen, characteristically concerned for individuals, who had arranged that Mansel should conduct Thomas of Savoy's daughter Margaret together with 'other ladies from overseas' to the hospitable safety of Louis IX's dominions. Edmund took control of Dover castle, while Mansel conveyed his charges across the Channel on 29 June. The rebels, elated by success, were not going to let the highly unpopular Mansel escape so easily. The chroniclers give slightly different stories here. Henry of Almain, close in Montfort's counsels at this point, either preceded Mansel in order to intercept him, or pursued him. Either way, it seems that the queen, getting wind of the plot, reacted so swiftly that Richard of Cornwall's luckless son was surprised, seized and imprisoned, probably at Boulogne, by the lightning action of the queen's faithful henchman Ingram de Fiennes. Mansel accomplished his mission safely.[101]

This incident electrified the barons and the first item in their conditions for peace became the release of Henry of Almain. All the evidence points to the queen's initiative. The St Albans chronicler reports that the arrest was thought to be her doing and records the barons' demand that Henry of Almain be freed 'by the king and the queen'.[102] In an undated communication Richard of Cornwall wrote to the justiciar, Philip Basset, sending him letters in the king's name directed to Ingram de Fiennes, but he asks urgently for letters patent to the same effect to be sent from the queen, with her own seal appended.[103] The king's letters presumably ordered the release of Henry of Almain, and letters to that effect dated 10 July were in fact sent.[104] However, Earl Richard's belief that the king's seal alone, without that of the queen, might not secure the obedience of Ingram de Fiennes is an astonishing fact.

The king was by now committing himself to far more than the release of his nephew. The baronial party, guided in political as well as military

[99] *Ann. Dunstable*, 222; date given as 26 June in *Gervase of Canterbury*, ii. 222.
[100] *Gervase of Canterbury*, ii. 222.
[101] *Flores*, ii. 481; *Ann. Dunstable*, 223; *Gervase of Canterbury*, ii. 222. For consideration of the different versions see Carpenter, '"Statute" against Aliens', 266, n. 4.
[102] *Flores*, ii. 482.
[103] SC 1/11/88.
[104] *CPR 1258–66*, 269.

strategy by Montfort, had stepped up their demands in pace with their success, and to match their growing awareness of the wide appeal of the anti-alien rallying cry. In the *forma pacis*, which formed the basis of the eventual peace with the king, they required not only Henry III's renewed adherence to the Provisions and the placing of all castles and governmental posts in the hands of men who were native-born, but also, and most bitter to the queen, the expulsion from England of all aliens 'never to return', except any whose residence in England was approved by the faithful men of the kingdom.[105] On 4 July the king had empowered his envoys to make peace with the barons and on 10 July, in addition to ordering Henry of Almain's release, the king instructed his son Edmund to surrender Dover castle.[106] Simon de Montfort was now in control of the south-east, and exhilarated by the prospect of complete victory.

The queen had never been so deeply opposed to her husband. She passionately resisted his reluctant decision to comply with the baronial demands; the St Albans chronicler says that 'she strove against it with all her strength'.[107] On 13 July she determined to leave the Tower and attempt to reach her son Edward in Windsor. Bereft of the advice of Peter of Savoy and John Mansel and at odds with her husband, Eleanor's instinct as ever was to take decisive action. Setting off upstream, she was rudely halted at London Bridge. Once the news had got round that she had left the Tower and was on the river, a rabble of Londoners crowded on to the bridge, roaring out their insults and seizing everything that lay to hand to pelt the little company in the approaching barge. In June the popular party in the city had overturned their patrician government and had found a protagonist in their new mayor, Thomas fitz Thomas. The crowd on the bridge shouted their predictable jibes of whore and adulteress, as the dirt, rotten eggs and stones fell around the boat. Eleanor of Provence must have known that her life was in danger. But the news which so quickly brought the ruffians also speedily brought the mayor to her rescue. Thomas fitz Thomas, radical though he was, would not countenance this. According to the Dunstable annalist the king refused her re-entry into the Tower, but she was conducted to the safety of the bishop of London's house.[108] Two days later the barons made their entry into London and on 16 July the king formally accepted the terms of peace, based on the *forma pacis*. Then, joined by

[105] *Flores*, ii. 482.
[106] *CPR 1258–66*, 268, 269. On 18 July Henry repeated his command to Edmund, *Foedera*, i. 427.
[107] *Flores*, ii. 481–2.
[108] Ibid.; *Ann. Dunstable*, 223; *Chron. Wykes*, 136.

his queen, he took up residence at Westminster.[109] Eleanor's policy had been shattered.

The dramatic scene at London Bridge was proof to the queen of the most personal kind, of the hatred which she had aroused. The attacks on her kinsfolk and political allies in the previous month had been proof of one kind but this was a harsh and bitter culmination. The respect and obedience due to an anointed queen had been thrown over in rough physical and verbal assault. The event marked her; that goes without saying. It also made a profound impression on others. The tone of the chroniclers makes this clear. The king and queen of France were greatly shocked and their support and sympathy for Queen Eleanor were enhanced by what had happened.[110] It also shocked her husband and her eldest son. References to it, implicit or explicit, are scattered through the account of later events, as when Henry III gave her the keeping of London Bridge after the civil war had ended, and part of the fine on the city.[111] No man, one suspects, felt it more than the Lord Edward. Later, when he flung himself into remorseless pursuit of the fleeing Londoners in the battle of Lewes in 1264, thereby playing his part in losing the battle, it is said that he was impelled by their treatment of his mother.[112] His relationship with his mother had been uneasy since 1258, when he had pulled himself free from her controlling hand. More recently he had perhaps allowed her to work on him in the victimization of Roger Leybourne. In the middle of a grave political and military crisis he would have heard the news of her terrible humiliation. It becomes evident that her honour as a lady and a queen and above all as his own mother was suddenly very dear to him. He had to wait his opportunity, but the Battle chronicler makes the telling comment that the queen could leave it to her son to avenge the insult.[113]

Although the Lord Edmund had been forced to surrender Dover, the great stronghold of Windsor remained in his elder brother's hands and the magnates were determined that if Edward would not submit, Windsor castle should be attacked in the king's name.[114] Edward did not let this happen. When the barons set out for Windsor, he too realized that for the moment he could do no more and he surrendered the castle. The foreign knights in the garrison were of course proscribed by the terms of the peace. On 26 July the king arranged for them to withdraw their

---

[109] *Cron. Maiorum*, 55; CPR 1258–66, 269–70.
[110] Maddicott, *Montfort*, 236.
[111] CPR 1266–72, 459.
[112] *Flores*, ii. 495–6; *Chron. Guisborough*, 194.
[113] Battle Chronicle in Bémont, *Simon de Montfort* (1st edn), 375.
[114] CR 1261–64, 308–9.

equipment from Windsor to Staines and then to proceed under escort to the coast.[115] Edward's humiliation was sharp and there is no account of his leave-taking with his companions, but by the chance survival of Eleanor's ring account, we have a record of their leave-taking with the queen. It was an impressive and courageous gesture on her part and it corroborates the evidence for her personal links with the aliens in Edward's retinue. On 1 August, the date given by the St Albans chronicler for the official surrender of the castle, over forty knights, many of them aliens and perhaps most, or all, from the Windsor garrison, were given rings by Queen Eleanor.[116] Despite her own recent experience at the hands of the Londoners, and in the face of what seemed total political defeat, Eleanor of Provence did not lose her sense of royal dignity and the proper expression of gratitude. Edward's knights may have honoured her for it.

Immediately after the king's submission to the baronial peace terms, the great offices of state were placed in the hands of Montfortian supporters.[117] Almost worse to bear than this, because more intimately felt, was the purge of aliens from the households of the king and queen. Since dismissed personnel had to be replaced, Simon de Montfort chose, in August 1263, to reassert and enhance the authority which he claimed as Steward of England, by appointing two new working stewards in the king's household. The Savoyard Ebulo de Montibus and the royalist Alan la Zuche were replaced by the baronial partisan John de la Haye and – most notorious among the rebels – Roger Leybourne himself.[118] The pressures which led to the choice of Leybourne are a matter for speculation. Some acknowledgement of the initiatives of the Marcher group, of which, although firstly a Kentishman, he was a prominent member, was required. Moreover he was regarded by his friends as a man who had been grievously wronged; he was a difficult candidate to pass over. It may even be that Leybourne put himself forward. He and his friends were not reformers; they were not even Montfortians; they had once been the Lord Edward's men and it was to the service of the Lord Edward that they wanted to return. The strength of the bond which had for the time been broken is revealed in an incidental remark in the *Flores*, under the year 1264; the chronicler writes that these men 'loved Edward greatly'.[119] In

---

[115] *Cron. Maiorum*, 57; *CPR 1258–66*, 272.

[116] E 101/349/26 mm. 8, 9; *Flores*, ii. 483.

[117] Maddicott, *Montfort*, 232.

[118] *Gervase of Canterbury*, ii. 224; Maddicott, *Montfort*, 239–40. Treharne seems to miss the significance of Leybourne's appointment (*Baronial Plan*, 312), as does L. B. Larking, 'On the Heart-Shrine in Leybourne Church', 170.

[119] *Flores*, ii. 503; Maddicott, *Montfort*, 235.

the summer of 1263 they wanted to work their way back to him and this they did with the help of their friends Henry of Almain and John de Warenne. As steward of the king's household Leybourne was in a strong position to make himself acceptable to the king and to seek to heal the breach with the Lord Edward. As early as 12 September he had received back the manor of Elham, recently such an object of contention, and on 18 September the whole group were formally pardoned by the king.[120] There can be no doubt that both Edward and his former friends were actively seeking this reconciliation and that Edward was prepared to reward these men generously. Already, on 10 August, Edward had made the important grant of Stamford and Grantham to John de Warenne, who claimed them in right of his father, although these two fiefs had been declared inalienable from the Crown in 1253 when they had formed part of the queen's dower.[121]

There is, as one would expect, no direct evidence of the queen's reaction. Montfort's appointment of Leybourne as steward, the man who two months previously had been ravaging the lands of her relatives and her friends and whom she herself had almost certainly victimized in 1261–2, would have been extremely bitter. In 1258 she had presumably hoped to wean Edward from the Lusignans and had failed. Now for a second time she had tried to destroy the friendships which he had made and again she had failed abysmally. Even by the time she again left for France on 23 September she would have been aware of what was happening. This development must surely have been deeply galling, even if she saw the advantage of such an access of strength to the royalist side. She was separated from Leybourne and his friends by deep mutual hostility. Her recent political ascendancy was completely destroyed, her own friends and partisans expelled. Her personal prospects could hardly have been more bleak.

Such situations can be sharply revealing. Like her Savoyard uncles, Eleanor of Provence had the courage, the resilience and the ultimate self-command to withstand even the deepest adversity. Despite the severe tensions, Henry III's family contrived to work together for a royalist recovery. Eleanor herself looked to the Continent. She saw the solution to the situation in England in terms of diplomatic help from France and from the papacy and massive military intervention by friends from abroad. She was almost certainly instrumental, along with the king, in

---

[120] E 368/94 m. 47; Larking, 'On the Heart-Shrine in Leybourne Church', 168, 175–6; *CPR 1258–66*, 278.

[121] *Ann. Dunstable*, 225; Studd, 'Acts of the Lord Edward', no. 893. Michael Prestwich (*Edward I*, 41) and Huw Ridgeway ('Politics', 400) emphasize the initiatives taken by Edward.

contriving that Louis IX should summon Henry, Eleanor and their two sons to a meeting of the French court at Boulogne towards the end of September, where the matters at issue between the English king and his barons might be considered.[122] The baronial council in England, by now a mere rump of the council of fifteen of 1258, made their reluctant agreement to this conditional on an oath to be sworn by the king, the queen and their sons that they would return to England within a fixed time.[123]

The queen had no intention of returning until she had amassed military support from abroad. Already her sister Margaret was trying to enlist the co-operation of Alphonse of Poitiers. Margaret urged Alphonse to cease oppressing Gaston de Béarn and to procure peace between Gaston and his own vassal the count of Comminges so that Gaston might go to the help of the king and queen of England. In a very cool response, Alphonse told the French queen that Gaston was the aggressor in the quarrel she mentioned.[124] Queen Margaret reiterated her request in August 1263 and asked Alphonse to provide Henry and Eleanor with ships from his port of La Rochelle by mid-October if the attempt to achieve a settlement at Boulogne failed.[125] Alphonse replied that he had no ships of his own at La Rochelle, as far as he knew.[126] The two queens were right in thinking that the peace attempt at Boulogne would fail. King Louis and his advisers seem to have been impressed by Montfort's presentation of the baronial case, and conceded the barons' claim that the matters at issue should be adjudicated before an English court, rather than that of the king of France.[127] According to the Tewkesbury annalist and the chronicler Robert of Boston, Louis went so far as to approve the Provisions, on condition that full reparations were made for the recent spoliations.[128] One must remember that Henry III himself had not yet publicly reneged on his renewed submission to the Provisions and that restitution to those whose lands had been attacked had already begun, as well as the undoubted fact that there were French magnates at Boulogne who were friendly to Montfort. The Boulogne meeting was a setback, if not exactly a defeat for the English king and his supporters. Eleanor of Provence was to change all that.

The problem of the recent violence in England was acute. When Henry arrived at Boulogne Archbishop Boniface, the queen's uncle, faced the

---

[122] *Ann. Dunstable*, 225.
[123] *CPR 1258–66*, 275; *CPL*, i. 397.
[124] *Correspondance d'Alfonse de Poitiers*, ii, nos 1866, 1867, 1988.
[125] Ibid., nos 2014, 2015.
[126] Ibid., no. 2016.
[127] *Ann. Dunstable*, 225; *Gervase of Canterbury*, ii. 224–5.
[128] *Ann. Tewkesbury*, 176; 'Robert of Boston', 114; Maddicott, *Montfort*, 243–4.

king with his complaints, and in a letter of 3 October the archbishop wrote in the strongest terms to his suffragans on the enormities committed against clergy and church property in the whole province of Canterbury, and ordered the bishops to pronounce the sentence of greater excommunication against the malefactors. Boniface was well informed and able to give a list of twenty-five names of perpetrators of these crimes, including Montfort's sons, Henry and the younger Simon, and the by now familiar group of Marchers, Roger Leybourne, Roger Clifford, Hamo Lestrange and John de Vaux, and finally, as supremely responsible, Earl Simon himself. This important letter has sometimes been seen simply as a protest by Boniface against violation of his own property and of ecclesiastical rights within the diocese of Canterbury, but he writes specifically of the 'province' of Canterbury and is referring to the full scope of the 1263 campaign. The report of the Canterbury/Dover chronicler that the Kentish knights had flocked to Earl Simon at this time may account for the narrower interpretation.[129] The bishops in reply prevaricated.[130] Henry III prevaricated too. Although as late as 4 January 1264 at Amiens he promised that the men named by Boniface should make competent amends for these injuries, Edward's former friends had by then been fully assimilated into the royalist camp, rewarded with lands, and Leybourne himself appointed to the key security post of warden of the Cinque Ports.[131]

A sharp cleavage in attitude among members of the royal family to the ex-Edwardians could have ruined the possibility of concerted effort against Montfort. In this the queen's attitude was crucial. She had more reason to hate these men than any one, and she would surely have shared Boniface's sense of outrage over the depredations of this militant Marcher group, but in this crisis of monarchical government she pushed aside the instinct for personal revenge so as to concentrate on the overriding aim of rallying diplomatic and military support for her husband. From her vantage point in France, she collaborated closely with Henry and Edward in England. They trusted her and her chief allies among the exiles, Peter of Savoy and John Mansel, to work with them and they trusted her to work on the French king who had to some extent failed them in the meeting at Boulogne.

[129] Bodleian MS 91, f. 136, printed by Wilshire, *Boniface of Savoy*, Appendix A; *Gervase of Canterbury*, ii. 222–3. Wilshire interprets the letter in the narrower sense (*Boniface of Savoy*, 73–4), followed by Ridgeway ('Politics', 398) and Maddicott (*Montfort*, 229).

[130] Reply of bishops, Bodleian MS 91, f. 136v, printed by Wilshire, *Boniface of Savoy*, Appendix B.

[131] CPR 1258–66, 378, 300. See also ch. 9, below.

While Eleanor and Edmund, in defiance of their oaths, remained in France, Henry and Edward returned to a parliament held at Westminster in October 1263, which was the scene of bitter recriminations over reparations and over Henry's demands that he should have power to appoint his own officials.[132] About 16 October Edward played a bold stroke; he left the parliament and on the pretext of visiting his wife, made once more for Windsor where he seized and occupied the castle. The king and other royalists almost immediately joined him and by the end of October the ex-Edwardians, together with John de Warenne and Henry of Almain, were with them too. Several chroniclers accuse Edward of bribery, probably with justification, although that was not the whole truth, as has been seen.[133] On 29 October the king left Windsor for Oxford and on 1 November the opposing parties agreed to submit their dispute formally to Louis IX.[134] But, despite the accompanying truce, the king continued to take steps to reassert his authority, replacing the baronial chancellor and treasurer and evicting John de la Haye from Winchester castle.[135] Early in December Henry attempted to seize the port of Dover, essential for the safe entry of the queen and the foreign knights and mercenaries whom she hoped to bring with her.[136] Eleanor meanwhile had lost no time in applying on her own account to Alphonse of Poitiers, begging him to supply ships and galleys 'as her sister would indicate more fully'.[137] Margaret's supporting letter of 31 October explains that the ships are needed because King Henry, Queen Eleanor and the Lord Edward have requested their friends to be at St Omer one month after 11 November.[138] Queen Margaret's specific reference to Henry and Edward, together with the timing of Henry's attempt to seize Dover, shows the closeness of the collaboration with Eleanor. Alphonse replied that he would not force any shipowners to supply their vessels, but he would not object to their doing so on a voluntary basis.[139]

For success in a co-ordinated military effort the vital prerequisite was money. Henry and Edward needed to tap with all speed as much as possible of the money still due to Henry under the terms of the Treaty of Paris. The men entrusted with negotiating this were Peter d'Aigue-

---

[132] *Cron. Maiorum*, 58.

[133] Ibid.; *Ann. Dunstable*, 225; *Gervase of Canterbury*, ii. 226; *Flores*, ii. 484–5; for the defection of Henry of Almain from Montfort to the king see *Chron. Rishanger*, 17.

[134] Maddicott, *Montfort*, 246–7.

[135] *DBM*, 264–7.

[136] *Ann. Dunstable*, 225.

[137] *Correspondance d'Alfonse de Poitiers*, ii, no. 2020 (15 October)

[138] Ibid., no. 2017.

[139] Ibid., nos 2019, 2021.

blanche, Peter of Savoy and John Mansel. Henry also requested the assistance of the queen of France and the dowager countess of Provence, Eleanor's sister and mother. Peter of Savoy and Mansel were further commissioned to attend to the pawning of the king's jewels.[140] One might almost say that it was the queen's 'affinity' who were entrusted with the war effort across the Channel. Military and financial preparations were not enough. They needed to be accompanied by a resounding diplomatic initiative directed at Pope Urban IV and King Louis of France. Eleanor's sister Margaret joined her husband in urging the pope to appoint a legate to tackle the troubled situation in England, and according to the Dunstable annalist Eleanor herself was instrumental in securing this. On 22 November Urban IV commissioned Guy Foulquois, a French ecclesiastic well known to King Louis, to this difficult post.[141] The pope would have been informed of the recent depredations in England from many sources and pre-eminently by Eleanor's uncle, Archbishop Boniface, whose stern letter to the suffragan bishops of his province finds an echo in the pope's instructions to Guy Foulquois. Pope Urban dwells on the injury to royalty, the attacks on the persons as well as the property of prelates and other clergy, the evictions from benefices and the many wrongful collations. The earl of Leicester is identified by the pope as reputedly 'the chief of the disturbers of the realm'. Urban's instructions are clear; the wrongs committed against the Church are to be remedied, the legate is empowered to preach a crusade against the king's enemies, property alienated from the Crown must be restored and oaths to the Provisions quashed.[142]

Such support was invaluable for the royalists, but the man called upon by both Henry III and the barons to make a formal adjudication on their dispute, an adjudication by which they swore to abide, was not the pope but the king of France. According to the Tewkesbury chronicler, Queen Eleanor, together with Aigueblanche and Mansel and others, had requested papal letters directing King Louis to quash the Provisions of Oxford entirely.[143] Judgement was to be pronounced on 23 January at Amiens and each side prepared its case with skill. In addition, Henry made a cunning move which had the double purpose of ensuring the continued loyalty of the great Marcher lord Roger Mortimer, who stood apart from the Edwardian group, and deflecting Simon de Montfort from the business of Amiens. The king granted to Mortimer, and

---

[140] *CPR 1258–66*, 293, 295.
[141] *CPL*, i. 396; *Ann. Dunstable*, 233 (where the appointment is mistakenly placed in 1264).
[142] *CPL*, i. 396–8.
[143] *Ann. Tewkesbury*, 179.

encouraged him to seize, a group of three Herefordshire manors which had been allocated to Montfort in the contentious settlement of the earl's claims by the reforming administration in 1259.[144] Henry knew, none better, Montfort's fiercely aggressive attitude to his own privileges and possessions, and he also knew that King Louis, who had admired and befriended Montfort over the years, was open to the accomplished earl's persuasiveness in argument. The October meeting at Boulogne had been recent proof of it. Montfort did arrange retaliation and he did not appear at Amiens, but in the event it was an unlucky fall from his horse that forced him to remain in England.[145]

Even without Montfort's attendance, the barons put forward a strongly argued case, which Montfort would undoubtedly have helped to frame, but which probably owed its final form to the scholarly Thomas Cantilupe, nephew of Montfort's close collaborator, the bishop of Worcester.[146] According to the baronial argument the Provisions of Oxford and the subsequent measures of reform followed naturally from the articles of Magna Carta itself, and all restrictions imposed upon Henry III were the result of his breaking of the terms of the Charter and then of the Provisions, which grew out of the Charter.[147] Ingenious and well put, the baronial case failed to convince the king of France, who was by now thoroughly informed on other aspects of the central issue at stake in the dispute.

Henry III's own statement concentrated on two major points. The first was the attack on his essential rights of kingship, as he saw them, in the appointment of officers of state, justices and even officials of his own household. The second was the scale of the malicious destruction, wrought by the barons in the recent rising, on the property of the king and the queen and the Lord Edward and of lay and ecclesiastical subjects who had remained loyal to them. Henry asked for a straightforward remedy, the quashing of the Provisions and of all statutes arising from them and the restoration of the king to his former state, together with the award of a heavy financial compensation to be paid by the barons to the king.[148]

Louis IX was by now fully open to the arguments of his fellow monarch. He could not have been other than aware of Henry III's

---

[144] DBM, 266–7; Gervase of Canterbury, ii. 232; Ann. Dunstable, 226; Maddicott, Montfort, 257.

[145] Ann. Dunstable, 227.

[146] Carpenter, 'St Thomas Cantilupe', 298–9; Stacey, 'Baronial Gravamina', 143.

[147] For the baronial statement see DBM, 256–79; for order and assessment of these documents see Stacey, 'Baronial Gravamina', 137–43.

[148] DBM, 252–7.

weaknesses and failings as a ruler, but Henry was a rightful king and one to whom he had obligations as his feudal vassal and his brother-in-law. Louis had become convinced that the essential point at issue was that of the inherent rights of kingship, and he continued to see the issue in those terms from now until the end of the struggle. The French king was also by this time deeply shocked, and moved, by the violence and destructiveness of the revolt of June 1263. He was aware of the maltreatment of the queen by the Londoners and the humiliation of her son Edward when the foreign knights of his household at Windsor, many of whom were known personally to Louis, were ignominiously ejected from England. Perhaps worst of all was the inhumane humiliation of King Henry when he had been obliged by Simon de Montfort to take part in an advance on Windsor castle at the end of July, which might have involved the king in open armed struggle against his eldest son.

Louis IX's judgement, the Mise of Amiens, pronounced on 23 January 1264, was a devastatingly thorough reassertion of Henry III's rights and a quashing of both the Provisions of Oxford and the 'statute against the aliens'.[149] Even a royalist chronicler such as Wykes was a little shocked at the entire lack of reservation in Louis's pronouncement, except for an acknowledgement of the validity of Magna Carta itself.[150] To some chroniclers Louis seemed to have made a complete volte-face since the conference at Boulogne. Yet one must remember that at Amiens Louis was presented with a single dispute on which to pronounce and that he had been provided with documentation from both sides. Moreover he had recently been listening not to the reasoning of Simon de Montfort, but to that of the queen of England and such highly articulate exiles as Boniface and Peter of Savoy and John Mansel, men who were as accomplished in diplomacy as Earl Simon himself. Three English chroniclers mention the personal influence of Queen Eleanor as a factor in bringing about Louis's judgement at Amiens, but it is the Tewkesbury chronicler who makes most of it. He rails against the woman whom he sees as the main culprit in changing the stance of the French king, who was 'deceived and beguiled by the serpentlike fraud and speech of a woman; the queen of England'.[151] The allusion to Eve has a particular significance here; the chronicler implies that it was not by tears and lamentations that Louis had been overcome, but by persuasive talking. It was a perceptive comment in relation to Eleanor of Provence.

---

[149] *DBM*, 280–91; Carpenter, '"Statute" against Aliens', 268.
[150] *Chron. Wykes*, 139.
[151] *Ann. Tewkesbury*, 177; *Ann. Dunstable*, 227; *Ann. Worcester*, 448.

9

War

The Mise of Amiens in January 1264 was a major diplomatic victory, for which the queen herself could take substantial credit, but the Mise fell far short of full political victory. It is true that the royalists had secured a significant political advantage for the English Crown in bringing Louis IX and the papacy to a firm and explicit support of Henry III's own interpretation of the essentials of his kingship. This continued to be of prime importance in the dramatic struggle which followed. What the Mise did not do was to end the political and military confrontation in England between the supporters of the king and the supporters of Earl Simon. Again, what it did not do was to secure any commitment on the part of King Louis to give material support to Henry III beyond what was already required of him by the terms of the Treaty of Paris.

As far as an armed struggle was concerned, the Mise of Amiens simply provoked its renewal. Montfort and his supporters would not accept Louis's adjudication, and no chronicler accuses Earl Simon of bad faith on that account.[1] Henry III and Edward had now to fight for the cause that had been sanctioned by the French king. Money and men were needed. It was here that Queen Eleanor, backed by Peter of Savoy and John Mansel, was intended by her husband and son to continue to complement their own strategies in England. Before he left France Henry determined to urge Louis's co-operation in allowing him immediate access to the sums of money still owing to him under the Treaty of Paris. Abandoning any elaborate and protracted arbitration, Henry had

---

[1] Maddicott, *Montfort*, 264.

agreed to an estimate of £58,000 of Tours (*c.*£14,500 sterling) as the balance owing to him from the total sum of £134,000 of Tours (*c.*£33,500 sterling), and the payment of the full sum was later acknowledged, on 14 May, the very day of the battle of Lewes, by a deed of acquittance drawn up by Richard of Cornwall's chancellor on behalf of Henry III.[2] However, the authority actually to receive this money had been placed with the queen, Peter of Savoy and John Mansel as early as 14 February, and Queen Eleanor drew up her own deed of acquittance for this sum on 1 June.[3] By this time she was the only person in a position to use the money and indeed much of it may already have been spent. On 14 February the same three had been further empowered by Henry to receive the king's jewels, deposited in the Temple in Paris, 'with power to dispose thereof as shall be most for his advantage and honour'.[4]

Henry returned to England on that day and, ominously, was still denied entry into Dover. During the next three months events moved towards their climax in the battle of Lewes on 14 May. In military terms Montfort's strength lay in his control of London where, as has been seen, the lower orders in the city had wrested power from the wealthier citizens, in the Cinque Ports, where the Mise of Amiens was immediately rejected, and in the midland shires where Montfort's affinity and wider influence had always been strong. In social terms, one chronicler notes that he had the support of 'most of the middling people of England', clearly a reflection of support for the legal and administrative reforms associated with the Provisions of Oxford.[5] The majority of the greater barons now gave their support to the king, though with varying degrees of commitment, and the division between the two parties among the lesser baronage and gentry again tended to be regional.[6] There can be no doubt that in terms of enthusiasm for the royalist cause and experience and competence in fighting, the Edwardians among the Marchers, together with Roger Mortimer, who was now on terms of bitter enmity with Montfort, formed one of the most important groups at the king's command. The king, as we have seen, had promised, on the eve of the Mise of Amiens, that Roger Leybourne and his friends would recompense those whom they had injured in the spoliations of the summer of 1263. Leybourne obviously feared that once again he might be called to

[2] *Foedera*, i. 434–5 (*CPR 1258–66*, 379); *Foedera*, i. 440 (*CPR 1258–66*, 317); Gavrilovitch, *Traité de Paris*, 60–1.

[3] *CPR 1258–66*, 381; Gavrilovitch, *Traité de Paris*, Appendix, 120–1.

[4] *CPR 1258–66*, 381.

[5] *Cron. Maiorum*, 61.

[6] For Montfort's affinity see Maddicott, *Montfort*, 59–72, Carpenter, 'Simon de Montfort', 226–9 and Knowles, 'The Disinherited', pt ii.

account for his misdeeds, by Boniface and the Savoyards. He had had enough of that in 1262. So indeed had the king and Edward; they wanted no recriminations against Leybourne now. On 28 February Henry promised Leybourne 'as a further grace' that he would answer for him to all who wished to proceed against him on the grounds of his recent trespasses.[7] Leybourne had been appointed to the wardenship of the Cinque Ports and the Weald in his native Kent, where his influence for good or ill was crucial. Henry knew he must stand by Leybourne now. The queen, humiliated as she may well have felt over this virtual exoneration of Leybourne, applied herself with single-minded determination to the support of her husband and her eldest son.

News from England, as it would have reached the queen, swung uneasily between good and bad. In March and April, in an outburst of ruthless and destructive violence, the Londoners made successive raids on the property of prominent royalists. Richard of Cornwall's manor of Isleworth was ransacked and attacks were made on the property of Peter of Savoy, William de Valence, Philip Basset and Walter Merton. There followed an even uglier outbreak in the plundering and murder of numerous London Jews, an incident in which Montfort and his supporters were mercilessly active, along with the wildly excited citizens.[8] For the queen, with her recent memories of the London mob, this news could only harden her resolve. But there was better news too. The king, who had been based in Oxford until 3 April, struck out for Northampton, where two days later he won an important victory, seizing the town for the royalists, capturing many prisoners and driving a wedge between Montfort's positions in the midlands and the south-east. On 25 April Montfort withdrew to London again and Henry was soon on the brink of recovering the vital south-eastern ports.

This was potentially of great moment for Eleanor. Her continuing task had been the assembling of men and ships for what she hoped would be a decisive intervention from abroad. She needed the ports of the south-east for entry. This was not in any way conceived by Henry, Edward and Eleanor as a substitute for the military effort in England but as a powerful supplement to it. One area to which they were looking for support was Gascony. On 28 March Henry de Cusances seneschal of Gascony gave a formal assurance to the citizens of Bayonne that the service provided by them for 'the great struggle of England' would not be drawn into a precedent.[9] On 19 April Gaston de Béarn himself was at

---

[7] *CPR 1258–66*, 382.
[8] *Chron. Wykes*, 140–3; Williams, *Medieval London*, 224.
[9] *Archives Municipales de Bayonne: Livre des Etablissements*, no. 15.

St Omer, no doubt with followers and ready to take his part in the projected expedition to England.[10] Ships were vital, and on 7 May Eleanor made another urgent appeal to Alphonse of Poitiers. She writes of the treachery of certain barons in England who, by open war (*vivam guerram*), are striving to disinherit the king and his children. She asks him to seize the English ships in his ports and to detain them as long as the war lasts, assuring him that such a detention of the ships would be perfectly in order 'since the aforesaid lord king is lord and prince of all the English and everything belongs to the prince in a case of urgent necessity', an interesting indication of her awareness of such reasons of state, in Roman law.[11] The letter brought a firm and speedy refusal from Alphonse, who told Eleanor that it seemed to many good men that what she asked could not be done without great harm and danger.[12] He was evidently not prepared to interfere with peaceful shipping activities in his ports, nor to involve himself in an armed struggle in England in which he had no personal stake.

This sharp snub, written on 12 May, two days before the fateful battle of Lewes, perhaps reached the queen at much the same time as the disastrous news from England. The open war, of which Eleanor had written, ended in a pitched battle in which Henry III's army was decisively defeated. David Carpenter's reinterpretation of that battle supersedes earlier accounts.[13] The king had by far the larger army but Montfort had the advantage of higher ground above the town, and better generalship. The attacks by Montfort's forces against the left and centre of the royal army, commanded respectively by the king himself and Richard of Cornwall, carried the day; the king was obliged to seek refuge in Lewes priory and the king of Almain found a less dignified retreat in a windmill. The Lord Edward was in command of the king's right, together with John de Warenne and William de Valence; here too were Guy de Lusignan, Hugh Bigod, Roger Mortimer and the Edwardian Marcher lords, Leybourne, Clifford and Lestrange.[14] Edward's grave mistake, after an initially promising offensive, was to lead this troop of the ablest fighting men on the king's side in pursuit of a contingent of Londoners whom he had quickly routed but then chose to track down in a hunt which ended in bloody slaughter. Several chroniclers commented that Edward's venom against the Londoners had been specially evoked by

[10] Archives Départementales des Basses-Pyrénées, E 351, transcribed by Ellis, 'Gaston de Béarn', Appendix 39, with her comments, ibid., 252.

[11] *Correspondance d'Alfonse de Poitiers*, ii, no. 2022.

[12] Ibid., no. 2023.

[13] Carpenter, *Battles of Lewes and Evesham*, 22–34.

[14] Ibid., 32; *Ann. Dunstable*, 232; *Chron. Guisborough*, 194–5; *Flores*, iii. 260.

their treatment of his mother at London Bridge.[15] If so, his avenging of his mother's honour must have seemed to Eleanor herself intolerably costly. Edward returned to the battlefield to find the day lost, and after some more fighting, in the course of which John de Warenne, Hugh Bigod, William de Valence and Guy de Lusignan escaped to the coast, Edward fought his way with his Marchers into Lewes priory to join his father.[16] In military terms the defeat could not be contested. Yet, as David Carpenter rightly points out, the king and Edward still had a little bargaining power, since Montfort would have hesitated to root them out of the priory by force. The Mise of Lewes, as the settlement was called, marked the king's defeat, but not unconditional surrender.[17]

Yet the terms of this settlement were hard and humiliating. Henry was in effect a captive; he swore once more to uphold the Provisions of Oxford and to remove all 'traitors' from his council. Edward and Henry of Almain were to be held by the barons as hostages for the carrying-out of the peace and on this condition the Marcher lords were allowed to go free.[18] This was to prove a disastrous concession from Montfort's point of view. Further, two panels of arbitrators were to be set up, the first of which, consisting of Englishmen, was to consider possible modifications to the Provisions of Oxford, but of this panel we hear no more.[19] The second panel is much more interesting. Louis IX was to be asked to convene a named group of three nobles and three bishops, all Frenchmen, who were to choose a further two Frenchmen; these two, after coopting an English arbitrator to join them, were to reconsider Louis's Mise of Amiens and other controversial matters.[20] Although Montfort had in practice paid no heed to the Mise of Amiens in the previous three months, he could not disregard it now, in a settlement with King Henry. Louis was Henry's feudal lord and had until recently been Montfort's personal friend; the earl desperately wanted Louis's co-operation at this point to confer an air of legitimacy on his provisional settlement with the king.[21] In fact the French king disdained to reply to Montfort's request and it later emerged that he had never passed on that

---

[15] *Flores*, iii. 194; *Flores*, ii. 495–6; *Chron. Rishanger*, 32.

[16] *Chron. Rishanger*, 33 and *Chron. Guisborough*, 194 imply lack of courage in those who escaped, but the author of the Merton *Flores* (iii. 260) describes them as going abroad to get help.

[17] Carpenter, *Battles of Lewes and Evesham*, 34–6. For the most authoritative recent discussion of the Mise of Lewes see Maddicott, *Montfort*, 272–8, incorporating earlier work by himself and by David Carpenter.

[18] *Chron. Wykes*, 152.

[19] *Cron. Maiorum*, 63.

[20] *Flores*, iii. 260–1; *Chron. Wykes*, 153.

[21] Maddicott, *Montfort*, 276–7.

request to the French nobles and bishops whom he had been asked to convene. The Mise of Lewes foreshadowed other troubles. The men who had escaped, Warenne, Valence and Bigod, together with the Marchers who had been allowed to go free, were to form the core of the forces which fourteen months later brought Montfort to his own defeat and death at Evesham. For the present, triumph rested with Earl Simon.

Warenne, Valence and Bigod, after they had escaped from the battle-field, rode fast to Peter of Savoy's castle of Pevensey and from there immediately crossed to France, where they sought out the queen.[22] Each of these men had at times been opposed to her, but she had their compassion and friendship now. The simple comment of the chronicler Wykes that they stayed with her a while and looked forward to better times has a chillingly authentic ring in hinting at the impossibility of comfort in such a situation.[23] Her husband and eldest son were now in effect both held captive in the hands of a man whose enmity to her husband and whose ruthlessness she well knew. This meant a measure of deep anxiety which went far beyond a mere political setback. The Dunstable chronicler, no friend of the queen, described her as 'anguished and wearied with grief'.[24] It is a measure of her capacity for endurance and her immense courage that she now rose to the leadership which for the present only she could give.

Eleanor probably went straight to the French court in Paris. She was certainly there by 1 June when, as has been seen, she acknowledged receipt of the sum due to Henry under the Treaty of Paris.[25] Business pressed upon her. It was essential that she should exercise authority in Gascony immediately, and as far as possible exclude that of Simon de Montfort, who would act in the name of her husband. On 3 June she took remarkably independent and assertive action on a complaint from the community of Dax. The question at issue was the right of their court to hear appeals from other parts of Gascony, a right which had been denied them by the seneschal, Henry de Cusances, acting with Erard de Valery and Jean de Grilly, Edward's officials. The delegates from Dax had been on their way to lay their complaint before the Lord Edward, but had been prevented by the warfare in England. They had therefore come to Queen Eleanor, asking her to act in Edward's place and remove this disability. Eleanor was quick to see that such an appeal to her own authority must be encouraged; she made a prompt judgement in their

---

[22] *Ann. London*, 64; *Chron. Rishanger*, 33; Battle Chronicle in Bémont, *Simon de Montfort* (1st edn), 377.

[23] *Chron. Wykes*, 151–2.

[24] *Ann. Dunstable*, 233.

[25] Above, n. 3.

favour, although prudently worded, and ordered the deputy seneschal of Gascony to ensure that it was carried out.[26] The queen knew too that Dax was traditionally loyal and politically important, for her visits to Gascony had given her more than a superficial knowledge of the duchy. Her aim now was to secure its loyalty, to tap its resources in men and money and to utilize its control of shipping.

In the same month that Eleanor dealt with the complaint from Dax she was faced with the need to complete one of those interminably protracted Gascon territorial disputes which, in the wake of the Treaty of Paris, were tossed to and fro between the courts in Gascony and the French *parlement*. The dispute between Renaud de Pons and his wife Margaret on the one hand and the English Crown on the other, over the castle of Bergerac, had dragged on for several years. It had been going badly for Henry III for some time before he placed the judgement in the hands of the queen of France in February 1264.[27] Queen Margaret had given her judgement quickly in favour of Renaud de Pons and his wife. It seems likely that Henry III had been informed of this in the six weeks which then elapsed before the battle of Lewes, but of his response we know nothing.[28] On 17 June, when Eleanor had to make a decision herself, she wisely accepted her sister's adjudication and her letter of enforcement to the seneschal of Gascony bore the great seal of the queen of England.[29]

The assumption of immediate authority in Gascony was a sign of Eleanor's rapid adjustment to the new situation created by Montfort's victory at Lewes. Up to this point she had been assembling forces to go to the support of the king's already large English army, a force considerably more numerous than Montfort's own. Now that army existed no more. She had to reconsider both the scale and the nature of her own effort. The maximum diplomatic pressure must be brought to bear on the new government in England, and here she relied on both the recently appointed papal legate to England, Guy Foulquois, and the king of France. But alongside this she also planned an army of invasion, a force large enough to inflict a military defeat on Montfort and his supporters, who were now in charge of the whole machine of government with all the strength which that implied. At the heart of it all was the determination to rescue her husband and son from captivity. To realize this plan she must build up a massive military armament and a fleet of ships capable of conveying large numbers of men, horses and equipment across the Channel.

---

[26] 'Livre Noir de Dax', 239–40.

[27] *Foedera*, i. 435.

[28] Trabut-Cussac, *L'Administration Anglaise*, 32.

[29] *Recogniciones Feodorum in Aquitania*, no. 503.

The logistics of war were well within Eleanor's experience and she had the campaigning ability of her Savoyard uncles at her service. She knew that the first requisite was money. Her accounts are lost. The relevant accounts of Hugh de la Penne for the queen's wardrobe only contain faint echoes of what was going on, most noticeably perhaps in the sums covering the purchase of horses and equipment and 'secret gifts and private alms'.[30] But this gives no idea of the scale on which Queen Eleanor was working.

The money which had been paid to Eleanor by 1 June under the terms of the Treaty of Paris caused Montfort to make an angry protest to the papal legate, that money which should have been spent for the succour of Holy Church and the benefit of the kingdom of England was patently going to the enemies of the realm, and he asked Guy Foulquois to prevent this. The legate replied laconically that the money was already spent (*pecunia iam soluta*).[31] The money which Eleanor made out of pawning the Crown jewels which Henry had urged her to dispose of 'for his honour' is revealed in an account drawn up in the next reign of the payments made by one Giles of Oudenard to redeem those jewels. £1,000 sterling was repaid to the queen of France, a sum equivalent to £500 sterling in part payment of debts was delivered to merchants of Paris, and a further £257 16s 3d to the executors of Bartholomew de Verders, citizen of Arras.[32]

The queen needed more, and in August 1264 she took a remarkable initiative. For £20,000 of Tours (*c.*£5,000 sterling) she sold back to Louis IX her husband's rights in the three bishoprics of Limoges, Cahors and Périgueux, secured to him under the Treaty of Paris. She did this in her own name and that of her son Edmund, but she knew that the step would lay her open to criticism and she recorded that she took it in accordance with the counsel of Peter of Savoy, John de Warenne, Hugh Bigod and John Mansel, 'counsellors of the Lord King of England'.[33] Louis IX clearly stood to gain, but he was not a man to make capital out of the dire misfortunes of his own vassal and brother-in-law, and he was in any case dealing with a queen and counsellors experienced in diplomacy. There was therefore an escape clause, allowing for the possibility of reversing the agreement, subject to an additional penalty payment of £10,000 of Tours; and this Henry III did later use to redeem his rights.[34]

---

[30] E 372/109 rot. 11d; E 372/113 rot. 1. Over £4,000 was spent in 'secret gifts and private alms', 1257–64, and over £5,000 on horses and equipment, 1264–69.

[31] Heidemann, *Papst Clemens IV*, nos 14 d, 16 c.

[32] E 372/118 rot. 18d.

[33] Gavrilovitch, *Traité de Paris*, Appendix V, 121–3.

[34] Ch. 10, below.

For the moment the contract provided a most necessary addition to Eleanor's resources. It seems to have taken some time for Earl Simon to hear of it, since it is not until 18 November that Henry, presumably at Simon's behest, wrote to Eleanor and also to King Louis, Queen Margaret and Peter of Savoy to repudiate a measure which he hears that 'certain people are putting forward' which he says will be to the disinheritance of himself and his heirs.[35] Henry was probably genuinely concerned about this, but no reliance can be placed on discerning his own attitude from any letters issued under Montfort's direction.

The queen's other main resource was obviously borrowing. There can be little doubt that much would have come from the firms of Florentine merchants with whom she was already accustomed to do business. Evidence for a loan from a different source happens to have survived among the archives of Peter of Savoy. Peter himself stood surety for the 2,500 marks which Eleanor borrowed from Henry of Castile, the Lord Edward's brother-in-law on 9 October 1264. Peter promises that the Lord Edward will repay the money after his release.[36] It is worth noting that Peter, who had succeeded his brother as count of Savoy in 1263, also borrowed large sums in his own name in order to help his niece.[37]

The army gathered around the port at Damme was said specifically by the St Albans chronicler to have been under the leadership of the queen and Peter of Savoy.[38] Of its composition we have little beyond the reports of chroniclers. Thomas Wykes mentions men from Germany, Brabant, Flanders, Normandy, Poitou, Gascony, Burgundy and France. The St Albans chronicler additionally writes of support from Brittany and Spain.[39] It is a plausible list. There had been many knights from northern France and Flanders in the mercenary forces coming to England in 1260–1, and there were knights from Flanders and Champagne in the Lord Edward's retinue in 1263. Gascony and Poitou were obvious sources of support, while John of Brittany, Henry of Castile and possibly Albert of Brunswick may have accounted for useful military help.[40] Advice too was available to the queen from men other than her Savoyard uncles. Warenne, Hugh Bigod and Mansel were all parties to Eleanor's deal with Louis IX over the Three Bishoprics, while John of Brittany and Peter

---

[35] *Foedera*, i. 448 (*CPR 1258–66*, 474).

[36] Wurstemberger, *Peter der Zweite*, iv, no. 664.

[37] Ibid., nos 647, 649; Cox, *Eagles of Savoy*, 316.

[38] *Flores*, ii. 499.

[39] *Chron. Wykes*, 154; *Flores*, ii. 502.

[40] Albert of Brunswick was betrothed to a relative of the queen, *CR 1261–64*, 259; see ch. 10, below.

d'Aigueblanche are mentioned by the London annals and William de Valence by the chronicler fitz Thedmar.[41]

For the distinctive contribution of Peter of Savoy we have something more than chroniclers' impressions. He looked to his own territories for support and there exists a list of more than forty names, some denoting individuals but others denoting sizeable groups of men, to whom he ordered payment for military service. This was dated 30 September 1264.[42] It is of some interest that Peter was paying his own men. Admittedly he was in a special relationship to the whole enterprise, but it gives added point to the remark of the St Albans chronicler that some of the men in the queen's army were stipendiary knights but that others were there at their own expense.[43] Edward and Queen Eleanor herself had many personal contacts abroad and personal loyalties counted in chivalric society. The author of the St Albans *Flores* was also impressed by the unfailing family solidarity of the house of Savoy.[44] Eleanor's mother had returned to her own territorial base where she could help to rally support for her daughter and to maintain stability in the Savoyard homeland.[45] Boniface was firm in his opposition to Simon, firm in his denunciation of the injuries against the Church. He had been given papal authority to exercise his archiepiscopal jurisdiction from the French side of the Channel and he scornfully refused to ease the path of the administration in England by sending anyone to deputize for him when his ecclesiastical services were urgently needed.[46] Peter himself was tireless in organization, to be found at Amiens on 6 August, at St Omer on 17 August and then, through most of September, with the army and fleet at Damme.[47] Philip of Savoy, also mentioned by the St Albans chronicler, was the queen's chief adviser in negotiations with the Montfort government conducted by the legate, based at Boulogne. King Louis himself had agreed to send ambassadors to Boulogne on 8 August in an attempt to facilitate peace negotiations, and there is evidence that both Peter of Savoy and the queen herself were at Boulogne in August.[48]

The capacity to invade England from the port of Damme depended in the end on ships. Some could be secured locally, but not enough. On 24 July Eleanor wrote again to Alphonse of Poitiers, sending messengers to

[41] Above, n. 33; *Ann. London*, 64; *Cron. Maiorum*, 67.
[42] Wurstemberger, *Peter der Zweite*, iv, no. 656.
[43] *Flores*, ii. 500.
[44] Ibid., 501–2.
[45] Wurstemberger, *Peter der Zweite*, iv, no. 644.
[46] *Reg. Urbain IV*, no. 1360; *CPR 1258–66*, 328.
[47] Wurstemberger, *Peter der Zweite*, iv, nos 646, 647, 649–56.
[48] *CR 1261–64*, 398–9; Gavrilovitch, *Traité de Paris*, 121–3.

go to La Rochelle, now asking him simply to instruct his bailiffs to encourage the ships' mariners in that port to receive her messengers favourably.[49] She had evidently accepted his point that only ships willing to serve her should do so. In Gascony she could order rather than solicit, and she evidently directed that English ships in Gascon ports should be seized. Her aim was not only to secure the ships for her own purposes but to prevent them falling into the hands of the Montfort government. That Bordeaux showed its traditional loyalty to the English Crown is evident from the anger of Montfort's government in England over ships of Bristol, Southampton and Dunwich, seized and detained in Bordeaux as early as July 1264.[50] The queen kept in close touch with the officials there. Some time later, on 29 October 1264, writing from St Omer, when her army and fleet were dwindling, Eleanor directed the constable of Bordeaux to let one Peter de Assalhit, a Gascon who had already served the queen well, to have a ship equipped with twenty mariners to be ready for her service when and where she should require it.[51] Bayonne was a different matter. This was the biggest shipping base in Gascony and the issue of its loyalty was of great moment to the queen. Some of the Bayonnais certainly opposed her. In the spring of 1265, at a later stage of the struggle, King Louis ordered the arrest of certain named Bayonnais at La Rochelle, by application to his brother Alphonse of Poitiers, and then had them brought to Paris where he only released them after the royalist victory at Evesham.[52] But not all Bayonnais withheld their services from Eleanor. On 24 July 1264, King Henry, under Montfort's direction, wrote to two shipmasters from Bayonne, Paschasius de Pino and Pelerin de la Poynte, then in Flanders, thanking them for resisting pressure to aid the aliens.[53] This was wishful thinking. In fact these mariners were collaborating energetically with the queen.[54]

The queen's land force gathered around Damme in the summer of 1264 was formidable in size and fighting capacity, and the fleet, reputed to be very large, may well have been at least adequate to convey the men, horses and equipment across the Channel. That force had a thoroughly experienced and skilful leader in Peter of Savoy, renowned for his fighting in his Alpine homeland, and there were many other hardened and vigorous knights under his command. In England the reaction to this

[49] *Correspondance d'Alfonse de Poitiers*, ii, no. 2025.

[50] *CPR 1258–66*, 363; *CR 1261–64*, 401.

[51] Archives Départementales des Basses-Pyrénées, E 172. I owe this reference and a transcription of the document to the kindness of Robin Studd.

[52] *Correspondance d'Alfonse de Poitiers*, ii, nos 2029, 2027.

[53] *CPR 1258–66*, 338.

[54] For recognition of their services see n. 96, below.

military threat was equally impressive, yet very different. In the king's name Montfort called out the feudal host and the men of the Cinque Ports, but then reached beyond this for the active co-operation of all such Englishmen as were able to bear arms, in the villages throughout the midland, southern and eastern counties. On 9 July the sheriff of Norfolk and Suffolk was ordered to organize men from every village, mounted or on foot and equipped with lances, bows and arrows and axes, to assemble near Canterbury in readiness to repel the alien invasion.[55] There was a huge response. Some men acted only under compulsion, but others because this call to leave even the urgent task of harvesting in order to defend their homeland from attack made a powerful appeal. Simon de Montfort's style of charismatic leadership and his acute discernment of populist psychology enabled him to play on such deep instinctive loyalties.[56] The English army which gathered on Barham Down and faced the army of aliens and exiles across the Channel had its own cause and its own cohesion.

According to the St Albans *Flores* the queen's army was straining with eagerness to come to battle. On the English side, the chronicler noted that the thirst for war was mainly to be found among the men of the Cinque Ports. The alien army was such, he writes, that there was little doubt that 'they would have subjugated this land'.[57] Why, then, did the queen's army never invade? For this in the end was a non-event; momentous in its political consequences. The chroniclers had their answers. Some, like the Elizabethans three centuries later, thanked God for his timely manipulation of the Channel winds; others put it down to the eventual failure of the queen's funds, and the Bury St Edmunds chronicler emphasized the importance of the effective English sea and coastal defences.[58] All these explanations have some element of truth and yet, even taken together, they fail to satisfy completely. The Channel winds may have been frequently adverse in the summer of 1264 but the queen's force was there in Flanders, perhaps indeed at varying strength, from June to late October or early November. The money for paying the stipendiaries was no doubt running out by October, but was there no earlier point at which she could have risked a crossing? Neither her army nor her fleet lacked men of experience and courage; quite the reverse.

It may be that there were other weighty factors which militated against an invasion. Chief among these, I suggest, was the work of the legate,

[55] *CPR 1258–66*, 360–1.
[56] Maddicott, *Montfort*, 231–2, 291; Carpenter, 'Simon de Montfort', 219.
[57] *Flores*, ii. 499–500.
[58] *Ann. Worcester*, 453; *Chron. Melrose*, 125; Battle Chronicle in Bémont, *Simon de Montfort* (1st edn), 378; *Chron. Bury St Edmunds*, 29; Maddicott, *Montfort*, 306.

Guy Foulquois, who was based at Boulogne in order to communicate rapidly with the Montfort government in England. That government must be briefly described. The parliament which Montfort had called in June 1264, following his victory at Lewes, confirmed a scheme of government by which effective power rested with a group of three, Montfort himself, Gibert de Clare, Montfort's most powerful baronial supporter, and Stephen Berksted bishop of Chichester, a man committed to the reforming aspect of the baronial programme and in this reflecting the supportive attitude towards Montfort among many churchmen and intellectuals. These three were to nominate a further nine who were to join with them in the 'counselling' of the king.[59] These provisions were said to be temporary, until the arbitrations envisaged in the Mise of Lewes took place. The scheme was given an even sharper edge when, in a proposal known as the Peace of Canterbury, sent to Louis IX himself on 15 August, it was stipulated that the arrangements for the Three and the Nine would continue either until the fulfilment of the terms of the Mise of Lewes or, failing that, for the whole of Henry III's reign and to an indefinite point in the reign of Edward.[60] It was against this background that the legate was working for peace. It is hardly surprising that historians have often regarded the negotiations as less than serious, since the legate and Louis IX were aiming at the restoration of Henry III to full rights of kingship. Yet this is greatly to underestimate their historical importance, as John Maddicott has recently shown in his detailed examination of the legate's register, a much under-used document.[61] It is impossible to read through that lengthy, closely reasoned record of the prolonged interchanges between the legate, the English bishops and the baronial representatives of Montfort's government without realizing that the legate was in full earnest. He felt his responsibilities keenly. His carefully drafted letters and his willingness to bring both sides together and make acceptable proposals when he saw a softening of the stance of his opponents show how hard and thoughtfully he was working. He also showed considerable psychological penetration in his handling of the English bishops. The bishops were in earnest, too. Montfort's regime depended a good deal on their moral support and Earl Simon knew he must take notice of their viewpoint. They were men of peace as surely as Montfort was a man of war.[62]

[59] *DBM*, 294–9; Maddicott, *Montfort*, 285–7.

[60] *CPR 1258–66*, 365–6; *DBM*, 294–301; *Foedera*, i. 443; Maddicott, *Montfort*, 293–4.

[61] Heidemann, *Papst Clemens IV*, esp. 198–247; Maddicott, *Montfort*, 291–306, *passim*.

[62] Maddicott, *Montfort*, 301–2; Powicke, *Henry III*, 484–6. Bémont underestimates the seriousness of the negotiations for peace, *Simon de Montfort* (2nd edn), 223–6.

The legate's relationship with the queen and her supporters has perhaps never been considered enough in seeking an explanation of the failure to launch an invasion. The legate opposed the invasion; he said so categorically to Montfort and there is no reason to doubt his sincerity. In a letter written late in July, Montfort refused the legate permission to enter England. In typically arrogant fashion, Earl Simon taunted Guy Foulquois with failing to make any attempt to stop the collecting of the invasion force.[63] The legate replied that he had in fact met Montfort's petitions *before* they were made (*praevenimus*).[64] He had laboured to prevent the assembly of knights, but had been unable to do so, and now it was bound to be harder because so much had been spent on recruiting both men and ships. It seems then that, if the legate was being honest, the queen and her advisers had declined to be guided by his advice in the matter of preparing for invasion. The question of giving the signal for the actual launching of the attack, however, was another matter. To sweep aside the legate's advice on this ultimate and irrevocable step, when his intervention had been solicited by both King Louis and Queen Margaret and by Queen Eleanor herself, would have been irresponsible. The queen and her army had to wait while the legate, with remarkable patience, conducted his negotiations.

It is conceivable too that the queen and her closest supporters would have been ready to avoid the bloody slaughter which they must now have known would be the outcome of a confrontation with the force gathered on Barham Down, if there was any possibility of peace on the legate's terms. This we do not know, but there happens to be one interesting piece of evidence which shows that Peter of Savoy regarded the possibility of peace seriously. On 17 August Peter sent letters by one William of London to his agent William Varnerii, who seems to have been in Ireland at the time. Peter proposed that William of London should return from Ireland either by way of La Rochelle or a port of Normandy, unless Varnerii had heard by then that peace had been made, in which case the messenger could travel back through England.[65] If Peter thought in these terms it is probable that the queen did too; it is a warning against assuming that the queen and her advisers were simply spoiling for a fight.

There is no need to trace again here the details of the legate's negotiations with the Montfortian government in England, a process which John Maddicott has revealed so fully for the first time.[66] The force of the

---

[63] Heidemann, *Papst Clemens IV*, no. 14.

[64] Ibid., no. 16.

[65] Wurstemberger, *Peter der Zweite*, iv, no. 648; for further comment see below.

[66] Maddicott, *Montfort*, 291–302.

feelings on both sides and the keen awareness of personal and political issues would have been part of the queen's experience in these months. There are moments when one can catch the sudden impulsive reactions of individuals when the tension of the detailed point and counterpoint drove them to an outburst of deeply felt underlying conviction. Louis IX reached such a moment when he saw the Peace of Canterbury and exclaimed that he would rather break sods behind a plough than have such kingship as that.[67] Another comes at Boulogne when the bishop of Winchester, momentarily overcome by the authority of the legate and his deep disapprobation, broke down and begged for absolution.[68] Queen Eleanor herself had such a moment too. Her advisers, led by Philip of Savoy, had taken the prudent line that they would stand by Louis IX's judgement at Amiens; beyond that, if there was any need for modification they would abide by the decision of King Louis or of the legate.[69] In fact the queen's desperate anxiety was for the safety of her eldest son. Henry III had already written a distressed letter to King Louis, explaining his fears for the hostages, the Lord Edward and Henry of Almain, if an invasion took place, and referring darkly to the *ius gentium*, the accepted code by which hostages might be put to death for the non-observance of the terms of a pact.[70] Whether Montfort would have gone so far as putting to death the heir to the throne may be doubted, but that fear probably helped to stay the queen's hand as effectively as the desire of the legate for a negotiated peace.[71] At an advanced point in the negotiations, very late in September, delegates from England brought the most moderate set of proposals they had yet made and these were shown to the queen. Her anger flashes out; she was outraged (*diminuatam*) that there was no mention of the release of the hostages.[72] In fact she was not alone in wanting the release of the hostages; the bishops wanted this and so did Gilbert de Clare;[73] the queen's stand was one which they could respect, but only for her was it a matter of deep personal anguish.

In October the negotiations broke down completely and the legate pronounced his sentences of interdict and excommunication, so long threatened, in Hesdin, in Artois, but from there they had little effect in England.[74] His mission had failed and he returned to Rome, where he

---

[67] Heidemann, *Papst Clemens IV*, no. 29 c.

[68] Ibid., no. 43 b.

[69] Ibid., no. 43 a.

[70] CR 1261–64, 390–1.

[71] Maddicott, *Montfort*, 284.

[72] Heidemann, *Papst Clemens IV*, no. 43 e.

[73] CPR 1258–66, 374.

[74] Heidemann, *Papst Clemens IV*, nos 50, 51, 52.

was soon to be elected pope as Clement IV; for the moment his links with England were at an end. It was also in October that the queen's army and fleet began to disperse, for her money to pay them had run out. She withdrew to France, 'not without confusion and distress'.[75] She had put all her strength into the assembling of that force, but now it was breaking up, the negotiations had failed, Montfort's regime in England seemed strong, her husband was still captive and her eldest son held as a hostage. The wretched sense of failure after great effort must have borne down on her inexorably.

Was the failure then as total as it seemed at the end of October 1264? In approaching this one must start with the magnificent tribute to the queen from the author of the St Albans *Flores*. He thanks God devoutly for his goodness in bringing about the dispersal of the alien army, but then with a burst of admiration and respect, he proclaims that it must always stand to the praise and honour of the noble lady of the English, Queen Eleanor, that for the sake of her lord the king and her son Edward, she strove so valiantly and vigorously like a heroine of old. In fact the Latin word he uses is *insudaverit*; she sweated at it.[76] That says it all.

The political importance of the efforts of both queen and legate during the summer of 1264 is worth reassessing. Together they had weakened the Montfort regime because they had shown it up as vulnerable and they had displayed the strength of the opposition to it from outside. Admittedly the bishops who had taken part in the negotiations remained loyal to the Montfort government and Walter Cantilupe, bishop of Worcester, was to absolve Simon's forces before the battle of Evesham. Assembled in council at Reading, the English prelates appealed to the pope against the sentences of the legate.[77] Even so, some of the bishops were men with troubled minds. They would stand by Montfort because they would stand by the principles of reform, justice and consent in government, yet Montfort's own often ruthless and acquisitive behaviour must at times have made them uneasy. They were troubled too by the many incidents of spoliation of the clergy during the fighting in 1263 and 1264 and by the continuing disorder in the country. Their primate Archbishop Boniface was opposed to the stand they were taking and they felt keenly the fact that they had been cast off by the legate, who had shown himself to be a man with an earnest desire for peace. A clear break with the authority of Rome was not to be contemplated. That the absence of the archbishop was already hampering is clear from the half-comic

[75] *Chron. Wykes*, 155.
[76] *Flores*, ii. 500.
[77] *Councils and Synods*, II, pt. i. 694–700; *Flores*, ii. 501.

predicament of Walter Giffard, son of the queen's friend Sybil Giffard, elected to the see of Bath and Wells on 22 May 1264, a highly unpropitious moment. Since Boniface refused to come to England or to depute his powers as metropolitan, Giffard, impelled by self-interest and perhaps by his curialist background, seems to have taken matters into his own hands.[78] He crossed to France to secure confirmation of his election and consecration.[79] Queen Eleanor would have followed all this very keenly. According to Wykes, Boniface obliged Giffard to swear that he would not act against the king, and on his return to England Giffard published the sentence of excommunication against Montfort and his accomplices, as his archbishop had enjoined. In Giffard's absence the baronial partisans are said to have ravaged his estates,[80] but he weathered the storm to become royal chancellor after Evesham, and later, archbishop of York. The incident lays bare a fundamental weakness in the position of the English Church and therefore in the whole Montfort regime; the stance of the prelates was ultimately untenable. As for Eleanor of Provence, throughout the critical months of 1264 she had shown a capacity for diplomacy and for organization and a readiness for action which even from her opponents won her the sparingly used accolade of *virago*. It was clear that she would not give in. Her friends took courage from this and among her enemies it rightly caused apprehension.

After the plan of invasion from Flanders had been abandoned there was a geographical shift in the royalist offensive and the action swung away from Flanders to the west – to Gascony, Ireland and the Welsh March. The planning and the action now became more complex, with secrecy and surprise essential. Because the queen's role is much less obvious to the chroniclers one is in danger of missing her centrality to the whole enterprise. The lands in the west had already featured in her planning even before the collapse of the invasion force. We have seen how she tightened her grip on Gascony to forestall the Montfort government.[81] Edward's lordship of Ireland was also a vital part of the royalist perspective. In the letter already mentioned, which Peter of Savoy sent from St Omer on 17 August 1264, he can be seen organizing the transport of money (*pecunia*), which would have been bulky and heavy, from Ireland to Amiens. Significantly, the money was to be handed over at the

---

[78] *CPR 1258–66*, 319, 328.

[79] HMC, *Cal. of MSS of the Dean and Chapter of Wells*, i. 103. *Chron. Wykes*, 164. The exact dating of Giffard's movements is not clear.

[80] *Chron. Wykes*, 164. The temporalities of the bishopric had been restored to Giffard as the incoming bishop on 1 September 1264, *CPR 1258–66*, 343.

[81] See above, nn. 50, 51.

lordship of Wexford, to two merchants of a firm based in Amiens, who would then bring it back to that base for delivery to Peter.[82] The man who carried Peter's letter of instructions to Ireland and was to return to him speedily with the merchants' letter of receipt for this valuable cargo was William of London, quite possibly the queen's clerk of that name. William, as has been seen, was to make his way back from Ireland to Flanders by way of La Rochelle or a port of Normandy, unless peace had been concluded meanwhile. Peter's letter presumes moderate ease of transport between the Irish ports and the Continent. In the view of Peter of Savoy and the queen, Ireland was far from seeming remote or marginal; it was already integral to their planning.

The Worcester annalist makes the general point that the queen sent to Ireland to ask for help from the magnates there, as she did to Gascony.[83] Robin Frame's discovery in the close rolls of another incident involving a trading vessel seems to bear this out.[84] In November 1264 the chances of a Channel storm brought a trading ship of St Mary's Abbey, Dublin, making its way back to its Irish base, into a port in the Isle of Wight. On board was a knight, said to have boarded the ship at Dieppe, by order of the mayor of that town, but against the wishes of the mariners (or so they insisted). Ship, mariners and knight were all seized in the Isle of Wight by the bailiffs of the pro-Montfortian countess of Aumale, because of a well-founded suspicion that the knight was carrying letters addressed to various magnates of Ireland. Here again we may be glimpsing the secret communication lines of the royalists.

Apart from these contacts under cover of trade, there were crucial political developments in Ireland in 1264–5 which highlight the vigorous initiatives of a man who was, as we have seen earlier, a relative by marriage of Peter of Savoy and a friend and protégé of the queen. Geoffrey de Joinville, lord of Meath in right of his wife, enjoyed an influence in Irish affairs that was enhanced by the fact that he spent appreciable time in Ireland instead of being a purely absentee lord. In December 1264 when the Lord Edward's justiciar of Ireland, Richard of La Rochelle, was captured by the aggrieved Geraldine family, it was Geoffrey de Joinville, assisted by the Geraldines' rival, Walter de Burgh, who brought the rebels to submission.[85] Joinville did not leave

---

[82] Wurstemberger, *Peter der Zweite*, iv, no. 648. For Ross see Powicke, *Henry III*, 29, n. 1; also *CPR 1247–58*, 297.

[83] *Ann. Worcester*, 452–3.

[84] Frame, 'Ireland and the Barons' Wars', 162; *CR 1264–68*, 80–1.

[85] Otway-Ruthven, *A History of Medieval Ireland*, 196–8. Walter de Burgh had been granted Ulster by the Lord Edward on 15 July 1263, Frame, 'Ireland and the Barons' Wars', 164.

matters there. In April 1265 he called an assembly of Irish magnates to Dublin, in which he evidently worked for a reconciliation of magnate factions and the consolidation of a royalist stance among them.[86] He had considerable success; Irish nobles from both sides of the quarrel of 1264–5 were to be found giving military support to the English Crown shortly after the battle of Evesham.[87] Joinville's personal assistance in furthering the affairs of the Lord Edward in the Welsh March in May 1265 will be seen later. I suspect that in the activities of Joinville we are touching on detailed political and military planning in the royalist interest.

How far, if at all, was Queen Eleanor involved? Was she in personal touch with Joinville? Her many contacts with Geoffrey de Joinville and his family have already been noted, with his wife Maud and his brothers Simon and William. Geoffrey had fought on Henry III's campaign in Gascony in 1253–4, had witnessed several of the Lord Edward's charters and had given his support in the king's dealings with the Welsh in 1260. There was a deep family commitment here. It seems inconceivable that Eleanor of Provence would not have made it her specific business to be in contact with Geoffrey de Joinville at the time when she needed his help most urgently.[88]

It was in November 1264, the same month in which letters to Ireland were intercepted in the Isle of Wight that, according to the chronicler Robert of Gloucester, a message from the queen got through to a group of former household knights of the Lord Edward who were holding out in Bristol. The message was of serious military importance since the queen was urging an attempt to rescue the Lord Edward and Henry of Almain from Wallingford castle, where they were held as prisoners.[89] Robert of Gloucester's report gains credence from his close personal contacts with Warin de Bassingbourne, one of the Bristol knights who led the venture. Another knight involved was Robert Walerand, a well-trusted ally of the queen. Eleanor believed that the guard placed at Wallingford at the time was not very strong, and one wonders where her evidence came from. According to the St Albans *Flores*, Walerand, Bassingbourne and a few others, with great daring, rode across to Wallingford and made an assault on the castle. Robert of Gloucester recorded that the attackers penetrated to the inner court but were then brutally warned that unless they withdrew, Edward would be hurled out to them by means of a mangonel; Edward himself spoke to them from the wall

---

[86] Frame, 'Ireland and the Barons' Wars', 163; Otway-Ruthven, *A History of Medieval Ireland*, 198.

[87] Frame, 'Ireland and the Barons' Wars', 161.

[88] Ibid., 163. For summary of Joinville's career see ch. 3, above.

[89] *Robert of Gloucester*, ii. 751–2.

above and begged them to go. There was no alternative and the immediate result was Montfort's removal of the hostages to the greater security of Kenilworth.[90]

The St Albans chronicler places the rescue attempt in the context of a new Marcher offensive in the course of which Hereford was sacked, the castles of Gloucester, Bridgnorth and Marlborough taken and a great deal of border country devastated.[91] Certainly the synchronisation of the rescue attempt and the rising makes it seem possible, or even probable, that the queen and her advisers were in communication with the Marchers.[92] Eleanor's own most likely personal contact in the March was Roger Mortimer, whose wife was undoubtedly known to the queen. On 1 January 1253, at the time of general present-giving at court, Maud de Mortimer had been given a valuable girdle by the queen.[93] Whether she may even have been attached to the queen's entourage at the time, one does not know, but the date and the value of the present imply more than a merely casual contact between Eleanor of Provence and Roger Mortimer's wife. The Marcher rising, like the rescue attempt, failed. With the help of Llywelyn ap Gruffudd, Montfort forced the lords of the March to submission and imposed hard terms on them in the Peace of Worcester in December 1264. They had to promise to go to Ireland for a year and a day, to leave their lands in Montfort's custody and to surrender the hostages they had taken at Northampton. Edward was to surrender his great Marcher lordship of Chester to Montfort, receiving uncertain compensation, but in return for all this it was promised that Edward and Henry of Almain would be released from custody at the forthcoming Hilary parliament.[94] In the event, the Marchers did not fulfil their side of the bargain, and Edward's release simply proved to be a slightly less restrictive form of surveillance. Yet a pattern had been set and was not forgotten. When the tide eventually turned against Montfort, it was set in motion by the well-planned escape of Edward and major military activity in the Welsh March.

At some point before mid February 1265 Eleanor of Provence had gone to Gascony. This was no doubt a carefully considered step and it would be a mistake to consider it as even a partial withdrawal. By residence in Gascony, where she had an official status as duchess, she could exercise control over its resources and encourage its loyalty the

---

[90] *Flores*, ii. 502–3; *Robert of Gloucester*, ii. 752.
[91] Ibid.
[92] Maddicott, *Montfort*, 307.
[93] E 101/349/13.
[94] *Flores*, ii. 503–4; *Ann. Osney*, 154–8; *Cron. Maiorum*, 70–1; *CPR 1258–66*, 394–5; *CR 1264–68*, 84–5; Maddicott, *Montfort*, 307–8, 321.

more effectively. On 13 February 1265 at Saint Macaire she granted letters patent to the community of the Isle of Oléron promising that the aid of £390 of Provins (*c*.£98 sterling), which they had granted her for the help of the Lord King and Edward, 'our dearest son', would not be drawn into a precedent.[95] From Gascony she would have been able to sustain a network of contacts by both land and sea routes. It would be interesting to know, for instance, something of the activities in 1265 of those two highly competent shipmasters from Bayonne, Paschasius de Pino, soon to be master of the queen's ship *La Reyne*, and Pelerin de la Poynte, who in the following April was granted special exemption from prise, for his services to the king, queen and Edward, beyond the seas.[96] I would suspect that both these men were active in the queen's service. From Gascony she could still have contact with Ireland, where Montfort's authority was minimal and where Geoffrey de Joinville, as has been seen, was swinging support towards the royalist cause. The queen would also have been able to sustain pressure on her supportive sister and brother-in-law in Paris and to maintain contact with William de Valence, whose Poitevin lands were not far from the Gascon border. We do not have evidence for contacts between Valence and Eleanor but one must consider the probabilities.

The movements of William de Valence in 1264 and the early part of 1265 give more than a hint of the plans which were to culminate in May in his landing in Pembroke with John de Warenne and a force of perhaps 120 men, carried in four ships, according to Montfort's own information.[97] At some point in 1264 Valence's marshal took twenty men in two ships from Bordeaux to La Rochelle, in other words from a port under Queen Eleanor's control and where she had herself ordered the fitting-out of such a ship for Peter de Assalhit in October of that year.[98] In February 1265 we catch a glimpse of William de Valence passing through the lands of Alphonse of Poitiers, together with men, horses and military equipment, heading north for 'England, Wales or Ireland, according to what seems best to him' – for Valence was lord of Wexford in the south-east of Ireland as well as Pembroke at the south-western tip of the Welsh March.[99] The words are those of Louis IX, requesting the bailiffs of

[95] *Gascon Register A*, ii, nos 166, 169.

[96] *CPR 1258–66*, 641, 583.

[97] *CR 1264–68*, 121.

[98] E 101/371/8/262, cited by Ridgeway, 'William de Valence and his *Familiares*', 245, n. 28, where the date is given as January 1265, but the date in the first line of the document is 1264; above, n. 51.

[99] *Correspondance d'Alfonse de Poitiers*, ii, no. 2030. For trans-regional landholding see Frame, *The Political Development of the British Isles*, 96–8, and 'Ireland and the Barons' Wars', 159; see also fig. 4.

Alphonse to permit William de Valence's passage. They show both that Valence was keeping his plans flexible and that Louis IX presumably had some idea of what he was about. So too, one surmises, had Queen Eleanor. Valence's companions in the May landing were John de Warenne and probably Hugh Bigod, two of the small group of men whom we know to have been her chief counsellors in the previous August.[100]

The great unknown factor in the early planning of the royalists in 1265 was Gilbert de Clare, earl of Gloucester, lord of Glamorgan in the Welsh March and also of Kilkenny in Ireland, and additionally, by grant of Montfort, guardian of Valence's own lordship of Pembroke. The mere list of names shows how crucial was his allegiance to either side. In the later part of 1264 Gilbert de Clare had become increasingly alienated by Montfort's blatant promotion of the interests of his sons, his reluctance to release the Lord Edward and Henry of Almain from their status as hostages and his use of alien mercenaries. Montfort's summary arrest of the young earl of Derby in February 1265 may have roused Clare's fear as well as his anger.[101] It was perhaps as early as the end of February that Clare's disillusion with Montfort caused him to withdraw to the Welsh March and soon to enter into negotiations with the royalist lords of that area.[102] In late April Montfort, now deeply suspicious of Clare's intentions, made his way with a group of his own friends and supporters to Gloucester, taking with him as usual, the king and the Lord Edward. It was Clare's eventual commitment to support the Lord Edward that made possible the great royalist breakthrough. The synchronization achieved was the outcome of masterly planning, as Montfort himself quickly realized. Before 10 May 1265 the small expeditionary force led by Valence and Warenne landed in Pembrokeshire without opposition. On 28 May, through a scheme which involved close collaboration and accurate timing on the part of Roger Mortimer and Gilbert de Clare's brother Thomas, the Lord Edward escaped.[103] Thomas de Clare was half-guard, half-companion to Edward and still well trusted by Earl Simon when he came in Edward's company to Hereford, where the prince and his father arrived from Gloucester about 8 May in Montfort's entourage. On the pretext of trying out the calibre of various horses, while taking exercise on the outskirts of Hereford, Edward contrived to ride off at great speed on the fastest horse, followed closely by Thomas de Clare and one or two others, to a pre-arranged meeting with a waiting group of Roger Mortimer's knights and so come to the Mortimer

---

[100] *Chron. Wykes*, 165; Gavrilovitch, *Traité de Paris*, 123.
[101] Maddicott, *Montfort*, 327–9.
[102] *Ann. Waverley*, 358; CR 1264–68, 43–4.
[103] CR 1264–68, 119–20, 121–2, 124–5.

stronghold of Wigmore. According to Robert of Gloucester he was there welcomed by Roger's wife, Maud, redoubtable descendant of Strongbow, enemy of Montfort and friend of Queen Eleanor.[104] We have no evidence (we need none) that the news of Edward's escape was immediately dispatched to his mother. The next day Edward and Gilbert de Clare held a crucial meeting at Geoffrey de Joinville's castle of Ludlow. It is clear that Joinville was privy to the whole plan. Edward made a solemn promise that the ancient laws and customs of the kingdom should be observed and that he would ensure that the king ruled through native Englishmen, and that he removed aliens from his council.[105] The actual terms of this concordat would not have pleased Eleanor, but they could by now have caused her no surprise. Edward, joined by Warenne and Valence from Pembroke and by Walerand and Bassingbourne and other knights from the loyal garrison until recently in Bristol, quickly gathered recruits and in a brilliant campaign lasting only a month proceeded to out-general Montfort himself.

The co-ordination of movements around the time of the royalist landing and Edward's escape, an achievement which turned the course of English history, has always been a matter of frustrated surmise rather than hard evidence for historians. In fact the excitement of the whole story is tantalizingly enhanced by the very fact that one knows so little of the secret royalist plans which produced it. What seems likely is that one should be thinking in terms of an overarching network of strategies which had its supports in the Welsh March, Bristol, Ireland, Poitou and Gascony and perhaps in Paris too. These considerations give a certain extra piquancy to the slight mystery surrounding Henry of Almain's diplomatic mission to Louis IX in April 1265, ostensibly on behalf of the Montfort government, still desperately eager for French approval. Montfort had shown some confidence in Henry of Almain as an intermediary at one stage in the negotiations with the legate in the previous autumn and he now released him temporarily from custody in order to send him to the French court on matters 'touching the state of the king and the realm', initially accompanied by the abbot of Westminster.[106] In mid-May Henry of Almain evidently asked to be allowed to stay longer to accomplish his business. With a certain discernible touch of impatience, this request was granted by Montfort on 18 May.[107] Ten days

---

[104] *Chron. Wykes*, 162–4; *Robert of Gloucester*, ii. 757–8; extract from Wigmore Chronicle, printed in Dugdale, *Monasticon*, vi. 351.

[105] *Chron. Wykes*, 164–5.

[106] *CPR 1258–66*, 418. For earlier use of Henry of Almain as an intermediary see Maddicott, *Montfort*, 296, 300–1.

[107] *CPR 1258–66*, 425. Montfort by now knew of the landing in Pembroke.

later Edward escaped and was soon reunited with Henry of Almain's close friends John de Warenne and William de Valence. Thomas de Clare, who assisted in Edward's escape, had certainly been playing a double role. What of Henry of Almain? Was there any venomous suspicion prompting Montfort's first act on hearing of Edward's escape – to have Henry of Almain's father and stepbrother, held at Kenilworth, actually put in irons?[108] We next hear of Henry of Almain in connection with Eleanor of Provence herself who, perhaps before she left Gascony, had begun to plan his marriage with Constance, daughter of Montfort's old arch-enemy Gaston de Béarn.[109] Since she would clearly only have done this in consultation with Henry of Almain himself, that may be significant too.

The queen remained in Gascony at least until 26 July 1265, the date on which she issued certain privileges, 'saving the approbation of her dear son Edward', to the inhabitants of Monségur in a document dated at Bordeaux.[110] She was obviously continuing to work hard at maintaining the authority of Edward and the king in the duchy. Apart from this, one of her major concerns was the action she was now urging on the papacy. In this she had a unique advantage. Guy Foulquois, now Pope Clement IV, was the legate whose advice she had followed, perhaps reluctantly, during those wearying months of negotiation at Boulogne in the summer and autumn of the previous year. He had an obligation to listen to her. As early as 23 March he assured her that he would indeed appoint a new papal legate to England as she asked, but he could not resist a sharp aside that 'remarking the contempt with which the English had treated him when he was in a lower office', he thought it better to wait for another month to give them time to come to a better frame of mind.[111] By early May he had made his appointment and his choice must have been so gratifying to Eleanor as to make up for any delay. The new legate to England was Cardinal Ottobuono de Fieschi, nephew of Innocent IV and brother of Thomas of Savoy's second wife, Beatrice de Fieschi. Eleanor had already met him and presented him with a ring whose value marked his high status, on his visit to England with Thomas of Savoy in May 1258.[112] The pope urged Louis IX's support for Ottobuono's difficult mission and he cautioned the new legate himself in respect of Montfort that he should not admit of a treaty of peace 'until the pestilent man with

---

[108] BL Cotton MS Cleopatra D. III (Hailes Chronicle), f. 45, cited by Maddicott, *Montfort*, 335.
[109] Studd, 'The Marriage of Henry of Almain', 169–70.
[110] *Archives Historiques du Département de la Gironde*, v, no. 1.
[111] *CPL*, i. 419.
[112] Ch. 7, above.

all his progeny be plucked out of the realm of England'.[113] Evesham still lay ahead, but the pope's tough stance must have satisfied even Queen Eleanor.

In England the pace of events had quickened and by late July was moving rapidly towards its climax. This is not the place to tell again the details of that campaign, which are readily available elsewhere.[114] It was brilliantly conceived and executed. By seizing control of the major fortified towns along the north/south barrier of the River Severn, Edward's forces gained an initial advantage which enabled them to pin Montfort behind the Severn at Hereford; they subsequently manoeuvred him into a desperate position at Evesham, cut off from help from his son's forces which were by then based at Kenilworth. At Evesham the second great battle of the civil war was fought, on 4 August 1265. Montfort and his men showed skill and courage to the last, but the battle turned into a merciless slaughter by the royalists, whose lust for vengeance now outweighed all other feelings. Henry III, decked out in Montfortian armour, barely escaped with his life since he was not immediately recognized. When the killing ended, Montfort's own body having been mutilated and dismembered, his severed head and testicles were carried triumphantly to a woman who had long hated him and who, from her later rewards, may have helped more than we know to bring about his downfall: Maud de Mortimer.[115] The fighting had drawn to its murderous close. Eleanor of Provence would have received the news with profound thankfulness.

---

[113] *CPL*, i. 426, 419.

[114] Maddicott, *Montfort*, 335–45; Carpenter, *Battles of Lewes and Evesham*, 37–66.

[115] *Cron. Maiorum*, 75–6. Maud de Mortimer was rewarded separately from her husband, to the sum of £100 yearly in land, *Rotuli Selecti*, 250.

10

A Troubled Peace

On 5 October 1265, as I have come to believe, two months after the
battle of Evesham, Eleanor's sister Queen Margaret wrote a letter to her
brother-in-law Henry III, a letter which is still extant.[1] Henry III, debilit-
ated by months of captivity, acute anxiety after Edward's escape and the
personal horror of the engagement at Evesham, was taken to Gloucester
to rest and recover after he had been rescued from the battlefield. He
stayed in Gloucester for three weeks, followed by ten days at Marlborough.[2] By this time he was presumably regaining his health and spirits
and he was eager to see his wife. Henry had evidently written to Queen
Margaret begging her not to delay Eleanor's return to England, from
which one may perhaps gather that she was returning from Gascony by

[1] SC 1/3/138. This interesting letter (see below) is usually thought to have been written
on 2 October 1235 (*Lettres des rois*, i, no. 34) or 14 January 1236 (*Diplomatic Documents*,
i, no. 244), in each case relating to one of two feasts of St Remigius, 1235/6. Either of these
dates raises problems. On 2 October 1235 Eleanor was in no sense queen of England, while
14 January 1236 was the very day of her marriage to Henry III, at Canterbury. The only
countess of Gloucester in 1236 was already married to Henry III's brother, Richard of
Cornwall. Queen Margaret's reference to her own (renewed) 'happy' state of pregnancy
does not fit with the birth of her first child in 1240. In 1265, at the age of 44, it is possible
that she believed herself to be again pregnant, although no child was born after Agnes (her
eleventh) in 1260. She may have been experiencing menopausal symptoms. The intimate
tone of the letter fits well with the relationship of the correspondents in the 1260s (see
Diplomatic Documents, i, nos 315, 362, 380, 424, 430), but it would have been strange in
1236. There was no other occasion for the writing of such a letter, referring to Eleanor's
'long delay', at any point in her marriage earlier than 1265. Agnes Strickland's suggestion
(*Lives of the Queens of England*, i. 397–8) that the letter was written in April 1264 is
untenable, since it is clearly dated in relation to the feast of St Remigius.
[2] Powicke, *Henry III*, 503.

way of Paris. Margaret is writing in reply and she writes from Paris. She rejoices with obvious sincerity over Henry's report that he is in good health; and then her letter changes to an altogether lighter tone:

> With regard to your request that we hasten the coming of our dear sister the queen of England, we let your excellency know that although we could very much wish for her company, especially in view of the happy state in which by the divine will we again find ourselves, yet since we are afraid lest you should make a marriage with another lady because of her long delay, we shall take all possible care to speed her on her way to you; and while I know that the countess of Gloucester is in your neighbourhood, I shall not rest until my sister is in your company. Dated Paris, the Monday after the feast of St Remigius.

This letter is charmingly touched by that *débonaireté* which marked the cultural ambience of the French and English courts. Perhaps deliberately, in view of the recent trauma of war, Queen Margaret strikes this note of family intimacy and playful humour in writing of her sister's return to England. Hence her frivolous suggestion that Henry, whose wife had been absent for two years, might think of having his marriage annulled and marrying someone else – perhaps for instance Maud de Lacy, the still eminently marriageable widow of Richard de Clare and the wealthiest dowager in England![3] Henry would no doubt have been amused.

In sober fact the timing and style of the return of Eleanor of Provence to England was of appreciable political importance. She disembarked at Dover on 29 October 1265 and she came with Cardinal Ottobuono, recently appointed legate to England.[4] Whoever advised her arriving in the legate's company advised her well. Curiously, it is a point which has been overlooked. The queen had been a prime target for popular hatred even before she had left England. Since then the threat of the army of foreign knights and mercenaries which she had gathered in Flanders 'thirsting for English blood' had roused intense patriotic feeling among the men whom Montfort had rallied to oppose it; this was all very recent. Eleanor's arrival with the legate presented her differently. It was the previous legate to England, the present pope, who had laboured for a settlement and restrained the queen from unleashing that force of foreign knights. The new legate, in that same tradition, came to England as a man of peace to work for reconciliation now that the royal victory had

---

[3] For the wealth of Maud de Lacy, widow of Richard de Clare see Altschul, *A Baronial Family*, 95–6.

[4] *Chron. Wykes*, 179; *Gervase of Canterbury*, ii. 243.

been won. Powicke's unforgettable portrayal of Ottobuono may be slightly roseate, but the legate was undoubtedly a remarkable man, of great integrity; his uncompromising support for royal authority was balanced by a constructive and compassionate attitude towards the vanquished.[5] This of course had yet to be revealed, but he commanded respect, and by arriving with Ottobuono Eleanor of Provence had tacitly associated herself with the forces of reconciliation.

In the event, peace proved to be a distant prospect and there lay ahead a further two years of bitter conflict with the former supporters of Montfort, and worse general disorder than the country had known during the period of official war.[6] A parliament held at Winchester in September 1265, following quickly upon the royalist victory at Evesham, had launched a provocative policy of outright confiscation of the property of former rebels, and a lavish, and too often indiscriminate, redistribution of these spoils as rewards for some of the most aggressive royalist supporters. Mortimer and his Marcher companions, together with Roger Leybourne and Robert Walerand, all gained substantially.[7] They were bitter and they were acquisitive, determined that the former rebels should now suffer in their turn. There were some among the magnates, and no doubt many in other ranks of society, both churchmen and laity, who wholly deplored this vindictive policy and three men disapproved so strongly that they withdrew from the parliament: Richard of Cornwall, Roger Bigod and Philip Basset.[8] For the present their wiser counsels of moderation were overruled and the policy of disinheritance began its evil work of driving the former Montfortians into continued resistance.

Immediately after the September parliament attention was turned to subjecting the capital. The citizens of London were punished by harsh reprisals, including the widespread and sometimes unjust confiscation of the property of individuals, and in due course the imposition of a very heavy fine on the city of 20,000 marks.[9] London Bridge was to be made over to Queen Eleanor.[10] By the time of the arrival of the queen and the legate the royalist *revanche* was in full swing. The previous few days had seen two particularly dramatic reversals of fortune. The Lord Edmund had been invested with Montfort's former earldom of Leicester, and Montfort's widow Eleanor had surrendered Dover castle to the

---

[5] Powicke, *Henry III*, 526–8; Jacob, *Studies*, 171 and n. 1.

[6] Jacob, *Studies*, 167–70; Powicke, *Henry III*, 503; Knowles, 'Resettlement', 25–6.

[7] *Ann. Dunstable*, 239; Knowles, 'The Disinherited', pt iii. 1–8; *CIM*, i, nos 609–940.

[8] *Ann. Waverley*, 367; *Robert of Gloucester*, ii. 768.

[9] Williams, *Medieval London*, 233–5.

[10] *CPR 1266–72*, 459.

Lord Edward, leaving England with her younger children, never to return.[11] When Queen Eleanor landed at Dover she was met by her son Edward and at Canterbury she was reunited with her husband. She was welcomed back to England by a great gathering of magnates, barons and prelates and, according to Thomas Wykes, she received joyful acclaim from the city of Canterbury.[12] One wonders in fact whether the memories of the patriotic army assembled on Barham Down in the previous year could have faded so quickly.

The Furness chronicler comments that after her return to England the queen was restored to her former state of honour and power.[13] It was an outsider's view. Technically of course the statement was true. The queen's official prerogatives were what they had always been. Her personal position, by contrast, was subtly different. She was bereft of her closest pre-war counsellors, Peter of Savoy, now fully occupied in his Alpine homeland, where he had succeeded as count in 1263, and John Mansel who had died in exile. The court was no longer rent by factious rivalries between Savoyards and Lusignans, nor between the supporters and the enemies of Montfort. New divisions of a different kind were to emerge, but there is no evidence that the queen attempted to play a divisive role. It is evident, however, that she took a full part in consultations on policy, at the highest level. The Dunstable chronicler shows her at Northampton around Christmas 1265 in discussion with the king and the legate on the handling of the individual submissions which followed Edward's campaign against the rebels in the Isle of Axholme.[14] It was the queen too who seems to have been given responsibility in relation to the award of dower to Simon de Montfort's widow.[15] The queen's experience both in diplomatic and military matters commanded respect and the evidence for her substantial role in the eventual suppression of recurrent outbreaks of rebellion has not previously been assessed.

In the spring of 1266 Eleanor was installed in Windsor. It had become clear that the fighting was by no means over and disorder was intensifying as the ruthless policy of disinheritance drove former rebels to a last desperate effort. They hoped for support from Montfort's sons Simon and Guy who were gathering troops overseas;[16] the seemingly impregnable Montfortian stronghold of Kenilworth still held out. Despite the

---

[11] CPR 1258–66, 470; *Chron. Wykes*, 178–9; *Gervase of Canterbury*, ii. 243.

[12] *Chron. Wykes*, 179–80.

[13] *Continuation of William of Newburgh*, 549.

[14] *Ann. Dunstable*, 240.

[15] CPR 1266–72, 141.

[16] CPR 1258–66, 664–5.

energetic efforts of the Lord Edward, John de Warenne, Henry of Almain and Roger Leybourne, the rebels in various parts of the country constantly regrouped. The queen had not been installed in Windsor simply for her own greater safety. When the rebel Robert Ferrers earl of Derby was captured by Henry of Almain in May 1266, he was sent forthwith to Windsor for safekeeping.[17] Edward meanwhile was attempting to clear up the resistance led by Adam Gurdon in Hampshire. This campaign ended in a dramatic encounter in single combat between the Lord Edward and Adam Gurdon himself. Edward hanged Adam's followers on nearby trees but spared their leader's life in tribute to his courage. At this point the accounts of the chroniclers differ. According to Nicholas Trivet, Edward had Adam sent to Guildford to the queen, with a recommendation that she should treat him kindly.[18] But Eleanor was at Windsor, not Guildford in May 1266 and an earlier and harsher account by Thomas Wykes is probably correct. According to Wykes, Adam was sent to the queen at Windsor, where he was imprisoned along with Ferrers, 'lest the earl should lack a companion', adds the chronicler with a touch of black humour.[19] Adam Gurdon was the queen's prisoner, not her guest, and his lands were eventually bought back from her under the terms of the Dictum of Kenilworth.[20] The dispatch of Ferrers and Gurdon to Windsor indicates that it was a top security prison and, as far as we know, the queen never let a prisoner in her charge escape. Windsor was strongly guarded. On 3 May 1266 the abbot of Abingdon was excused from the general feudal summons to Northampton because he was performing his full service of thirty knights at the castle of Windsor 'where the queen is now staying'.[21]

At Windsor the queen was in charge of relatives and high-powered guests as well as prisoners. She had Eleanor of Castile in her care, who gave birth to her son John in June 1266. Even more costly, and Queen Eleanor was running out of funds, was the entertainment of the duke of Brunswick. Eleanor accompanied the duke to Kenilworth, where the king was investing the Montfortian stronghold, so that Brunswick's marriage to the queen's kinswoman, sister of the marquis of Montferrat, might take place in the presence of the king himself. Back in Windsor she found herself saddled with the expense of entertaining both Albert of Brunswick and John of Brittany for a time.[22]

[17] *Chron. Wykes*, 189.
[18] Nicholas Trivet, *Annales*, 269; Prestwich, *Edward I*, 36.
[19] *Chron. Wykes*, 189.
[20] CR 1264–68, 284.
[21] CPR 1258–66, 592.
[22] CR 1268–72, 49.

The scale of these financial worries was domestic, but Eleanor of Provence was currently involved in much weightier problems, as the result of the war. One transaction indeed had to be reversed. Both Henry III and the Lord Edward were determined that the queen's sale of the rights of the English Crown in the dioceses of Limoges, Cahors and Périgeux must be revoked, and the fine from the Londoners was used to reverse the agreement of August 1264.[23] There were many other financial claims to be met. The queen was indebted to Flemish and Gascon merchants, individuals and groups. One Walter Espeye and his fellows, merchants of Flanders, had lost goods to the value of £1,100 at the hands of the men of the Cinque Ports, and must be helped to recover their losses 'in consideration of the services of the said merchants to Queen Eleanor.[24] There were also debts to men of a different style. In December 1265 the king stated that he was bound to the count of St Pol in 400 marks for his expenses in the king's service beyond the seas with Queen Eleanor.[25] But the indispensable St Pol stood to gain much greater rewards; he was granted the lands of the northern rebel John de Vescy, which brought him in due course a redemption fine of 3,700 marks.[26] These examples simply reveal the fringes of a problem of daunting size. While she was abroad the queen had borrowed freely and may also in some cases have taken goods without payment. To meet her obligations she needed financial support on an exceptional scale, and for this she appealed to the papacy. Again, Clement IV felt bound to respond.

In March 1266 the pope agreed to the levy of a triennial tenth on clerical incomes to relieve the financial problems of the Crown. It is not always recognized that Eleanor of Provence took a personal initiative in eliciting from the pope a stipulation that a sum of £60,000 of Tours (*c*.£15,000 sterling) should be reserved for the payment of her own debts, incurred during her time abroad.[27] The tax was unpopular and there was some resistance to payment. The attempt to extend the triennial tenth to Scotland and to levy the queen's share from that country was turned down flat by Alexander III in June 1266.[28] The tenth was therefore levied in England, Wales and Ireland and it raised in all between £44,000 and

---

[23] *CPR 1258–66*, 658–9, 662. Although Henry III apparently temporized over the payment of the £10,000 of Tours (£2,500 sterling) required by the penalty clause of the agreement of 1264 (*CPR 1258–66*, 667–8), there seems to be no clear evidence to justify Powicke's surmise that Louis waived this (*Henry III*, 515, n. 1); see Louis's letter in Gavrilovitch, *Traité de Paris*, 123–4.

[24] *CPR 1258–66*, 651.

[25] Ibid., 516.

[26] E 159/42 m. 24, cited by Knowles, 'The Disinherited', pt iv. 108.

[27] *Foedera*, i. 473. For detail on this tax see Lunt, *Financial Relations*, 292–310.

[28] *CPL*, i. 433.

£49,000 sterling.[29] The queen was purposefully involved in the collection of her share. Walter Giffard's register shows her clerk Henry Sampson active within the province of York.[30] When the levy from the northern province proved inadequate, the king asked the legate and the other distributors of the tenth to pay the queen what remained due from the Irish bishoprics and the bishopric of Exeter.[31] Payment continued sluggish. In 1270 Eleanor was said to be troubled 'in no small degree' about the collection of the tenth in Ireland; in 1275, 370 marks was still owing from the Chichester diocese and as late as 1280 the bishop of Llandaff was still triumphantly resisting all payment.[32] A little over £1,000 due to Eleanor from the tenth was paid into her wardrobe, but the bulk of the issues from the tax would presumably have gone into her treasury at the exchequer, or direct to debtors.[33]

The pope's concession in the spring of 1266 came at a moment when the situation in England appeared increasingly grave. Rebellion was hydra-headed and the legate was coming close to despair as he watched the appalling results of the vindictive policy of disinheritance, of which he profoundly disapproved. He begged the pope to recall him from what seemed an utterly overwhelming task. Clement IV would have none of it. Knowing that Ottobuono must persist against all odds, he painted the alternative in the darkest colours. If the legate were to leave England his object would have been completely defeated and 'the king and queen and their family delivered to death'.[34] These were strong words but the pope was mindful of his own anxieties as legate to the English in the autumn of 1264, and suggest that at that time he may indeed have felt that the lives of Edward and of Henry of Almain were in real danger as hostages in Montfort's hands.

Ottobuono recovered his nerve, and by the summer of 1266 many among the king's counsellors had come to see the folly of the policy of disinheritance.[35] Gradually they moved towards the alternative policy of redemption, by which former rebels were enabled to recover their lands on payment of fines. At Kenilworth between August and October 1266 a workable scheme was hammered out by a committee of twelve, all of them Englishmen, but of varying viewpoints. According to the final Dictum of Kenilworth fines from former rebels were to be paid to the

---

[29] Lunt, *Financial Relations*, 309.
[30] CPR 1266–72, 175; *Reg. Walter Giffard*, 119.
[31] CPR 1266–72, 234–5.
[32] Ibid., 458–9; CPR 1272–81, 80, 365.
[33] E 372/111 rot. 1.
[34] CPL, i. 420.
[35] Knowles, 'Resettlement', 27–9.

grantees of their lands on a scale which related both to the value of the property and to their guilt as rebels.[36] The Dictum, however, had one serious defect; it did not provide for former rebels to have seisin of their estates *before* they had completed the payment of their fines. This flaw kept dangerous numbers of the wealthier and more hardened rebels from availing themselves of the new policy.[37]

The sequel was the final flaring-up of armed resistance to the Crown. Early in 1267 there were serious threats from three directions. John de Vescy led a rising in the north which required the personal attention of the Lord Edward. In the east, the militant group of rebels led by John d'Eyvill, now based on the Isle of Ely, was ravaging the countryside for supplies and angrily resisting all the legate's attempts at negotiations.[38] The final and most serious threat came from Gilbert de Clare earl of Gloucester, disaffected against the court and sharply at odds on both political and personal grounds with the hard-liner Roger Mortimer. Gloucester absented himself from the parliament at Bury St Edmunds in January/February 1267 and again he made clear his own demands – the removal of aliens from royal counsels and the immediate restoration of the lands of the disinherited as soon as they submitted and before they completed payment of their fines.[39] The king's curt dismissal of these proposals prompted Gloucester to join forces with Eyvill.

Control of London was crucial to the whole situation. So too, as ever, was control of the the Cinque Ports and the south-east, since help from the Continent was a possibility for either side. In the strategic deployment of the king's military strength the queen was evidently regarded as a key figure. Windsor was presumably left in the care of its capable Savoyard constable, Ebulo de Montibus, while by 12 March 1267 the queen had moved to Dover. Here she remained until 7 July.[40] She had undertaken during these crucial months to assume control in the port which looked across the Channel; the constable was her own trusted servant Matthias Bezill.[41] Eleanor evidently took an active part in the provisioning of Dover castle. As late as August 1268 a merchant was paid £25 for corn previously 'taken by the king's consort for the munition of Dover castle'.[42] Her own merchant Deutatus had advanced 26 marks for the

[36] *DBM*, 316–37; Powicke, *Henry III*, 533–8.
[37] Knowles, 'Resettlement', 30.
[38] *Chron. Wykes*, 192–8.
[39] *Ann. Dunstable*, 244–5; Knowles, 'The Disinherited', pt i. 37–8.
[40] *Gervase of Canterbury*, ii. 245.
[41] *CPR 1258–66*, 512.
[42] *CLR 1267–72*, no. 386.

same purpose.[43] She also found it convenient to take immediately from some clergy of the Canterbury diocese the money that would be due to her from the levy of the triennial tenth.[44] It was no moment for meticulous assessment and that anxious man, Henry of Ghent, later claimed that he had handed the queen 100 marks on the understanding that the amount would be adjusted if he had paid too much or too little.[45]

On 8 April 1267 the earl of Gloucester entered London with a large armed force. Initially he did so with the consent of Ottobuono, now based in the capital, for the legate at first trusted him and tried to conduct discussions with him. The London chronicler fitz Thedmar excuses the leading citizens from failing to resist the earl by explaining that they had been commanded to obey the legate 'by the king and by the queen'.[46] The comment shows the queen's prominence in political and military decision making. John d'Eyvill, now in collusion with Gloucester, arrived in Southwark on 11 April, having avoided Roger Leybourne's plans to intercept him, and encamped with his followers just outside the city. The popular party in London rose against the aldermen, royalist property was seized, exiled Montfortians began to return and Newgate prisoners were freed. The situation was explosive.[47]

It was clear that Gloucester and the rebels were likely to prove stubborn and although Gloucester acted with restraint, his control of Eyvill's followers in Southwark was uncertain; they had already broken out in an ugly attack on the royal palace of Westminster.[48] In early May the king took up his headquarters at the abbey of Ham at Stratford Langthorne in Essex, ready if need be for a siege of London; Edward had returned from the north and the legate escaped from the Tower of London to join the king's camp.[49] A firm royal initiative was required and attention was focused on the south-east. The queen's distinctive role now emerges. The king was looking once more to foreign mercenaries to secure the decisive military advantage which he and his advisers felt to be the necessary prerequisite for negotiations with the rebels. One can hardly doubt that this was a decision which had been taken in full consultation with Queen Eleanor. The man who was chosen to execute the plan was Roger Leybourne who was now dispatched to Dover, presumably to discuss ways and means with the queen. According to his own record,

---

[43] *CPR 1266–72*, 547.
[44] Above, n. 33.
[45] *CPR 1266–72*, 345–6.
[46] *Flores*, iii. 14; *Cron. Maiorum*, 90.
[47] *Cron. Maiorum*, 90–1; *Ann. London*, 77; Williams, *Medieval London*, 239–40.
[48] *Chron. Wykes*, 203; *Cron. Maiorum*, 92.
[49] *Cron. Maiorum*, 91; *Chron. Wykes*, 202–3 for a variant version.

Leybourne arrived at Dover on 6 May 1267 'on this business' (*pro predictis negotiis*).[50] The business specified was the munitioning of Dover and Rochester castles, the provisioning of the king's army at Stratford Langthorne and Leybourne's own mission abroad. He spent considerable time at Dover in the next few weeks before receiving the king's official mandate, dated 24 May, directing him to cross to France to urge the counts of St Pol and Boulogne to come speedily to the king's assistance, with all available knights.[51] Leybourne sailed from Dover the next day, an indication that preparatory work had already been done, and his mission overseas lasted a week.[52] The two French counts responded with their usual alacrity and landed at Dover on 31 May with men and horses, a substantial force of 100 knights. On disembarking they would surely have been welcomed once again by Queen Eleanor; she knew them well. Roger Leybourne was awaiting them at Rochester.[53]

Was this final resort to foreign aid necessary? This was an issue which was debated at the time. The Canterbury/Dover chronicler commented that the king felt his own force insufficient to conduct a siege of London; Wykes, however, believed that the aliens were called in unnecessarily.[54] Clive Knowles, the scholar who has made the most detailed study of these events, believes that it was this sudden substantial reinforcement of the king's military strength which did push Gloucester to negotiate a settlement.[55] The earl came to terms with the king on 16 June and it was probably through the mediation of Henry of Almain and Philip Basset that he was able to secure his point that grantees of confiscated lands should be urged to allow the original owners immediate seisin, pending the payment of the redemption fines. The king was able to re-enter London on 18 June.[56] In the wake of Gloucester's submission came that of John d'Eyvill on 1 July.[57]

Between the arrival of the mercenaries and the king's entry into London, the queen had remained at Dover. On 3 June the king had ordered the men of the Ports to pursue one Henry Pethun, a pirate, and his accomplices, who were holding out in Portland and the Isle of Wight; the Portsmen were to defend the sea coast 'as Queen Eleanor and Roger

---

[50] E 101/3/9 m. 4 (printed by Lewis, 'Roger Leyburn', 213); ibid., 207; *Gervase of Canterbury*, ii. 246.

[51] E 163/1/41 no. 11.

[52] E 101/3/9 m. 4 (Lewis, 'Roger Leyburn', 213–14).

[53] Ibid.; *Gervase of Canterbury*, ii. 246.

[54] *Gervase of Canterbury*, ii. 246; *Chron. Wykes*, 207.

[55] Knowles, 'The Disinherited', pt i. 58.

[56] CPR 1266–72, 72; *Cron. Maiorum*, 92–3; *Chron. Wykes*, 206.

[57] CPR 1266–72, 73.

Leybourne will let them know on the king's behalf'.[58] Again one sees Eleanor of Provence and Leybourne, by the curious twist of events, acting in close concert as agents of the king's will. Eleanor was still at Dover when the counts of St Pol and Boulogne left England and one wonders whether there were rings available to grace this final leave-taking.

On 1 July Henry III wrote a letter to his wife, who was still at Dover, seeking her favourable reaction to what might be unwelcome news. The lands of the rebel leader John d'Eyvill had originally been granted to the queen, but by the terms of the recent settlement Eyvill could now receive immediate seisin of that property, provided that in due course he paid the queen the value of his lands over five years. However, in view of the importance of Eyvill's personal submission, the king and his advisers had made a further concession; they had remitted the first year of that fine – and the queen must be told. The king is gently persuasive; he says he depends on her magnanimity and he lovingly requests her to accept this decision 'for reasons which he will explain more fully at their next talk together'.[59] The letter illuminates a relationship. The king has made a concession which involves some material sacrifice on Eleanor's part, but one suspects that he is more apprehensive of her feeling that John d'Eyvill deserves no such consideration than her resentment at the loss of the money. Henry knows that the news will initially anger her, but he knows too that she will listen to reason, if all the facts are put before her. The implication of detailed rational discussion between Henry and Eleanor is significant. Slightly over a year later, when Henry III was planning a visit to Louis IX to settle certain matters of business outstanding between them, he asks that he may bring the queen with him 'so that we may be cheered by the sight of her, and by talking with her'.[60] In these two letters, official though they happen to be, we see the evidence for the role of Eleanor of Provence as the king's indispensable *compagne*.

In the years immediately following her return to England, one dominant preocupation of Eleanor of Provence was the question of property. She naturally received her share of the lands of the disinherited, the greater part of eight major lordships belonging to prominent rebels, with a total annual value of more than £300.[61] In due course redemption fines were substituted for control of the lands themselves, the largest fine being that of John d'Eyvill, calculated at 900 marks.[62] The queen's share

---

[58] Ibid., 142.
[59] Ibid., 74.
[60] CR 1264–68, 552.
[61] *Rotuli Selecti*, 248; Jacob, *Studies*, 154, n. 2, where the queen's gains are summarized.
[62] E 159/42 m. 24d; E 159/44 m. 12d; Knowles, 'The Disinherited', pt iv. 108–9.

of the confiscation spoils was comparable to that of other members of the royal family, with the exception of the very large endowment of the Lord Edmund.

Far more contentious were Eleanor's various claims upon the inheritance of her uncle Peter of Savoy, who died on 16/17 May 1268. These could have caused bitter ill will within the royal family. Peter's three English lordships of Richmond, Pevensey and Hastings were open to other claims than her own. She had no intention of meekly yielding whatever her uncle had bequeathed to her, but family solidarity depended upon an equitable settlement, especially in relation to John of Brittany and the Lord Edward. It was a situation calling for calm temper and political realism.

Edward was no doubt still angry about Peter's acquisition of the lordship of Hastings by the exchange of property into which he had been pressured in 1262; the prince was determined that this time his own interests should not be overridden.[63] Above all, the king and his advisers and the Lord Edward seem to have been unanimous on one major issue, that the lands of Peter's inheritance should not drift into the ambit of the counts of Savoy. This was a real danger. Although in 1255 Peter had bequeathed all his English possessions to Eleanor, in a later will, of 1264, Eleanor had only been left the usufruct of those possessions, with reversion of the lands to his own daughter Beatrice on Eleanor's death.[64] On 11 May 1268 he dictated a codicil to his final will, which had been drawn up only a few days earlier. By this Peter left Richmond to Eleanor, but all his other possessions in England to the sons of Thomas of Savoy.[65] On receiving news of Peter's death, Henry III and his advisers acted quickly. On 3 June 1268, as a preliminary step, the Lord Edward was given custody of all Peter's English lands.[66] This gave time for consideration. Queen Eleanor was no less decisive. Her least questionable claim was to the honour of Pevensey, since here she could depend on the public bequest which Peter had made her in 1259 in the king's court.[67] On 15 July the king and his council, which included the Lord Edward, confirmed this grant, with the important proviso that the honour must revert to the Crown on her death.[68] The situation was uneasy, and it seems that the Lord Edward was far from satisfied. This must surely explain the

[63] Ch. 8, above.

[64] Wurstemberger, *Peter der Zweite*, iv, nos. 407, 657.

[65] For Peter's death and his vacillations over his will in the previous week see Cox, *Eagles of Savoy*, 368–71.

[66] *Excerpta e Rotulis Finium*, ii. 472.

[67] C 47/9/1; ch. 7, n. 47, above.

[68] *Foedera*, i. 475–6.

king's grant of Pevensey to Edward on 28 December 1268, a startling reversal of Henry's previous confirmation of the grant to the queen. The memorandum that this deed was sealed not only with the seal of the king but also with the seal of the queen 'in testimony of her good will' may indicate that hard bargaining had been going on, especially between Edward and his mother.[69] It had in fact already been agreed that Eleanor would hold the honour of Pevensey from Edward during her own life-time.[70]

The settlement of Eleanor's claim to Richmond was also subject to careful negotiation on the part of the king, the queen and the Lord Edward. By the same instrument by which she was granted Pevensey on 15 July 1268, Eleanor was also granted compensation for Richmond to the value of 2,000 marks a year, provided she could satisfy the king as to the bequest and the terms on which it had been made. The earldom itself was to go to John of Brittany. As with Pevensey, she had to accept that the compensation, whether in money or in lands, would revert to the Crown on her death, but in this case she was to be allowed to dispose of the issues in her will up to the sum of 10,000 marks. The Richmond compensation was made up of Louis IX's annual payment of 1,200 marks under the agreements of 1259, for as long as Joan of Poitiers retained the Agenais, and of lands in England yielding 800 marks a year. These sums were subject to adjustment when the Agenais itself became available on Joan's death.[71] Negotiations continued into 1269 and it emerges that, as with Pevensey, the Richmond compensation was the subject of a separate covenant between the queen and the Lord Edward.[72] In regard to Hastings, it does not seem that Eleanor ever pushed her claim, and here there was an adjustment of the interests of the Lord Edward and John of Brittany. As for the claims of the Savoyard boys, these were simply brushed aside with a token payment of an annual fee of £100 from the exchequer.[73] These complicated negotiations, extending over many months, reveal tensions in the royal family. Both John of Brittany and Edward may have been edgy and jealous in guard-ing their own interests and in watching the queen. The outcome was an achievement for fair dealing, and would have required a combination of determination and restraint on Eleanor's part. She emerged on good terms with her son-in-law John of Brittany and presumably the honour and interests of the Lord Edward had been satisfied. After her return to

---

[69] *CPR 1266–72*, 312.
[70] Ibid., 320.
[71] *Foedera*, i. 475–6; Powicke, *Henry III*, 251–5.
[72] *CPR 1266–72*, 383–4, 362.
[73] Ibid., 375, 487.

England in 1265 the queen never again risked a breach with her eldest son.

The queen now felt the urgency of helping to shape the future of her second son, Edmund. This presented an old challenge in a completely new guise. Sicily had recently become a prize for Charles of Anjou, but in England in the later 1260s there were other opportunities, which might not come again. In receiving the grant of Montfort's earldom of Leicester in October 1265 Edmund had become by far the greatest beneficiary of the lands of the disinherited. On 30 June 1267 the king additionally granted him the honour of Lancaster. But this was still not considered sufficient as an appanage for the king's second son.. Another tempting possibility beckoned, the earldom of Derby, the inheritance of the twice-treasonable Robert Ferrers, who, as we have seen, was held a prisoner at Windsor. The story of his subsequent fate is a tale of ugly and heartless chicanery. On 1 May 1269 he was brought before the king's council at Windsor and his lands technically restored on condition of a fine payable to the Lord Edmund, who was their custodian.[74] The enormous redemption fine of £50,000 was deliberately imposed on impossible conditions of payment, which Ferrers was later intimidated into accepting. When he failed in immediate payment, as he was bound to fail, and intended to, his lands were declared forfeit, and Edmund added the earldom of Derby to those of Leicester and Lancaster.[75]

The trickery practised against Robert Ferrers had been promoted by the friends of the Lord Edward, who himself hated the earl, and it was condoned by the king. One suspects that it had the full support of the queen. Her ambition for Edmund was keen and, viewed in retrospect, the timing of the plot against Ferrers certainly fitted neatly with her planning of Edmund's marriage, which was also intended to secure a fitting place for him within the English social structure and to help make his fortune. The bride was to be Aveline, daughter of Isabella de Forz, and heiress to both the Aumale and Devon earldoms. Queen Eleanor was determined to secure this match for Edmund. The rights over the marriage were divided between Aveline's mother Isabella de Forz and the girl's grandmother, Amice, dowager countess of Devon. The amount payable to each was £1,000. Edmund could not afford to pay this himself at present and the matter was urgent. His supportive mother undertook both payments for him. By an instrument of 6 April 1269 the queen undertook to pay Isabella de Forz £1,000 in two instalments, the payment to be completed

---

[74] Ibid., 336.
[75] CR 1268–72, 122–6; Knowles, 'The Disinherited', pt iv. 97–8; Powicke, *Henry III*, 523–6. For the grant of Lancaster, *CChR 1257–1300*, 78 and *CPR 1266–72*, 100.

by 1 November.[76] Three days after the agreement was made the marriage took place.[77] The arrangements with Amice for her £1,000 were less hasty, but then Amice was a friend of the queen. The settlement of this part of the debt was not finalized until 20 July, and the payments were to be spread over three years.[78] This money was to come from the issues of properties granted to Eleanor in her compensation for Richmond. The various financial arrangements were evidently closely intertwined. So too, perhaps, was the treatment meted out to Ferrers and the marriage of Edmund. Edmund was married on 9 April 1269 at Westminster in the presence of the king and queen, the Lord Edward and many of the magnates of England, and, as we have just seen, it was on 1 May that Robert Ferrers was brought before the king's council at Windsor in the first move towards defrauding him of his inheritance.

Marriage was a prime instrument of family aggrandizement and international diplomacy alike. While Eleanor of Provence was engaged in an initiative over the marriage of her son Edmund, she was bringing to a successful conclusion her scheme for the marriage of Henry of Almain to Constance, daughter of Gaston de Béarn. The queen's partner in this venture was the Lord Edward. Gaston de Béarn remained a restive vassal, who still tended to look across the Pyrenees for his alliances. His prime political objective for many years had been to give effect to his wife's claims to the neighbouring county of Bigorre, in which he had been thwarted by the ambitions of Simon de Montfort, and he may have hoped that his co-operation in Eleanor's scheme for the marriage of Constance would prove beneficial to his prospects in Bigorre.[79] In fact no promises were made but at least steps were taken to meet Gaston's many financial claims on the English Crown.[80] The queen and the Lord Edward presumably hoped to secure Gaston's present loyalty and to see the eventual establishment of the heirs of Constance and Henry of Almain in Béarn and its various dependencies. Edward had reason to depend heavily on his mother's lead in the whole matter, but he gave her his full support.[81] By contrast, Richard of Cornwall stood conspicuously

---

[76] *CChR 1257–1300*, 121–2. Scott Waugh (*Lordship of England*, 228) missed the involvement of Isabella de Forz.

[77] *Cron. Maiorum*, 108–9; *Gervase of Canterbury*, ii. 248 (correct in text but misdated in margin).

[78] Confirmed by the king four days later, *CPR 1266–72*, 358.

[79] Studd, 'The Marriage of Henry of Almain', 165–70. For Bigorre see ch. 3, n. 64, above, also Maddicott, *Montfort*, 134, 173, 184.

[80] Studd, 'The Marriage of Henry of Almain', 172–3.

[81] Ibid., Appendix, 178; *Chron. Wykes*, 222.

aside from his son's marriage and there is no evidence that he was consulted on it.[82]

It was barely six weeks after the marriage of Edmund and Aveline at Westminster that Henry of Almain and Constance de Béarn were married at Windsor, on 21 May 1269.[83] Queen Eleanor may have regarded both marriages as being in some sense personal triumphs. If so, it is well that she could not foresee the tragedies which befell them. In 1274 the young Aveline died in giving birth to twins.[84] According to Wykes, her husband had come to love her for more than her estates and was deeply grieved by her death.[85] Her 'small and dainty tomb', as Binski describes it, stands in the choir of Westminster Abbey, not far from that of her husband, two masterpieces of Gothic craftsmanship.[86] The marriage of Constance de Béarn to Henry of Almain was cut short more savagely when Henry was stabbed to death by Guy de Montfort and his brother Simon, in a church in Viterbo in March 1271. Henry of Almain's marriage into the family of their enemy, Gaston de Béarn, would itself have angered the young Montforts but they also clearly felt that Henry bore some responsibility for their father's death at Evesham.[87] The arid task which remained to Eleanor of Provence was to supervise the administration of the dower of the widowed Constance.[88] In political terms the marriage had accomplished very little, since Gaston became rebellious again, failing to keep his promise to accompany the Lord Edward on crusade and springing a fresh revolt in 1273, and Constance herself was unstable in her allegiance.[89]

The last five years of Henry III's reign reveal a tension between two royal lifestyles, that of the monarch and that of the heir to the throne; a phenomenon that has occurred at other times in English history. Queen Eleanor, in age poised almost exactly mid-way between her husband and her son, may have had some sympathy with each. The gap between the two was not only of generation but of temperament. The ageing king was concerned primarily for the security and peace of the realm and his deep personal piety may have been intensified by his humiliations at the hands of Montfort, followed by his restoration to full kingly power. The trans-

---

[82] Studd, 'The Marriage of Henry of Almain', 171.

[83] *Chron. Wykes*, 222.

[84] BL Arundel MS 56, f. 72.

[85] *Chron. Wykes*, 261.

[86] Binski, *Westminster Abbey*, 113 and plate 156.

[87] Ch. 9, above; Maddicott, *Montfort*, 370–1; Studd, 'The Marriage of Henry of Almain', 177.

[88] *CPR 1266–72*, 619, 660.

[89] Ellis, 'Gaston de Béarn', 290–314; Trabut-Cussac, *L'Administration Anglaise'*, 42–5, 57; Prestwich, *Edward I*, 300–1.

lation of the body of his patron saint Edward on 13 October 1269 was conceived as a richly evocative royal and religious pageant and as an act of profound thanksgiving. A great assembly of magnates, prelates and leading citizens of towns throughout England had been summoned to attend the ceremony, enhanced by the pristine freshness and beauty of the newly built church at Westminster.[90] It was now for the first time, according to Thomas Wykes, that the monks celebrated mass beneath the vaults of the new chancel. Paul Binski has recently developed the theme that this richly appointed building, so close to the royal palace of Westminster, was itself a statement on kingship and government, part of the political culture of the Plantagenet court, as well as a statement of intense personal religious devotion.[91] At the high point in this ceremony of translation, King Henry, his sons the Lords Edward and Edmund and his brother Richard of Cornwall helped to support the body of the saint as it was transferred to its gold and jewelled shrine.[92] For the king himself there was an intimately personal aspect to the translation ceremony, which could be shared by no one, for he intended the now empty coffin, which had held the Confessor's body, to be his own future resting place.

Whereas the imagination of Henry III was dominated by intense piety and by a quite exceptional aesthetic sensitivity, the mind of his eldest son was gripped by the absorbing excitements of chivalry and warfare. Edward was more active and decisive than his father and his forceful personality had a strong militaristic bent. The old king had, throughout his reign, habitually prohibited tournaments; he had no wish to take part in them and he had rightly regarded them as disruptive of order and politically suspect.[93] Edward had as yet no such fears, he delighted in the sport, had led his friends on tourneying expeditions abroad in the early 1260s and wanted the prohibition lifted at home. He had his way. In 1267 a proclamation legitimizing tournaments was issued and the king's two sons and Henry of Almain led the rush.[94] The young aristocrats of the prince's generation were eager to join in the enthusiasms of the man who would soon be king.[95]

[90] *Chron. Wykes*, 226–7.
[91] Binski, *Westminster Abbey*, 1–9.
[92] For state of completion of the shrine in 1269 see Carpenter, 'King Henry III and the Cosmati Work at Westminster Abbey', 409–25.
[93] Denholm-Young, 'The Tournament in the Thirteenth Century', 245–53; Barker, *The Tournament in England*, 56; Prestwich, *Edward I*, 60; Wait, 'Household and Resources', 251, 258–9.
[94] *Chron. Wykes*, 212.
[95] Coss, *The Knight in Medieval England*, 120.

Eleanor of Provence had to live in both these worlds. She had long identified with her husband's religious devotion, but, like her eldest son, she had an active temperament; she was socially at home with men like her Savoyard uncles or the count of St Pol or Ingram de Fiennes, men who were accustomed to the use of force in solving problems. John of Howden's poem, written so close to this time, extols knightly prowess because he knows that the queen delights in such stories herself.[96] She could hardly have been unsympathetic to Edward's aspirations, and she could hardly have been surprised when he determined to accompany Louis IX on a crusade to the Holy Land.

By far the most serious issue between the Lord Edward and Henry III in the last years of the reign was the crusade. On 24 June 1268 at Northampton both Edward and Edmund, along with their friends Henry of Almain, John de Warenne, their uncle William de Valence and many others, took the Cross in the presence of the legate Ottobuono; so too did Gilbert de Clare.[97] It was the intention of all of them to depart on crusade in the near future. The Lord Edward's motives have been perceptively analysed by Simon Lloyd. He wanted scope for his energies, he wanted independence of action and the excitement and exhilaration of crusading warfare. At home there seemed to be nothing for him. His father was by no means so enfeebled as to think of giving up his habitual personal direction of government, and even in the lands of Edward's appanage Henry tended to interfere. On the Welsh March the treaty of Montgomery, concluded with Llywelyn under the legate's supervision, had brought a temporary lull in fighting, although it was probably not to Edward's liking.[98] Edward had played a decisive part in the military operations of 1265–7, but that phase of the settlement of England was over. He wanted to stretch out to adventure overseas and the opportunity to join Louis IX's crusade to the Holy Land provided just that.

The king was dismayed, much more deeply concerned than Edward about the possibility of renewed disturbance at home. Not that Edward was blind to this; which explains his determination, with the help of his uncle Richard of Cornwall, to secure a settlement of the disputes between himself and Gilbert de Clare and to exact Gilbert's firm promise to join the crusade himself, as an essential precondition for Edward's own departure.[99] It was no more than a year since Gilbert

---

[96] Ch. 4, above.

[97] *Chron. Wykes*, 217–18; *Cron. Maiorum*, 107.

[98] Lloyd, 'The Lord Edward's Crusade', 123–4; Studd, 'The Lord Edward and Henry III', 11, 17.

[99] *Chron. Wykes*, 228–32; Lloyd, 'Gilbert de Clare, Richard of Cornwall and the Lord Edward's Crusade', 52–60.

had been in hostile occupation of London. Even Clement IV considered that Edward was being precipitate in contemplating a crusade so soon, and it was initially Edmund, not Edward, who was to be entrusted with bearing Henry III's own Cross to the Holy Land.[100] Edward overcame all this caution and opposition. For the view of Edward's mother we have no evidence. She knew that she might lose either of her sons, or even both. Some men were killed and others died from illness on crusade, and indeed this was the crusade from which Louis IX did not return. Eleanor was aware too of the political dangers at home, which could burst into a renewal of civil war if Henry III should die in Edward's absence; and in fact Henry did die before Edward's return. Yet Eleanor, despite her restraint in the long summer and autumn of 1264, was a woman used to taking risks, and whatever her fears, she would have shared in that sense of religious exaltation and excitement which still characterized the knightly crusades of the thirteenth century, and gloried in the adventure on which her sons were to embark.

The arrangements for the crusade and for the security of the kingdom in the absence of the crusaders overshadowed all other considerations in 1268–70. The quarrel between Gilbert de Clare and Edward, which, as Simon Lloyd has shown, all but vitiated the whole enterprise, was settled by Richard of Cornwall's award of 27 May 1270.[101] This was to be somewhat modified in response to Gilbert's complaints, but the basic conditions by which he gave security for embarking on crusade in the next passage after Edward himself, were now laid down, and the matter was regarded as sufficiently settled for the king to take the remarkable step on the following day of effecting a massive transfer of castles and counties throughout England into the control of the Lord Edward for five years.[102] These were to be placed in the hands of Edward's agents while he was abroad and the whole transaction, which was decided upon after consultation with the royal councillors, was said to be 'for the conservation of the peace and security of the realm'. In short, if the king died, Edward's men were already in control and were in a position to keep the peace in Edward's name. It remained to decide who should exercise central authority over his lands and take responsibility for the care of his children in his absence. His children were placed in the care of Richard of Cornwall and in the event of Richard's death, of Henry of Almain. The men to be associated with Richard of Cornwall in the

[100] *Reg. Clément IV*, no. 1288; Lloyd, 'The Lord Edward's Crusade', 122–3.

[101] Lloyd, 'Gilbert de Clare, Richard of Cornwall and the Lord Edward's Crusade', 55–6, 59–62.

[102] Hilary Wait, 'Household and Resources', 136–53, citing E 371/34 mm. 1, 2, has thrown new light on the significance of this transfer.

control of Edward's lands and castles were Walter Giffard, now archbishop of York, Philip Basset, Roger Mortimer and Robert Walerand,
soon to be replaced by Edward's clerk Robert Burnell.[103]

The striking omission in these arrangements is surely Eleanor of Provence. Of her ability there could have been no doubt. She was barely fifty,
still vigorous, and with eighteen more years to live. She had previous
experience as regent, in 1253–4, when she had worked in partnership
with Richard of Cornwall and she had more recently shown a remarkable capacity for leadership and initiative in the events of 1264–7. Her
absolute devotion to the interests of her family had been proved repeatedly. Yet Edward deliberately excluded her completely. Admittedly the
decisions were made with the assent of the council, but one cannot but
think that they reflected his own wishes, and his own judgement.

This calls for explanation. Edward and his mother were now on terms
of deep mutual respect, and she loved him dearly. She had accommod-
ated herself to accepting and working with those of his friends, like
Leybourne, who had previously injured her. Yet Edward's instinct was
to leave her out of his arrangements, and one can see why. In the country
as a whole the past and its enmities were still very close and Eleanor of
Provence was the alien queen, convener of the armed force which had
threatened to subdue England in 1264. The patriotic feeling which
had then been roused and had been assiduously worked upon by Montfort was still alive; miracles were said to be happening at Simon de
Montfort's tomb. The Lord Edward was himself far from being xeno-
phobic, but his close contacts with men who were, had taught him what
was politically prudent. The men whom he now left in charge of his
affairs were all Englishmen. The chief potential trouble maker in England, if in the end he should stay in England, which he did, was Gilbert de
Clare. Gilbert had made an issue of rule by native Englishmen when he
had consented to give his vital support to Edward in May 1265. The
rebels in 1267 had been insistent on that same point and although it had
not then been specifically conceded, Edward knew of the deeply rooted
and widespread support for the principle.[104]

We know nothing of the queen's feelings about this exclusion. She had
learned acceptance on many points, and perhaps even on this. When her
grandson John died in August 1271, Richard of Cornwall conveyed his
body to Westminster to be buried in the abbey church, and Wykes refers
to the grief of the king and the queen.[105] Two other children of Edward
remained in England, Eleanor and Henry. When, within two years, the

[103] *Foedera*, i. 484; Powicke, *Henry III*, 583.
[104] Ch. 9, above; *Chron. Rishanger*, 64.
[105] *Chron. Wykes*, 246.

death of Richard of Cornwall and the murder of Henry of Almain removed both the men whom Edward had appointed to the custody of his children, it was Queen Eleanor who characteristically took on the task which lay to hand and looked after them until the return of their parents.[106]

In sharp contrast to the initial exclusion of Eleanor of Provence from the affairs of Edward in his absence were the arrangements made by her younger son, Edmund. Here Eleanor was involved to the hilt. Early in 1271 Edmund issued a statement that for the duration of the crusade Queen Eleanor was to take his place and authority in England, detailing her full powers, her rights of appointment and dismissal over all his ministers, her right to present to vacant churches in his gift, to sell or lease his lands and to contract loans for his use. His trust in her was absolute.[107] In 1264–5 he had been with her abroad and had seen her cope with crushing adversity and he also knew her high administrative competence. Since then she had promoted his marriage and he clearly felt that his extensive lands and privileges could not be better entrusted. In Edmund's case his mother's image as an alien queen was no impediment to his choice; he was not inhibited by considerations of future kingship. Eleanor needed to use her wide powers, for Edmund was soon short of cash. On 3 August 1271 the king ratified a loan of 1,000 marks from Richard of Cornwall to the queen and three other attorneys, for Edmund's use.[108] On 28 July 1272 she made over the issues of a substantial portion of Edmund's honour of Leicester for four years to her own nephew Edmund of Cornwall, Sanchia's son, for a cash payment of 3,500 marks, handed over to the queen for the use of his cousin and namesake.[109] Eleanor arranged such transactions with assurance.

The departure of the crusaders left the government in England vulnerable. Levels of crime were high and the renewed ban on tournaments was not enough to stave off the constant threat of disorder.[110] John Maddicott's analysis of the unease and apprehension of those in power and the very real justification for their anxiety carries greater conviction than Powicke's optimistic picture of the end of the reign.[111] Henry III himself had no illusions and when news came of Louis IX's death at Tunis in

[106] Ch. 12, below. Ultimate responsibility for the children now rested with Edward's agents.
[107] CPR 1266–72, 668; and, more fully in the original, as cited by Lloyd, *English Society and the Crusade*, 169.
[108] CPR 1266–72, 566.
[109] Ibid., 668–9; Lloyd, *English Society and the Crusade*, 195.
[110] CPR 1266–72, 528, 611.
[111] Maddicott, 'Edward I and the Lessons of Baronial Reform', 1–3; Powicke, *Henry III*, 583.

August 1270, the prospects for the crusade itself looked grim. In the early spring of 1271 Henry became seriously ill and on 6 February he wrote to his eldest son urging him to return home, especially as he understood that Philip, now king of France, had decided to do so.[112] Edward disregarded his father's advice and pressed on to Acre and the fulfilment of his crusading vow.

The death of Richard of Cornwall in April 1272 removed one of the most stable figures, as well as one of the most powerful, from the political scene. There was now no one with the rank of earl among the Lord Edward's agents, whereas the prestigious earl of Gloucester, kept at home by renewed attacks from the Welsh, had a record of dubious allegiance. The harsh reaction of the government to the riot which broke out in Norwich in the summer of 1272, and the brutal punishments meted out to the condemned citizens was perhaps a measure of the insecurity of the men advising King Henry.[113]

The king's serious illness in the spring of 1271 would have given Eleanor of Provence warning that her husband's health was failing.[114] She already knew that the mood in many parts of the country was uncertain and that the spectre of rebellion still hovered. With her habitual vigour and political acumen she took care to strengthen her personal position. Only a month before her husband died she gained her point that the provision for her household should be met by augmenting the wardships under her control to a notional figure of £1,000 a year.[115] This was preferable to relying on uncertain payments from the exchequer. Eight days later, on 23 October, the queen was granted custody of Windsor castle, with its appurtenances, to answer for them at the exchequer, as the previous constable, Nicholas de Yattingden had done.[116] Yattingden had belonged to a family with long-standing associations with the queen's household, but on his recent death the queen evidently felt that her best security lay in her personal control of Windsor, one of the two premier royal strongholds outside the capital. It was presumably also at her request, with an eye to ensuring that her affairs were in order, that an extent of all her lands in fifteen counties was ordered.[117] This was only four days before her husband died.

As Henry lay dying, in his chamber in the palace at Westminster, a large and noisy mob of London citizens swarmed around the building

---

[112] CR 1268–72, 397–8.
[113] *Bartholomaei de Cotton, Historia Anglicana*, 146–9.
[114] CPR 1266–72, 591–2; Denholm-Young, *Richard of Cornwall*, 148.
[115] CPR 1266–72, 682; SC 1/16/207.
[116] CPR 1266–72, 684.
[117] Ibid., 716.

shouting out their demand that the radical Walter Harvey should be their new mayor. Walter was with them and whipped up the excitement, and there was talk in the city of an armed rising against the aldermen once the old king was dead.[118] It seems almost certain that the queen would have been with the king at this time; his death was far from sudden and one recalls the drawing in the *Estoire* of Queen Edith grieving by the death-bed of her husband.[119] The behaviour of the Londoners would not have surprised her; she knew them by now, but it no doubt angered her. The threat of a revolt was in fact averted. On the morning of the day on which the king died, 16 November 1272, Gilbert de Clare was sum-moned to Henry's bedside and made his solemn promise of loyalty to Edward, and it was Gilbert who, after the king's death, played a major role in calming the Londoners.[120]

On 20 November Henry III's body, dressed in his royal robes and crowned, was carried on an open bier to its resting place in the church which he had reconceived and rebuilt and which consecrated his vision of kingship.[121] His body was traditionally adorned in the regalia appropri-ate to a coronation, his final affirmation of his royal state.[122] According to his wish, he was buried in the Confessor's coffin, where his body remained until it was placed some years later in the fine Cosmati tomb which still stands today in the Chapel of the Kings. The whole ceremony was conducted with striking splendour and dignity and Thomas Wykes observed that the king shone more gloriously in death than in life.[123] The great men of the realm had come to see the old king lifted to his burial place, and at the conclusion of the ceremony the chief magnates present, headed by Gilbert de Clare, John de Warenne and Humphrey de Bohun, swore fealty to the new king, Edward.[124]

In all of this the queen is entirely lost to view. Her marriage partner-ship of thirty-six years had ended, and her son Edward, still in the Holy Land, did not yet know of his father's death; none of her children was with her or even in England. In 1265 her gracious and clever mother had died, in 1268 her uncle Peter of Savoy, and in 1270 his brother Arch-bishop Boniface, both men of vigour and distinction. There had been other deaths too within the last eight years, which for her signalled the

[118] *Cron. Maiorum*, 148–53; Williams, *Medieval London*, 243–4.
[119] *Estoire*, (ed. James), plate 50, f. 51.
[120] *Cron. Maiorum*, 155.
[121] *Chron. Wykes*, 252–3.
[122] For the significance of Henry III's burial see Carpenter, 'The Burial of King Henry III', 427–59.
[123] *Chron. Wykes*, 252.
[124] *Flores*, iii, 28; *Cron. Maiorum*, 153–4.

end of an era; Simon de Montfort himself, John Mansel, Richard of Cornwall, Henry of Almain, Ebulo de Montibus, Ingram de Fiennes and Roger Leybourne. Some were friends, some adversaries and some had been both at different times, but they all belonged to the reign of her husband, while she had to press on into the reign that was beginning, one of the most remarkable in English history. This seems an appropriate point at which to reflect on the character and significance of her queenship.

11

Queenship: Image, Practice and Resources

The image of queenship was a visual concept of endless fascination in the medieval West. The subtle and sophisticated interplay of images of secular queenship and images of the queenship of the Virgin Mary, especially during the flowering of the cult of the Virgin in the twelfth and thirteenth centuries, has been the subject of extensive recent analysis. No justice can be done here to this rich field of scholarship; yet an understanding of the queenship of Eleanor of Provence must have initial reference to it, at however basic a level. There are two caveats. The first is the deliberate care taken by artists to distinguish heavenly queenship from all secular forms.[1] This disassociation could never be entirely successful, but the attempt was made. Secondly, however potent the Marian symbolism in the minds of sculptors, illuminators and liturgists and of those who responded to their imagery, more secular concepts of queenship normally prevailed.

Three aspects of Marian symbolism, as it touched earthly queenship, need to be mentioned. The first, and by far the most important in relation to Eleanor of Provence, is that of the queen as the vital link in a royal lineage. The coronation liturgy for a queen stressed by allusion, both verbal and visual, the intimate association of queenship and marriage, with its end in the birth of heirs to the royal line.[2] Henry III, as we have seen, deeply imbued with a sense of his own specially sanctified ancestry, had the Tree of Jesse depicted in the window of his wife's bedchamber at Windsor castle. Later, it was presumably Eleanor herself who asked her

---

[1] R. Muir Wright, 'The Virgin in the Sun and in the Tree', 36–7.
[2] Ch. 1, above; Parsons, 'Ritual and Symbol', 61–2, 67.

husband to commission the window at Clarendon, which depicted her kneeling before the figure of the Virgin and Child.[3] The concepts of royal fecundity and maternity went deep within her own self-perception.[4] It has already been suggested that a sense of empathy with the Virgin as mother was almost inescapable for a devout thirteenth-century queen. Yet even in relation to this particular image one must remember more mundane reality. The need for an heir to the throne was a matter of political pragmatism. The news of the birth of the Lord Edward was received with straightforward rejoicing, a matter of patriotic pride and political relief to all loyal subjects. Magnates sent congratulatory presents and the citizens of London enjoyed themselves in boisterous celebration, until Henry III demanded such lavish gifts that the Londoners began to complain sourly, 'God gave us this child, but the king sells him to us.'[5] We are some distance here from a near-mystical approach to royal childbirth.

A second queenly image, essentially secular, but one which developed Marian connotations is that of the queen as an authority figure. The authority attributes in representations of the Virgin were in the first place borrowed straight from the regalia of secular queens. That was the inescapable starting point. In a German sacramentary of the tenth century the Virgin, crowned and enthroned, bearing a sceptre and a book, is exquisitely represented in the guise of an Ottonian queen, complete with elaborate royal draperies and jewels. As Rosamund McKitterick crisply remarks, it was 'a compliment to earthly queens then in power ... if not to the heavenly one'.[6] Those same royal attributes of crown and sceptre are seen in the representations of the Triumph of the Virgin above the portals of the northern French cathedrals at Senlis, Mantes and Laon, dating from the late twelfth or early thirteenth century. Penny Schine Gold distinguishes the tone of these sculptures in which the Virgin, already crowned and sometimes bearing a sceptre, is seated as Queen of Heaven beside the figure of Christ, from later representations of the actual Coronation of the Virgin, where she is a more passive, suppliant figure.[7] The sculptures of the Triumph of the Virgin perhaps gave added force to purely secular images of queenly authority. The figure of Eleanor

[3] *CLR 1245–51*, 324. For a composition which would have been visually similar see plate 10.

[4] Nigel Morgan notes the popularity in the thirteenth century of the physically evocative image of the Virgin suckling the Child, 'Texts and Images of Marian Devotion', 93–4. See plate 10.

[5] *CPR 1232–47*, 417 (William de Warenne's grant); *CM*, iii. 539–40.

[6] McKitterick, 'Women in the Ottonian Church: an Iconographic Perspective', 88–9 and plate 3.

[7] Gold, *The Lady and the Virgin*, 52–61 and plate 4 (Senlis).

of Provence on her first great seal, crowned and bearing both sceptre and virge, conveys an impressive regal image.[8]

A third visual and conceptual image with implications for secular queens was that of the Virgin as intercessor. This is an image evocatively linked with the immensely popular representations of the Coronation of the Virgin, which are found in profusion in medieval churches from the thirteenth century onwards, and which virtually superseded the earlier Triumph of the Virgin.[9] The emphasis here is on the humility of Mary, who appears with head and body inclined towards the figure of Christ, receiving her crown at his hands, and holding herself poised for intercession.[10] This brings us to the evidence for a remarkable transmission of ideas from the religious to the secular sphere. On an early thirteenth-century tympanum above the north portal at Chartres is a representation of the Virgin as Queen of Heaven, which shows her already crowned but inclined towards the Christ figure and with her hands spread out in suppliant *orans* gesture.[11] It has a quite uncanny likeness to an illumination in a *bible moralisée* which was made for the use of Blanche of Castile around 1235. Here Queen Blanche and her son Louis IX both sit enthroned, regarding each other. Blanche is dressed in a Marian blue mantle; she inclines gently towards her son and holds out her hands towards him with that same *orans* gesture.[12] One can only conclude that for Blanche this was a potent image of intercession which in some sense she was prepared to transfer to her own relationship with her son. This in itself is significant, but further inference requires caution. Blanche was a masterful woman, at home in the council chamber and even in siege warfare, the *virago* admired by Matthew Paris; intercession was not her most characteristic posture. What is certain is that Eleanor of Provence too would have been familiar with visual representations of the Virgin as queenly intercessor and with the theological concept which lay behind it.[13]

John Parsons has suggested that the image of a secular queen as intercessor distanced her from the legalistic authority of her husband and conveyed the hope of merciful intervention on behalf of individual subjects. He notes that a petition to Eleanor of Castile from the citizens of St Albans has explicit Marian overtones and suggests that this queen

---

[8] BL Cotton Charter XVII. 6; Tout, *Chapters*, v. 286; see also n. 89, below.

[9] Gold, *The Lady and the Virgin*, 61–5.

[10] For the Coronation scene over the portal at Rheims cathedral (*c*.1260) see Hurlimann and Bony, *French Cathedrals*, plate 52.

[11] Gold, *The Lady and the Virgin*, plate 6.

[12] Warner, *Alone of All her Sex*, 114–15 and plate 15.

[13] Morgan, 'Texts and Images of Marian Devotion', 95–6.

on various occasions manipulated her role as intercessor in order to enhance the impression of her own influence.[14] Was this true of Eleanor of Provence? Eleanor certainly interceded effectively for individuals, both with Henry III and with Edward I, and her intercession would normally have been in response to a personal approach. Some of these occasions were politically significant, as in the case of her plea on behalf of Walter Marshal in 1241 or her intercession for William Raleigh in respect of the see of Winchester in 1243; others were not.[15] She regarded intercession as inherent in her role as queen, both as consort and dowager, and her letters of intercession were persuasive, although never servile.[16] The analogy with the Virgin's role as intercessor would have been one of which any thirteenth-century queen, steeped in Marian devotion, would have been conscious. Yet this facet of queenship needs to be understood in a broader context than this. Eleanor's token intercession on the day of her coronation relates, as has been seen, to ancient precedents.[17] Again, queenly intercession was only one type of all wifely intercession.[18] Nor was the right of intercession with the king in thirteenth-century England a unique privilege of the queen. Among women it did indeed belong only to ladies with royal connections; however, this stretched not only to the king's daughters but to Eleanor de Montfort, as his sister, to Sanchia (before she became a queen herself), Alice de Warenne and Alice de Lacy.[19] It was perhaps a matter of propriety that it did not stretch further. Among men, however, the practice was apparently open-ended. A perusal of the patent rolls reveals a mass of male intercessors, lay magnates, knights, clerks and chaplains. Intercession therefore was far from being exclusively a queenly prerogative, and although it could be touched by Marian overtones, as Blanche of Castile's Bible and other evidence makes clear, men mixed their metaphors as easily then as now.

One exceptionally thoughtful churchman who had taken part in the coronation of Eleanor of Provence had a high regard for queenly intercession. Robert Grosseteste believed it to be the natural duty of a wife to soften the heart of her husband. At a level of high opportunity this role belonged to the queen. He urged that she be asked to use her persuasion in the individual case of William Raleigh, but he also pleaded with her

---

[14] *Gesta Abbatum Monasterii Sancti Albani*, i. 411–12; Parsons, 'The Queen's Intercession in Thirteenth-Century England', 151–3 and n. 21.

[15] *CM*, iv. 158, 349.

[16] Ch. 12, below.

[17] Ch. 1, n. 87, above.

[18] Farmer, 'Persuasive Voices', 517–43.

[19] *CPR 1247–58*, 388, 394, 398, 425, 455, 457; *CPR 1258–66*, 523; *CPR 1266–72*, 673.

earnestly to use her influence with the king much more broadly, to rectify his policy towards the Church and people.[20] His model for her was Queen Esther, and in this he may have been a little old-fashioned, but Grosseteste was a clear thinker and he may have regarded any analogy with the Virgin as inappropriate. Eleanor's task was to incline the heart of an erring king towards the good, as Esther's had been. The role of the Virgin was to tap the springs of mercy already existing in a wholly righteous Saviour. Although Grosseteste uses images of light dispelling the darkness (Ecclesiasticus 26: 16), which have Marian associations in other contexts, his well known preoccupation with the metaphor of light would sufficiently explain his language, especially since the image is found in the Book of Esther (11: 11).[21] Grosseteste's view of the queen as intercessor was an exalted one and broadly based, but I doubt whether it was Marian.[22]

There were other influences hovering over the images of queenship in the thirteenth century, which had nothing to do with the Virgin Mary. Eleanor's son Edward was the first English king to capitalize on Arthurian romance in royal image-making. He and his wife, Eleanor of Castile, were present at Glastonbury in 1278 when the supposed bodies of King Arthur and Queen Guinevere were ceremonially reinterred in front of the great altar in the abbey church, and in the following year they took part in the lavish display at the Round Table held by Roger Mortimer at Kenilworth.[23] Such Round Tables had obvious Arthurian associations. Edward himself later held Round Tables at Nevyn and Falkirk. These events were great chivalric pageants in which aristocratic ladies were prominent as well as knights.[24] In 1283 Edward's success against the Welsh was followed by the presentation to the victorious English king of what was alleged to be Arthur's crown.[25] Although one must not casually read back evidence from Edward I's reign, Arthurian romance was already popular in court circles in the middle years of the century and the imagery of queenship as well as kingship in these romances might play on men's imaginations.[26]

---

[20] *Roberti Grosseteste Epistolae*, nos 86, 103.

[21] Apocryphal version. Southern, *Robert Grosseteste*, 217–19. For the earlier popularity of the 'Esther topos' see Huneycutt, 'Intercession and the High-Medieval Queen', 126–46.

[22] For a different view see Parsons, 'The Queen's Intercession in Thirteenth-Century England', 154.

[23] *Chron. Wykes*, 281–2; Prestwich, *Edward I*, 120–1.

[24] Barker, *The Tournament in England*, 90–1, 101–2.

[25] *Ann. Waverley*, 401.

[26] In a tournament at La Hem (1278) a sister of the lord of Longueval presided as Queen Guinevere, Barker, *The Tournament in England*, 88.

To change key even more decisively; images of queenship were not created solely by ritual, symbol and religious or romantic analogy, but by the personalities and achievements of real queens, as people experienced them. Michael Prestwich recently gave the salutary warning that thirteenth-century writers 'found character hard to describe'.[27] For this reason one is often left with stereotypes, of men as well as women, but even these can extend significantly the range of images of queenship. One recurrent thirteenth-century image, with no Marian overtones at all, is that of the superbly competent woman of affairs, who could deal with political crises, day-to-day rule or the logistics of war; she is described as a *virago*.[28] Matthew Paris wrote of Blanche of Castile as *sexu femina, consilio mascula*, and Eleanor of Provence, like Queen Blanche, evoked this image.[29] As Pauline Stafford has shown, it was an image which had implicit biblical allusion to the queenly figures of Judith and Esther, but it was an image sustained by the personal qualities of living queens, with whom men in the thirteenth-century courts of France and England were fully familiar.[30]

Kaleidoscopic images of queenship partially relate to an institutional reality which must now be approached from different evidence. The prerogative quality of the queenship of Eleanor of Provence stands within a tradition, partly insular but partly Western European. The development of that tradition down to the early twelfth century has been greatly elucidated by Pauline Stafford, and in relation to France by Marion Facinger.[31] The late eleventh and early twelfth centuries in both England and France saw queens consort as active formal participants in royal government. In France this style of queenship reached its apogee in the career of Adelaide of Maurienne (1115–37), wife of Louis VI.[32] In England it is exemplified by the Conqueror's wife, Matilda of Flanders (1068–87) and the first wife of Henry I, Edith-Matilda (1100–18). These queens were associated by name in royal acts, they had their own household officers, including, in Edith-Matilda's case, a chancellor, and they had control of the lands which supported them during their husband's lifetime. They readily undertook the responsibility of regency in the husband's absence.[33] The circumstances of the Empress Matilda,

[27] Prestwich, *Edward I*, 559.

[28] Stafford, *Queens, Concubines and Dowagers*, 30. For appreciative use of 'virago', to describe Adela countess of Blois, see Farmer, 'Persuasive Voices', 524.

[29] *CM*, v. 354; *Flores*, ii. 500; *Flores*, iii. 72.

[30] Stafford, *Queens, Concubines and Dowagers*, 25–6.

[31] Ibid., chs. 4, 5, 6; Facinger, 'Medieval Queenship: Capetian France', *passim*.

[32] Facinger, 'Medieval Queenship: Capetian France', 27–33.

[33] Parsons, *Eleanor of Castile*, 71–4; for chancellors of both Henry I's queens see Brett, *The English Church under Henry I*, 107.

daughter of Henry I, who claimed the throne as her father's chosen heir, and of Matilda of Boulogne, wife of the Empress's rival King Stephen, cannot be considered as typical, but there is certainly no evidence here for any falling off of queenly authority.

The nature of that authority is tellingly reflected in a revised English coronation order of the second recension, the so-called 'William Ordo', compiled after the Conquest. There is no evidence that it was in fact used at any coronation of an English queen, but it is the key to a concept of queenly authority which was evidently currently influential and certainly in keeping with the authority actually exercised by queens of the late eleventh and early twelfth centuries. The significance lay in the Benediction, which called upon the Lord to bless his handmaiden the queen who has now become *regalis imperii particeps*. The English people are to rejoice in being ruled by the king's power and by the queen's justice and prudence.[34]

The mid-twelfth century marks something of a watershed in English as in French queenship, witnessing the beginning of a decline in the queen's formal participation in government. This has been seen in France as resulting in part from the increasing bureaucratization of the king's government, and this could certainly have been a factor in England too, in view of the striking developments in law and administration in Henry II's reign.[35] Yet the change seems to predate the major measures of that reign. Eleanor of Aquitaine did not issue writs in her own name after 1163 and earlier still she had ceased to witness Henry II's acts.[36] The distancing of the queen from the king's public acts was naturally accentuated when personal relations broke down, and it is not until after Henry II's death that Richard I's reliance on his mother's loyalty and competence resulted in her playing an influential political role in England, in which her authority as a crowned and anointed queen may have been important.[37] Berengaria of Navarre, Richard's queen, never came to England, while Isabella of Angoulême, judging by her subsequent behaviour, was unsuited to governmental responsibility. Yet the view that in the late twelfth century, queenship itself entered a phase of steep and irreversible decline cannot be accepted in relation to England. It was the form and style which changed.

[34] Bruckmann, 'English Coronations, 1216–1308', 50; Schramm, *A History of the English Coronation*, 29–30; Richardson, 'The Coronation in Medieval England', 122–3 and 'The Marriage and Coronation of Isabella of Angoulême', 309.

[35] This is strongly emphasized by Facinger, 'Medieval Queenship: Capetian France', 40, 46, but less by Stafford, *Queens, Concubines and Dowagers*, 195.

[36] Parsons, 'The Queen's Intercession in Thirteenth-Century England', 149–50; *Eleanor of Castile*, 72–3.

[37] Richardson and Sayles, *Governance*, 153.

Queenship continued to be firmly rooted in the English body politic. A relevant thirteenth-century image is the remarkable painting ordered by Henry III in 1243 for the dais of a new hall in Dublin castle; the subject was a king and queen sitting with their baronage. Since this could hardly be a conversation piece, we are left fumbling for its precise significance, but as an image relating to the queenship of Eleanor of Provence, it should certainly be borne in mind.[38] Queenship was obviously to be understood in relation to kingship, yet its prerogatives were occasionally distinctive. An interesting example is the queen's alleged prerogative to present a nun to every English nunnery on the occasion of her coronation. Henry III exercised this right in Eleanor's name in 1236, at least in respect of some nunneries, and refers to it in a letter to the abbess of Wilton in July of that year.[39] This was symbolic royal patronage on a grand national scale. It was of course the acquisitive side of that patronage, but behind the claim lay a tradition of the queen's special relationship with the many communities of women religious scattered throughout England. This had more benevolent implications. Richard le Poore may have had it in mind when he gave his Wiltshire nunnery of Tarrant Keynes to Eleanor 'when she came to England'.[40] This suggests that it was not for any personal merits of Eleanor that he made his gift, but perhaps because he perceived the queen as the traditional protectress of communities of nuns. It is likely that Henry III regarded his queen in this light too. When he made a gift to a nunnery he sometimes directed it through the queen's officials, as in the case of Ankerwyk in 1248 and again in 1256.[41] On other occasions the king would grant a nunnery protection, a present or a privilege – as he did to Marlow, Cookhill, Westwood and Catesby respectively – 'at the queen's instance'.[42] This perception of the queen's role as the special patron of nuns may even stem from a tradition going as far back as the tenth-century *Regularis Concordia* in which the king and queen are seen as the 'patrons and guardians of the whole monastic institute', the queen having special responsibility for the nuns.[43] This is one of the points where prerogative right and the image of queenship meet.

The foremost queenly prerogative was the right to the levy of queen's gold. In the seventeenth century William Prynne told Catherine of Braganza that this was 'one of the antientest, royalest, richest civil prerog-

---

[38] CR 1242–47, 23.
[39] CPR 1232–47, 155.
[40] CM, iii. 392, 479.
[41] CLR 1245–51, 184; CLR 1251–60, 340.
[42] CPR 1232–47, 280; CLR 1240–45, 37; CPR 1247–58, 599.
[43] *Regularis Concordia*, 2, 7.

atives'.[44] By the thirteenth century the right had already become standardized as a levy of ten per cent on voluntary fines of ten marks or more, made with the king.[45] Although all provision for the queen was ultimately under the king's surveillance, this was a right which Prynne saw as 'absolutely vested in the queen'.[46] The exercise of the right by Eleanor of Provence will be considered in relation to the wider question of her total resources, but its very existence enhanced the image of distinctive queenly power. In the practical problem of the collection of the gold, Eleanor enjoyed a privilege of royal status which applied to the collection of all her debts. Debts to the queen were collected by sheriffs and bailiffs second only to the debts of the king himself.[47] The memoranda rolls of Henry III's reign show the barons of exchequer continuously active in ordering sheriffs to distrain for debts to Queen Eleanor or requiring her debtors to be brought before the exchequer.[48]

Many of the queen's prerogatives arose directly from the fact that queenship was considered to partake of the nature of kingship. This gave the queen a special status in relation to landholding and also in relation to the processes of law. In the holding of landed property the queen had privileges which were enjoyed by no other married woman.[49] She could hold land in her own right and on occasion dispose of it, although this later facility was severely limited in the case of Eleanor of Provence since the great bulk of her property, both that which she held of the gift of Peter of Savoy, and later that which she held in dower, were enjoyed under the specific condition of reversion to the Crown on her death. On the other hand, lands which she acquired through her exploitation of other people's debts to the Jews, in accordance with a very common practice in the thirteenth-century royal court, were disposable, and a dispute over such landholding could force into the open a very explicit awareness of the queen's royal status. One important example has been brought to my notice.[50] In October 1256 Nicholas de Lenham acknowledged before a Grand Assize that he held the Norfolk manor of Redenhall, with the advowson of its church from Earl Roger Bigod for a rent of 100s and the service of two knights.[51] Less than a year later the

[44] Prynne, *Aurum Reginae*, 1.
[45] Howell, 'The Resources of Eleanor of Provence', 373–80.
[46] Prynne, *Aurum Reginae*, 7.
[47] Ibid., 23; Parsons, *Eleanor of Castile*, 70.
[48] E.g. E 159/28 mm. 1d, 15; E 159/29 m. 15d; E 159/30 mm. 15, 17d, 20; E 159/43 m. 15d; E 159/45 m 4d. There are also frequent recognitions of debt to the queen, which may have been prompted by the exchequer.
[49] Blackstone, *Commentaries on the Laws of England*, i. 189–90.
[50] I am grateful to David Carpenter for drawing my attention to this case.
[51] CP 25(1), 158/84/1269.

earl was at odds with Lenham because, in return for a loan, Lenham had given the manor of Redenhall at farm to the queen for a period of sixteen years. Lenham was deeply in debt to the Jews and it is likely that the queen had in return acquitted him of such a debt; this was her usual way of entry into the land market. On gaining seisin of Redenhall Eleanor had promptly taken fealty of the free tenants of the manor by her attorneys. The earl equally promptly ejected the attorneys and claimed that Nicholas de Lenham had no right to give or sell this land to the queen.[52] The point at issue was Earl Roger's right, as capital lord of the tenement, to enforce the payments and service attached to it. He could enforce such dues against Lenham, but not against the queen in view of her royal status. 'What is demised to the Lady Queen is demised to the Lord King.'[53] The king took the point. It was agreed that the queen could have seisin, provided that the king guaranteed to the earl by letters patent the rights of distraint which Roger held as superior lord of the fee. Yet it is interesting that matters were not left there. In July 1258 a different agreement was made. The queen and Roger Bigod seem to have withdrawn from the scene. Peter of Savoy now emerges as superior lord of Redenhall, holding directly from the Crown.[54] It seems that in a situation like this, the queen's prerogative status could threaten to frustrate her own strategies.

That was rarely the case. The queen's special status was normally an immensely powerful asset. She was not an ordinary subject; by her royal status she was set aside from all other subjects of the Crown. The queen could not be sued by writ in the courts of law, but she could herself sue others, with or without her husband.[55] In a society in which control and defence of property was a highly litigious matter, these prerogatives gave the queen a powerful advantage against any adversary. As Eleanor of Provence acquired more property, in wardship or later in fee, the number of cases in which she was involved increased. An investigation of the *curia regis* rolls gives a sense of the extent to which the scales were tipped in the queen's favour. This does not mean of course that she never lost a case; even kingship itself was in some senses 'below the law'. Nevertheless, the queen was entrenched in a highly privileged position which may have weighed heavily on the spirits of her adversaries.

The queen's closeness to the king is regularly emphasized in the legal records. In a case where the king believed his own right to be imperilled,

---

[52] JUST 1/567 m. 13. Lenham is said to have let the manor at farm to the queen 'pro commodo suo faciendo'.

[53] Ibid.

[54] CP 25(1), 283/15/351.

[55] Ehrlich, *Proceedings against the Crown 1216–1377*, 206–7; Parsons, *Eleanor of Castile*, 70.

he pleaded along with the queen. In 1267/8 the bailiffs of Southampton were summoned to answer to the king and queen for the seizure and despoiling of a ship carrying goods for the queen from Gascony.[56] Again, the king and queen pleaded together in 1272 when the queen's right to an escheat arising from the wardship of the lands of John de Grey, granted her by Henry III, had been resisted.[57] In the next reign Edward I pleaded alongside his mother in the dispute over her patronage of St John's hospital in Cambridge.[58] More usually the queen pleaded on her own account by her attorney, although that attorney was frequently one of those whom the king himself used for his own litigation. Gilbert de Chalfont, who acted in many cases for the king, also acted in several pleas for the queen.[59]

The wording of entries on the *curia regis* rolls frequently implied that an offence against the queen touched the king's own dignity. The intimacy of their association is stressed by such phrases as *karissima consors* and *dilecta consors*.[60] An attack on the queen's servants or an infringement of her rights prompted more emphatic phrases. In 1257 an attack on one Richard de Folville attempting to collect scutage for the queen within the bailiwick of the mayor of Northampton was said to be 'in contempt of the king and of the queen'.[61] The parson of the church of Twyning who drove off the queen's pigs from her property had likewise acted 'in manifest contempt of the king and of the queen'.[62] One feels the immense prestige of the queen's position at law, the fact of her regality.

Eleanor of Provence made full use of her privileged position in the courts. In 1274, when she was dowager, she sued Philip de Coleville for hindering her presentation to the Cambridgeshire church of Stanton St Michael, which she claimed as her advowson. Initially both parties had agreed to the summoning of a local jury, but when the jury met, the queen's attorney repudiated the inquisition and said that 'in no wise would she place herself on any inquisition concerning the right of the aforesaid heir, who is in her custody through the lord king's grant, without the lord king himself'. Eleanor insisted that the case be heard before the king's council. In fact the council decided in favour of Philip de Coleville 'notwithstanding the opposing claim of the aforesaid queen or

[56] *Abbrevatio Placitorum*, 172.
[57] KB 26/207 m. 13d.
[58] *Select Cases in King's Bench*, i, intro., cx, n. 1.
[59] KB 26/197 m. 20d; KB 26/200B m. 9; KB 26/201 m. 19d; KB 26/204 mm. 27d., 31; KB 26/207 mm. 7d, 10, 15.
[60] KB 26/198 m. 16d; KB 26/201 mm. 8, 11; KB 26/204 m. 6d.
[61] KB 26/158 m. 13.
[62] KB 26/189 m. 3; KB 26/190 m. 1; KB 26/193 m. 11d.

king'.[63] In this case Eleanor was worsted, but she had pushed her rights to the full.

A second case shows the queen able to victimize her opponent by pursuing him simultaneously on two fronts. William Heringaud was one of the disinherited whose lands had been granted to Eleanor of Provence. In 1268 he was pardoned by the king and his lands restored according to the Dictum of Kenilworth.[64] On the dorse of the close roll he is recorded as owing the queen a fine of £40, but he never had this in writing from Eleanor, who came to believe that his lands had been assessed at far too low a figure.[65] In 1270, through Gilbert de Chalfont's pleading, she won her case before the king and council and was able to seize William's lands until he could redeem them at a higher figure.[66] Matters now took on a more sinister tone. When we turn to the Jewish plea rolls for Trinity term 1279, it becomes evident that William Heringaud was still struggling with his father's debts to the Jews. There was a debt of £116 owing to the Jew Bernard Crispin but this debt had been made over to Eleanor of Provence as payment for Crispin's own debt in queen's gold.[67] So Heringaud was now caught on two counts, his fine for his lands and his debt in Jewry, which had been transferred to the queen. When the justices of the Jews demanded payment of the debt, no doubt prompted by Eleanor's aggressive collector of queen's gold, John de Whatley, Heringaud responded bitterly that the queen had seized his lands as surety for the debt, and had had sufficient profit, to the value of £116 and more, and that he had therefore nothing to answer. Eleanor of Provence was using her position to play the system.

The institutional presence of queenship in England in the thirteenth century was inescapable. Marion Facinger has seen the relegation of the French queen to her own household in the twelfth century as marking a significant and irreversible step in the removal of the queen from power in government, but this view perhaps underestimates the potential of a queen's household as a separate institution.[68] A queen's household, operating within the court setting, in close proximity to the institutions of central government, could be a sturdy support to her queenship and a sensitive and effective vehicle through which it could operate. This potential deserves examination in relation to Eleanor of Provence.

---

[63] *Select Cases in King's Bench*, i. 7–9.
[64] CPR 1266–72, 205.
[65] CR 1264–68, 523.
[66] KB 26/197 m. 20d; Knowles, 'The Disinherited', pt iv. 96.
[67] E 9/32 mm. 2, 2d.
[68] Facinger, 'Medieval Queenship: Capetian France', 35–7.

For a substantial part of the year, the provision for the daily needs of the queen and her entourage was subsumed into the provision for the king's own household and the expenses of both were accounted for in the enrolled accounts of the king's wardrobe, without differentiation.[69] Yet the queen's household never lost its identity even at these times. It had its physical base in the queen's apartments, which ensured that a degree of separation was possible, even when the queen's domestic officers were rendering their daily accounts to officials of the king's own household. In the absence of the king, the queen's household easily resumed its functions as a self-sufficing entity, which indeed it always was in all activities that were not purely domestic.

The household of Eleanor of Provence, in its heyday, probably numbered upwards of a hundred people, of varied status and functions, ladies, knights, *valetti*, senior domestic functionaries such as marshal and steward, cooks and tailors; there were nurses and laundresses, messengers, grooms and carters, together with many serving in much more humble capacities.[70] There was also an important core of clerks employed on financial and administrative business and, sharing that clerical status, there were doctors and chaplains. Several of these categories have been considered in describing the queen's lifestyle.[71] The unifying purpose of the household was to sustain the queen. She and her entourage had to be fed and clothed, her accounts kept in order, her letters written and dispatched, her religious and recreational needs met and her entertaining arranged, all in grand royal style. Yet, if the purpose of Queen Eleanor's household was constant, the scale of its operations and the controls to which it responded changed dramatically between the queen's arrival in England as a girl of twelve and her achievement of full maturity in the late forties and early fifties of the century, when her household had reached institutional stability. After the king had set up a household for his young wife and established a small wardrobe to service it in January 1236 the total receipts for the first twenty months or so amounted to a little over £562.[72] By contrast, in an account for two years, beginning 24 June 1250, the receipts totalled £3,360 and spending on the *hospicium* (essentially the food departments) had steadied at some

---

[69] E.g. king's wardrobe accounts on E 372/83 rot. 7, E 372/88 rot. 14.

[70] For the personnel of the household of Eleanor of Provence see Ridgeway, 'Politics', Table 8. John Parsons has estimated Eleanor of Castile's household in 1289/90 at about 150 persons, *The Court and Household of Eleanor of Castile in 1290*, 153–60. See also Parsons, *Eleanor of Castile*, 87–92

[71] Ch. 4, above.

[72] *CPR 1232–47*, 196.

£1,000 a year, or rather for that portion of each year when the queen was apart from the king.[73]

Change in the scale of operation was matched by change of control, and both are explained by the simple fact of a young girl growing into womanhood. The household was a personal institution and its dynamism was that of the queen's own development. The first two wardrobe keepers, John of Gatesden (1236–42) and Guy de Palude (1242–7) would have been chosen by the king.[74] Both were men at a high level of royal service, employed by the king in a variety of business within which their responsibility for the queen's wardrobe was unlikely to have been their major commitment. Both men would have looked to the king for direction. Palude deputed most of the wardrobe business to two less eminent clerks, Walter de Bradley and Robert de Chaury, who were spending their time and establishing their professional careers in the service of the queen herself.[75] Bradley became keeper of the wardrobe in 1249, with Chaury as controller until 1254, when Chaury moved to the exchequer to act there as keeper of queen's gold. Both men remained in the queen's service, Bradley until his death in 1255, and Chaury until his elevation to the bishopric of Carlisle in 1257.[76] It was to the queen herself that Bradley and Chaury looked for direction.

The queen's household had by now settled into established patterns, its wardrobe accounting at the exchequer, and not at the king's wardrobe, whereas the wardrobe of Eleanor of Castile and of later queens consort accounted at the wardrobe of the king.[77] Accounting at the exchequer implied a measure of institutional independence. There were occasions when Eleanor of Provence seems to have pushed this independence further than the barons of exchequer found acceptable. In 1257, on the resignation of her wardrobe keeper James d'Aigueblanche, it was the queen who ordered the exchequer to accept his accounts, having first accepted them herself and acquitted him. One wonders whether it was the exchequer officials who asked the king for his own authorization.[78] Certainly, at the beginning of Edward I's reign, the exchequer showed itself hesitant about accepting the account of her wardrobe keeper Hugh de la Penne for the years 1269–72. The new king was in Acre and they

---

[73] E 372/95 rot. 6. Over two years the total was £2,027 4s 1d. See also Howell, 'The Resources of Eleanor of Provence', 387–8.

[74] Above, n. 72; *CPR 1232–47*, 408.

[75] Howell, 'The Resources of Eleanor of Provence', 388 and n. 5; Tout, *Chapters*, i. 252–5; v. 233–5.

[76] E 372/93 rot. 1; E 372/95 rot. 6; E 372/97 rot. 9; *CM*, v. 535; Howell, 'The Resources of Eleanor of Provence', 377.

[77] Tout, *Chapters*, ii. 42–3; v. 236.

[78] *CPR 1247–58*, 558.

were not happy to act without his authorization, since these payments concerned the previous reign. In the end they did hear the account and enrol it 'at the instance and petition of the queen', but they insisted on regarding it as a 'view of account', not as the final account itself, since they said they were obliged to act without writ or other warrant from the king, and they made a note to this effect at the end of the enrolment.[79] Both incidents indicate an assertive attitude on Eleanor's part.

Able queens of the twelfth and thirteenth centuries stamped their households with their own distinctive personal style. In the factious struggles between Savoyards and Lusignans in the mid-thirteenth century the very existence of the queen's household within Henry III's court was a threat and an obstacle to the Lusignans. Eleanor of Provence had a power base which they could never touch or emulate. This source of power and prestige was enhanced, as we have seen, by the queen's close links with the households of her children. Although there were fluctuating patterns here, this network of contacts was in a sense the institutional aspect of her royal motherhood. Men such as Ebulo de Montibus, Bartholomew Pecche, Geoffrey de Cauz, Nicholas de Yattingden and Simon of Wycombe moved between service of the queen and service of the royal children, but they moved very much within the queen's orbit.[80] Provision for arrangements in the event of the king's death, both in 1242 and 1253, endued Eleanor of Provence with an unassailable position as mother of the king's heirs; her authority was explicitly carried forward into the future, and in case of the king's death would have given her ultimate royal authority over the children and the kingdom.[81] Meanwhile she held the reins of an institution second only to the king's own household as a focus of court life.

At court, Eleanor of Provence was close to the centre of politics and close to the centre of government, and she was prepared at all times to maximize the opportunities which that proximity gave her. She was by instinct a politician. Despite her occasional disputes with her husband she retained his regard, not only in her familial role but for her political capacity. Within the ambience of the court Eleanor had the support of men who themselves had political influence with the king, Peter of Savoy, Peter d'Aigueblanche, John Mansel, Robert Walerand among the most important. In the years 1261–3 her own political influence rose to a peak where it became totally unacceptable to her opponents and was directly responsible for the political revolution in 1263.

[79] E 372/116 rot. 1d.
[80] Ch. 4, above.
[81] Chs 3 and 5, above.

Apart from her personal links with men in the king's own household, some of whom have been mentioned, she also had links with those three great bastions of government over which the reformers always wanted to establish control; the chancery, exchequer and judiciary. Her personal contacts with various keepers of the great seal, Mansel, Kilkenny and Wingham, prepares us for the voluminous correspondence with Robert Burnell, John Kirkby and William Hamilton in the next reign when many of her letters to officials of chancery happen to be extant.[82] Her access to the courts of law has already been mentioned. At the exchequer her presence was marked by her keeper of queen's gold, who was probably in charge of all her income except that which was specifically designated for the support of her household.[83] Access to the exchequer of the Jews was also required in relation to many of the problems concerning queen's gold.[84] This was another contact which could be utilized by the queen in a more private capacity. In 1273 Eleanor discovered that the land of Rainham in Kent, which she had bestowed upon the hospital of St Katharine, had been seized into the king's hand because of the debts in Jewry of one Reginald de Cornhill. She promptly required the justice of the Jews that 'for love of us you respite all debts and demands affecting our said hospital until after Michaelmas and so we shall be holden to you in special gratitude'.[85] Eleanor of Provence knew how to be gracious and she knew how to insist. In exerting pressure in chancery, exchequer or courts of law, the queen could of course depend on expert advice, but there was no substitute for an informed grasp of institutions and procedure on her own part. Eleanor was intelligent, assertive, and, as time went on, increasingly knowledgeable. Some of her letters as dowager, written in her most characteristic style, show a personal grasp of legal and administrative procedure which proclaim her as a seasoned practitioner.

That a queen of England in the thirteenth century enjoyed exceptional privileges and that she was potentially an influential figure in political affairs is clear. There remains the vexed question of the constitutional significance of queenship. In this respect Eleanor of Provence as a queen consort has exceptional interest. In the later eleventh and early twelfth centuries in England, as has been seen, the queen could be regarded as *regalis imperii particeps*.[86] As late as the end of the twelfth century King

---

[82] Ch. 3, above, and ch. 12, below.

[83] Howell, 'The Resources of Eleanor of Provence', 379–80. For Eleanor of Castile's exchequer and treasury see Parsons, *Eleanor of Castile*, 94–5.

[84] *Select Pleas, Starrs and Other Records*, 67–8, 71, 78; *Cal. of Plea Rolls of Exchequer of the Jews*, i. 151, ii. 15, iii. 153.

[85] Ibid., ii. 65–6.

[86] Above, n. 34.

John could speak of his wife as being crowned with the assent of the people of England.[87] In the 1240s Grosseteste spoke of the people of England as being within the queen's *domus*.[88] In short, there was a continued awareness that the queen had a relationship, albeit very ill-defined, with the community of the people of England. This receives visual confirmation in the representation of Queen Eleanor on both her great seals, standing erect, crowned and bearing a sceptre.[89] Sceptres were and still are symbols of authority.[90] It may be that the fleur-de-lis which often topped a queen's sceptre both in England and France had symbolic association with the flowering stem of Jesse and therefore spoke messages of fertility and intercession, but this could hardly have been its sole association;[91] it was a royal symbol *par excellence* and was to be found on the sceptres of kings and princes as well as queens.[92] The queen on her seal appears as an authority figure, and her sceptre was probably presented to her at her coronation, even though at this stage it had no place in the liturgy of the coronation orders which have come down to us.[93] Here we are touching an interesting ambivalence in the attitude to queenly authority. The queen took no coronation oath, such as bound the king in a formal constitutional relationship with the community of the realm. Certainly the queen might act as regent, as Eleanor of Provence did in 1253–4, but it was possible for another member of the royal family or, in the twelfth century the justiciar, to exercise the king's deputed power in his absence. In the case of Edward I, as has been seen, the power was exercised by a group of senior advisers to the king. A regent, however, exercised power in the king's name, by the king's authority, not in his or her own right.

It was the revolution of 1258–9 in the first place, and then the powerlessness of the king in the hands of Simon de Montfort in 1264–5 which thrust the question of queenship to the fore. Even then it is doubtful whether the issue would have been faced as it was, if Eleanor of Provence had been less politically active and less influential in the counsels of the king. At some point between 1258 and 1261 she took an oath to

---

[87] Ch. 1, n. 73, above.

[88] *Roberti Grosseteste Epistolae*, no. 103.

[89] For Eleanor's seals before and after the Treaty of Paris see BL Cotton Charter XVII. 6 and BL Harleian Charter 43. C. 42; Birch, *Catalogue of Seals*, i. 98–9; Sandford, *A Genealogical History of the Kings and Queens of England*, 57. On her second great seal Eleanor is seen without the virge, presumably because this now replaced the sword on Henry III's seal, Carpenter, 'The Burial of King Henry III', 441.

[90] Crouch, *The Image of Aristocracy in Britain*, 211–14.

[91] Parsons, 'Ritual and Symbol', 65.

[92] Crouch, *The Image of Aristocracy in Britain*, 212.

[93] Ch. 1, above.

maintain the Provisions of Oxford, and was released from that oath, along with the king and his sons, in 1261 and again in 1262.[94] The oath to maintain the Provisions did bind her formally in a matter concerning the government of the realm. This fact made her rejection of her oath in 1261 and her encouraging of the king in his own rejection of the Provisions a particularly heinous crime in the view of the reformers. In 1263 Simon de Montfort accused Eleanor as well as Henry III and Edward of the guilt of perjury.[95] In the end Eleanor was prepared to make a more obdurate stand for royal authority than Henry III himself. When she refused to accept the Montfortian peace plan of July 1263 she was attempting to take a stand in defiance not only of the victorious baronial party but in defiance of her husband's reluctant submission to their terms. She had to retract.

Simon de Montfort's victory at Lewes again threw queenship into sharp relief. During the captivity of Stephen in the mid-twelfth century, his queen, Matilda of Boulogne, had acted for him. Eleanor of Provence now acted for Henry III, but the situation was even more irregular since Henry III was technically still exercising kingship in his own name, and even countermanding initiatives which Eleanor was taking on his behalf and in the name of his royal authority, as with the sale of the Three Bishoprics to Louis IX.[96] Yet Louis treated Eleanor as having a right to act for her husband, just as the majority of Henry's Gascon subjects were prepared to accept her authority in defiance of writs issued from England in Henry's name. The situation was clearly highly anomalous. The Montfort government itself seems to have been careful to avoid direct reference to the activities of the queen of England; instead it contented itself with oblique references to the machinations of certain persons. Although the period of revolution and war was quite exceptional, it revealed the latent significance of English queenship in a particularly interesting way.

Throughout the years of her maturity Eleanor of Provence was politically assertive both in her influence over her husband and in the factious power struggles within the court. It could be argued that her role was disastrous, especially in her commitment to the business of Sicily and her hostility to the reform movement. But not all her policies were divisive; she was a steady supporter of peace with France. She was of course a vigorous defendant of monarchy itself. She opposed what she saw as the negation of kingship, the removal of the king's powers of appointment and his right to take counsel where he would. Because she was never

[94] Chs 7 and 8, above.
[95] *Chron. Wykes*, 133.
[96] *CPR 1258–66*, 474.

moved by sheer ambition and acquisitiveness she won respect among those who knew her, and she saw her first duty as queen in the service of her husband and family. In 1264–5 she played a major part in eroding the confidence of the Montfort regime, in drawing attention to the partisan quality of its support and in keeping the king's cause alive and publicized. On her return to England her promotion of good will within the royal family, at some cost to herself, helped to bring the reign to a reasonably calm end.

As queens consort, Eleanor of Aquitaine and Isabella of France were politically important because they threw over the bonds of loyalty to their husbands. Eleanor of Provence set herself to work within those bonds; personal loyalty was one of her most deeply held values. Within those constraints she pushed queenship to its political limits. Among those who experienced contact with her masterful personality one man probably pondered more than most in these critical years on the authority of a queen. Edward revered his mother, appreciated her courage and knew that he and his father had been saved in part by her indomitable energy and commitment. This is true and he never forgot his debt. It is also true that he would never have tolerated queenship of this style in his own wife. It was Henry III who made possible the queenship of Eleanor of Provence. This should not be attributed simply to Henry's alleged weakness, but to the fact that Henry recognized in his own wife what Louis IX recognized in his mother – an exceptionally able woman, in whom he had a deep basic trust.

One essential element in the queenship of Eleanor of Provence remains to be considered; the matter of resources. Here, Eleanor's lucid grasp of the problems and the potential of her position as queen provides a clear insight into specific facets of her personality and her ability. It is a fascinating success story. She began with very little. Her father could only afford her a moderate marriage portion and this was never fully paid. From her arrival in England she was heavily dependent upon the generosity of her husband.[97] If she was to realize her potential as a queen she would need wealth and wealth was what she conspicuously lacked. At first she had no lands under her personal control; her household was financed by *ad hoc* grants of money from the king, drawn mainly from his own wardrobe or the exchequer.[98] On the other hand there was queen's gold. That too was initially under the king's personal control. He appointed the first two gold keepers, Laurence de Castellis (1236–7)

[97] Howell, 'The Resources of Eleanor of Provence', 372.
[98] Ibid., 384, n. 3.

and John Francis (1237–54), as he had appointed her first two wardrobe keepers, and at first it was the king who arranged the spending of the gold, some of it in the building of the queen's new chamber at Westminster.[99] Yet the levy of queen's gold was in essence a prerogative right of the queen herself, whereas payments into her wardrobe were simply at the king's discretion.

As she progressed through her teens, Eleanor of Provence got the measure of this situation. She began to reach out after maximum control of the resources which underlay the role she sought to develop as queen. By 1254 she had the appointments to the keeperships both of her wardrobe and of her gold in her own hands.[100] The style of provision for her household was beginning to change too. As early as 1242 she received the wardship of the lands late of Ralph de Tony.[101] Other wardships followed, including some major ones such as those of the fiefs of William Longespee (1257), Reginald de Mohun (1258) and Margaret, countess of Lincoln (1266).[102] Most of the wardships granted to her were under her direct control and some extended to rights over the marriage of the heirs and over escheats, wardships of mesne tenants and even advowsons. This was the style of provision for which Eleanor pressed, and between 1257 and 1269 she received a total of £9,014 into her wardrobe from lands in her wardship.[103] However, it was not until very shortly before her husband's death that she finally achieved an arrangement by which the full provision of £1,000 a year for her *hospicium*, that is her household in the more restricted sense, would be covered by wardships, while the king retained his customary responsibility for providing her with wines and cloth in kind.[104]

As Eleanor of Provence reached out for maximum control of her resources she also reached out for maximum returns. She evidently condoned ruthless exploitation of estates in her wardship. Matthew Paris gave a vivid picture of her estates steward William of Tarrant as a man who thirsted after money as a horse-leech after blood. 'He sold or pledged all her lands and manors for the queen's benefit, substantially increasing her wealth, but by the loss and peril he caused to others he damaged his own reputation irreparably.' It was not only Tarrant's reputation that was at stake; the queen was careless of her own in this respect. She was in touch with Tarrant, and according to Paris she

---

[99] *CR 1234–37*, 235, 264; *CPR 1232–47*, 176; *CLR 1226–40*, 258, 268, 276, 285, 300.

[100] Howell, 'The Resources of Eleanor of Provence', 377, 388–9.

[101] *CPR 1232–47*, 283.

[102] *CPR 1247–58*, 536, 614; *CPR 1258–66*, 574.

[103] E 372/109 rot. 11d; E 372/113 rot. 1.

[104] SC 1/16/207; Howell, 'The Resources of Eleanor of Provence', 387–8.

cunningly excused his deeds.[105] She had evidently received complaints but her reaction is clear. When she received custody of the Longespee lands in 1257 the bailiffs already in office, according to Paris, 'assumed the horns of audacity from being under the patronage of a lady of such high rank, and practised such oppression on all their neighbours that their sufferings might have drawn tears from the eyes even of their enemies'.[106] Even though some allowance must be made for Paris's customary rhetoric, Eleanor's management of other property under her control substantiates his verdict. She aimed at quick and substantial returns.

It was not only in respect of wardships that Eleanor of Provence pressed her financial claims to the limit. When she was granted lands to the value of 800 marks in part compensation for her claims to the honour of Richmond, she initially received from the royal exchequer the issues of the lands allocated to her. She was not satisfied, and in 1270 the king ordered the exchequer to allow the queen to take the farms from those manors which were at farm 'by her own hands or the hands of her bailiffs' and the other manors she was to have in demesne.[107] She exploited the various properties which came to her in 1268 as vigorously and as unscrupulously as she had exploited her wardships. Richard of Pevensey, who administered her Sussex lands after she had acquired the honour of Pevensey, was a man of the same style as William of Tarrant. The Hundred Rolls reveal Pevensey as a thoroughly oppressive steward, fabricating faults for which he then imposed amercements, taking gifts for the appointment of officials and imprisoning men in Pevensey castle without judgement.[108] It is the Hundred Rolls too which make plain the anger and concern of the citizens of London over the queen's abysmal failure to maintain the fabric of London Bridge which had been given into her keeping by the king in 1265. The bridge came within imminent danger of collapse. Again we know that she was approached on the subject and at one point agreed to hand it over to the citizens, but then repented of her decision.[109]

The neat series of enrolled accounts of Eleanor of Provence's wardrobe, covering most of the period in which she was consort, has produced a distorted and greatly over-simplified view of the range and complexity of her financial activity. Substantial income which we know was accruing to her in the later part of Henry III's reign from certain wardships granted

---

[105] *CM*, v. 716; ch. 6, above.
[106] *CM*, v. 612, 621.
[107] *CPR* 1266–72, 433–4.
[108] *Rotuli Hundredorum*, ii. 204–8.
[109] Ibid., i. 403, 406, 419–22, *passim*; *Cron. Maiorum*, 141–2.

her by the king, from others which she had bought, from the issues of the lands which had come to her through the death of Peter of Savoy and from various other sources, did not touch her wardrobe. She was apparently steering her financial business increasingly in the direction of her office of receipt at the exchequer where it would be dealt with by the keeper of her queen's gold, the official concerned by definition with the receipt of monies to which she had a prerogative right.[110] Although the lands of the disinherited, granted to her on her return to England, were stated by the king to be granted *ad sustentationem suam*, that is, for the provision of the daily needs of her household, the queen saw to it that the redemption fines for those lands were directed not into her wardrobe but to the keeper of her gold.[111] When money was paid into her office of receipt at the exchequer the management seems to have been entirely under her control. From the exchequer memoranda rolls in the later part of Henry III's reign we glimpse Simon of Wycombe, the keeper of Eleanor's gold, applying himself to a range of financial business for the queen. He received an instalment of John d'Eyvill's redemption fine and £500 from a royal tallage, money especially granted to Eleanor by the king.[112] The treasurer told Henry III that this money had been dealt with entirely by Queen Eleanor's clerks.[113] Together with Adam de Stratton, Wycombe was responsible for overseeing the payments due from the queen to Amice, countess of Devon, in connection with the marriage of the Lord Edmund to Amice's granddaughter.[114] Wycombe was therefore concerned with disbursement as well as receipt.

Even more ambitious was the queen's attempt to extend the range of incidence of queen's gold itself. This became an issue in 1258–9 when the queen's claim to take her gold on reliefs as well as entry-fines was denied in the Petition of the Barons in 1258 and when, in the following year, the reformers placed decisions as to the lawful occasions for the levy of queen's gold in the hands of the small committee which was also dealing with wardships.[115] At the end of the reign Queen Eleanor even made a spirited, though unsuccessful attempt to extend the levy of queen's gold to the 'gracious aids' which were granted to the king to help with the financing of the impending crusade. This was the most aggressive financial bid that she ever made, and it was to be sharply rebuffed by Edward I.[116]

---

[110] Howell, 'The Resources of Eleanor of Provence', 379–80, 390–1.
[111] *Rotuli Selecti*, 248; E 159/42 m. 24d.
[112] Ibid.; CR 1268–72, 49.
[113] Ehrlich, 'Exchequer and Wardrobe in 1270', 553–4.
[114] E 159/45 m. 6.
[115] *DBM*, 78–9, 152–3.
[116] Howell, 'The Resources of Eleanor of Provence', 379.

Eleanor of Provence had opportunities of acquiring wealth and using wealth that were quite different from those open to earlier medieval queens. She had to operate within a complex, sophisticated and in some respects fast-changing economic environment. A detailed analysis is not possible here, but brief mention must be made of her dealings with the Jews and with foreign merchants. In her initial attitude to the Jews she was a child of the Midi. Jews played a prominent and respected part in Raymond-Berengar's financial administration and it is significant that Eleanor of Castile, also from the south, twice attempted to appoint a Jew as her keeper of her queen's gold.[117] Eleanor of Provence took under her special protection the London Jewish family of Evesque, the sons and grandsons of the wealthy Benedict l'Evesque.[118] In 1256 Benedict's son Jacob was exempt from tallage for life at the queen's instance and in the following year, when Jacob died, his own son Benedict was granted the same privilege 'at the prayer of the queen'; Benedict's brother Salomon was granted quittance of tallage for two years in 1261, again at the instance of the queen.[119] No doubt the various members of the family made themselves useful to the queen and Jacob had been a prominent agent of the Crown within the Jewish community, where the establishment of a 'court faction' was integral to royal policy.[120]

The exaction of queen's gold also brought the queen into close contact with Jewish finance. She was entitled to gold on the exceedingly heavy fines which the king levied on individual Jews such as Abraham of Wallingford, Aaron of London and Aaron of York.[121] When a Jew died the queen received gold on the third part of his property, which went to the Crown, and she even received her ten per cent on the 60,000 mark tallage levied on the Jews in 1244.[122] The queen's gold which a Jew owed might sometimes be paid to the queen in bonds rather than in cash. There were occasions when it was the money that she wanted and in 1272 there was a sharp clash over a debt of £100 owed to the queen by Cok, son of Cresse, a Jew of London, who claimed his right to pay her in bonds, whereas her gold keeper, John de Whatley, claimed that the queen must be satisfied in cash.[123] On other occasions she accepted the bonds and

[117] Parsons, 'Eleanor of Castile: Legend and Reality', 30 and n. 29.

[118] Stokes, *Anglo-Jewish History*, 12.

[119] *CPR 1247–58*, 528, 542; *CPR 1258–66*, 177.

[120] Stokes, *Anglo-Jewish History*, 15; *Select Pleas, Starrs and Other Records*, intro., xxviii.

[121] Howell, 'The Resources of Eleanor of Provence', 375.

[122] *CPR 1258–66*, 88; E 159/24 m. 6 for Aaron of York's debt for queen's gold on the tallage of 1244; see *CR 1247–51*, 389 for tallage of 1250.

[123] *Select Pleas, Starrs and Other Records*, 67–8.

plunged straight into the land market, since the gage for such bonds was often the land of the original Christian debtor. In this way she acquired land of William de Lascelles, worth £20 a year, the gage for his debt to Aaron of York, contracted in 1257.[124] But Eleanor was involved in Jewish finance apart from queen's gold, especially in the later part of her husband's reign and the early years of Edward I's. In 1271 she bought the debts owed by Roger Bertram to Hagin son of Moses and his family, and in 1272 those of Peter Scrapin to Benedict of Winchester; in 1271 her husband granted her the debts of Herbert Barre to the Jews of Canterbury.[125] The sums involved here were small, but some transactions were on a larger scale and more clearly related to real estate, as with her acquittance of the 300 mark debt in Jewry of her ward, heir of Barnabas de Stiucle, lord of the Bedfordshire manor of Warden. The queen confirmed a thirteen-year lease of the manor to the abbey of Warden, profiting substantially as she went.[126] Occasionally she might wish to keep the property in her own hands. This seems to have been the case in her elaborate transaction of 1273 with the impoverished Humphrey de Bassingbourne, which brought her a twenty-five-year seisin of the castle and manor of Benefield in Northamptonshire, together with the advowson of the church; for this she had to acquit his Jewish creditor of the large sum of 2,150 marks.[127] In other cases Eleanor seems to have let the property slip quickly through her hands and to have been mainly interested in profit, as was probably the case in the transactions with Geoffrey de Langley and Nicholas de Lenham described earlier.

In a recent study of the aristocratic exploitation of the land market in the thirteenth century, Sandra Raban suggested that it was the two queens consort, Eleanor of Provence and Eleanor of Castile, who seem to have taken a strikingly active interest.[128] Yet there was a marked difference of style between the two. Eleanor of Castile, working in close collusion with her husband, carefully planned her acquisitions of land so that she built up consolidated enclaves of property in well-chosen areas. The impressively extensive and systematic scale on which she was working has now been revealed in full detail by John Parsons.[129] There

---

[124] *Cal. of Plea Rolls of Exchequer of the Jews*, iii. 18. The queen transferred the lands to Richard of Otteringham, on whose death Lascelles tried to reclaim them from Richard's heir.

[125] CPR 1266–72, 532, 715, 606. For exercise of usury by Christian purchasers (as in the Herbert Barre grant) see Richardson, *The English Jewry under Angevin Kings*, 7.

[126] CPR 1247–58, 635; CR 1259–61, 501.

[127] CCR 1272–79, 112–13; CChR 1257–1300, 189.

[128] Raban, 'The Land Market and the Aristocracy in the Thirteenth Century', 257.

[129] Parsons, *Eleanor of Castile*, 126–38 and Appendix 1.

was nothing comparable to this in the case of Eleanor of Provence, whose supreme aim was liquidity.

In respect of the Jews Eleanor of Provence and her advisers needed up-to-date knowledge of current financial and legal practice both within the Jewish community and in the relation of that group to the wider community within which it operated. Here the problems and opportunities scarcely reached outside England. However, expertise on a much wider scale was required for business dealings with foreign merchants. Individual merchants could be used by Eleanor of Provence for purchase of goods, in semi-diplomatic work or, during 1264–5, for the needs of war. In the last context the activities of the Bayonnais merchants Paschasius de Pino and Pelerin de la Poynte have already been mentioned, and as master of the queen's ship *La Reyne*, Paschasius traded as an ordinary merchant on the queen's behalf after the war had ended.[130] Especially in the latter part of Henry III's reign there are several prominent merchants who are described by the term 'merchant of the queen'. Henry Wale-mund was a citizen of London, but most of the others were foreign or based abroad, Robert de Renham at Douai, Peter Bonyn at Bruges, and Nicholas de Lyon, also in Flanders.[131] Such men looked to the queen for personal support and protection. She intervened to protect the interests of Peter Bonyn in his controversy with the civic authorities in York;[132] she secured exemption from arrest for Nicholas de Lyon, Robert de Renham and Gamelin Vylens at the time of Henry III's reprisals against Countess Margaret of Flanders, and in 1273 she requested protection for Nicholas de Lyon's widow.[133]

The most favoured and long-serving of all the individual merchants associated with Queen Eleanor was Deutatus Willelmi. Deutatus was a citizen of Florence, a member of the king's household, frequently engaged in purchasing and other business for both the king and the queen, but he is often referred to simply as the queen's merchant and he remained in the service of Eleanor of Provence into the 1280s, an association lasting some thirty years.[134] He has been described as 'banker to Queen Eleanor' and he was indeed able to advance moderate sums for royal business, as required.[135]

---

[130] Ch. 10, above.
[131] *CPR 1258–66*, 503; *CPR 1266–72*, 462, 523, 530, 531.
[132] KB 26/198 mm. 16d, 22d.
[133] *CPR 1266–72*, 462; SC 1/7/10.
[134] *CPR 1247–58*, 177, 423; *CPR 1258–66*, 519; *CPR 1281–92*, 109, 154.
[135] Kaeuper, *Bankers to the Crown*, 13; *CPR 1258–66*, 570; *CPR 1266–72*, 547; CLR *1267–72*, no. 1537.

For larger loans Eleanor of Provence frequently turned to the Florentine firm of Maynettus Spine and Rustikellus Cambii. They had enjoyed the protection of Peter of Savoy since 1253 and during the regency the queen borrowed from them on the king's behalf.[136] In 1257 they were one of the firms used by the king, the queen and Edward for the loan of 10,000 marks of gold in one of the payments to the papacy for the business of Sicily.[137] In the same year they obliged the queen and Peter of Savoy to the extent of at least 4,500 marks in the notorious loan which was based on the security of certain English religious houses[138] When Eleanor was securing loans for the Lord Edward in 1261 she used both Maynettus Spine and another Florentine firm, the Simonetti brothers, and it was Maynettus Spine who helped finance Eleanor's army in 1264.[139] In these various large-scale transactions Eleanor of Provence showed a mastery of the use of credit to further her political purposes. Her ability to command extensive credit was in part the result of her reputation for reliability. Her responsible attitude to the repayment of her war debts, her concern for the proper satisfaction of the claims of her sons-in-law, her undertaking of the business affairs of Peter of Savoy and of her son Edmund in their respective absences from England and her role as executrix for such old friends as Ebulo de Montibus and Matthias Bezill, all suggest that Eleanor of Provence had both high competence and an underlying sense of honour in her financial dealings.[140] To depict her, as has been done, as a carelessly extravagant woman is a judgement very wide of the mark.

From the very beginning of her reign a queen looked to the end of it. Her future affluence, in the event of her husband's death, and a good deal of her present prestige depended on her dower, a prime element in the total pattern of her resources. Henry III's initial provision for the dower of Eleanor of Provence and its main modifications have been noted in the course of earlier chapters. She did not have control of her dower lands during her husband's lifetime, with one interesting exception. When the queen received a revised compensation for Richmond in June 1270, five of the towns allocated to her had already been nominated among her future dower towns; Basingstoke, Andover, Kingston, Ospringe and Marlborough.[141] This left open the question of what would happen

---

[136] *CPR 1247–58*, 198; *CLR 1251–60*, 157.

[137] *CPR 1247–58*, 562.

[138] Ibid., 557–8.

[139] *CPR 1258–66*, 219; BL Harleian Charter 43. C. 42; Wurstemberger, *Peter der Zweite*, iv, no. 649.

[140] For Eleanor as executrix see *CPR 1266–72*, 352; E 159/46 mm. 4, 14.

[141] *CPR 1266–72*, 433–4; ibid., Appendix, 736–7.

about these towns on her husband's death. On one thing Eleanor was quite determined, as one would readily expect; she would not allow them to be counted twice. If they were to be part of her dower after her husband's death, then she must be given further compensation for Richmond. When Henry III died in 1272 Eleanor of Provence was a wealthy woman but her various property claims held contentious issues for herself and her eldest son.

Eleanor of Provence, like other queens, exercised patronage. Patronage was both a material resource and an aspect of the queen's prestige, but it is difficult to quantify. Henry III's disposal of his own vast reserves of patronage was highly contentious politically, as Huw Ridgeway has shown in his detailed studies in this field. By comparison, the patronage at the disposal of Eleanor of Provence was exiguous, but its special character and her own management of what was available to her, reflect on her style of queenship.

Much of the queen's patronage was exercised in the shadow of the king. Even appointments to posts within the queen's household may have been subject ultimately to the king's confirmation, and the frequent transfer of personnel from one royal household to another suggests consultation among the heads of the households concerned. In the case of the queen, patronage quickly shades off into influence. Her influence over appointments to posts in the Lord Edward's household, which has been described as 'merely an extension of the queen's service' before Edward's marriage, cannot be thought of as the disposal of posts in her indisputable gift.[142] On a fairly limited number of occasions the king granted small wardships to members of the queen's household, sometimes mentioning that it was at her request, but not always.[143] This indicates an insuperable problem in quantifying the queen's patronage 'by influence'. When a handful of concessions to the queen herself and to those broadly associated with her occurs on the chancery rolls, which happens not infrequently, one is tempted to detect the queen at the elbow of the king, but much must be surmise. A clearer indication than usual of this unrecorded influence may be inferred in the case of patronage received by the queen's more highly placed clerks. Walter d'Aubigny, John de Sancta Maria, Hugh of Evesham and John of Scarborough were presented to benefices in the queen's own gift through her direct

---

[142] Ridgeway, 'The Lord Edward', 92. On queen's household see above and ch. 4.

[143] *CPR 1232–47*, 423; *CPR 1247–58*, 106, 632; *CPR 1258–66*, 353; *CPR 1266–72*, 608, all as cited by Scott Waugh, *Lordship of England*, 184, n. 1.

patronage from rights of wardship.[144] But such senior clerks were men whose status marked them out as eligible not merely for the gift of churches but of prebends. Here she could not help them directly since prebends in the major churches were never in her gift; they were in the gift of bishops or of the king *sede vacante*. Yet such prizes were not out of the reach of these men. Walter d'Aubigny came to hold a prebend in Salisbury, John de Sancta Maria in St Paul's, London, Hugh of Evesham in York, John of Scarborough in Hereford, while Eleanor's wardrobe keepers Walter de Bradley and Hugh de la Penne held prebends in St Martin's, London and Salisbury respectively and her gold keeper Robert de Chaury proceeded from the archdeaconry of Bath to the bishopric of Carlisle.[145] None of these presentations came to these officials through the queen's gift, but it is possible that some of them at least would not have gained their benefices but for their association with her.

Patronage of institutions, as distinct from individuals, touched on public prestige, and Eleanor of Provence sought such prestige. This is not to deny her religious motivation; patronage was notoriously ambivalent. In 1275 Eleanor founded a Dominican house at Guildford in memory of her grandson Henry, who was in her care towards the end of his life. Guildford was one of Eleanor's main dower residences and the Dominicans were the order for which the boy's mother had a special affection.[146] Yet, despite the royal predilection for the friars, neither Eleanor nor her husband ever lost interest in earlier religious traditions. Eleanor's generosity to her Cistercian nunnery of Tarrant, given to her by Richard Poore, may have caused her to be remembered in the house as its actual foundress.[147] She watched over the interests of these nuns with characteristic kindness and sharpness, sending them herrings, directing money from the chattels of a hanged felon for their use, protecting the legal claims of the abbess against the local lord of Tarrant Keynes, and finally asking for all their charters to be enrolled on the charter rolls, which was done in 1280.[148] The queen also granted the community properties at Kingsbere and Idsworth.[149] The Cistercian house of Bindon in Dorset, by contrast with Tarrant, had only come into the patronage of Eleanor of Provence, jointly with her husband, shortly before Henry III's

[144] *Reg. Walter Giffard (Bath and Wells)*, 9; *Reg. Walter Giffard (York)*, 80; *Reg. William Wickwane*, 32; *Reg. John le Romeyn*, i. 76, 101.

[145] Le Neve, *Fasti* (ed. Greenway), iv. 105; ibid., i. 87; *Reg. William Wickwane*, 2; Le Neve, *Fasti*, i. 518; *CPR 1247–58*, 327; Le Neve, *Fasti* (ed. Greenway), iv. 85; *CPR 1247–58*, 541.

[146] Hinnebusch, *The Early English Friars Preachers*, 82–3.

[147] Dugdale, *Monasticon*, v. 619.

[148] E 101/349/18; *CLR 1240–45*, 58; *CR 1242–47*, 13; SC 1/16/200.

[149] *CChR 1257–1300*, 227, 230.

death in 1272, but Eleanor promptly took Bindon under her wing in characteristically proprietary fashion.[150] In 1276 she made a grant to the house of land in Wool in Dorset for the salvation of her husband's soul and probably at the same time made over the patronage of the abbey itself to her son Edward.[151] In order to make her point quite clearly she writes to him that she hears he has been spending a little time at his ease at Bindon, 'your new house, which you have of our gift'.[152]

When faced with a challenge, this proprietary instinct led Eleanor of Provence into assertive and high-handed behaviour. In two of her dower towns there were prestigious hospitals, the hospital of St John in Cambridge and that of God's House in Southampton. In each case she attempted to assert her patronage. By 1274 she had appointed a Master to the hospital in Cambridge, but Hugh Balsham Bishop of Ely rejected the appointment, refusing to admit him, and the dispute came before the *curia regis*. The bishop won.[153] The struggle in Southampton was more prolonged. The town only became part of her dower settlement in 1280 and it was not until 1285 that the wardenship of the hospital became vacant. There was an immediate dispute over the patronage between the Southampton burgesses and the bishop of Winchester, but the brethren themselves cannily approached the queen mother for permission to elect their own warden, treating her as their patron. Eleanor of Provence was as ready to challenge the bishop of Winchester as she had been to challenge the bishop of Ely and the brethren sensibly elected her almoner Robert de Stoke as their warden. The struggle continued, with physical violence at Southampton where the queen's warden was forcibly ejected, and in more seemly fashion in the king's court where Edward I eventually recovered the right of patronage which Queen Eleanor was judged to have exercised in his name.[154]

Eleanor's attempts to assert her patronage claims in Cambridge and Southampton do no more than reveal her as sharing the characteristic attitudes of the landowning classes. It was otherwise with her vindication of her claims over the hospital of St Katharine by the Tower of London. Here we have a series of incidents which encapsulate both the image and practice of the harsher aspect of her queenship in remarkably circumstantial detail. The successive steps by which Eleanor attained her object in this instance not only show her as aggressive and intransigent in

---

[150] *CPR 1272–81*, 337.
[151] Ibid., 133; *CChR 1257–1300*, 216–17.
[152] SC 1/16/160.
[153] *CCR 1272–79*, 131; *Abbrevatio Placitorum*, 263.
[154] *The Chartulary of God's House, Southampton*, i, intro., xli–xlv; *Rotuli Parliamentorum*, i. 18–20, 30, 39–40; *Reg. Johannis de Pontissaria*, ii. 695–711.

pursuing her goal, but they also reveal how her position as queen enabled her to grind down the opposition. The hospital had been founded and modestly endowed in 1147–8 by King Stephen's queen Matilda, and had been given by Matilda into the custody of the Augustinian priory of Holy Trinity Aldgate.[155] It is in the cartulary of that house that the story unfolds.[156] Hostility between the priory and the hospital on matters of management was embittered around 1253 when the prior of Holy Trinity forced one of his own canons upon St Katharine's as its Master; a step that was evidently *ultra vires*.[157] The brothers of St Katharine's saw the queen as their natural ally – as those of God's House, Southampton were to do later – and at some point before 3 May 1257 the queen asserted her own right of patronage, based on Queen Matilda's endowment, in a letter to Fulk Basset, bishop of London. She deplored the mismanagement of St Katharine's hospital by the priory of Holy Trinity and complained that the latter refused to admit her own rights. She urged Basset to investigate the matter.[158] Fulk Basset was not a man to be easily intimidated, but he saw sufficient reason, after a personal visitation of the hospital, to remove it from the custody of Holy Trinity and to place it under a chaplain of the hospital itself. There is no evidence, however, that he made any admission of the queen's rights of patronage; he simply took disciplinary action as Ordinary.[159]

The queen presumably bided her time. When Henry of Wingham, recently royal chancellor and a clerk high in the favour of both king and queen, was consecrated as Basset's successor in February 1260 the queen seized her chance. Conveniently, there was now a new prior of Holy Trinity too. At this point the sharp edge of queenship is witnessed in action. The year, significantly, was 1261, when Henry III vigorously reasserted his rights of kingship. Henry of Wingham, in association with Robert de Chaury bishop of Carlisle and former keeper of queen's gold, and Giles of Bridport bishop of Salisbury, supported by other members of the queen's council, summoned the new prior of Holy Trinity before them and browbeat him into a verbal surrender of his house's

---

[155] *Regesta Regum Anglo-Normannorum, 1066–1154*, iii, nos 406, 503, 504.

[156] The cartulary was compiled in the fifteenth century, based on earlier material. For calendared version of entries concerning St Katharine's see *Cartulary of Holy Trinity Aldgate*, nos 973–94, but important items are printed *in extenso* by Ducarel, *History of the Royal Hospital and Collegiate Church of St Katharine*, 1–126. The best modern account is by C. Jamison, *History of the Royal Hospital of St Katharine*, 102–6.

[157] Ibid., 11–13.

[158] Ducarel, *History of the Royal Hospital and Collegiate Church of St Katharine*, 103–4; *Cartulary of Holy Trinity Aldgate*, no. 985.

[159] Ducarel, *History of the Royal Hospital and Collegiate Church of St Katharine*, 104–5; *Cartulary of Holy Trinity Aldgate*, no. 986.

ancient rights over St Katharine's hospital, although those rights were backed by episcopal, papal and even royal confirmations. They proceeded by a mixture of persuasion and threat, pointing out that the prior and canons of Holy Trinity would be well advised to yield to the queen's wishes, since she could incite the king's anger against them, which they would be unable to withstand, 'firmly asserting that the will of the king has the force of law'.[160]

Whether this well-known tag from Roman law was indeed quoted by Wingham one cannot be sure. What is certain is the prior's very reluctant surrender in the face of such formidable opposition. He knew he was in the right but we are told that he was a meek man and he evidently could not stand up to the authority of the queen's council. The clinching argument used by the bishops, according to the cartulary account, is of interest for the contemporary image of queenship, whether or not it represents accurate reporting. They moved the scene in imagination to the royal bedchamber where the queen, who was the night-bird (*nicticorax*) of the king, could incite him to great anger against the priory of Holy Trinity.[161] This hint at influence in ultimate privacy seems to have broken the prior's nerve.

After 1261 Eleanor of Provence faced further stiff resistance to her rights of patronage over St Katharine's, this time from the papacy. In 1264 Urban IV made a stern protest to the queen and professed himself scarcely able to believe what he had heard of her action. The protest left her unmoved.[162] The hospital was to be further endowed and given a new charter by Eleanor in 1273 when it was virtually re-founded in memory of her husband, without displacing the existing personnel. Provision was made for a Master and three brethren, who were priests, as well as twenty-four poor men, six of whom were to be scholars, and there were also three sisters.[163] The hospital had become for her a highly cherished institution. Moreover, its prestigious position beside the Tower of London had implications for the image of queenship. The long-term sequel to Eleanor's determined struggle for St Katharine's has its own slightly ironic interest. She had provided that the patronage of St Katharine's should be vested in all future queens of England after her own death, and it became customary that, as in her own case, they should retain the

---

[160] Ducarel, *History of the Royal Hospital and Collegiate Church of St Katharine*, 105–6; *Cartulary of Holy Trinity Aldgate*, nos. 986, 987, 988, 989.

[161] Ducarel, *History of the Royal Hospital and Collegiate Church of St Katharine*, 105.

[162] SC 7/33/2. In 1267 Clement IV granted further confirmation of the rights of Holy Trinity over the hospital, SC 7/10/1B.

[163] *CChR 1257–1300*, 409–10; *Foedera*, i. 439; Jamison, *History of the Royal Hospital of St Katharine*, Appendix 2, 179–81 and trans., 19–21.

patronage as dowagers. With extraordinary persistence, Queen Eleanor's foundation, albeit modified and deprived of its original buildings, has survived every disaster, including the sixteenth-century Reformation and the nineteenth-century flooding of St Katharine's dock. It continues to exist as the Royal Foundation of St Katharine, and the rules of patronage are unchanged.[164]

English queenship in the thirteenth century had great potential, but not for the passive or incompetent. The achievement of Eleanor of Provence depended on keen political sense, an intelligent grasp of management and a determination to seize opportunities. It also depended on a husband who allowed room for all these qualities to come into play.

[164] See e.g. Alexander and Binski, *Age of Chivalry*, no. 469.

12

Queen Mother

With the death of her husband in 1272 Eleanor of Provence assumed a new role, that of queen dowager. It was fourteen years before she changed her style yet again, to 'a humble nun of the order of Fontevrault of the convent of Amesbury'.[1] Throughout her widowhood she was most frequently referred to as queen of England, mother of the king, but she did not hesitate on certain occasions, particularly in business letters, to refer to herself by her full title of 'queen of England, lady of Ireland, duchess of Aquitaine'.[2] The fact that after 1272 there was another queen of England, Eleanor of Castile, who also bore those exact titles, was evidently of no hindrance; she was an anointed queen and continued so until her death in 1291, after almost twenty years of widowhood.

Recent work on the state of England between the death of Henry III and the arrival of Edward I on 2 August 1274 has revealed just how unsettled the country was.[3] The succession itself went reasonably smoothly. The judicious intervention of Gilbert de Clare averted the threat of a rising in London; the magnates swore fealty immediately after Henry's burial and then proceeded to the New Temple where they approved the assumption of authority by Edward's agents, the breaking of the old seal and the making of the new and the declaration of the new king's peace.[4] According to Nicholas Trivet the transfer of authority was

---

[1] SC 1/16/151 (*Letters of the Queens of England*, 66–7); SC 1/16/156 (*Letters of the Queens of England*, 66).

[2] SC 1/7/10; SC 1/16/158, 162, 184; SC 1/23/5 (Sayles, 'The Sources of Two Revisions of the Statute of Gloucester', 467–9, 473); SC 1/23/39.

[3] Maddicott, 'Edward I and the Lessons of Baronial Reform', 1–9.

[4] *Cron. Maiorum*, 152–4; *Flores*, iii. 28.

done with the assent of Eleanor of Provence, and this is very likely, as she was the only person in the realm anointed to royal estate.[5] If so, it was done quietly; it was no moment for an alien queen to appear centre-stage. During the months that followed, serious disorder and violence were rife, the conduct of local government was often corrupt and oppressive, royal liberties were quietly appropriated and there was serious feuding among the nobility, with Eleanor's younger son Edmund much in evidence.[6]

The queen mother established herself at Windsor, the castle which had been placed in her custody shortly before her husband's death. The Lord Edmund went straight to Windsor to see her on his return to England in December 1272.[7] She had not yet been granted her dower lands, which she could only enter with her elder son's formal consent. Besides, there were royal children at Windsor, Henry aged six, now the heir apparent to the throne, his sister Eleanor aged four, and Beatrice of Brittany's son John aged eight, known in the financial accounts by his pet name of Brito. To watch over these very young grandchildren and to gain entry to her dower lands were probably Queen Eleanor's main preoccupations. The keeper of young Henry's wardrobe was the royal clerk Thomas de Pampesworth, several of whose accounts survive. The children's household was modest but each child had his or her own nurse and one can glean details of their daily lives.[8] Perhaps the queen mother's strong maternalism had found, as is not unusual, a late additional outlet.

On 24 September 1273 Eleanor of Provence left Windsor for Guildford.[9] The reason is almost certainly to be found in the writs of 23 August, issued in the king's name, ordering the transfer of her dower lands to her own hands.[10] Practical and prudent in matters of property, Eleanor evidently thought it advisable to visit some of her major dower properties without delay. Guildford was a royal palace close beside the walls of the castle, and it has been said that 'with its chapels, cloister and gardens it was clearly one of Henry's most attractive residences'.[11] It was

---

[5] Nicholas Trivet, *Annales*, 283.

[6] Maddicott, 'Edward I and the Lessons of Baronial Reform', 8–9.

[7] *Ann. Winchester*, 112; *Chron. Wykes*, 253.

[8] E 372/125 rot. 2d; E 101/350/15, 16, 17, 18, 20; entries of issues to keepers of the children: E 403/23 mm. 1, 2; /25 m. 1; /27 mm. 1, 2, 3; /28 m. 2; /30 m. 1. For discussion of the household accounts see Johnstone, 'The Wardrobe and Household Accounts of the Sons of Edward I', 37–40 and 'Wardrobe and Household of Henry, son of Edward I', 384–420, where E 101/350/18 is printed, pp. 400–20. Page references to her edition are given in brackets in subsequent footnotes. She rightly mentions that the sequence of the entries in the account is confused (p. 389). Her own numbering of the membranes has been superseded.

[9] E 101/350/18 m. 1 (400).

[10] *CPR 1272–81*, 27–8; E 159/48 m. 2d.

[11] *King's Works*, ii. 953.

the residence at which Eleanor as dowager probably spent more time than any other. Apart from an October visit to Kempton, Eleanor spent most of the autumn and early winter in Guildford and her grandchildren were with her. Between 4 February 1274 and early August, when she took her protégés to Canterbury to meet their parents, Eleanor again visited Kempton, and also Windsor, Havering, Marlborough and Ludgershall.[12] The last three manors were her dower properties. It is easy to see what she was about, but one wonders why she imposed all this travelling on the children, especially since Henry seems to have been in weak health. Eleanor presumably wanted to watch over him herself and the evidence suggests that she had a warm personal attachment to the little boy, named after her own husband. When Henry was ill he received the attention of two physicians in whom the queen mother had great confidence, William le Provençal and Hugh of Evesham.[13] In the autumn of 1274, after the excitements of his parents' coronation, the young Henry again fell ill and he spent the last short stretch of his life at Guildford, presumably again in the care of his grandmother. Spiritual as well as human help was invoked; *mensurae* (candles measuring his height) were sent to neighbouring shrines and two were sent to Westminster, one to the shrine of St Edward and one to the tomb of Henry III.[14] When Prince Henry died, probably on 16 October, his grandmother mourned him.[15] When the king made a grant of £10 a year from a wardship to Henry's nurse, Amicia de Derneford, it was at the queen mother's instance that the gift was made permanent.[16] It was Eleanor of Provence too who founded the Dominican priory at Guildford in his memory and it was there that his heart was buried after his body had been taken to Westminster.[17]

Was there any comparable bond between the queen mother and Henry's companions, his sister Eleanor and his cousin Brito? The younger Eleanor certainly continued to visit her grandmother from time to time.[18] On 15 February 1282, when the girl was between twelve and thirteen years old, she was again at Guildford, when her grandmother's seal was used to confirm her betrothal to Alfonso of Aragon, since she had as yet no seal of her own. A few months later Eleanor of Provence joined with

---

[12] E 101/350/18 mm. 1, 2 (400–7).

[13] Ibid., m. 3 (412).

[14] Ibid., m. 3 (409).

[15] Parsons, 'The Year of Eleanor of Castile's Birth', 259–60.

[16] CPR 1272–81, 79.

[17] Hinnebusch, *The Early English Friars Preachers*, 82; Johnstone, 'Wardrobe and Household of Henry, son of Edward I', 399 and n. 4.

[18] Parsons, *Eleanor of Castile*, 39.

Eleanor of Castile in urging Edward I not to send his daughter to the Aragonese court until she was appreciably older.[19] Young Brito, later earl of Richmond, made his career in England at the court of Edward I. He evidently continued to think of his kindly grandmother with affection. In 1294 the king made a gift to his nephew of an oak in the forest of Windsor to repair a cross erected in memory of the king's mother.[20] Much less grand no doubt than the memorial crosses commissioned by the king in memory of Eleanor of Castile, but a cross with its own significance.

Edward had returned to England by way of Sicily, Savoy and Paris, where at each stage he was given hospitality by his mother's kinsmen; and so finally to Gascony to crush the renewed rebellion of Gaston de Béarn against the English Crown. His itinerary is a reminder of Eleanor's own continuing personal contacts outside England. On his return in 1274 Edward proceeded almost immediately to his coronation, which took place in Westminster Abbey on 19 August, the first royal coronation in England since Eleanor's own in 1236. It was an occasion of lavish entertainment and fine spectacle, intended as a great national celebration. The crowning and anointing of her son Edward, in succession to his father, and in the presence of her daughters Margaret and Beatrice, with their husbands, would have been deeply gratifying to Eleanor, even though her younger son Edmund may have boycotted the ceremony in personal pique over the matter of his claim to the hereditary stewardship of England.[21] He surrendered his claim the next day and accepted the grant of the stewardship as a life appointment. For Eleanor of Provence, in terms of hopes fulfilled and terrible dangers past, her eldest son's coronation was an occasion of deep thanksgiving.

This was a high moment, only to be followed by a year of shattering bereavements. The death of Eleanor's grandson Henry in October 1274 was quickly followed by the death in childbirth of Edmund's young wife Aveline, whose twin babies died with her. Eleanor had done much to promote Edmund's marriage and Edmund himself was said by Thomas Wykes to have grieved deeply for his young wife.[22] The coming winter brought deeper tragedy. At the beginning of 1275 it was clearly Eleanor's intention to go abroad. Royal protections and in some cases licences for

---

[19] Chaplais, *English Medieval Diplomatic Practice*, Part I, ii, no. 248 (a), in the context of a full discussion of the negotiations; *Rôles Gascons*, ii, no. 597; Parsons, 'Mothers, Daughters, Marriage, Power', 63; Prestwich, *Edward I*, 321.

[20] *CCR 1288–96*, 352. He succeeded his father and namesake as earl of Richmond.

[21] *Cron. Maiorum*, 172–3; *Chron. Wykes*, 259–60; *Flores*, iii. 44–5; Richardson, 'The Coronation of Edward I', 97–8; Prestwich, *Edward I*, 89–91.

[22] Ch. 10, above.

the appointment of attorneys were issued for various senior members of her household who were to accompany her. Among those chosen to go were her lady Christiana de Marisco, her clerk John of Scarborough, her chaplain Alexander de Bradenham and her physician William le Provençal.[23] Eleanor herself was given permission to make her will of all her goods and movables and had confirmation of her right to make bequests up to the sum of 10,000 marks from the revenues representing her compensation for Richmond.[24] All these provisions were made in January or early February 1275. Yet this proposed visit remains a mystery and there seems no evidence as to whether it took place or not, or what its purpose was. Perhaps events overtook Eleanor in the crushing double bereavement which now struck her. On 26 February her eldest daughter, Margaret queen of Scotland, died and less than a month later, on 24 March, came the death of Margaret's sister Beatrice. Both were in their early thirties and their beauty had drawn the attention of chroniclers on the occasion of Edward I's coronation when they had so recently been together at Westminster. To Eleanor of Provence this sudden loss of both her daughters must have brought devastating grief. Death in childbirth was common, but the cause of Margaret's death is unknown and it appears that Beatrice did not die in giving birth to her daughter Eleanor, although her death may have been linked with that. The influence of their mother on both young women had been profound, and both came to share her particular devotion to the Franciscan order. When she was nearing death Margaret would have no other cleric with her except her Franciscan confessor, and Beatrice had chosen to be buried in the Franciscan convent in London.[25] Eleanor of Provence was to act as Beatrice's executrix, along with her husband, John of Brittany, who did not marry again and who seems to have remained devoted to the memory of his wife.[26] Thomas Wykes comments that the severity of Eleanor's grief at the loss of her daughters was tempered only by her joy in their children.[27]

In the early years of her widowhood, one of the major preoccupations of Eleanor of Provence was the matter of resources, as it had always been. Two main sources of her wealth as consort were cut off with the death of her husband. She could no longer claim queen's gold, although her gold keeper John de Whatley continued to press her retrospective

[23] *CPR 1272–81*, 75–80, *passim*; *CCR 1272–79*, 226–7.

[24] *CPR 1272–81*, 76, 77.

[25] *Chron. Lanercost*, 97; Kingsford, *The Grey Friars of London*, 71; Green, *Princesses*, ii. 220, 265.

[26] Green, *Princesses*, ii. 265–6; *CPR 1272–81*, 270.

[27] *Chron. Wykes*, 262.

claims with great vigour.[28] Nor did she have any claim on the king for direct sustenance of herself and her household. Instead, as queen dowager she had her dower properties, and as an individual she had the two large grants which had come to her from Peter of Savoy, the honour of Pevensey and the compensation for the honour of Richmond. Eleanor pressed her claims assertively. At her husband's death, as we have seen, some of her dower towns were doubling as compensation for Richmond. Moreover, a number of towns mentioned in the 1262 dower settlement were missing from the allocation of 1273.[29] To make up the shortfall in his mother's dower Edward allowed her an annual payment of £1065 16s 7d at the exchequer.[30] Eleanor insisted on regarding this as a temporary arrangement and would not be satisfied until she was compensated in actual property. She was equally determined that she should see fair play over the extending of the Agenais, which in 1279 had finally come into the hands of the English Crown, according to the terms of the Treaty of Amiens, concluded with France in that year, and which represented a large part of her compensation for Richmond.[31] She sent her own proctors, her knights Guy Ferre and Benedict de Blakenham and her clerk William de Estden to supervise the making of the extent, along with Edward I's representatives. She wrote to the chancellor Robert Burnell, asking him to ensure that the king's agents did not arrive in the Agenais before her own, whose departure had been slightly delayed.[32] This is not the place to trace the frequent adjustments and rearrangements which culminated in the major settlement of 24 May 1281, which covered both dower and Richmond, presumably to her satisfaction. When the king described himself as granting his mother 'full satisfaction of the whole dower demanded by her of the king' the wording suggests a steely determination on Eleanor's part to realize all that was due to her.[33] It was an attitude which Edward himself could appreciate.

Eleanor of Provence was by now a woman of impressive wealth. Her dower assignment had been officially fixed since 1262 at £4,000 a year, and more recently Richmond had been valued at £1,805.[34] In addition to this she held the honour of Pevensey. Since 1275 she further enjoyed certain highly profitable rights over her dower properties; fines and amercements taken before the itinerant justices, pleas of the forest, and

---

[28] Howell, 'The Resources of Eleanor of Provence', 379.
[29] *CPR 1272–81*, 27–8; E 159/48 m. 2d.
[30] *CPR 1272–81*, 142. For payments see E 403/3110; /35 m. 1; /36 m. 1; /37 m. 1.
[31] *Foedera*, i. 571–2.
[32] *CPR 1272–81*, 361; SC 1/23/11 (*Rôles Gascons*, iii, p. xxxi).
[33] *CPR 1272–81*, 438–9.
[34] Ibid., 386.

tallage when the king tallaged his own demesnes.[35] Wealth on this scale placed her in the top bracket of English aristocratic landowners. The management of her wealth and of her affairs rested in the hands of able and long-serving administrators, among whom the names of Benedict de Blakenham, steward of her household, Guy of Taunton, her estates steward, Luke de la Gare, bailiff of Pevensey, John of Scarborough, Guy Ferre and William de Estden stand out. Their names occur as witnesses of her charters and as agents in financial, legal and administrative matters.[36] Her contacts with them were close and she showed them favour. In 1279 she granted Guy Ferre and his wife the Norfolk manor of Fakenham, and in 1287 she presented John of Scarborough to the benefice of Spofforth in the diocese of York.[37] Scarborough, Ferre and Estden, together with the Lord Edmund, were the executors of her will.[38] After her death William de Estden set aside a rent from his lands in Combe, Littlecote and Enford for the salvation of Eleanor's soul.[39] A professional relationship had evidently fostered substantial personal regard.

All Eleanor of Provence's lands would revert to the Crown on her death. Only rarely did she add to her properties and this was usually done to provide an additional endowment for a favoured religious house or, in one historically interesting case, to make a gift to her son Edmund. She bought back Peter of Savoy's palace in the Strand, which he had granted to the house of St Bernard, Mont Joux, and in 1284 she presented it to Edmund as a gift.[40] Its troubled and exciting history is well known, but the site still belongs to the duchy of Lancaster and a modern life-size gilded statue of Peter of Savoy commands the entrance of the present hotel.

The evidence for the interests and influence of Eleanor of Provence as dowager lies above all in her letters. There are some one hundred and sixty of them which survive, many written to whoever was chancellor at the time, and another substantial group written to her eldest son. In the first place they indicate where she spent her time. She was mainly to be found in one of three royal residences which were among her dower properties, Guildford, Marlborough and Ludgershall, or at Amesbury where she was eventually to take the veil in 1286 and where she evidently

---

[35] Ibid., 81.
[36] Ibid., 361, 429; *CPR 1281–92*, 405; *CChR 1257–1300*, 189, 217, 410; SC 1/8/104, 105; SC 6/1089/20 mm. 2, 3, 4.
[37] *CPR 1272–81*, 355; *Reg. John le Romeyn*, i. 76, 101.
[38] *CCR 1288–96*, 179, 247, 313; SC 6/1089/21 m. 1.
[39] *VCH, Wiltshire*, iii. 247.
[40] *CPR 1281–92*, 189.

visited frequently in the previous decade.[41] Occasionally there is a record
of a visit to other dower properties. Gillingham, in Dorset, she disliked
because of 'the greasy smoky vapours which rise in the evenings'; King's
Cliffe, in Northamptonshire, and Gloucester were sometimes visited.[42]
She may have spent more time in Gloucester than her extant letters
indicate since, as has been seen, she had taken trouble to secure permission to walk in the gardens of Llanthony priory across the river from the
castle. Although there seem to be no surviving letters dated from Havering after 1275 it is known from other evidence that she spent time there
since payments were made into her wardrobe at Havering in 1280/1 and
1284/5.[43] It was in the chapel at Havering that she had made provision in
1274 for daily masses to be said for the soul of her husband.[44] On a visit
there in the 1280s she clashed sharply with her tenants, who had defied
her authority by hunting in the woods which had been designated royal
warren at her request. When twelve local men, summoned before her,
sturdily declined to give her information on these trespasses, she had
them confined for three days with only rushes to lie on, until they
submitted. As very old men some of them recalled the incident vividly.[45]
From her letters and other evidence it is clear that on occasion, as one
would expect, Eleanor travelled to places other than her dower manors,
to Westminster, Windsor, Winchester, Clarendon, Canterbury and
Northampton.[46]

Many of the queen dowager's letters deal with business matters, enlist-
ing the help of the chancellor or the king in dealing with problems or
establishing her rights. She writes of an unlawful distraint upon the men
of Colchester, her wish for a weekly market at Pevensey and for the
Wiltshire court to meet at Marlborough.[47] Her gaol at Milton Regis
should be delivered and the sheriff of Sussex should keep prisoners at
Guildford rather than Arundel castle.[48] Most of these letters, ostensibly
from the queen, were prompted by the initiatives of her administrators,
but occasionally there is a flash of indignation which is characteristically
her own. In accordance with the king's concession to Eleanor in 1275
that no Jews should remain in her dower towns, her steward Guy of

---

[41] Letters dated at Amesbury before 1286 include: SC 1/16/164, 200, 201; SC 1/23/34,
35, 37–44; SC 1/47/108; SC 1/48/18, 19.

[42] SC 1/16/157 (*Letters of the Queens of England*, 60); SC 1/16/184, 185; SC 1/10/45

[43] SC 6/1089/20 m. 3; /21 m. 7.

[44] CPR 1281–92, 378.

[45] McIntosh, *The Royal Manor of Havering*, 57–8.

[46] SC 6/1089/21 m. 7; SC 1/16/188, 154, 159, 202; SC 1/10/41.

[47] SC 1/10/43; SC 1/23/25, 26.

[48] SC 1/23/27; SC 1/60/110.

Taunton evicted the Jew Jacob Cok from Andover. When Jacob Cok retaliated by bringing an action for felony and robbery against Guy of Taunton, Eleanor wrote a superbly angry letter to the king himself.[49]

The most interesting letters are undoubtedly those written to her son Edward, partly for the light which they throw on the relationship which now existed between them. In her claims to a share in the county of Provence, which Eleanor pursued more vigorously than before, after the death in 1267 of her youngest sister Beatrice, wife of Charles of Anjou who was now king of Sicily, she looked to Edward to defend her rights as a matter of filial duty. Together with her sister Margaret, dowager queen of France, she strongly opposed a proposed marriage between Charles Martel, grandson of Charles of Anjou, and the daughter of Rudoph of Hapsburg, king of Germany, from whom Provence was held as a fief.[50] The two queens, who regarded Charles of Anjou as their inveterate enemy, saw the proposed marriage as a threat to any chance of vindicating their own claims to Provence. Edward I's mother 'prays and requires' that he shall write to the king of Germany on her behalf. This is no timorous plea; she is emphatic.[51] Edward was aware that he had exceptional obligations to his mother, although he was reluctant to cause a breach between himself and Charles of Salerno, Charles Martel's father. In 1281 Edward wrote to Charles of Salerno to this effect, but emphasized how much he owed to his aunt Queen Margaret for the help which she gave him in his time of trouble, and above all to his mother 'to whom, since the death of my father, I am more bound than to any living creature'.[52] In the following year Eleanor wrote herself to Philip III of France, asking him to help her to secure her rights in Provence. She sent the letter first to Edward, asking him to send it on his own authority after making any necessary amendments.[53] She was not prepared to let him forget. Eleanor never did realize her claims in Provence but she never yielded them either and, with Edward's assent, she transferred them in 1286 to the children of her second son, Edmund, who had married Louis IX's niece Blanche of Artois in 1276, as his second wife.[54]

The anguish and the effort of the years 1264–5 left their permanent mark on Eleanor of Provence. She remained deeply mindful of those who had helped her in that extremity and who by implication had helped her

[49] SC 1/16/158, and n. 76, below.

[50] Cox, *Eagles of Savoy*, 404–33.

[51] SC 1/16/180 (*Letters of the Queens of England*, 60). See also SC 1/16/173 (*Foedera*, i. 573).

[52] *Treaty Rolls*, i. 77.

[53] SC 1/16/168 (*Letters of the Queens of England*, 65).

[54] *CPR 1281–92*, 243.

eldest son. She frequently recalled him to such indebtedness. She felt the claims of Philip her uncle, now count of Savoy, who had been her chief adviser in the anxious negotiations of the summer and autumn of 1264 between the papal legate and the Montfortian government. When she urged Edward to support Philip in his dispute with Otto of Burgundy, she added 'think that he was your friend in your great need over England'.[55] Count Philip had confidence in Eleanor's diplomatic ability as well as that of Edward and drew upon the help of both in tackling the dynastic problems in Savoy itself.[56] There were other claimants to Eleanor's (and Edward's) gratitude; the burgesses and merchants of Bruges who asked to have their privileges confirmed and the burgesses of St Omer who sought confirmation of the charter granted to them by Henry III. Eleanor told her son that they had done much for his father and herself in the time of trouble.[57] This line of appeal could hardly fail to carry weight with the king when urged by the mother who had undergone so much on his behalf. Her own personal sacrifice, however, was the one lever Eleanor of Provence never used.

Most of Eleanor's letters to her eldest son include requests, either for herself, or more often for other people; the key phrase is *nous prioms*. The scene is set by her usual form of address: 'Eleanor by the grace of God queen of England, to our very dear son Edward by the same grace king of England, greeting and our blessing'.[58] There is implicit here an equality of rank, together with a relationship of mother to son, a son who is expected to value her maternal blessing. Her further address of *tres cher fiz, douz fiz, beau fiz* are forms used frequently and spontaneously within the course of the letters. The approach is warm and direct, as in writing to someone she knows intimately. She takes trouble to catch his personal interest. In asking him to excuse some debts of Amaury Pecche, incurred during the time of trouble, she writes that she asks the more willingly 'because his father looked after you when you were a child'.[59]

Only rarely can Edward's response to his mother be inferred, but these hints are invaluable. Despite Eleanor's endearments, these two spoke their minds to each other openly. In 1279 a letter of Eleanor to John Kirkby at the chancery shows the queen dowager pressing for the election of her almoner Richard de Tellisford as prior of Kenilworth.[60]

---

[55] SC 1/16/179 (*Lettres des rois*, i, no. 240).
[56] *Foedera*, i. 649; Cox, *Eagles of Savoy*, 448.
[57] SC 1/16/197; SC 1/47/108.
[58] E.g. SC 1/16/152.
[59] SC 1/16/203.
[60] SC 1/10/42.

Meanwhile she had asked Edward to treat the priory leniently in the approaching vacancy. This had been in conversation with her son at Clarendon. Edward had told her bluntly that he could not let the vacancy go for nothing, but that when the time came he would put in a good keeper, so that the priory did not suffer injury. She wrote to remind him and tactfully asked for the appointment of a keeper known to him, one whom he knows to be good and moderate.[61] The touch of flattery in reference to his judgement is delicately calculated. It was again at Clarendon, on the same or another occasion, that she had evidently been ready for him with a list of requests. She wrote shortly afterwards to say that she had put down the points on an *escroe* (a scrap of parchment), which she is sending by her *valettus*, asking the king to deal with them.[62] The deprecating word *escroe* does not conceal the fact that she thought it prudent to follow up her initial approach by putting things in writing. Indeed it seems to have been her wise custom to reinforce her requests in this way. In a meeting at Wilton the king had said that he would send her the two justices, John de Lovetot and Walter de Helion, to counsel her in her business. Again, she wrote to remind him.[63]

Edward did not always accede to his mother's requests. When Eleanor de Percy, mother of Eleanor of Provence's ward John de Percy, died the queen dowager asked to have the custody of Eleanor de Percy's dower lands.[64] This Edward would not allow; he had promised the custody to his friend John de Vescy and in a writ of 16 June 1285, addressed to his mother the king pointed out sharply that it was within his right to resume the two parts of the custody of the lands and heirs of Henry de Percy which she already had.[65] He rarely gave her wardships, evidently feeling that she was already well provided for. When Eleanor made a twofold request in a matter of patronage, asking that he would present her priest Henry de Kemeseye to a chantry at Southampton and her cousin Raymond de Laudon to the church of Downton in the diocese of Winchester, Edward conceded the first request but presented first William de Hamilton and then John de Montibus to Downton.[66] On a personal matter, not involving any grant, Eleanor on one occasion received a particularly curt response from her son. She had written to him to excuse her old friend Geoffrey de Joinville, who had visited her at Guildford on his way to Edward's court in March 1282; Geoffrey had a tertian fever, she said,

[61] SC 1/16/205.
[62] SC 1/16/192.
[63] SC 1/16/157; *CPR 1272–81*, 308.
[64] SC 1/16/159.
[65] *CPR 1281–92*, 175.
[66] SC 1/16/152; *CPR 1281–92*, 1; *CPR 1272–81*, 427; *CPR 1281–92*, 30.

and she was detaining him until he was better.[67] In a draft reply which is full of irritable crossings-out and interlining, Edward, dictating to his scribe, had obviously struggled to find words to express his strong displeasure.[68]

Eleanor could be angry too. Trivet tells the story, often cited, of Edward's visit to his mother at Amesbury soon after she had been approached by a knight who claimed to have had his sight miraculously restored at the tomb of Henry III. When Edward sturdily assured his mother that the man was a rogue and an impostor she ordered him from her room – and he went. Edward certainly intended no disrespect to his father and told the Dominican Provincial, Hugh of Manchester, who was about to go in to the queen, that his father's sense of justice was such that he would have been more likely to have had the rascal's eyes put out rather than to have restored his sight.[69] He was taking his mother to task for her gullibility. These sharp interchanges could no longer dent a relationship between the king and his mother that was founded on deep regard on each side. They were well matched in strength of personality and they had crossed swords dangerously in the past, but they were now bound by a mutual loyalty that was indestructible and by ties that went beyond loyalty.

Eleanor of Provence made intercession an art. She had the qualities of imagination and quick sympathy which enabled her to enter into the problems of others and she had the skills of the highly articulate letter writer. A formulary drawn up at Salisbury in the later thirteenth century included a letter from the queen mother to John Burton, the precentor, under a heading *Littere precum peroptime* (exceptionally good letters of request).[70] Most frequently she was writing on behalf of an individual. Eleanor had faced harsh suffering herself through humiliation, desperate anxiety and the grief of sudden and severe bereavement. This did not blunt her sensibility to lesser worries in other people and did not check her outgoing disposition. Her sympathy for Margaret Neville, deprived of access to her son, or for Eleanor de Percy, summoned before the justices at York at short notice and the need to take her mother with her across country (a matter not to be undertaken lightly) show the queen mother's understanding of human predicaments and her willingness to ease them if she could.[71] Her ready concern went beyond the practice of

---

[67] SC 1/16/171.
[68] SC 1/12/164.
[69] Nicholas Trivet, *Annales*, 302–3.
[70] BL Royal MS 12. D. XI, f. 87v.
[71] SC 1/16/151 (*Letters of the Queens of England*, 66–7); SC 1/16/195 (Sayles, *The Functions of the Medieval Parliament of England*, 162).

a queen's acknowledged role as an intercessor. It had been noticed all through her life by those who had observed her. The author of the *Estoire* had praised her *bonté* and *franchise*.[72] Adam Marsh referred to her liberality of heart.[73] After her death Oliver Sutton, bishop of Lincoln, in the letter to his archdeacons in which he asked for prayers for Eleanor's soul, wrote that the whole of England was injured by her death because of the help which she was ready to give to all who were oppressed by any kind of trouble.[74]

In 1290, the year before Eleanor's death, Edward I expelled the Jews from England. Both at the time and since, the influence of Eleanor of Provence has been seen as one of the reasons for this act.[75] There is in fact no evidence to support such a view, which may be no more than an inference from her own expulsion of the Jews in 1275 from all towns which she held in dower.[76] The year 1275 was that in which Edward issued his Statute of Jewry, forbidding the Jews to practise usury, and therefore a time when the principles of Jewish activities were under discussion.[77] In fact Eleanor's likely motives in 1275 were very different from those of her son in 1290. It is true that both were subject to the same ideological pressures, but it may be that the queen dowager was more sensitive than her son to the steadily growing antagonism of the friars to the Jews.[78] It is noticeable that in Cambridge, which was included in Eleanor's dower, the growth in the presence of the Dominicans and Franciscans coincided with her expulsion of the Jews from that town.[79] Eleanor took a continuing interest in the conversion of Jews and interceded with Edward for the admission of a converted Jewess into the *Domus Conversorum* in London, which had been founded by Henry III and of which she was a joint patron.[80] Edward's own act of expulsion can readily be explained in financial and political terms. He had already expelled the Jews from Gascony in 1287, confiscating their wealth. In 1290 he was hard pressed for cash to meet his debts and refill his treasury.[81] The clearing-up of Jewish assets would bring a modest immediate profit but the expulsion carried a far greater financial

---

[72] *Estoire* (ed. Wallace), 2.

[73] Adam Marsh, 'Epistolae', no. 153.

[74] *The Rolls and Register of Bishop Oliver Sutton*, iii. 132.

[75] *Ann. Waverley*, 409; Stokes, 'The Relationship between the Jews and the Royal Family of England in the Thirteenth Century', 165.

[76] CPR 1272–81, 76.

[77] *Statutes of the Realm*, i. 220–1.

[78] Cohen, *The Friars and the Jews*, 13–14.

[79] Stokes, *Anglo-Jewish History*, 108–9, 188.

[80] SC 1/16/177.

[81] Richardson, *The English Jewry under Angevin Kings*, 226–8.

significance. The measure was highly popular politically, especially with the Commons, and Edward was able to use it as a quid pro quo for a desperately needed grant of parliamentary taxation.[82] Although Edward had respect for his mother's views on matters concerning her own affairs or concerning the family, his expulsion of the Jews is readily explained without any reference to her influence.

In the 1280s Eleanor of Provence was making preparations for the last phase of her life; not just for death, although death was a part of it. She had decided to take the veil in the Wiltshire nunnery of Amesbury and she set about the arrangements in good time and with her usual practical sense. As early as May 1280 the king ordered the keeper of Chute forest to deliver to the prioress of Amesbury ten oaks 'for certain works that Queen Eleanor the king's mother is causing to be made at Amesbury', and the bailiff of Clarendon was to provide twenty oaks for the same purpose.[83] No work in the convent church or community buildings is specified and it seems altogether likely that the new building was for the approaching entry of the queen mother and two of her granddaughters into Amesbury in a few years' time. In 1281 a further fifteen oaks were cut down in the forest of Chute and twelve in the forest of Melksham for Eleanor's projects at Amesbury.[84]

Eleanor of Provence had decided, and Nicholas Trivet, who was likely to know, was quite specific that it was her personal decision, that her namesake Eleanor, daughter of Beatrice of Brittany, and Mary, daughter of Edward I, should enter Amesbury shortly before her. Eleanor of Brittany, born in 1275, was veiled first, on 25 March 1285, together with seven companions. Although Eleanor of Castile was apparently reluctant to let her daughter Mary enter Amesbury, Mary too was received into the house, on 15 August 1285, at the age of six, accompanied by thirteen other girls from aristocratic families, in a grand ceremony attended by the king and queen, by bishops, abbots and priors and lay magnates.[85] Eleanor of Provence herself, by contrast, made her entry into Amesbury quietly on 7 July 1286 after her son and daughter-in-law had left for their prolonged visit to Gascony.[86] The queen mother's insistence that these two granddaughters should be received into Amesbury ahead of her own arrival there may seem merely a piece of blatant selfishness. In part it probably was. The two girls and their

---

[82] Prestwich, *Edward I*, 343–6 and forthcoming article by Robert Stacey in *TCE*, vi (1997).

[83] *CCR 1279–88*, 14.

[84] Ibid., 96.

[85] BL Arundel MS 56, f. 75; *Ann. Worcester*, 491.

[86] *Ann. Worcester*, 492; *Flores*, iii. 65; *Chron. Wykes*, 307; *Ann. Waverley*, 404.

young companions would have added considerably to the interest and sociable intercourse which Queen Eleanor would be able to enjoy there. This is not a completely anachronistic judgement, but it is partly so. The presentation of a young girl to the religious life was still considered an act of piety on the part of her family and a close parallel is to be found in the arrangement at Lacock where Ela, countess of Salisbury, the founder and later abbess of the house, had two granddaughters with her.[87]

Eleanor of Provence intended that her granddaughters should live in conditions of comfort and dignity at Amesbury. Provision for Mary she could safely leave to the girl's father, but for the support of the young Eleanor the queen dowager made a gift to Amesbury of the manor of Chaddleworth (Berkshire) and the advowson of Poughly priory.[88] When Amesbury came to be troubled by debt the manor was farmed out for three years with Queen Eleanor's consent to help tide the house over its difficulties, but in 1293 Eleanor of Brittany, showing spirit and outlook which reflected that of her late grandmother, requested the king in council that the revenues of the manor should be restored to their original purpose of her own personal maintenance. It was granted that this should be done, once the three-year period had run its course.[89]

Personal financial provision for a lady of high rank entering a religious house was not unusual, but the provision which Eleanor of Provence envisaged and achieved for herself was quite exceptional. She was prepared to relinquish some of her property but she intended to retain a large landed endowment. The cynical chronicler of Osney abbey poured scorn on her assumption of a nun's habit on these terms; purely delusory, he considered it.[90] A final arrangement of her affairs had been made urgent by the king's intended departure for a prolonged stay in Gascony. Yet two writs of 23 January 1286 show Eleanor apparently still hedging her bets. The first writ granted her the right to retain all her possessions in England and Gascony until Michaelmas 1287. This was assured 'whether she entered any religious order and whether professed or not'. There seems to be a hint of uncertainty here. This writ was witnessed by her son Edmund, Robert Burnell as chancellor and by two friars, the Dominican Provincial and one Brother Solomon, a Franciscan. The second writ, issued on the same day, was a provision for the rest of Eleanor's life and again it was to obtain whatever her status 'whether in the religious habit or not and whether professed or not'.[91] The provision

---

[87] Wood, *English Monasteries and their Patrons in the Thirteenth Century*, 122, n. 1.
[88] CPR 1281–92, 128.
[89] *Rotuli Parliamentorum*, i. 96; VCH, *Wiltshire*, iii. 247.
[90] *Ann. Osney*, 329.
[91] E 159/59 m. 30 (less explicit versions in *CPR 1281–92*, 218–19).

was very substantial indeed, including most of her dower property, most of the Richmond compensation in England and the whole honour of Pevensey. She had admittedly given up a number of valuable and prestigious English properties including Cambridge, Kingston, Guildford and Havering. Even more, she had given up her substantial Gascon revenues. All this was far from being a negligible gesture, but Eleanor had not embraced poverty. A few weeks later the king granted that in order to provide her with the 10,000 marks which had been promised her for the execution of her will, she should retain all her lands in Gascony until Michaelmas 1289.[92]

The signs are that Eleanor of Provence may possibly have been having some difficulty with ecclesiastical authority in retaining all this property. Certainly the Waverley chronicler specifically notes that she kept her dower in England in perpetuity and that she had papal letters of confirmation for this.[93] They do not survive, and there may have been some unease at Rome, or indeed at Fontevrault, over this highly irregular territorial arrangement. None of these lands would come to Amesbury after Eleanor's death; all would revert to the Crown. The wording of the writs cited above further indicates the two stages of entry into religion. Eleanor of Provence, as has been seen, was veiled at Amesbury on 7 July 1286. Her two granddaughters, who had been veiled a little earlier, both went on to be fully professed, but not until late in 1291, after their grandmother's death.[94] Was Eleanor herself ever professed? The two writs of 1286 concerning her property indicate that her intentions in this respect were unsure, and no chronicler records that she took that final step. It is probable that Eleanor of Provence never became a fully professed nun.

The queen mother was apparently very far from feeling that she had gone further than she should in reserving to herself such ample resources. Quite the contrary. On 6 June 1290 the king, obviously at her request, regranted to her several of the English properties which she had let go in 1286, to the amount of an additional £1,000 a year.[95] This was 'to aid in the maintenance of herself and her household'. Droitwich, Cambridge, Kingston, Colchester, Alton, Cookham, Havering and Middleton were now back among her possessions, together with sundry other revenues. Eleanor had only made a partial retreat from the things of this world.

---

[92] *CPR 1281–92*, 220.

[93] *Ann. Waverley*, 404.

[94] It is likely that both girls were professed at about this time. For Mary see Parsons, 'The Year of Eleanor of Castile's Birth', 264 and Douie, *Archbishop Pecham*, 323. For Eleanor see letter of Godfrey Giffard in HMC, *Report on MSS in Various Collections*, i. 347–8 (but this could refer to Mary), and *VCH, Wiltshire*, iii. 247.

[95] *CPR 1281–92*, 368; *CCR 1288–96*, 85 (8 June).

Is it then possible to regard Queen Eleanor's entry into Amesbury as true 'conversion of life'? The Osney chronicler obviously thought not, but the queen mother herself was quite clear about her change of status. Hitherto in letters to her son Edward she had placed her own name first, as queen of England, but now it was the king's name which came first and Eleanor's second as 'a humble nun of the order of Fontevrault of the convent of Amesbury'.[96] The change of style was clearly a very conscious one. She was a sincerely devout woman and the Lanercost chronicler records her liberality while she was at Amesbury. She had five pounds of silver given to the poor every Friday in reverence for the five wounds of Christ.[97] Almsgiving, attendance at mass and the office and devotional reading were occupations which her religious directors would have encouraged and there is no reason to suppose that in these respects she failed them. Oliver Sutton, bishop of Lincoln, too was convinced of her genuine piety. She moved within a community where a round of religious devotion was regularly practised and that community was sufficiently large and prosperous to allow the dignity of ceremonial and setting which her husband had taught her to cherish. It is also possible that at this late stage of her life Eleanor of Provence came to feel a sense of moral responsibility for the misdeeds of her own bailiffs. In July 1290 she requested from the king a commission of *oyer* and *terminer* to inquire into trespasses committed by her stewards or bailiffs throughout her lands.[98] Her daughter-in-law Eleanor of Castile was also to ask for such an inquiry into the misdeeds of her officials, but only on her death-bed.[99]

The queen dowager's choice of Amesbury rather than any other house as her final home is interesting. The abbey of Fontevrault, of which Amesbury was a daughter house, was a twelfth-century establishment founded by the reformer and evangelist Robert of Arbrissel. From humble beginnings Fontevrault soon began to attract ladies of high birth and to become the mother house of a sizeable order. Yet two marked characteristics of the original foundation were preserved and recent historians have pointed to them as factors in Fontevrault's success. The first was the substantial quality of the male support for the nuns. A nunnery needed priests to administer the sacraments and to act as confessors; it needed clerks and lay brothers to give protection, to manage commercial activity and to act in the law courts. Few Benedictine or Cistercian nunneries had this style of support built into their constitutions. At

[96] E.g. SC 1/16/151, 156 (*Letters of the Queens of England*, 66–7).
[97] *Chron. Lanercost*, 141.
[98] CPR 1281–92, 405.
[99] Parsons, *Eleanor of Castile*, 113–15.

Fontevrault there were enough men, and this was a factor of stability.[100]
At Amesbury itself in the mid-thirteenth century there were said to be
sixteen lay brothers and six chaplains, headed by a prior, to care for the
needs of a prioress and some seventy-six nuns.[101] Robert of Arbrissel
showed his practicality in another matter. The whole community at
Fontevrault had been placed under the undisputed control of the abbess
and he wanted the abbess to be a widow with experience of the world
rather than a virgin bred in the cloister.[102] This provision was later
modified, but one begins to sense that the general tone of the order
would be congenial to Eleanor of Provence.

The order of Fontevrault had in any case special claims on the royal
family of England. The fine tombs of Henry II, Eleanor of Aquitaine and
Richard I are still there. In Henry III's reign the links were still close. His
mother Isabella of Angoulême was buried there and Henry's heart was
taken there after Eleanor's death, in 1291. The heart of Eleanor and
Henry's daughter Beatrice was also buried there and it seems fitting that
Beatrice's daughter Eleanor, brought up at Amesbury, later became an
abbess of Fontevrault.[103] Why then did Eleanor of Provence not enter
Fontevrault itself? This was a question which probably rankled with the
abbess and prioress of Fontevrault. They certainly wished to have Eleanor's
granddaughter Mary at Fontevrault and they reminded Edward I that he
had once promised this. They even resorted to a little spiritual blackmail,
explaining to the king that if he did not let them have his daughter they
would find it more difficult to pray for him. It was to no avail. Edward had
promised his mother that she should settle Mary's destiny and Eleanor
wanted Mary at Amesbury.[104] When in due course Eleanor of Provence
died, the nuns of Fontevrault wanted to have the queen mother's body
buried in their church and they again urged that Mary should move to
Fontevrault, especially now that she was no longer needed as a companion
for her grandmother.[105] But Mary remained at Amesbury.

Amesbury had much to commend it. Originally a pre-Conquest foun-
dation, the house had been re-founded for the order of Fontevrault by
Henry II and it had regularly attracted royal and aristocratic ladies.
Henry III's cousin Alpesia had been a nun there and Eleanor, sister of
Arthur of Brittany, had chosen to be buried there.[106] Yet Fontevrault was

[100] Gold, *The Lady and the Virgin*, 110–13.
[101] Thompson, *Women Religious*, 128.
[102] Gold, *The Lady and the Virgin*, 96–7; Thompson, *Women Religious*, 116.
[103] VCH, *Wiltshire*, iii. 247.
[104] SC 1/17/115 (*Lettres des Rois*, i, no. 329).
[105] SC 1/17/116, 117.
[106] VCH, *Wiltshire*, iii. 245–6.

certainly the more illustrious name. Eleanor of Provence, linked by ties of kinship and friendship to many aristocratic continental families, would have been perfectly at ease in the social ambience of Fontevrault. But she chose Amesbury. Maurice Powicke, in one of his remarkable flashes of insight, remarked that 'Eleanor of Provence made England her home'.[107] This was the crux of it. She preferred to settle in Wiltshire close to her family and friends, in the realm where her son Edward was king and where her husband Henry III lay buried in the abbey church at Westminster. It was in England that she had lived her life and it was in England that she wished to end it.

The matriarchal role which Eleanor of Provence could fulfil even near the end of her life is revealed by an important document dated at Amesbury on 17 April 1290.[108] It recorded an oath taken by Gilbert de Clare earl of Gloucester, who was about to marry Edward I's daughter Joan, to uphold the succession to the English Crown as it had been laid down by the king. Gloucester swore that in the event of the king's death he would give his allegiance to Edward I's surviving son, Prince Edward, who was of course a grandson of Eleanor of Provence. The boy was six years old at the time, and it was intended that he should marry Eleanor's great-granddaughter Margaret, daughter of King Eric of Norway and heiress to the Scottish throne. On the same day that Gloucester made his oath, Edward I dispatched a letter to King Eric, asking him to send his daughter to England without delay, a papal dispensation for the marriage having now been secured.[109] The importance attached to the gathering at Amesbury, in which these arrangements were finalized, is clear from the list of those present as witnesses. These included the king's brother Edmund, William de Valence, Henry de Lacy, John Pecham archbishop of Canterbury, Robert Burnell bishop of Bath and Wells who was the king's chief minister, Otto de Grandson justice of Wales, Anthony Bek bishop of Durham and three other bishops. The name of Eleanor of Provence is of course nowhere mentioned, but the purpose of holding the meeting at Amesbury would have been a sense of the propriety of her own involvement in this dynastic settlement.

The enactment of these matters at Amesbury in April 1290 may be seen as a prelude to the last fourteen months of Eleanor's life, which ostensibly were spent very quietly. In fact this short period raises many unanswered questions which touch closely on relationships within Eleanor's nearer family and on concepts of royalty, of death and of

---

[107] Powicke, *Thirteenth Century*, 73.
[108] *Foedera*, i. 742.
[109] Ibid., i. 731.

commemoration. Death may be a great leveller, but commemoration in death may be the reverse.

On 11 May 1290, less than a month after the gathering at Amesbury, the body of Henry III was removed from its temporary resting-place in the old grave of Edward the Confessor, near to the high altar at Westminster, to the fine Cosmati tomb which had been prepared for it and where it still rests, alongside the Confessor's shrine. It was noticed at the time that this transfer of King Henry's body was done with scant ceremony – 'on the night of Our Lord's Ascension, suddenly and unexpectedly' – in the words of the Bury St Edmunds chronicler.[110] Most chroniclers do not notice it at all, but the author of the *Annals of London* makes the interesting comment that the king's body appeared intact (*integrum*), with a luxuriant beard.[111] Perhaps there was an implication here that there was little sign of corruption. This interest in the state of the body would fit well with David Carpenter's recent suggestion that Henry III's family, no doubt partly conditioned by the rapidly developing cult of Louis IX in France, may have been looking forward to a different ceremony. They perhaps hoped up to this point that the much more feeble cult of Henry III in England might have grown and culminated in a triumphant translation of Henry as a figure of generally acknowledged sanctity to a tomb which, from its construction, could indeed have served as a shrine. Dr Carpenter sees the unceremonious transfer on 11 May as possibly marking the final disappointment of any such hopes.[112]

This seems to me a very likely surmise. Moreover, there can be no doubt that one of those who hoped most for the sanctification of Henry III was his widow, and that his eldest son was more sceptical. This is clear from the incident related by Nicholas Trivet, and already mentioned, when Edward had 'tried to dissuade his mother' from her ready acceptance of the claim made by a disreputable knight to have had his sight miraculously restored at the tomb of Henry III.[113] This was in 1281, but already in 1274, as has been seen, it was almost certainly Eleanor herself, in the last illness of her dearly loved grandson Henry at Guildford, who sent two special votive candles to Westminster, one to the shrine of the Confessor and one to the tomb of Henry III.[114] A further indication of the devotion of Eleanor of Provence to the memory of her husband concerns his heart-burial. Henry had promised that his heart should be buried at Fontevrault, but it seems that Eleanor of Provence would not

---

[110] *Chron. Bury St Edmunds*, 94.
[111] *Ann. London*, 98.
[112] Carpenter, 'Henry III and the Cosmati Work at Westminster Abbey', 423–4.
[113] Nicholas Trivet, *Annales*, 302.
[114] E 101/350/18 m. 3.

allow that to happen during her own lifetime. It was not until 10 December 1291 that a ceremony took place in the abbey church at Westminster in which the king's heart was handed over to the abbess of Fontevrault, who had come to England to claim it.[115] The Lord Edmund and William of Valence were present, together with two bishops, but apparently not Edward I himself. The continued devotion of Eleanor of Provence to her husband's memory should be remembered when considering the significance of the events relating to her own death and burial.

Between the transfer of Henry III's body to its final resting-place and the death of Eleanor of Provence at Amesbury on 24 June 1291, there is interposed the death of Edward I's wife, Eleanor of Castile. The queen consort died unexpectedly at Harby, not far from Lincoln, on 28 November 1290, with literally spectacular results. Of Edward's deep personal grief there has never been any question, but grief was not the only motive for the nature of his commemoration of his queen. He appears to have decided almost immediately, at least in outline, on a programme of royal commemoration which proved unparalleled for the scale and splendour of its conception and the high artistic quality of its execution. No other English monarch or consort before or since has been honoured in death so lavishly or so beautifully as Eleanor of Castile.[116] At each of the twelve places where her bier rested on its journey from Lincoln to Westminster a site was marked out for the future erection of a memorial cross.[117] These crosses have a striking stylistic significance in the history of English art, but they are also significant historically as a deliberate statement of royal authority in visual terms.[118] In a more restricted context the crosses clearly emulated the *montjoies* which were raised along the route taken by the bearers of Louis IX's body on its journey through France in 1270.[119] On arrival in London, the body of Eleanor of Castile was first taken in solemn procession to the churches of the Franciscans and the Dominicans, but the ultimate destination of the funeral cortège was the Confessor's chapel in the abbey church at

---

[115] WAM 6318B (Edward's confirmation, dated 11 December 1291, of the transfer of his father's heart on 10 December); *Foedera*, i. 758, where the date is incorrectly given as 3 December 1291.

[116] *King's Works*, i. 479–85; Coldstream, 'The Commissioning and Design of the Eleanor Crosses', 55–60.

[117] *Ann. Dunstable*, 362–3.

[118] Hallam, 'The Eleanor Crosses and Royal Burial Customs', 18; Lindley, 'Romanticizing Reality', 82–3; Coldstream, 'The Commissioning and Design of the Eleanor Crosses', 65.

[119] Coldstream, 'The Commissioning and Design of the Eleanor Crosses', 60; *King's Works*, i. 484–5; Parsons, *Eleanor of Castile*, 209.

Westminster, close to the shrine of St Edward, and even closer to the tomb of Henry III. There, at the foot of Henry III's tomb, the body of Eleanor of Castile was buried.[120] The Dunstable chronicler, whose only comment on the character of the late queen was that she had acquired many fine manors, also noted that she was buried *in sepulcro Henrici regis* (in the burial place of King Henry).[121]

The stately Eleanor crosses were only part of Edward I's tribute to his wife and, as is now accepted, to the dynastic glory of Plantagenet kingship. Eleanor of Castile had wished to be buried in Westminster Abbey, with a heart-burial in the church of the London Dominicans, of which she was a benefactor and where her son Alfonso's heart was also reserved for burial.[122] But Edward decided on a further memorial, in the cathedral at Lincoln, where he had arranged for her entrails to be buried before the funeral cortège had begun its slow procession to London. For the tombs at Lincoln and at Westminster the king commissioned two life-size gilded bronze effigies, a virtually new venture in English funerary art, and a dramatic one. The Lincoln effigy was destroyed in the seventeenth century, but it is known to have been virtually identical with the effigy at Westminster.[123] It is the Westminster effigy which is of especial significance, for it is essentially one of a pair. The effigy which in one sense truly complements it is not the replica at Lincoln but the effigy which Edward I had commissioned, at the latest by May 1291, for the tomb of his father Henry III.[124] The craftsman who executed these two masterpieces and who worked on them simultaneously and in identical style was the English goldsmith William Torel. He set up special sheds for the work in the churchyard near to the abbey and repeated payments are made to him in the financial accounts of the executors of Eleanor of Castile 'for the making of the images of the king and of the queen'.[125] The association of the two effigies was much more than incidental. They are in every sense a pair visually, and the effect is intentional. It would be quite mistaken to regard the commission of the gilded effigy for his father as simply a happy afterthought on Edward's part, although it was no doubt conceived in the context of the effigy of his wife. The two effigies are idealized portraits, impressively regal and formal. As Paul Binski has pointed out, the king and queen are here seen as holders of royal office and the treatment in style and materials is very different from the more

[120] *Flores*, iii. 71–2.
[121] *Ann. Dunstable*, 362.
[122] Parsons, *Eleanor of Castile*, 206. Alfonso died in 1284.
[123] Lindley, 'Romanticizing Reality', 72.
[124] *CCR 1288–96*, 171.
[125] *Manners and Household Expenses*, 108, 110, 112, 113.

relaxed and elaborate style of the tombs of the Lord Edmund and his wife Aveline de Fortz, which were only slightly later and which are executed throughout in stone.[126] In the two royal effigies at Westminster Edward was making a particularly explicit statement about the dignity and power of royal estate. He now knew that his father would not be canonized and he could not realistically have had any such ideas about his wife. Yet the proximity of these tombs to the Confessor's shrine, like the proximity of Eleanor of Castile's Lincoln tomb to the shrine of St Hugh, carries messages of the spiritual as well as the secular authority inherent in royalty.[127] There was a spirit of emulation at work here too. Edward was consciously working within the funerary traditions of the French as well as of the English monarchy and his achievement was of such a high order as to make actual royal canonization perhaps seem almost supererogatory.

This apparent diversion from the affairs of Eleanor of Provence in fact provides the essential context for a consideration of her own death, burial and commemoration. By the time of her death at Amesbury on 24 June 1291 it is likely that she knew the outlines of Edward's plans for the erection of the twelve crosses, and more importantly from her own point of view, for the two Westminster effigies, one for his wife and the other for her own husband, although the work could not as yet have progressed very far. Edward visited Amesbury in February 1291 and he may have told her something of his plans at that point. She is likely to have been in frail health since she lived only four months longer. Was any mention made of her own burial and commemoration?

In 1246, Henry III had recorded his intention to be buried in the abbey church at Westminster, where he had recently begun his rebuilding. Eleanor of Provence, at the same time and in virtually the same words, had recorded her own wish to be buried there too.[128] There is no reason to think that at the time of Henry III's own death in 1272, his queen was any less constant in that decision, and one must assume that Henry died in full confidence that in due course his wife would be buried near to him at Westminster within the ambience of the Confessor's shrine, in the church where their daughter Katharine rested under her own silver effigy. Henry could hardly have thought at that point that the queen so firmly linked to him in death and commemoration would not be his wife but his daughter-in-law, Eleanor of Castile. Since there is evidence, as we have seen, that Eleanor of Provence remained loyal to the memory of her

[126] Binski, *Westminster Abbey*, 108–16; 'The Cosmati at Westminster', 6–7.
[127] Lindley, 'Romanticizing Reality', 83; Parsons, *Eleanor of Castile*, 213.
[128] WAM Domesday, f. 62v.

husband, her burial at Amesbury, reversing her previous decision to be buried at Westminster, requires consideration.

Eleanor's heart-burial at the church of the Franciscans in London causes no surprise in view of her long-standing devotion to that order and her love for her daughter Beatrice, who had been in her mother's company at court until her marriage at the age of seventeen. On her death in 1275, as has been seen, Beatrice had been buried with the London Franciscans.[129] It is the burial of the body of Eleanor of Provence at Amesbury which is problematic. There were indeed some uncertainties about her place of burial in the few weeks after her death, which occurred while Edward I was in Scotland. The Osney chronicler comments that the nuns of Amesbury did not dare to bury 'so magnificent a body' without the king's assent and his presence, and the body was therefore embalmed and kept in a secret place until the king's return.[130]

The nuns did well to pause. Very quickly after the death of the queen mother, Margaret abbess of Fontevrault and Gila the prioress of that house wrote separately to Edward I begging him to allow his mother's body to be buried in their own church at Fontevrault.[131] They clearly assumed that the last word about his mother's burial rested with Edward. Even more interesting is the incidental comment in a letter from an official of Henry of Eastry, prior of Canterbury, written about the same time. The writer of the letter gives Prior Eastry the news that the Lord Edmund was on his way to London 'for the burial of his mother', but the writer adds that he does not yet know whether the queen mother should be buried (*debeat sepeliri*) in London or at Amesbury.[132]

It seems likely, although not entirely certain, that Eleanor of Provence intended, upon entering the convent at Amesbury, that she should be buried there, and that this would have been in conformity with custom.[133] It must be added that it is also likely that Edward I was very content that his mother should be buried at Amesbury rather than Westminster, and that the final decision rested with him. His plans at Westminster were in a sense complete. The two gilded effigies 'of the king and of the queen' were already under way and it must be considered highly unlikely that Edward felt any impulse to idealize the queenship of his mother.

---

[129] Kingsford, *The Grey Friars of London*, 71.

[130] *Ann. Osney*, 330.

[131] SC 1/17/116, 119.

[132] HMC, *Report on MSS in Various Collections*, i. 259–60. For the use of London to include Westminster see Carpenter, 'Henry III and the Tower of London', 211–12.

[133] Blanche of Castile, for instance, was buried at Maubuisson, where she adopted the Cistercian habit shortly before she died.

The burial of Eleanor of Provence at Amesbury on 8 September 1291 was marked 'with great reverence'. Edward was present himself, with his brother Edmund and a large gathering of magnates and prelates.[134] According to the account in the Lanercost chronicle, which was based on an earlier Franciscan text, Edward handed the gold-encased heart of his mother, which he described as a treasure most dear to him, to the Franciscan Minister General for burial in the London church of the Franciscans.[135] The heart-burial took place early in December 1291, when the magnates and prelates had been summoned to London to attend this ceremony and also the elaborate celebration of the first anniversary of Eleanor of Castile's death, which took place in Westminster Abbey on 29 November.[136]

Henry III had planned that the anniversaries of his own death and that of Eleanor of Provence should be permanently celebrated at Westminster, and he had envisaged providing an endowment of some £100 a year for this purpose. Partly through the failure of the abbey to secure the lands of the rebel Richard de Culworth, which were allocated to this purpose, Henry's endowment never exceeded the modest income of the church of Feering, which Innocent IV had permitted the monks to appropriate in 1249 to finance the anniversaries of Henry and Eleanor.[137] However, although Henry III's anniversary was celebrated at Westminster throughout the Middle Ages, there is no evidence that his queen's anniversary was ever celebrated there.[138] At Amesbury Eleanor of Provence was somewhat better remembered. The nuns stated in 1327 that at the request of Edward I, they had provided a daily celebration for his mother Queen Eleanor for the last thirty-six years. Edward had promised them an endowment of £100 a year to establish this; they had received nothing.[139]

Whatever monuments the queen mother may have had at Amesbury and in the Franciscan church in London would have been destroyed at the time of the Dissolution. But Eleanor of Provence has her own unofficial, and therefore particularly moving, memorial in the Chapel of the Kings at Westminster. It is a small, delicate engraving on the underside of the gilded plate which bears William Torel's fine effigy of King Henry III, and it remained unseen until November 1871, when the plate was lifted

---

[134] *Ann. Osney*, 330.

[135] *Chron. Lanercost*, 141.

[136] *Ann. Dunstable*, 366; *Flores*, iii. 72. In the text of the Lanercost chronicle (*Chron. Lanercost*, 143) there seems to be a confusion between the queen consort and the queen mother.

[137] WAM 1692; WAM Domesday, f. 61v; for Feering, *Reg. Innocent IV*, no. 4570; Harvey, *Westminster Abbey and its Estates*, 29, 391, 406.

[138] For Henry III see WAM 33351, 5258B.

[139] *CIM*, ii, no. 1002.

for an inspection of the tomb.[140] The engraver, who may of course have been Torel himself, has drawn a crowned and veiled figure of a queen, together with a very young nun; their hands are lifted in prayer to a larger, unfinished figure which possibly represents the Virgin. W. R. Lethaby was almost certainly right in identifying the queen and the nun as Eleanor of Provence and one of her granddaughters at Amesbury, probably Mary.[141] Paul Binski refers to them as 'votive figures engraved by way of trial',[142] but it seems doubtful whether the underside of the plate of Henry III's effigy would have been considered an appropriate place for making random experimental drawings. It may be that these small figures were engraved in a spirit of some deliberation.

The day on which Eleanor of Provence died, 24 June 1291, saw the close of a life of quite exceptional excitement and opportunity. The thirteenth century was an age of outstanding achievement by any standards and Eleanor moved freely in that world. She had close contact with men of action and men of government, of the calibre of Edward I, Louis IX and Simon de Montfort. As a young woman she had known the saintly scholar bishops, Edmund of Abingdon, Roger Niger and Richard Wych and also one of the most eminent scholars of the Middle Ages, Robert Grosseteste. Later she had worked alongside the papal legates Guy Foulquois and Ottobuono de Fieschi, who both became popes. In the formation of her taste she had the experience of close family ties with two of the most discerning and lavish royal patrons, Henry III and Louis IX. Eleanor of Provence had the capacity to respond to distinction in those around her and she played her own individual role with immense vigour and conviction.

The style of Eleanor's queenship was made possible by her husband and probably deplored by her eldest son, but it is likely that both men would have agreed that her career and personality were touched by greatness. Politically she was one of the foremost protagonists of English monarchy in the thirteenth century. A loyal friend, a loving but possessive mother, a harsh property owner, she was both blessed and cursed with a strongly active temperament. She had many triumphs, but it was in defeat that she showed her calibre. Faced by disaster or by grief, she met adversity with a resilience of spirit which enabled her to reach the last years of her life without ultimate bitterness. 'Generosa et religiosa virago' was the verdict of the Westminster chronicler, and it would be hard to improve on that contemporary judgement.[143]

---

[140] Plate 9; Carpenter, 'The Burial of King Henry III', 427.
[141] Lethaby, *Westminster Abbey and the King's Craftsmen*, 285–6.
[142] Binski, *Westminster Abbey*, 170.
[143] *Flores*, iii. 72.

Bibliography

The bibliography provides details of works cited in shortened form in the notes and lists the principal secondary sources which have assisted in the preparation of the book.

A Unprinted Primary Sources

Public Record Office, Kew

Chancery

C 47   Miscellanea
C 61   Gascon Rolls

Exchequer

E 9   Jews' Plea Rolls
E 101   King's Remembrancer, Accounts Various
E 159   King's Remembrancer, Memoranda Rolls
E 163   Miscellanea
E 368   Lord Treasurer's Remembrancer, Memoranda Rolls
E 372   Pipe Rolls
E 403   Issue Rolls

Judicial Records

CP 25   Feet of Fines
JUST 1 Eyre and Assize Rolls
KB 26   Curia Regis Rolls

Special Collections

SC 1   Ancient Correspondence
SC 6   Ministers' and Receivers' Accounts

SC 7   Papal Bulls

British Library, London

Additional MSS 33385, 62925
Arundel MS 56
Cotton MSS Augustus II. 14, Cleopatra D. III, Cleopatra E. I., Julius D. VII
Cotton Charter XVII. 6
Harleian MS 3674
Harleian Charter 43. C. 42
Royal MSS 12. D. XI, 14. C. VII

Westminster Abbey Muniment

WAM Book 11 (Westminster Abbey 'Domesday')
WAM 1692, 5258B, 6318B, 33351

Muniments of the Dean and Chapter of Durham

Locellus 1, no. 60

Chetham Library, Manchester

MS 6712 (on loan to the British Library)

Archives Départementales des Basses-Pyrénées

E 172, E 354

B Printed Primary Sources

Abbrevatio Placitorum (Record Commission, 1811).
Adam Marsh, 'Epistolae Ade de Marisco', in *Monumenta Franciscana*, ed. J. S.
  Brewer and R. Howlett (2 vols, RS, 1858–82).
*Annales Londonienses (London), Chronicles of the Reigns of Edward I and
  Edward II*, i, ed. W. Stubbs (RS, 1882).
Annales Monasterii de Burton (Burton), in *AM*, i.
Annales Monasterii de Oseneia (Osney), in *AM*, iv.
Annales Monasterii de Theokesberia (Tewkesbury), in *AM*, i.
Annales Monasterii de Waverleia (Waverley), in *AM*, ii.
Annales Monasterii de Wintonia (Winchester), in *AM*, ii.
Annales Monastici, ed. H. R. Luard (5 vols, RS, 1864–9).
Annales Prioratus de Dunstaplia (Dunstable), in *AM*, iii.
Annales Prioratus de Wigornia (Worcester), in *AM*, iv.

Archives Historiques du Département de la Gironde, v (Paris and Bordeaux, 1863).

Archives Municipales de Bayonne: Livre des Etablissements, ed. E. Dulaurens (Bayonne, 1892).

Bartholomaei de Cotton, Historia Anglicana, ed. H. R. Luard (RS, 1859).

The Book of Fees, Commonly Called Testa de Nevill (3 vols, HMSO, 1920–31).

Calendar of Charter Rolls (HMSO, 1903–).

Calendar of Documents relating to Ireland, ed. H. S. Sweetman (5 vols, HMSO, 1875–86).

Calendar of Inquisitions Miscellaneous, i, *1219–1307* (HMSO, 1916).

Calendar of Liberate Rolls (HMSO, 1916–).

Calendar of Papal Letters, i, *1198–1304* (HMSO, 1893).

Calendar of Patent Rolls (HMSO, 1906–).

Calendar of Plea Rolls of the Exchequer of the Jews, ed. J. M. Rigg and others (5 vols, JHSE, 1905–72).

The Cartulary of Holy Trinity Aldgate, ed. G. A. J. Hodgett (London Record Society, 1971).

The Chartulary of God's House, Southampton, ed. J. M. Kaye (2 vols, Southampton, 1976).

Christine de Pisan, *The Treasure of the City of Ladies*, trans. S. Lawson (London, 1985).

The Chronicle of Bury St Edmunds, 1212–1301, ed. A. Gransden (London, 1964).

The Chronicle of Melrose, introduced by A. O. and M. O. Anderson (London, 1936).

The Chronicle of Walter of Guisborough, ed. H. Rothwell (Camden Society, 1957).

The Chronicle of William de Rishanger of the Barons' Wars, ed. J. O. Halliwell (Camden Society, 1840)

Chronicon de Lanercost, ed. J. Stevenson (Maitland Club, 1839).

Chronicon vulgo dictum Chronicon Thomae Wykes, 1066–1288, in *AM*, iv.

Close Rolls of the Reign of Henry III (HMSO, 1902–75).

A Continuation of William of Newburgh's 'History' to A.D. 1298, in *Chronicles of the Reigns of Stephen, Henry II and Richard I*, ed. R. Howlett (4 vols, RS, 1884–9), ii.

Correspondance Administrative d'Alfonse de Poitiers, ed. A. Molinier (2 vols, Paris, 1894–1900).

Councils and Synods, II, A.D. 1205–1313, ed. F. M. Powicke and C. R. Cheney (2 pts, Oxford, 1964).

The Court and Household of Eleanor of Castile in 1290, ed. J. C. Parsons (Toronto, 1977).

Cronica Maiorum, see *De Antiquis Legibus Liber*.

De Antiquis Legibus Liber. Cronica Maiorum et Vicecomitum Londoniarum, ed. T. Stapleton (Camden Society, 1846).

Diplomatic Documents Preserved in the Public Record Office, i, *1101–1272*, ed. P. Chaplais (HMSO, 1964).

Documents of the Baronial Movement of Reform and Rebellion, 1258–1267, ed. R. F. Treharne and I. J. Sanders (Oxford, 1973).

Dugdale, W., *Monasticon Anglicanum*, ed. J. Caley and others (6 vols, London, 1817–30).

English Coronation Records, ed. L. G. Wickham Legg (Westminster, 1901).

English Historical Documents, 1189–1327, ed. H. Rothwell (London, 1975).

La Estoire de Seint Aedward le Rei, ed. M. R. James (Roxburghe Club, 1920).

La Estoire de Seint Aedward le Rei attributed to Matthew Paris, ed. K. Y. Wallace (Anglo-Norman Text Society, 41, 1983).

Excerpta e Rotulis Finium, ed. C. Roberts (2 vols, Record Commission, 1835–6).

Flores Historiarum, ed. H. R. Luard (3 vols, RS, 1890).

Foedera, Conventiones, Litterae et Acta Publica, ed. T. Rymer, new edn, vol. i, ed. A. Clark and F. Holbrooke (Record Commission, 1816).

Gascon Register A, ed. G. P. Cuttino and J. P. Trabut-Cussac (3 vols, Oxford, 1975–6).

Gervase of Canterbury, see *Historical Works*.

Gesta Abbatum Monasterii Sancti Albani, ed. H. T. Riley (3 vols, RS, 1867–9).

Les Grandes Chroniques de France, ed. J. Viard (Paris, 1932).

Guillaume de Nangis, 'Vie de St Louis', in *Receuil des Historiens des Gaules et de la France*, xx (Paris, 1740).

Guillaume de Saint-Pathus, *Vie de Saint Louis*, ed. H. F. Delaborde (Paris, 1899).

Heidemann, J., *Papst Clemens IV: Das Vorleben des Papstes und sein Legation-register* (Münster, 1903).

Historical Manuscripts Commission:
Calendar of MSS of the Dean and Chapter of Wells (2 vols, 1907–14).
Middleton MSS (1911).
Report on MSS in Various Collections, i (1901).

The Historical Works of Gervase of Canterbury, ed. W. Stubbs (2 vols, RS, 1880).

The Langley Cartulary, ed. P. R. Coss (Dugdale Society, 1980).

Layettes du Trésor des Chartes, ed. A. Teulet and others (5 vols, Paris, 1863–1909).

Lettres des rois, reines et autres personnages des cours de France et d'Angleterre, ed. J. J. Champollion-Figeac (2 vols, Paris, 1839–47).

Letters of the Queens of England, 1100–1547, ed. A. Crawford (Stroud, 1994).

Livre Noir de Dax, in *Archives Historiques du Département de la Gironde*, xxxvii (Paris and Bordeaux, 1902).

Manners and Household Expenses of England in the Thirteenth and Fifteenth Centuries, ed. T. H. Turner (Roxburghe Club, 1841).

Matthaei Parisiensis, Monachi Sancti Albani, Chronica Majora, ed. H. R. Luard (7 vols, RS, 1872–83).

Matthaei Parisiensis, Monachi Sancti Albani, Historia Anglorum, ed. F. Madden (3 vols, RS, 1866–9).

Memorials of St Edmund's Abbey, ed. T. Arnold (3 vols, RS, 1890–6).

The Metrical Chronicle of Robert of Gloucester, ed. W. A. Wright (2 vols, RS, 1887).

Nicholas Trivet, *Annales*, ed. T. Hog (London, 1845).

Poems of John of Hoveden, ed. F. J. E. Raby (Surtees Society, 154, 1939).

Receuil des Actes des Comtes de Provence appartenant à la Maison de Barcelone, ed. F. Benoit (2 vols, Paris, 1925).

Receuil des Historiens des Gaules et de la France (24 vols, Paris, 1734–1904).

Recogniciones Feodorum in Aquitania, ed. C. Bémont (Paris, 1914).

Regesta Regum Anglo-Normannorum, 1066–1154, iii, ed. H. A. Cronne and R. H. C. Davis (Oxford, 1968).

Regeste Genevois, ed. E. Mallet and others (Geneva, 1866).

The Register of Eudes of Rouen, ed. J. F. O. Sullivan (New York and London, 1964).

The Register of John le Romeyn, Lord Archbishop of York, 1286–1296, i, ed. W. Brown (Surtees Society, 123, 1913).

The Register of Thomas de Cantilupe, Bishop of Hereford (1275–1282), ed. R. G. Griffiths and W. W. Capes (Canterbury and York Society, 2, 1907).

The Register of Walter Giffard, Bishop of Bath and Wells, 1265–6, and of Henry Bowett,...1401–7, ed. T. S. Holmes (Somerset Record Society, 13, 1899).

The Register of Walter Giffard, Lord Archbishop of York, 1266–1279, ed. W. Brown (Surtees Society, 109, 1904).

The Register of William Wickwane, Lord Archbishop of York, 1279–1285, ed W. Brown (Surtees Society, 114, 1907).

Les Registres d'Alexandre IV, ed. C. Bourel de la Roncière and others (3 vols, Paris, 1895–1953).

Les Registres de Clément IV, ed. E. Jordan (6 vols, Paris, 1893–1945).

Les Registres d'Innocent IV, ed. E. Berger (4 vols, Paris, 1884–1919).

Les Registres d'Urbain IV, ed. L. Dorez and J. Guiraud (4 vols, Paris, 1899–1958).

Registrum Epistolarum Fratris Johannis Peckham, Archiepiscopi Cantuariensis, ed. C. T. Martin (3 vols, RS, 1882–5).

Registrum Johannis de Pontissaria, Episcopi Wintoniensis, 1282–1304, ed. C. Deedes (2 vols, Canterbury and York Society, 19, 30, 1915–24).

Regularis Concordia, ed. T. Symons (London, 1953).

'Robert of Boston' in *Historiae Anglicanae Scriptores Varii*, ed. J. Sparke (London, 1723).

Robert of Gloucester, see *Metrical Chronicle*.

Roberti Grosseteste Episcopi Lincolniensis Epistolae, ed. H. R. Luard (RS, 1861).

Rôles Gascons, ed. F. Michel and C. Bémont (4 vols, Paris, 1885–1906).

The Rolls and Register of Bishop Oliver Sutton, 1280–1299, ed. R. M. T. Hill (8 vols, Lincoln Record Society, 1948–86).

Rotuli Chartarum, ed. T. Duffus Hardy (Record Commission, 1837).

Rotuli Hundredorum, (2 vols, Record Commission, 1812–18).

Rotuli Parliamentorum, i (Record Commission, 1832).

Rotuli Ricardi Gravesend, diocesis Lincolniensis, ed. F. N. Davis (Lincoln Record Society, 20, 1925).

Rotuli Selecti, ed. J. Hunter (Record Commission, 1834).

Royal and other Historical Letters Illustrative of the Reign of Henry III, ed. W. W. Shirley (2 vols, RS, 1862–6).

Select Cases in the Court of King's Bench under Edward I, i, ed. G. O. Sayles (Selden Society, 55, 1936).

Select Charters and other Illustrations of English Constitutional History, from the earliest times to the reign of Edward I, 9th edn, revised by H. W. C. Davis (Oxford, 1921).

Select Pleas, Starrs and other Records from the Rolls of the Exchequer of the Jews (1220–1284), ed. J. M. Rigg (Selden Society, 15, 1901–2).

Statutes of the Realm, i (Record Commission, 1810).

Thomas of Eccleston, 'Liber de Adventu Minorum in Angliam', in *Monumenta Franciscana*, ed. J. S. Brewer and R. Howlett (2 vols, RS, 1858), i; translation by L. Sherley-Price, *The Coming of the Franciscans* (London, 1964).

Treaty Rolls, i, 1234–1325, ed. P. Chaplais (HMSO, 1955).

Two Chartularies of the Priory of St Peter at Bath, ed. W. Hunt (Somerset Record Society, 7, 1893).

C Secondary Sources

Alexander, J. and Binski, P., eds, *Age of Chivalry: Art in Plantagenet England, 1200–1400* (Royal Academy of Arts, London, 1987).

Altschul, M., *A Baronial Family in Medieval England: The Clares, 1217–1314* (Baltimore, 1965).

Backhouse, J., *Books of Hours* (London, 1985).

Baratier, E., *Histoire de la Provence* (Toulouse, 1969).

Barker, J. R. V., *The Tournament in England, 1100–1400* (Woodbridge, 1986).

Barry, F., *Les Droits de la Reine sous la Monarchie Française jusqu'en 1789* (Paris, 1932).

Baylen, J. O., 'John Maunsell and the Castilian Treaty of 1254', *Traditio*, 17 (1961).

Bell, S. G., 'Medieval Women Book Owners: Arbiters of Lay Piety and Ambassadors of Culture', in *Women and Power in the Middle Ages*, ed. M. Erler and M. Kowaleski (Athens, GA and London, 1988).

Bémont, C., *Simon de Montfort*, 1st edn (Paris, 1884) (*Simon de Montfort*, trans. E. F. Jacob, 2nd edn (Oxford, 1930)).

—— 'La Campagne de Poitou (1242–1243): Taillebourg et Saintes', *Annales du Midi*, 5 (1893).

Biles, M., 'The Indomitable Belle: Eleanor of Provence, Queen of England', in *Seven Studies in Medieval English History and Other Historical Essays Presented to Harold S. Snellgrove* (Jackson, MI, 1983).

Binski, P., *The Painted Chamber at Westminster*, Society of Antiquaries Occasional Paper 9 (London, 1986).

—— 'Reflections on La Estoire de Seint Aedward le Rei: hagiography and kingship in thirteenth-century England', *JMH*, 16 (1990).

—— 'The Cosmati at Westminster and the English Court Style', *Art Bulletin*, 72 (1990).

—— *Westminster Abbey and the Plantagenets: Kingship and the Representation of Power, 1200–1400* (New Haven and London, 1995).

Birch, W. de Gray, *Catalogue of Seals in the Department of Manuscripts in the British Museum* (6 vols, London, 1887–1900).

Blackstone, W., *Commentaries on the Laws of England* (4 vols, London, 1765–9).

Boase, R., *The Origin and Meaning of Courtly Love* (Manchester, 1977).

Boffey, J., 'Women authors and women's literacy . . .', in *Women and Literature in Britain, 1150–1500*, ed. C. M. Meale (Cambridge, 1993).

Borenius, T., 'The Cycle of Images in the Palaces and Castles of Henry III', *Journal of the Warburg and Courtauld Institutes*, 6 (1943).

Brett, M., *The English Church under Henry I* (Oxford, 1975).

Brieger, P., *The Trinity College Apocalypse* (London, 1967).

Brown, R. A., Colvin, H. M. and Taylor, A. J., *The History of the King's Works: The Middle Ages* (2 vols, HMSO, 1963).

Brown, W., 'The Institution of the Prebendal Church of Howden', *Yorkshire Archaeological Journal*, 22 (1912).

Bruckmann, J. J., 'English Coronations, 1216–1308: The Edition of the Coronation *Ordines*' (Toronto doctoral thesis, 1964).

Brundage, J. A., *Law, Sex and Christian Society in Medieval Europe* (Chicago, 1987).

Bullock-Davis, C., *Register of Royal and Baronial Minstrels, 1272–1327* (Woodbridge, 1986).

Busquet, R., *Histoire de Provence des Origines à la Revolution Française* (Monaco, 1954).

Carpenter, D. A., 'Westminster Abbey: some characteristics of its sculpture, 1245–59: The workshop of the censing angels in the South Transept', *Journal of the British Archaeological Association*, 3rd series, 35 (1972).

—— *The Battles of Lewes and Evesham, 1264/65* (Keele, 1987).

—— *The Minority of Henry III* (London, 1990).

—— *The Reign of Henry III* (London and Rio Grande, 1996). This book includes the essays listed below, with places of original publication noted. The pagination followed in my footnotes is that of the book.

—— 'St Thomas Cantilupe: His Political Career', reprinted from *St Thomas Cantilupe, Bishop of Hereford*, ed. M. Jancey (Hereford, 1982).

—— 'What Happened in 1258?', reprinted from *War and Government in the Middle Ages*, ed. J. Gillingham and J. C. Holt (Woodbridge, 1984).

—— 'King, Magnates and Society: The Personal Rule of King Henry III, 1234–58', reprinted from *Speculum*, 60 (1985).

—— 'The Lord Edward's Oath to Aid and Counsel Simon de Montfort, 15 October 1259', reprinted from *BIHR*, 58 (1985).

—— 'Simon de Montfort: The First Leader of a Political Movement in English History', reprinted from *History*, 76 (1991).

—— 'King Henry III's "Statute" against Aliens: July 1263', reprinted from *EHR*, 107 (1992).

—— 'King Henry III and the Tower of London', reprinted from *The London Journal*, 19 (1995).

—— 'King Henry III and the Cosmati Work at Westminster Abbey', reprinted from *The Cloister and the World*, ed. J. Blair and B. Golding (Oxford, 1996).

—— 'The Burial of King Henry III, the *Regalia* and Royal Ideology', not previously published elsewhere.

Chaplais, P. 'The Making of the Treaty of Paris (1259) and the Royal Style', *EHR* 67 (1952), reprinted in *Essays in Medieval Diplomacy and Administration* (London, 1981).

—— 'Le Duché-Pairie de Guyenne: l'Hommage et les Services Féodaux de 1259 à 1303', *Annales du Midi*, 69 (1957), reprinted in *Essays* (as in previous note).

—— *English Medieval Diplomatic Practice, Part I* (2 vols, London, 1982).

Chaytor, H. J., *The Troubadours and England* (Cambridge, 1923).

Chibnall, M., *The Empress Matilda: Queen Consort, Queen Mother and Lady of the English* (Oxford, 1991).

Clanchy, M. T., *England and its Rulers, 1066–1272* (Glasgow, 1983).

—— *From Memory to Written Record*, 2nd edn (Oxford, 1993).

Cockayne, G. E., *Complete Peerage of England, Scotland, Ireland, Great Britain and the United Kingdom*, ed. V. Gibbs and others (12 vols in 13, London, 1912–59).

Cohen, J., *The Friars and the Jews* (Ithaca, NY, 1982).

Coldstream, N., 'The Commissioning and Design of the Eleanor Crosses', in *Eleanor of Castile, 1290–1990*, ed. D. Parsons (Stamford, 1991).

Contamine, P., *War in the Middle Ages*, trans. M. Jones (Oxford, 1984).

Coss, P. R., 'Sir Geoffrey de Langley and the crisis of the Knightly Class in Thirteenth-Century England', *Past and Present*, 68 (1975).

—— *The Knight in Medieval England, 1000–1400* (Stroud, 1993).

Cowdrey, H. E., 'The Anglo-Norman *Laudes Regiae*', *Viator*, 12 (1981).

Cox, E. L., *The Eagles of Savoy: The House of Savoy in Thirteenth-Century Europe* (Princeton, 1974).

Crouch, D., *The Image of Aristocracy in Britain, 1000–1300* (London, 1992).

Cuttino, G. P., 'A Chancellor of the Lord Edward', *BIHR*, 50 (1977).

Davies, R. R., *Conquest, Coexistence and Change: Wales, 1063–1415* (Oxford, 1987).

Delaborde, H. F., 'Un frère de Joinville au service de l'Angleterre: Geffroy, sire de Vaucouleurs', *Bibliothèque de l'Ecole des Chartes*, 54 (1893).

Denholm-Young, N., *Richard of Cornwall* (Oxford, 1947).

—— 'The Tournament in the Thirteenth Century', in *Studies presented to F. M. Powicke*, ed. R. W. Hunt and others (Oxford, 1948).

Donovan, C., *The de Brailes Hours: Shaping the Book of Hours in Thirteenth-Century Oxford* (London, 1991).

Douie, D., *Archbishop Pecham* (Oxford, 1952).

Duby, G., *Medieval Marriage: Two Models from Twelfth-Century France*, trans. E. Forster (Baltimore and London, 1978).

—— *The Knight, the Lady and the Priest*, trans. B. Bray (Harmondsworth, 1983).

Ducarel, A. C., *The History of the Royal Hospital and Collegiate Church of St Katharine near the Tower of London from its earliest foundation in the year 1273 to the present time*, 2nd edn (London, 1790).

Duncan, A. A. M., *Scotland. The Making of the Kingdom* (Edinburgh, 1975).

Eales, R., 'Henry III and the End of the Norman Earldom of Chester', *TCE*, i, (1986).

Eames, E. S., 'A tile pavement from the queen's chamber, Clarendon Palace, dated 1250–2', *Journal of the British Archaeological Association*, 3rd series, 20–21 (1957–8).

—— 'The royal apartments at Clarendon Palace in the reign of Henry III', *Journal of the British Archaeological Association*, 3rd series, 28 (1965).

—— *English Tilers* (London, 1992).

Ehrlich, L., 'Exchequer and Wardrobe in 1270', *EHR*, 36 (1921).

—— *Proceedings against the Crown, 1216–1377* (Oxford, 1921).

Ellis, J. O., 'Gaston de Béarn: A Study in Anglo-Gascon Relations, 1229–1290' (University of Oxford D.Phil. thesis, 1952).

Emden, A. B., *A Bibliographical Register of the University of Oxford to A.D. 1500* (3 vols, Oxford, 1957–9).

Facinger, M., 'A Study of Medieval Queenship: Capetian France, 987–1237', *Studies in Medieval and Renaissance History*, 5 (1968).

Farmer, S., 'Persuasive Voices: Clerical Images of Medieval Wives', *Speculum*, 61 (1986).

Fauriel, M., *Histoire de la Poésie Provençale* (3 vols, Paris, 1846).

Forey, A. J., 'The Crusading Vows of the English King Henry III', *Durham University Journal*, 65 (1973).

Fournier, P., *Le Royaume d'Arles et de Vienne* (Paris, 1891).

Frame, R., 'Ireland and the Barons' Wars', *TCE*, i (1986).

—— *The Political Development of the British Isles, 1100–1400* (Oxford and New York, 1990).

Gavrilovitch, M., *Etude sur le Traité de Paris de 1259* (Paris, 1899).

Gibbs, M. and Lang, J., *Bishops and Reform, 1215–1271* (Oxford, 1934).

Gold, P. S., *The Lady and the Virgin: Image, Attitude and Experience in Twelfth-Century France* (Chicago and London, 1985).

Green (née Wood), M. A. E., *Lives of the Princesses of England from the Norman Conquest* (6 vols, London, 1849–55).

Hajdu, R., 'Castles, Castellans and the Structure of Politics in Poitou, 1152–1271', *JMH*, 4 (1978).

Hallam, E., *Capetian France, 987–1328* (London and New York, 1980).

—— 'Royal Burial and the Cult of Kingship in France and England, 1060–1330', *JMH*, 8 (1982).

—— 'The Eleanor Crosses and Royal Burial Customs', in *Eleanor of Castile, 1290–1990*, ed. D. Parsons (Stamford, 1991).

Harriss, G. L., *King, Parliament and Public Finance in Medieval England to 1369* (Oxford, 1975).

Harvey, B., *Westminster Abbey and its Estates in the Middle Ages* (Oxford, 1977).

Harvey, J., *Medieval Gardens* (London, 1981).

Harvey, P. D. A., *Mappa Mundi: The Hereford World Map* (London, 1996).

Hill, B., 'The Luve-Ron and Thomas de Hales', *Modern Language Review*, 59 (1964).

Hill, M. C., *The King's Messengers, 1199–1377: A Contribution to the History of the Royal Household* (London, 1961).

—— *The King's Messengers, 1199–1377: A list of all known messengers, mounted and unmounted, who served John, Henry III and the first three Edwards* (Stroud, 1994).

Hilpert, H. E., 'Richard of Cornwall's Candidature for the German Throne and the Christmas 1256 Parliament at Westminster', *JMH*, 6 (1980).

Hinnebusch, W., *The Early English Friars Preachers* (Rome, 1951).

Horrall, S. M., 'Thomas of Hales OFM: His Life and Works', *Traditio*, 42 (1986).

Houseley, N., *The Italian Crusades* (Oxford, 1982).

Howell, M., 'The Resources of Eleanor of Provence as Queen Consort', *EHR*, 102 (1987).

—— 'The Children of King Henry III and Eleanor of Provence', *TCE*, iv (1992).

Huneycutt, L., 'Intercession and the High-Medieval Queen: The Esther Topos', in *Power of the Weak*, ed. J. Carpenter and S. B. Maclean (Chicago, 1995).

Hurlimann, M. and Bony, J., *French Cathedrals* (New York, 1951).

Isenburg-Budingen, W. C. H. von, *Stammtafeln zur Geschichte der Europaïschen Staaten*, ed. D. Schwennicke, xv (Berlin, 1936–7).

Jacob, E. F., 'A Proposal for Arbitration between Simon de Montfort and Henry III in 1260', *EHR*, 37 (1922).

—— *Studies in the Period of Baronial Reform and Rebellion* (Oxford, 1925).

James, T. B. and Robinson, A. M., with E. Eames, *Clarendon Palace. The History and Archaeology of a Medieval Palace and Hunting Lodge near Salisbury, Wiltshire*, Society of Antiquaries Report, no. 45 (London, 1988).

Jamison, C., *The History of the Royal Hospital of St Katharine* (Oxford, 1952).

Jeanroy, A., *La Poésie lyrique des Troubadours* (2 vols, Toulouse, 1934).

Johnstone, H., 'The Wardrobe and Household of Henry, son of Edward I', *Bulletin of the John Rylands Library*, 7 (1922–3).

—— 'The Wardrobe and Household Accounts of the Sons of Edward I', *BIHR*, 2 (1925).

Kaeuper, R. W., *Bankers to the Crown* (Princeton, 1973).

Kantorowicz, E. H., *Laudes Regiae. A Study in Liturgical Acclamations and Medieval Ruler Worship* (Berkeley, 1946).

Keen, M., *Chivalry* (New Haven and London, 1984).

Kemp, E. W., *Canonization and Authority in the Western Church* (Oxford, 1948).

Kennett, W., *Parochial Antiquities attempted in the History of Ambroseden, Burcister (Bicester)* ... 2nd edn (2 vols, Oxford, 1818).

Kingsford, C. L., *The Grey Friars of London* (Aberdeen, 1915).

Knowles, C. H., 'The Disinherited, 1265–1280: A Political and Social Study of the Supporters of Simon de Montfort and the Resettlement after the Barons' War' (University of Wales Ph.D. thesis, 1959).

—— 'The Resettlement of England after the Barons' War', *TRHS*, 5th series, 32 (1982).

Lamborn, E. A. Greening, 'The Shrine of St Edburg', *Oxfordshire Archaeological Society Report*, no. 80 (1934).

Larking, L. B., 'On the Heart-Shrine in Leybourne Church', *Archaeologia Cantiana*, 5 (1863).

Lawrence, C. H., *St Edmund of Abingdon* (Oxford, 1960).

Legge, M. D., 'The Anglo-Norman Sermon of Thomas of Hales', *Modern Language Review*, 30 (1935).

Le Goff, J., *The Medieval Imagination*, trans. A. Goldhammer (Chicago, 1988).

Le Nain de Tillemont, L. S., *Vie de Saint Louis*, ed. J. de Gaulle (6 vols, Paris, 1847–51).

Le Neve, J., *Fasti Ecclesiae Anglicanae*, ed. T. Duffus Hardy (3 vols, Oxford, 1854); editions compiled by D. Greenway: i, *St Paul's, London* (1968), iv, *Salisbury* (1991).

Lethaby, W. R., *Westminster Abbey and the King's Craftsmen* (London, 1906).

Lewis, A., 'Roger Leyburn and the Pacification of England, 1265–7', *EHR*, 54 (1939).

Lewis, F. R., 'William de Valence (*c.*1230–1296)', *Aberystwyth Studies*, 13 (1934).

Lewis, S., *The Art of Matthew Paris in the Chronica Majora*, (Berkeley, 1987).

—— *Reading Images: Narrative Discourse and Reception in the Thirteenth-Century Illuminated Apocalypse* (Cambridge, 1995).

Lindley, P., 'Romanticizing Reality: The Sculptural Memorials of Queen Eleanor and their Context', in *Eleanor of Castile, 1290–1990*, ed. D. Parsons (Stamford, 1991).

Lloyd, S. D., 'The Lord Edward's Crusade, 1270–2: its setting and significance', in *War and Government in the Middle Ages: Essays in Honour of J. O. Prestwich*, ed. J. Gillingham and J. C. Holt (Woodbridge, 1984).

—— 'Gilbert de Clare, Richard of Cornwall and the Lord Edward's Crusade', *Nottingham Medieval Studies*, 31 (1986).

—— *English Society and the Crusade, 1216–1307* (Oxford, 1988).

—— 'King Henry III, the Crusade and the Mediterranean', in *England and her Neighbours, 1066–1453: Essays in Honour of Pierre Chaplais*, ed. M. Jones and M. Vale (London, 1989).

Lodge, R. A., 'Language Attitudes and Linguistic Norms in France and England in the Thirteenth Century', *TCE*, iv (1992).

Lunt, W. E., *Financial Relations of the Papacy with England to 1327* (Cambridge, MA, 1939).

Maddicott, J. R., 'Magna Carta and the Local Community, 1215–59', *Past and Present*, 102 (1984).

—— 'Edward I and the Lessons of Baronial Reform: Local Government, 1258–80', *TCE*, i (1986).

—— *Simon de Montfort* (Cambridge, 1994).

Marks, R., *Stained Glass in England during the Middle Ages* (London, 1993).

Marsh, F. B., *English Rule in Gascony, 1199–1259* (Ann Arbor, 1912).

McIntosh, M. K., *Autonomy and Community: The Royal Manor of Havering, 1200–1500* (Cambridge, 1986).

McKitterick, R., 'Women in the Ottonian Church: an Iconographic Perspective', in *Women in the Church*, ed. W. J. Sheils and D. Wood (Oxford, 1990).

Meekings, C. A. F., 'Walter de Merton', reprinted in *Studies in 13th Century Justice and Administration* (London, 1981).

Millar, E. G., *The Rutland Psalter*, facsimile edn (Roxburghe Club, 1937).

Moor, C., *Knights of Edward I*, (5 vols, Harleian Society Publications, 80–4, 1929–32).

Moorman, J., *A History of the Franciscan Order from its Origins to the year 1517* (Oxford, 1968).

Morgan, N., *Early Gothic Manuscripts* (2 vols, London, 1982–8).

—— 'Texts and Images of Marian Devotion in Thirteenth-Century England', in *England in the Thirteenth Century*, ed. W. M. Ormrod (Harlaxton Medieval Studies, i, 1991).

Mugnier, F., *Les Savoyards en Angleterre au xiiie siècle et Pierre d'Aigueblanche, évêque d'Hereford* (Chambéry, 1891).

Orme, N., *From Childhood to Chivalry: The education of English kings and aristocracy, 1066–1530* (London, 1984).

Otway-Ruthven, A. J., *A History of Medieval Ireland* (London, 1968).

Parsons, J. C., 'The Year of Eleanor of Castile's Birth and her Children by Edward I', *Medieval Studies*, 46 (1984).

—— 'Eleanor of Castile (1241–1290): Legend and Reality through Seven Centuries', in *Eleanor of Castile, 1290–1990*, ed. D. Parsons (Stamford, 1991).

—— 'Ritual and Symbol in the English Medieval Queenship to 1500', in *Women and Sovereignty*, ed. L. O. Fradenburg (Edinburgh, 1992).

—— 'Family, Sex and Power: The Rhythms of Medieval Queenship', and

—— 'Mothers, Daughters, Marriage, Power: Some Plantagenet Evidence, 1150–1500', in *Medieval Queenship*, ed. J. C. Parsons (Stroud, 1994).

—— 'The Queen's Intercession in Thirteenth-Century England', in *Power of the Weak*, ed. J. Carpenter and S. B. Maclean (Chicago, 1995).

—— *Eleanor of Castile: Queen and Society in Thirteenth-Century England* (New York, 1995).

Paterson, L. M., *The World of the Troubadours: Medieval Occitan Society, c.1100–c.1300* (Cambridge, 1993).

Powicke, F. M., 'The Archbishop of Rouen, John de Harcourt and Simon de Montfort in 1260', *EHR*, 51 (1936).

—— *King Henry III and the Lord Edward* (1947), reprinted, 2 vols in 1 (Oxford, 1966).

—— *The Thirteenth Century, 1216–1307* (Oxford, 1953).

Prestwich, M., *Edward I* (London, 1988).

Prynne, W., *Aurum Reginae* (London, 1668).

Raban, S., 'The Land Market and the Aristocracy in the Thirteenth Century', in *Tradition and Change. Essays in Honour of Marjorie Chibnall*, ed. D. Greenway and others (Cambridge, 1985).

Regnier-Bohler, D., 'Imagining the Self', in *A History of Private Life, II: Revelations of the Medieval World*, ed. G. Duby, trans. A. Goldhammer (Cambridge, MA and London, 1988).

Rhodes, W. E., 'Edmund, Earl of Lancaster', *EHR*, 10 (1895).

Richard, J., *Saint Louis: Crusader King of France*, trans. J. Birrell, ed. S. D. Lloyd (Cambridge, 1992).

Richardson, H. G., 'The Coronation of Edward I', *BIHR*, 15 (1937–8).

—— 'The Marriage and Coronation of Isabella of Angoulême', *EHR*, 61 (1946).

—— *The English Jewry under Angevin Kings* (London, 1960).

—— 'The Coronation in Medieval England: the Evolution of the Office and the Oath', *Traditio*, 16 (1960).

Richardson, H. G. and Sayles, G. O., *The Governance of Medieval England from the Conquest to Magna Carta* (Edinburgh, 1963).

Ridgeway, H., 'The Politics of the English Royal Court, 1247–65, with Special Reference to the Role of Aliens' (University of Oxford D.Phil. thesis, 1983).

—— 'The Lord Edward and the Provisions of Oxford (1258): A Study in Faction', *TCE*, i (1986).

—— 'King Henry III and the "Aliens", 1236–72', *TCE*, ii (1988).

—— 'King Henry III's Grievances against the Council in 1261', *Historical Research*, 61 (1988).

—— 'Foreign Favourites and Henry III's Problems of Patronage, 1247–58', *EHR*, 104 (1989).

—— 'William de Valence and his *Familiares*', *Historical Research*, 65 (1992).

—— 'The Ecclesiastical Career of Aymer de Lusignan, Bishop Elect of Winchester, 1250–1260', in *The Cloister and the World: Essays in Medieval History in Honour of Barbara Harvey*, ed. J. Blair and B. Golding (Oxford, 1996).

Rosser, G., *Medieval Westminster, 1200–1540* (Oxford, 1989).

Round, J. H., 'The Heart of St Roger', *Transactions, Essex Archaeological Society*, new series, 16 (1923).

Russell, J. C., and Hieronimus, J. P., *The Shorter Latin Poems of Master Henry of Avranches Relating to England* (Cambridge, MA, 1935).

Salter, E., *English and International: Studies in the Literature, Art and Patronage of Medieval England*, ed. D. Pearsall and N. Zeeman (Cambridge, 1988).

Sanders, I. J., *English Baronies* (Oxford, 1960).

Sandford, F., *A Genealogical History of the Kings and Queens of England and Monarchs of Great Britain from 1066 to the Year 1707* (London, 1707).

Sayles, G. O., 'The Sources of Two Revisions of the Statute of Gloucester', *EHR*, 52 (1937).

—— *The Functions of the Medieval Parliament of England* (London, 1988).

Schramm, P. E., *A History of the English Coronation*, trans. L. G. Wickham Legg (Oxford, 1937).

Shahar, S., *Childhood in the Middle Ages*, trans. Chaya Galai (London, 1990).

Sivéry, G., *Marguerite de Provence: Une reine au temps des cathédrales* (Paris 1987).

Snellgrove, H. S., *The Lusignans in England, 1247–58* (Albuquerque, 1950).

Southern, R. W., *Robert Grosseteste: The Growth of an English Mind in Medieval Europe* (Oxford, 1986).

Spufford, P., *Handbook of Medieval Exchange* (London, 1986).

Stacey, R. C., *Politics, Policy, and Finance under Henry III, 1216–1245* (Oxford, 1987).

—— 'Crusades, Crusaders and the Baronial *Gravamina* of 1263–1264', *TCE*, iii (1991).

Stafford, P., *Queens, Concubines and Dowagers: The King's Wife in the Early Middle Ages* (Athens, GA, 1983).

Staniland, K., 'The Nuptials of Alexander III of Scotland and Margaret Plantagenet', *Nottingham Medieval Studies*, 30 (1986).

Stokes, H. P., 'The Relationship between the Jews and the Royal Family of England in the Thirteenth Century', *Transactions, JHSE*, 8 (1918).

—— *Studies in Anglo-Jewish History* (Edinburgh, 1913).

Stone, L., 'Jean de Howden, poète Anglo-Normand du xiiie siecle', *Romania*, 69 (1946–7).

Storey, R., 'The First Convocation, 1257?', *TCE*, iii (1991).

Strickland, A., *Lives of the Queens of England from the Norman Conquest*, 2nd edn (8 vols, London, 1851).

Studd, R., 'A Catalogue of the Acts of the Lord Edward, 1254–1272' (University of Leeds Ph.D. thesis, 1971).

—— 'The Lord Edward and King Henry III', *BIHR*, 50 (1977).

—— 'Chancellors of the Lord Edward: A Supplementary Note', *BIHR*, 51 (1978).

—— 'The Marriage of Henry of Almain and Constance of Béarn', *TCE*, iii (1991).

Talbot, C. H. and Hammond, E. A., *The Medical Practitioners in Medieval England: A Biographical Register* (London, 1965).

Thirteenth Century England: Proceedings of the Newcastle upon Tyne Conference, ed. P. R. Coss and S. D. Lloyd (5 vols, Woodbridge, 1986–95).

Thompson, S., *Women Religious: The Founding of English Nunneries after the Norman Conquest* (Oxford, 1991).

Tobin, R. B., 'Vincent of Beauvais on the Education of Women', *Journal of the History of Ideas*, 35 (1974).

Tout, T. F., *Chapters in the Administrative History of Medieval England* (6 vols, Manchester, 1920–33).

Trabut-Cussac, J. P., *L'Administration Anglaise en Gascogne sous Henry III et Edouard I de 1254 à 1307* (Geneva, 1972).

Trease, G. E., 'The Spicers and Apothecaries of the Royal Household in the Reigns of Henry III, Edward I and Edward II', *Nottingham Medieval Studies*, 3 (1959).

Treharne, R. F., *The Baronial Plan of Reform, 1258–1263*, 2nd edn (Manchester, 1971).

Tristram, E. W., *English Medieval Wall Painting: The Thirteenth Century* (2 vols, Oxford, 1950).

Tyerman, C., *England and the Crusades, 1095–1588* (Chicago, 1988).

Vale, M., *The Angevin Legacy and the Hundred Years War, 1250–1340* (Oxford, 1990).

Vaughan, R., *Matthew Paris* (Cambridge, 1958).

—— 'The Chronicle of John of Wallingford', *EHR*, 73 (1958).

Viard, F., *Béatrice de Savoye* (Lyon, 1942).

Victoria County History: Essex, ii (1907); *Wiltshire*, iii (1956).

Wade, M. M. (Labarge), 'The Personal Quarrels of Simon de Montfort and his Wife with Henry III of England' (University of Oxford B.Litt. thesis, 1939).

Wait, H. A., 'The Household and Resources of the Lord Edward, 1239–1272' (University of Oxford D.Phil. thesis, 1988).

Warner, M., *Alone of All her Sex*, 2nd edn (London, 1985).

Watson, G. E., 'The Families of Lacy, Geneva, Joinville and La Marche', *The Genealogist*, new series, 21 (1904).

Waugh, S. L., *The Lordship of England: Royal Wardships and Marriages in English Society and Politics, 1217–1327* (Princeton, 1988).

Williams, D. T., 'Aspects of the Career of Boniface of Savoy, Archbishop of Canterbury, 1241–70' (University of Wales Ph.D. thesis, 1970).

Williams, G. A., *Medieval London: From Commune to Capital* (London, 1963).

Wilshire, L. E., *Boniface of Savoy, Carthusian Archbishop of Canterbury, 1207–1270* (Salzburg, 1977).

Wolff, P., *Western Languages, A.D. 100–1500*, trans. F. Partridge (London, 1971).

Wood, C. T., *The French Apanages and the Capetian Monarchy, 1224–1328* (Cambridge, MA, 1966).

Wood, S., *English Monasteries and their Patrons in the Thirteenth Century* (Oxford, 1955).

Wright, R. Muir, 'The Virgin in the Sun and in the Tree', in *Women and Sovereignty*, ed. L. O. Fradenburg (Edinburgh, 1992).

Wurstemberger, L., *Peter der Zweite* (4 vols, Berne, 1856–8).

Yates, W. N., 'Bishop Peter de Aquablanca (1240–1268): A Reconsideration', *Journal of Ecclesiastical History*, 22 (1971).

Index